# THE PLIGHT OF CRIME VICTIMS
# IN MODERN SOCIETY

*Also by Ezzat A. Fattah*

A STUDY OF THE DETERRENT EFFECT OF CAPITAL PUNISHMENT
FEAR OF PUNISHMENT (*co-author*)
FROM CRIME POLICY TO VICTIM POLICY (*editor*)

# The Plight of Crime Victims in Modern Society

Edited by

Ezzat A. Fattah, Ph.D
Professor of Criminology, Simon Fraser
University, Vancouver, Canada

MACMILLAN

First published in 1989

Published by
THE MACMILLAN PRESS LTD
Houndmills, Basingstoke, Hampshire RG21 2XS
and London
Companies and representatives
throughout the world

Printed and bound in Great Britain by
Antony Rowe Ltd, Chippenham, Wiltshire

10  9  8  7  6  5  4  3  2
06  05  04  03  02  01  00  99

British Library Cataloguing in Publication Data
The Plight of crime victims in modern
society.
1. Victims of crimes
I. Fattah, Ezzat A.
362.8'8    HV6250.25
ISBN 0–333–40775–X

# Contents

# Notes on the Contributors

**Richard Block** is a professor of sociology at Loyola University of Chicago, a fellow of the University of Chicago Law School Center for Study in Criminal Justice, and a Research Associate of the North-western University Center for Urban Affairs and Policy Research. He has been studying victims of crime since the First US National Victim Survey of 1966. Currently he is studying the dynamics of victim-offender interaction and the effect of resistance on the completion of crimes.

Another continuing interest of his has been comparative research on violent crime. This cross-national research began with a comparison of Amsterdam and Chicago and has continued with a published (1982) volume *Victimization and Fear of Crime: World Per- spectives*, which he edited for the US Bureau of Justice Statistics.

**Raymond R. Corrado** is an associate professor in the Department of Criminology at Simon Fraser University in Burnaby, British Columbia. He received his Ph.D. in Political Science from Northwestern University. He has published articles and chapters on various aspects of terrorism. His current research interest in terrorism is focused on why and how governments employ terrorism in pluralist democratic societies.

**Donald G. Dutton** is an associate professor of psychology at the University of British Columbia, Vancouver, Canada. Trained as an experimental social psychologist, his early research interests were in interpersonal attraction, inter-racial altruism and attribution theory. Since 1974 he has worked in areas of psychology related to the Criminal Justice system, including police training, programme evaluation, policy research, and his current research interest: spouse assault.

**Ezzat A. Fattah** is a professor of criminology at Simon Fraser University. He studied law at the University of Cairo where he obtained an LL.L. degree. He worked for 13 years as a prosecutor in his native country, Egypt. This was followed by 3 years of graduate work at the Institute of Criminology, University of Vienna, Austria. In 1964 he moved to Canada where he obtained an M.A. and a Ph.D.

from the University of Montreal. He taught criminology at that University until 1974 when he was invited to found and chair a Department of Criminology at Simon Fraser University in Vancouver.

Dr Fattah is a pioneer in victimology and first wrote on the topic as early as 1966. His list of publications includes 6 books and 80 papers published in learned journals. He received several honours including the Beccaria Prize and the Alex Edmison Award. He served for many years as a national councillor for the Canadian section of Amnesty International and is currently a member of the Board of Directors of the International Society of Criminology.

**Edith E. Flynn** is professor of criminal justice, Northwestern University in Boston, Massachusetts. She served on several National Committees and was one of the key figures in the National Advisory commission on Criminal Justice Standards and Goals. Dr Flynn is author/co-author of numerous publications including *The New and the Old Criminology* (1978); 'Political Prisoners and Terrorists in American Correctional Institutions' in *Terrorism and Criminal Justice* (1978); 'Crime Victims: an Agenda for the 1980s', in *An Anatomy of Criminal Justice* (1980); *Crime and Violence in American Society, American Behavioral Scientist* (1980); 'Theory Development in Victimology' in *The Victim in International Perspective* (1982); 'Women as Criminal Justice Professionals' in *Judge, Lawyer, Victim, Thief* (1982).

**Curt T. Griffiths** is an associate professor, Department of Criminology, Simon Fraser University, Burnaby, British Columbia. He received his Ph.D. in Sociology from the University of Montana in 1977. His major areas of teaching and research include Native North Americans and the law; Formal and Informal Systems of Social Control; Delivery of Criminal Justice Services in the Canadian North. Dr Griffiths co-authored *Criminal Justice in Canada: an Introductory Text* (1980) with S. N. Verdun-Jones and J. F. Klein, and *Corrections in Canada: Policy and Practice* (1984) with J. W. Ekstedt, and has published several articles in learned journals.

**Susan W. Hillenbrand** is the co-ordinator of the Victim/Witness Assistance Project funded by the American Bar Association (section of criminal justice). The project developed a set of guidelines for fair treatment of victims and witnesses in the Criminal Justice System.

**Marja Korpilahti** took her Master of Laws degree in 1981 at the University of Uppsala, Sweden. She is now a postgraduate student at the University of Helsinki.

Ms Korpilahti has studied child abuse and neglect at the University of Uppsala with grants from the Scandinavian Research Council of Criminology and the Research Institute of Legal Policy in Helsinki, Finland. She now works at Kalervo Insurance Ltd, in Helsinki. Ms Korpilahti has published results of her studies on child abuse in Finland and Sweden in the report series of the Research Institute of Legal Policy.

**André Normandeau** received his Ph.D. from the University of Pennsylvania. Since then he has been teaching at the School of Criminology, University of Montreal. In addition to his teaching duties he is currently director of the International Centre for Comparative Criminology, University of Montreal. He also served as the secretary for a task force set up by the Quebec provincial government to study armed robberies in the province. Dr Normandeau has written several books and articles dealing with various aspects of criminology.

**Teuvo Peltoniemi** took his M.A. in Sociology in 1974 at the University of Tampere and his Lic.Pol.Sc. in 1980 at the University of Helsinki where he is now a doctoral student. Mr Peltoniemi has worked as researcher at the University of Tampere, the Finnish Foundation for Alcohol Studies and Research Institute of Legal Policy. He is presently the principal investigator in a health education study at the Provincial Board of Uusimaa, Helsinki, and a lecturer in Sociological Alcohol Research at the University of Tampere. Mr Peltoniemi is the author of a forthcoming book on family violence in Finland and the editor of a book on Alcohol Sociology.

**Ab Thorvaldson** received a B.A. in Political Science from the University of Manitoba, an M.A. in experimental psychology from the University of British Columbia, and a Ph.D. in criminology from the Institute of Criminology, Cambridge for his thesis on the aims and effectiveness of community service by offenders. He is presently the Director of the Research and Evaluation Division of the Ministry of Attorney General, British Columbia, having previously served the same ministry as probation officer, director of offender classification in the provincial prison system, and corrections research director. He is the author of many published articles on reparative sanctions and other topics.

**Irvin Waller** is a professor of criminology at the University of Ottawa, Canada. From 1966 to 1974 he was at the Centre of Criminology, University of Toronto, where he published *Men Released from Prison* and *Burglary, the Victim and the Public*. Dr Waller was the first Director General of Research and Statistics for the Solicitor General of Canada where he initiated and spearheaded a 'research program for policy', which includes major initiatives on crime prevention, victims, sentence disparity, policing, and alternatives to prison use. He is a Director of the National Organization of Victim Assistance and is on the executive of the World Society of Victimology.

**Linda F. Weafer** received her B.A. in Criminology from Simon Fraser University in 1982. She is currently enrolled in the Graduate Studies Program in the Department of Criminology at Simon Fraser University, Burnaby, British Columbia. Major areas of interest include, Justice in the North, Native Justice, and Minorities and the Criminal Justice System. She has recently co-authored *Native North Americans: Crime, Conflict, and Criminal Justice: a Research Bibliography*, with Curt Taylor Griffiths and Gregory F. Williams.

**Diane Wood** has held several federal government positions in the public relations and information field. Since 1982, she is Chief of Social Policy and International Relations at Status of Women Canada. Among other things, she co-ordinates federal response around the issue of family violence through an interdepartmental committee.

**J. Colin Yerbury** is currently Director, Directed Independent Study courses, Continuing Studies, Simon Fraser University, Burnaby, British Columbia. His major areas of teaching and research include: Minorities and the Criminal Justice System; Ethnohistory; Ethnology of Law; Anthropological Theory; and Cultural Ecology and Cultural Evolution. Among his recent works is a book entitled: *The Subarctic Indians and the Fur Trade: 1680–1869* (University of Toronto Press) and his research papers have appeared in the *Journal of Ethnic Studies, Alberta History, Arctic Anthropology, Current Anthropology. Ethnohistory*, and the *Western Canadian Journal of Anthropology*. He is currently writing a book with Curt Taylor Griffiths: *Native North Americans: Crime, Deviance and Criminal Justice*.

**Eduard A. Ziegenhagen**, Ph.D., is an associate professor of Political Science, State University of New York at Binghamton, Research Associate, Center for Social Analysis. He is the author of the following publications: *Techniques for Political Analysis* (1971); with George Bowlby, *Victims, Crime and Social Control* (1977); 'The Recidivist Victim of Violent Crime, *Victimology*, vol 7. (1976); 'Toward a Theory of Victim-Criminal Justice System Interactions in William F. McDonald (ed.) *Criminal Justice and the Victim* (1976); 'Victim Interests, Victim Services and Social Control' in Bert Galaway and Joe Hudson (eds) *Perspectives on Crime Victims* (1981); 'Controlling Crime by Regulating Victim Behavior' in H. J. Schneider (ed.) *International Perspectives on the Victim* (1980). He was Director, Crime Victim's Consultation Project, 1973–74.

# Foreword

The international course in criminology has an impressive history and is universally considered to be one of the major scholarly events in the field of criminology. Organized jointly by the International Society of Criminology (Paris) and one of the world's leading universities, the course has been held in various cities and capitals all over the globe. Each year the course is devoted to a general theme chosen for its importance and currency. The theme selected for the 33rd international course was 'Victims of Crime', a most timely topic. The course was held at the Westin Bayshore Hotel in Vancouver, Canada, in March 1983 and was generously funded through grants from Simon Fraser University, the Solicitor-General of Canada and the Federal Department of Justice. The course dealt with both theoretical and applied aspects of victimology and examined in depth the problems of research and practice encountered in this young and growing discipline. The course was attended by 150 participants from Canada, the United States, Europe, Africa, and Asia. The international faculty for the course consisted of some of the world's best experts and recognized authorities in the field of victimology. Each faculty member invited was asked to prepare one or two original papers for the course. This yielded over 40 previously unpublished papers. A first volume, *From Crime Policy To Victim Policy – Reorienting the Justice System* was published in 1986, also by Macmillan, and was devoted mainly to research and policy issues. The present volume contains chapters of a more applied nature, focusing on victims, victimization, and victim services. Together, the two volumes constitute an invaluable reference to all those interested or involved in victim research, victim services, or in the administration of justice.

A few years ago, the organization of an international course on victims of crime and the publication of the ensuing papers seemed like an impossible dream. With the publication of this volume, the dream has become a reality and it is with a great sense of relief and gratification that I see the whole project come to fruition. I wish, therefore, to express my warm and sincere thanks to the contributors who gave generously of their time, to Dr Denis Szabo, past President of the International Society of Criminology, for asking me to organize and direct the course, to my colleagues at Simon Fraser

University for their encouragement and support, to my family for their understanding, and finally to Ann Marangos for her editorial assistance.

# Acknowledgements

The 33rd International Course in Criminology on Victims of Crime (Vancouver, 1983), for which most of the papers in this volume were prepared, was generously funded by grants from Simon Fraser University, the Solicitor-General of Canada, and the Federal Ministry of Justice. Their contribution is acknowledged with sincere thanks.

The editor and publishers wish to thank the following who have kindly given permission for the use of copyright material: International University Press, Inc., for the extracts from Henry Krystal's *Massive Psychic Trauma*; A. B. Raben and Sjögren Bokförlag, for the table from Karin Alfredsson's Den Man Älskar Agar Man; and the *Revue Internationale de Droit Pénal* for permission to reproduce Ezzat Fattah's article 'The Child as Victim'.

They also wish to thank Rusins Kaufmann for his kind permission to reproduce the cartoon (Chapter 11) which first appeared in the *Ottawa Citizen* in September 1981.

# Prologue
# On Counting Victims

# 1 A Comparison of National Crime Surveys[1]

## Richard Block

In the past two decades a new method, the crime survey, has evolved to measure the total volume of crime independently from the records of the police, court, and correctional systems. Criminologists have long searched for a measure which could come close to describing the total volume of criminal behaviour. They realized that the closer the measurement of crime was to the actual commission of a criminal act, the fewer the filtering decisions that would affect that measure and the greater the volume of crime. They were especially concerned with the 'dark figure' of crimes which never became known to the police. The first crime statistics measured court activities. By the 1930s, these had been rejected as the basic crime statistic in favour of 'crimes known to the police'. Until the mid-1960s, these police-recorded crimes were the most feasible measure, close to the criminal act. However, it was recognized that the police were never notified of many crimes, and that, in some jurisdictions, the police failed to act on some crimes of which they were notified (Block and Block, 1980).

In the mid-1960s, in the US, officially known crime rates increased and concern for personal safety developed. A new method began to supplement police statistics. A large random sample of the population of an area was asked whether or not they had been criminally victimized during a fixed time period (usually 6 months or a year). This methodology, first developed for the *United States President's Commission on Crime* in 1966 (NORC) (Biderman *et al.*, 1967), was incorporated into the continuing *National Crime Panel* (NCP) in the early 1970s. As concern for crime grew in other countries, similar surveys were conducted. While none of these replicates the NCP, all stem from a common heritage. Thus, the crime surveys of many countries reflect similar concerns, methods, and a common development history. They represent a unique opportunity for cross-cultural comparison.

The object of this chapter is to carry out the background work for such a comparison by documenting similarities and differences in method and content of several national surveys of crime, and by giving one example of the potential usefulness of cross-national comparison.

Eight national crime surveys are compared:

1. the first national crime survey of the United States (NORC/USA);
2. the continuing United States, National Crime Panel (NCP/USA);
3. the continuing Dutch national crime survey;
4. the Australian survey of 1974;
5. the Swedish surveys of 1978 and 1982;
6. the Israeli surveys of 1979 and 1981;
7. the survey of England and Wales/Scotland of 1981;
8. the Canadian Survey of 1981.

While some surveyors are content to include only questions on victimization and a few demographics, many surveyors included questions on the aetiology of victimization and attitudes toward the criminal justice system. These may be put in a separate questionnaire or as part of an integrated questionnaire. While these questions were relatively unfocused in the NORC survey, as befits an inventory in a new field, in recent surveys, four main areas have been covered:

1. precautions to prevent crime – locking doors and windows;
2. life-style characteristics which may prevent or promote crime – going out at night or avoiding dangerous places;
3. guardianship – physical characteristics of dwelling or community, neighbourliness;
4. criminal behaviour of the respondent;
5. attitudes and experiences concerning the criminal justice system – evaluation of the police.

Generally these questions have not been asked of all respondents but only of a sample.

These aetiological questions reflect the concerns of many victimologists with opportunity theory and the routine activity approach to crime. The mid-range theories see different rates of crime as reflecting the differing characteristics of communities, physical structures, and the behaviour of individuals.

The questionnaires always contain a series of demographic questions which might also be related to victimization. Residents of big cities are more likely to be targets of crime than residents of rural areas. Young people are more frequently victims than the elderly.

Generally, the aetiological variables considered are at an individual level. One major purpose of cross-cultural comparison is to discover if the same theories of victimization hold true in several societies, and to examine possible differences across cultures in crime patterns. In a later section of this chapter we will show how cross-cultural comparison both demonstrates similarities in the causes of victimization in Holland and the US and point to cultural differences which explain differences in crime patterns.

## SAMPLING AND QUESTIONNAIRE DESIGN

Crime surveys were developed as an alternative estimate of the rate or amount of crime in an area. The surveys were expected to generate estimates which were comparable to police statistics. In order to do this, all crime surveys had to confront two different problems.[2] *Firstly*, crime is a relatively rare phenomenon which is often rapidly forgotten. If crime was either more common or could be remembered over long periods of time, then a survey of normal size might be used (1500–2000). However, in order for the surveys to be comparable to police statistics which are generally issued on a yearly basis, their time frame had to be a year or less and the number of respondents had to be very large. The smallest survey reported here interviewed 5700 respondents (Israel). The largest survey interviews more than 135 000 respondents each six months. *Secondly*, questions about crime must be asked in such a way that they are both simple enough for non-criminal justice personnel to understand, but in sufficient detail to allow for comparison with official police statistics.[3] This requirement has typically resulted in a series of screen questions followed by detailed incident questions. Sometimes the screen questions are part of a separate questionnaire. Sometimes both screen and detail questions are integrated into a single questionnaire.

Table 1.1 compares the sample design of the eight surveys. All except the NORC/USA survey are limited to victimization of households, older teenagers, and adults. All are random samples, and all except the Canadian survey are predominately conducted using in person interviews.[4] All exclude most commercial crimes and crimes committed against non-residents. These exclusions may have been unimportant in the design of the NCP. In the US commercial crimes

Table 1.1 A Comparison of Sampling Design

NORC/USA
>Estimated year 1965–66 – victimization for stratified random
>sample of households – all residents.
>10 000 household informants age 18+ reporting 33 000
>individuals.
>Each victim or surrogate adult interviewed, two incident max. per
>respondent.

NCP/USA
>Estimated years 1973–present
>Stratified random longitudinal panel sample of addresses.
>All residents age 12+ reporting on personal victimization (12 and
>13   adult surrogate).
>One reports on household victimizations.
>60 000 households, 135 000 respondents interviewed each 6
>months.
>Each address remains in the sample for 7, 6 month periods.

Netherlands
>Estimated years 1973–present.
>Stratified random sample of citizens age 16+.
>11 000 respondents, one per household.
>Personal victimizations for respondent interviewed and household
>victimizations.

Australia
>Estimated year 1974.
>Victimization for all address residents age 15+ and household.
>Stratified random sample of addresses excluding northern
>territories rural areas and small towns.
>8414 households all eligible adults (15+) interviewed.
>18 694 respondents.

Israel
>Estimated years 1979, 1981.
>Victimization for households and all residents.
>Stratified random sample of jewish households excluding
>Kibbutzim and institutions. One interview per household.
>5700 respondents.

Canada
>Estimated years 1981; 1983 replicated
>Victimization for households and individual respondents age 16+.
>Random interview per household digit dialling of residential
>telephones in seven urabn centres.
>61 000 respondents age 16+.
>6910—9563 per urban area.

England and Wales/Scotland
>Estimated years 1981; 1983 replicated.
>Victimization for households and individual respondents age 16+.
>Stratified random sample interview per household, addresses
>based on electoral registry.
>Non-institutional:
>>16 000 total respondents
>>11 000 England and Wales
>>5000 Scotland

Sweden
>Estimated year 1978, 1982.
>Victimization for households and individuals.
>Stratified random sample of households 1978.
>1000 interviews Head and Spouse – Cohabitant (age 16–74).
>1982 – 8000 interviews – 1 interview per household, age 16–85.

are a relatively small proportion of the UCR and proportionately few US crimes occur to international tourists. However, these exclusions may be very significant in small countries with many tourists (e.g. Israel). In some countries, businesses are victim to a high proportion of property crimes (e.g. the Netherlands, to be discussed later in this chapter).

All surveys ask about victimization which occurred to the respondent him/herself, and all surveys ask the respondent to report about some victimizations which occurred to the household as a whole (usually, burglary and auto-theft). Some surveys also attempt to measure victimizations which occurred to any household member. Others limit this enumeration to the respondent. The NORC and Israel surveys asked a single respondent to enumerate victimizations which occurred to all household members. This technique probably underestimated personal victimizations which occurred to household members other than the respondent. The NCP and the Australian survey interviewed all members of the household within the survey's age range. The 1978 Swedish survey interviewed household head and co-habitant or spouse. Interviewing more than one respondent per household, while economical for achieving a large sample at reduced costs, probably violated assumptions of the independence of observations.[5] While the samples for the other surveys are quite large, they are drawn in a way which is typical for national surveys – one randomly chosen respondent per household.

No sample is an exact representation of a population. These crime surveys exclude many possible respondents. However, unlike some surveys, the sample selection process may be systematically related to the dependent variable. There is good reason to believe that persons excluded from the samples may have higher rates of victimization than those included. All eight surveys exclude transients and, effectively, exclude persons who do not speak the official language(s) of the country.[6] Thus, many recent immigrants and temporary residents are not included. The Dutch, English and Israeli surveys include only citizens. The Israeli survey includes only Jews. In Holland and Sweden, the lowest socio-economic rungs are occupied by guest workers. In Israel, these rungs are occupied by non-Jews. While we cannot know, it is likely that non-citizens have a higher rate of victimization. The Canadian and Australian surveys exclude rural areas. The Canadian survey includes only seven urban centres. Regardless of country, all research has indicated that urban areas have higher rates for most crimes than rural areas. Therefore a comparison of the Canadian or Australian survey to those of other countries without controlling for urbanization would be misleading.

*Finally*, the sampling structure of the NCP is different from all others. All other surveys, even those which are periodically repeated, make no attempt to reinterview the same respondents. The NCP is a quasi-panel survey. Each address is interviewed eight times over a three and one-half year period. A family may move from the address (perhaps because of crime) but the address remains in the sample. Unfortunately, this design which might be of great use in describing victimization careers, precautions taken, and changes made has never been effectively used. It mainly creates problems for the researcher attempting to analyse the survey.

Table 1.2 examines the questionnaire design of the eight surveys. In all except the Swedish survey, a screen question is asked about a particular type of victimization (e.g. rape, robbery, theft, etc.). Then, either following immediately or in a second questionnaire, the respondent is asked to describe the victimization in sufficient detail that it can be placed into crime categories which correspond to police definitions.[7] An important difference among the surveys is the placement of these detailed questions. In those surveys in which the crime-screen filters directly into a series of additional questions, the detail of those questions is necessarily limited. In those surveys in which the crime-screen leads to the completion of a second questionnaire, the detailing of the incidents can be quite elaborate. However, this detail is both expensive and time consuming and may limit the number of additional questions which can be asked.

Series victimization is a major problem for crime surveys. This problem was discovered during analysis of the NORC survey, and all following surveys have attempted to deal with it. Series victimizations are a number of crimes occurring to the same respondent which are so alike that the respondent cannot differentiate among them. Spouse beatings or repeated robberies by the same offender are examples of this type of crime. Each survey has attempted to handle these victimizations usually by asking the respondent to describe the last victimization. Unfortunately, each survey defines series victimization quite differently. These differences make comparison of personal violence rates between the surveys very difficult, especially for non-stranger crimes.[8]

The basic design of the NCP has changed little over the years despite the rapid development of victimology. Many questions about the causes of victimization which the respondent might answer are still not asked. The NCP has remained from its inception to the present only an alternative to the UCR index of crimes known to the police.

The design of the Dutch, English, and Canadian surveys allows for flexibility in attitudinal and behavioural questions while leaving crime questions nearly intact. The Swedish survey is part of a continuing general survey of living conditions which contains many questions on neighbouring and recreational behaviour that might be related to victimization.

The much more systematic and focused questions of the most recently designed surveys of Canada and the United Kingdom, are evidence of the increasing maturity of the field of victimization research. The Canadian survey, especially, moves beyond victimization to consider the victim in the criminal justice system and the potential usefulness of victim assistance schemes.

## WHICH CRIMES ARE MEASURED?

Each of the eight surveys measures a different set of crimes. Table 1.3 catalogues the crimes which are measured in each questionnaire. Only two crimes, burglary and car theft are measured in all eight, and as we shall show in Table 1.5 even these are measured somewhat differently. Of the remaining crimes, some form of assault is measured in all surveys. Although robberies are sometimes included as assaults, other times they are treated as a separate crime. Theft and theft from a car are included in seven surveys. Vandalism is included in six surveys. Rape and sexual molestation are included in five surveys.

However, even though the same crimes are included in several surveys and the description of these crimes must be in language a lay person can understand, the questions asked are different. This makes comparison across published reports very difficult. Table 1.5 lists the screening questions used to detect burglary/breaking and entering in each of the eight surveys.

The NORC and Swedish questions exclude burglaries during which nothing was taken. The Dutch and Swedish surveys exclude attempted break-ins. Several surveys include only houses and flats while others include outbuildings, second homes, and even small stores. The wording of the NCP and Canadian surveys are almost identical. There is little similarity in the wording of the other surveys.

Table 1.2   Questionnaire Design

| | Crime Screener | Attitude and Behaviour | Detailed incident |
|---|---|---|---|
| **NORC/USA** | | | |
| Stand Alone Survey | | | |
| 3 questionnaires | | | |
| | | | |
| No special provision for series victimization | | | |
| | Crime Screener | Detailed Incident | |
| **NCP/USA** | | | |
| Stand Alone survey | | | |
| 2 questionnaires | | | |
| | | | |
| Was incident part of a series of 3 or more undiffereniateable crimes? | | | |
| If so reported on last incident. | | | |
| | Crime Screen questions followed immediately by description/1979–present Screener/Detailed incident | | |
| **Netherlands** | | | |
| Part of a larger survey questionnaire | | | |
| | Screen questions/Detailed incident | | |
| **Australia** | | | |
| Part of a larger survey questionnaire | | | |
| | | | |
| How often did it happen? | | | |

| | | | | | |
|---|---|---|---|---|---|
| Israel | Part of a larger survey | How many times – year and month<br>Further questions refer to incidents in general | Crime screen questions followed by brief description to place in legal categories. | | Detailed Incident |
| Canada | Stand Alone Survey<br>2 questionnaires | How many times?<br>If series, incident questionnaire refers to most recent incident. | Crime<br>Screen questions | With attitude &<br>behavioural<br>questions | Detailed Incident |
| England and Wales/Scotland | Stand Alone Survey<br>3 questionnaires | Screener how many times<br>Series all very similar in type, done under the same circumstances and probably by the same offender.<br>Details only on most recent | Few attitude &<br>crime screen<br>questions | Attitudes &<br>behaviour | Detailed Incident<br>report |
| Sweden | Part of a larger survey<br>number of times | | Crime screen questions followed immediately by description. | | |

Table 1.3   A Comparison of Crimes Measured*

| | NORC/USA | NCP/USA | Netherlands | Australia | Israel | Canada | England/Wales/Scotland | Sweden |
|---|---|---|---|---|---|---|---|---|
| *Against Person* | | | | | | | | |
| Rape | X | X | | X | | X | X | X |
| Sexual molestation | X | | X | X | X | X | X | |
| Assault/battery | X | X | X** | X | X | X | X | X |
| Robbery | X | X | | X | | X | X | |
| *Against Property* | | | | | | | | |
| Burglary/Breaking and entering | X | X | X | X | X | X | X | X |
| Motor vehicle theft | X | X | X | X | X | X | X | X |
| Theft from auto | X | X | X | | X | X | X | X |
| Bicycle theft | X | | X | | | | X | X |
| Pickpocketing | X | X | X | | | X | X | |
| Simple theft | X | X | | X | X | X | X | |
| Vandalism | X | | X | | | | X | X |
| Fraud | X | | | X | | | | X |

*Definitions vary from country to country
**Some year to year variation
☐Indicates inclusive questions.

Table 1.4 Burglary: Incidence per 10 000 Households Using Non-Standardized Definitions

|  | *Year* | *Per 10 000 Households* | *% Notification* |
|---|---|---|---|
| NORC/USA | 1965 | 213 | 58 |
| NCP/USA | 1975 | 915 | 49 |
|  | 1980 | 843 | 51 |
| Netherlands | 1976 | 110 | 81 |
|  | 1980 | 160 | 90 |
| Australia | 1974 | 393 | 67 |
| Israel | 1979 | 610 | 68 |
| England/Wales | 1981 | 410 | 66 |
| Canada | 1981 | 938 | 64 |
| Sweden | 1978 | 275 | 65 |

The wording of these questions probably has significant effects on both the overall rate of burglary reported in each country, and on details of crimes reported.

Table 1.4 presents the incidence rate per 10 000 households and the percentage of burglaries resulting in police notification using the definition of burglary in each survey. No attempt is made at standardization. Of the eight surveys analysed here, the Netherlands consistently has the lowest overall rate of household burglaries and the highest percentage of burglaries which resulted in police notification. While, as I argue later in this chapter, some of this difference may be real, it is clear that the exclusion of attempted burglaries from the Dutch survey affects both the overall crime rate and the percentage of crimes which became known to the police. Similarly the low rate of burglary in the NORC survey may both reflect a quieter time period and the exclusion of crimes without loss from the questionnaire. The exceptionally high burglary rate reported in the Canadian survey probably reflects the urban nature of the sample. Cities are known to have higher burglary rates than rural areas.

## Table 1.5 An Example: (Breaking and Entering) Burglary

1. NORC

   First, in the last 12 months did someone break into your (home/apartment) and take something, attempt to break in or just walk in and take something?

2. NCP

   During the last 6 months – between _____ and _____ did anyone break into or somehow illegally get into your (apartment/home) garage or another building on your property.

   (Other than the incident(s) just mentioned did you find a door jimmied, a lock forced, or any other signs of an attempted break in?

3. Australia 1974

   Within the last 12 months did anyone break into your home or attempt to break in?

4. Netherlands

   Was your house broken into?
   If so, when? This year? Last year? and/or earlier?
   Exactly where was your house broken into last time? Was that in your home, in a cellar, garage, outbuilding, second home, or in a shop (R.B. under the home)
   Where exactly?

5. Israel

   Did someone break into your apartment or has someone tried to break in and failed:

   (a) break in and steal something?
   (b) break in and not steal anything?
   (c) tried to break in and did not succeed?

6. Canada

   Did anyone break into or illegally enter your (home/apartment), garage or any other building on your property? (Other than in the incident(s) already mentioned) (R.B. robbery, purse snatching, pickopocketing)?

   During 1981 did anyone find a door jimmied, a lock forced or any other signs of attempted illegal entry (other than the incident(s) already mentioned)?

7. England/Wales, Scotland

   During the _____ months since the first of January, 1981, has anyone got into your house/flat without permission and stolen anything?

   Apart from this, in that time has anyone gotten into your house/flat without permission and caused damage?

   And apart from this, in that time have you ever found anything that showed that someone had tried to get in without permission to steal or cause damage?

   (Theft from garages is handled in a separate question)

8. Sweden (1982 differs)

   Have you (or anybody in your household) been victim to any of the following crimes in the last year?

   (Show card. Theft or damage in Ordinary Dwelling, Attic, Cellar, Garage, Holiday Dwelling, was it theft, damage or both?)

While the Swedish burglary rate is expectedly low, given the many crimes that are excluded, the percentage of crimes reported to the police is higher than might be expected. The very similar percentages of notification of the Israeli, English, and Canadian surveys, may reflect a similarity of crime coverage, but it may also reflect a difference in the relationship between police and citizen when these countries are compared to the US.

## OTHER INFORMATION

Table 1.6 compares the surveys on questions which go beyond merely measuring the crime rate. While not included in Table 1.6, all eight surveys asked enough demographic questions to allow for age, sex, and urbanization-specific crime rates. Many also asked questions about labour force participation.[9] All eight included questions which allowed for some description of the criminal event. The purpose of seven of these surveys is comparison with police statistics. Therefore, it is not surprising that all except the Swedish surveys asked if the police were notified of the crime, and that all seven asked those who did not notify the police why they did not.

A secondary purpose of the surveys was to measure the impact of crime. Therefore, all except the Swedish asked, at least for some crimes, whether the offence was attempted or completed. The Swedish survey measured only completed crimes. All asked about injury during violent crimes, and most also asked about the value of property lost and insurance coverage. Many asked about this loss in great detail. Beyond these questions only some offender characteristics (not always the same), the means of entry during burglaries, incident location, and time of day were asked in most surveys. These questions, however, might be very interesting for cross-national comparison and might suggest some possibilities for crime-prevention policy. For example, many crime control experts have compared technical prevention (locks on doors) to physical presence of observers as methods to reduce burglary. Cross-cultural comparison of incident location, means of entry, and time of day, might shed light on factors that are important for burglary prevention.

Several surveys continue today (*Fall*, 1983). The NCP continues to interview more than 130 000 respondents each 6 months. While many subtle changes have occurred in the NCP over the years, only a very dedicated examiner could tell that the survey of 1973 was different from that of 1979. On the other hand, the other surveys have changed

Table 1.6 A Comparison of Information Asked on Incidents, Attitudes, and Behaviours

| | NORC/USA | NCP/USA | Netherlands | Australia | Israel | Sweden* | Canada | England* |
|---|---|---|---|---|---|---|---|---|
| Attempt/Compl. | X | X | X | X | X | | X | X |
| Notification | X | X | X | X | X | X | X | X |
| Reason Non notif | X | X | X | X | X | | X | X |
| Value of Prop. loss | X | X | X | X | | | X | X |
| Injury | X | X | X | X | | X | X | X |
| Off.Charac. | X | X | X | X | X | X | X | X |
| Weapons | | X | | | | | X | X |
| Resistance | | X | | | | | X | X |
| Police Evaluation | X | | | | | | | |
| Burg. — means of entry | X | X | X | | | | X | X |
| Incid. Locat. | X | X | X | | | | X | X |
| Time of Day | X | X | X | X | | X | X | X |
| Safety in neighbour. | X | | | X | | X* | X | X |
| Change over time in crime | | | | | | | X | X |
| Opinion of Police | X | | | | | | X | X |
| Precautionary behaviour | X | | X | | | X* | X | X |
| Going out | X | | X | X | | X* | X | X |
| Envir. Descrip. | X | | X | | | X* | X | X |

*Content varies by year
This table assumes that all questionnaires include standard demographic and employment information.

significantly. Only crime questions have remained fairly constant. The English, Swedish, Canadian, and Dutch surveys systematically ask questions which might explain why some people become crime victims and others do not. The model proposed in all three studies is similar. It is the routine activity/opportunity approach advocated by Garofalo and Hindelang (1977) and Cohen and Felson (1979). Essentially this theory states that the less difficulty in committing a criminal act and the greater the exposure of the potential victim to crime the greater the probability that a crime will occur. Thus, to take an extreme example, a young man who lives alone in the city and goes out drinking every night without locking his door, has a higher probability of becoming a victim of robbery, burglary, or assault than an older woman who lives in the country, rarely goes out or drinks, and always keeps her door locked. Van Dijk and Steinmetz have demonstrated that this theory has some validity when tested with the Dutch survey. While the data of the Canadian and England/Wales/Scotland survey have yet to be analysed, both should be good tests of this theory. In the following section I will test this theory, comparing the results of the Dutch and NCP surveys and through comparison of differences between the two cultures.

## A COMPARISON OF THE NETHERLANDS AND THE UNITED STATES

### The Two Victimization Surveys

The basic data sources used for this comparison are the Dutch National Crime survey of 1977 and the United States National Crime Survey of 1976.[10] The United States survey is set equal to the Dutch survey. The Dutch survey asks about completed household burglaries, so comparison will be limited to completed crimes.

As we have previously discussed, starting with the same objective the two surveys used far different methods, samples, and questionnaires. These differences do not mean comparison is impossible, but they do mean that conclusions based on these comparisons should be both cautiously made and tentatively accepted.

### Rates of Burglary

Rates of home burglary are far higher in the United States than in the

Netherlands – five times as high. Much of the difference in property crime rates is primarily a result of the opportunities available.

Burglary induces fear because of its potential for violence, and because of the impact of home invasion on the individual's concept of his own domain. Yet studies of burglars have shown that they do not want to confront their victim, and generally choose targets to minimize the probability of confrontation. Recent research has described a relationship between guardianship and burglary. The most likely targets of property crimes are those which are relatively unguarded. Thus, most of the recent increase in burglary rates in the United States has been a result of a great increase in daytime burglaries (Cohen and Felson, 1979). Cohen and Felson demonstrate that the overall level of officially known burglaries is inversely related to the percentage of women in the labour force.

The rate of burglary reported to the police in the United States is much higher than in the Netherlands. In 1976, 5670 burglaries were reported to the police per 100 000 households in the United States and 3051 in the Netherlands (*Maandstatistiek,* May 1977). However, in the Netherlands there are two and one-half times as many officially reported burglaries as there are in the victim survey. In the United States the number of victim survey burglaries exceeds the number of burglaries known to the police. This difference between the two countries probably results from a difference in the burglar's target choice. In the Netherlands, stores, factories, and offices are the targets of most officially known burglaries. Only 15% of reported burglaries are against households (*Maandstatistiek,* 1977). In the United States a large majority of officially known burglaries (63%) are against households (*UCR,* 1976).

This difference in reported target in the two countries probably reflects a difference in opportunities. In 1977, most Dutch stores, factories, and offices could legally be open no more than 37.5 hours per week, and moonlighting ('black work' in Dutch) was often criticized. Thus, not only were businesses, factories, and offices unlikely to be operating at night, but also were unlikely to be well guarded. As compared to the Netherlands, United States stores and factories are open long hours, moonlighting is widely practised and accepted, and a much greater percentage of women have a paying job. Thus, occupancy of offices and factories is greater and of houses is less than in the Netherlands. In the Netherlands, the structure of labour makes commercial organizations a likely target of attack, while in the United States, homes are a more likely target.

In the United States, 83% of the population aged 20–65 was in the labour force in 1976. Women were far less likely to work in paid occupations in the Netherlands than in the United States (31% vs. 56%). Of Dutch married women with children 16% work; 4% work more than 20 hours per week. In 1976, 45% of married American women with children 0–18 years old worked; 32% worked more than 35 hours per week.

Table 1.7 Rates of Household Burglary by Time of Day and Occupancy per 100 000 Households

| | Day | | Evening | | Night | | Total | |
|---|---|---|---|---|---|---|---|---|
| | US | Nether-lands | US | Nether-lands | US | Nether-lands | US | Nether-lands |
| Someone home | 160 | 45 | 126 | 99 | 168 | 324 | 455 | 468 |
| No one home | 2320 | 189 | 1160 | 216 | 1160 | 99 | 4638 | 513 |
| Total | 2480 | 234 | 1286 | 315 | 1328 | 423 | 5093 | 981 |

Thus, it is likely that Dutch homes are occupied a far greater percentage of the day, and are therefore less easily available for burglary than United States homes. Table 1.7 dramatically illustrates these differences in target availability. There is no difference in burglary rates between the two countries for occupied homes. In both countries these are exceedingly rare. However, burglaries of unoccupied homes are nine times more likely in the United States than in the Netherlands. Daytime burglaries of unoccupied homes are 12 times more likely in the United States than in the Netherlands.

If Cohen and Felson's observation of changes in opportunities for burglary over time can be extended to comparisons across countries, then their findings are strongly supported by this comparison of Dutch and American households.

My general impression of life style and household security precautions in the United States corresponds to the reality of the burglary rates of the two countries. Homes both in Amsterdam and the Hague and in rural areas were protected with locks which, by American standards, were exceedingly insecure. These were often invalidated or unused during the day. During working hours, Dutch businesses and offices are very well protected with porters checking all ante-rooms and with store detectives and electronic surveillance. In major cities, for example, bank tellers have no cash. However, most stores close at mid-afternoon Saturday and reopen Monday afternoon. They are open one night per week. In the United States homes are far better protected by locks, but less well protected by people than in the Netherlands. American stores, offices, and factories are occupied, and therefore guarded, a far greater percentage of the day and night than in the Netherlands.

### Discussion

If much of the difference between the Netherlands and the United States is dependent on opportunity structure, is it possible to predict changes in patterns of crime as these structures change? Day-time burglaries of unoccupied houses account for a major proportion of the difference between the two countries in rates of burglary. Therefore, the rate of household burglary should vary inversely with unemployment and directly with employment of women. Given the current American pattern of high unemployment and female labour force participation and shortened work hours, rates of household burglary should remain about constant in the United States. The Netherlands, too, suffers from higher than normal unemployment; however, in the Netherlands unemployment has resulted in a decline in female labour force participation, and perhaps a decline in the number of household burglaries. Recent crime survey statistics from both countries support these predictions.

It is unlikely that patterns of crime in the Netherlands will ever be similar to those in the United States. They may become more alike if the nations become more similar. However, differences in history and culture will remain even as opportunities for crime change.

### CONCLUSIONS

In this chapter, the groundwork has been laid for an international comparison of victims of crime. While this research would not be easy, the common heritage of crime surveys makes it possible. Comparative research could include:

1. rates of crime;
2. notification of the police;
3. basic demographic and urbanization comparisons;
4. the aetiology of victimization;
5. the consequences of victimization.

While these comparisons could be made using published reports, this paper has demonstrated, analysing the Dutch and US surveys, that using original data is far more effective. Direct data comparison can take into account differences in sample and design among the different surveys. With greater confidence in the comparison and with knowledge of both theories of crime and victimization and cultural differences, the researcher can sort general explanations of victimization from explanations which are limited to a single culture. The research can consider crime prevention proposals which have been applied in one culture, but may be applicable to another.

We can learn little or nothing about criminals or victims without comparison. A discussion of victims of crime without comparison to non-victims cannot build an explanation of the causes of victimization. Without comparison to non-victims, we cannot know if the characteristics we cite are those of most people or are especially true of victims. Similarly, if comparison is limited to a single country, we have difficulty differentiating cultural characteristics from more universal explanations of crime. If, for example, we find that opportunity is a partial but universally applicable explanation of victimization, it may be possible to alter the environment to reduce the risk of victimization.

Through comparative victimization research we can look at the impact of crime and assess programmes with potential for reducing this impact. Just as crime surveys have been conducted in many countries, crime prevention or victim assistance programmes which have been shown to be successful in one country may be adopted in another (Reeves, 1983).

We have had little success in improving the behaviour of criminals. Neither punishment nor rehabilitation has convinced many offenders to abandon a life of crime. On the other hand, it may be more in the interest of potential victims to reduce their chance of crime attack. However, a programme for reduction of crime based upon reduction of risk must be strongly grounded in theory or it will fail. Cross-cultural research can affirm, reject, or show the limitations of theory more rapidly than can studies limited to victims or comparisons limited to a single time or place.

**Notes**

1. Thanks go to Carl Steinmetz and Jan Van Dijk (Netherlands), Ake Lindblom (Sweden), Mike Hough and Pat Mayhew (England, Wales/ Scotland), Menachim Amir and Shai Javetz (Israel), John Braithwaite (Australia), Dorothy Hepworth (Canada), and Wes Skogan for their help in preparation of this report.

   I would also thank the Netherlands American Committee for International Exchange for the financial aid which first led me to study victimization across cultures.

2. Crime surveys have many problems. Among them are the difficulty which many victims have in recalling incidents, and the limitation of these surveys to crimes which are discrete events occurring to individuals. It is not the purpose of this chapter to review the problems or the history of crime surveys. For good reviews see Sparks, 1981; Skogan, 1981; and Block and Block, 1984. Crime surveys are not an alternative measure of the same crime universe as police reports.

3. There are several types of crimes which are included in police reports but not in crime surveys. For example, crime surveys measure only non-commercial crimes committed against residents. Police statistics include commercial crimes and those occurring to non-residents.

4. As a cost control measure, the NCP beginning in 1980, required three of the seven panels to be interviewed by telephone. Prior to this change, telephone interviews were allowed only if in person interviews were impossible or very difficult.

5. It also vastly complicates computer analysis.

6. There are, of course, French and English versions of the Canadian survey. While the NCS was translated into Spanish in 1976, the interview is rarely given in Spanish.

7. The detail questions included in the Swedish survey are probably insufficient to place crimes into legal categories. The Swedish survey seems to view crime more as a public health problem than a legal problem.

8. Most published reports of the NCP totally exclude series victimizations. This exclusion seriously distorts the reported rates of assaultive violence. For example, if series victimizations were included in the simple assault estimate for 1979, the rate of this crime would increase by 49%. Fortunately, other countries have not followed the NCP lead in this respect.

9. Indeed, several surveys were combined with labour force questionnaires.

10. The following discussion is an abridgement of my paper, 'The Impact of Victimization, Rates and Patterns: a Comparison of the Netherlands and the United States'.

**Bibliography**
Australian Bureau of Statistics (1975), *General Social Survey: Crime Victims* (Canberra, ACT: Australian Bureau of Statistics, May).
Australian Bureau of Statistics (1979), *General Social Survey: Crime Victims May 1975*. Cat. No. 41050 (Canberra).
Biderman, Albert D., Johnson, Louise, McIntyre and Wier, Adrianne (1967), *Report on a Pilot Survey in the District of Columbia on Victimization and Attitudes Toward Law Enforcement* (Washington, DC: President's Commission on Law Enforcement and Administration of Justice).
Block, Carolyn R. and Block, R. L. (1984), 'Crime Definition, Crime Measurement and Victim Surveys' *Journal of Social Issues*, vol. 40.
Block, R. L. and Block, Carolyn R. (1980), 'Decisions and Data: the Transformation of Robbery Incidents into Official Robbery Statistics', *Journal of Criminal Law and Criminology*, vol. 71 (winter) pp. 622–36.
Block, Richard (ed.) (in the Press) *Victimization and Fear of Crime Round the World* (Washington, DC: Bureau of Justice Statistics), contributions by Aromaa (Finland), Braithwaite and Biles (Australia), Kirchhoff and Kirchhoff (Germany), Manzanera (Mexico) and Schwind.
Braithwaite, John and Biles, David (1979), *Crime Victimization and Reportability Rates: a Comparison of the United States and Australia* (Canberra, ACT: Australian Institute of Criminology).
Braithwaite, John and Biles, David (1980), 'Crime Victimization in Australia: a Comparison with the US', *Journal of Criminal Justice,* vol.III, pp.95–110.
Braithwaite, John and Biles, David, 'Crime Victimization Rates in Australian Cities', *Australia & New Zealand Journal of Sociology*, vol.16, no.1 (Mar.), pp.79–83.
Buikhuisen, Wouter (1975), *Registered and Non-Registered Crime*, Report no.XVII (The Hague, Netherlands: Research and Documentation Centre, Ministry of Justice).
Catlin, Gary and Murray, Susan (1979), *Report on Canadian Victimization Survey Methodological Pretests* (Ottawa: Statistics Canada).
Central Bureau voor de Statistiek (1982), *Slachtoffers van Misdrijven, 1980* (Victims of Crime, 1980) (Voorburg, Netherlands).
Cohen, L. E. and Felson, M. (1979 'Social Change and Crime Rate Trends: a Routine Activity Approach', *American Sociological Review*, vol. 44, no. 4, pp. 588–608.
Corrado, Raymond, Glackman, William and Roesch, Ronald (1979), *Vancouver Victimization Survey 1979: Extent and Distribution of Victimization* (Vancouver, BC: Criminology Research Centre, Simon Fraser University).
*Criminal Victimization in the United States: 1973–78 Trends* (1981), Bureau of Justice Statistics (Washington, DC: US Department of Justice).
*Criminal Victimization in the United States, 1979* (1981), Bureau of Justice Statistics (Washington DC: US Department of Justice).
Ennis, Philip (1967), *Criminal Victimization in the United States: a Report of a National Survey*, US President's Commission on Law Enforcement and Administration of Justice, Field Survey II (Washington DC: US Government Printing Office).

Garofalo, James and Hindelang, Michael J. (1977), *An Introduction to the National Crime Survey* (Washington, DC: National Criminal Justice Information and Statistics Service, Law Enforcement Assistance Administration, US Department of Justice).

Hough, Mike and Mayhew, Pat (1983), *The British Crime Survey: First Report*, Home Office Research Study, No.76 (London: HMSO).

Inter-University Consortium for Political & Social Research (1978), *National Crime Surveys, National Sample 1971–77* (Ann Arbor, Michigan).

Israeli Central Bureau of Statistics (1981), *Victimization Survey, 1979*, Special Series #664 (Jerusalem).

Javetz, Shai (1982), 'National Victimization Household Survey', *Memorandum*, Israel Police HQ Research & Development Division (Jerusalem, 10 Jan.).

*Maandstatistiek* (Netherlands Ministry of Justice, Monthly Bulletin of Judicial Statistics) (May) (1977). The Hague: Central Bureau of Statistics.

National Central Bureau of Statistics (1981), Living Conditions, Report No.24, *Victims of Violence & Property Crimes in 1978* (Stockholm).

Nederlands Instituut voor de Publieke Opinie (1978), *Rapport over Misdrijeum* (Amsterdam).

Peltonieme, Tewo and Aromaa, Kauko (1982), *Family Violence Studies & Victimization Survey in Finland*, paper presented at the International Symposium on Victimology, Siracusa, Italy, 3–9 Jan.

Reeves, Helen (1983), *Third Annaul Report 1982/83: National Association of Victims Support Schemes* (London).

Skogan, W. G. (1981), *Issues in the Measurement of Victimization* (Washington, DC: US Department of Justice).

Sparks, R. F. (1981) 'Surveys of Victimization – an Optimistic Assessment', in Tonry, M. and Morris, N. (eds), *Crime and Justice: an Annual Review of Research*, vol. 3 (University of Chicago Press).

Sparks, Richard F., Genn, Hazel and Dodd, David J., *Surveying Victims: a Study of the Measurement of Criminal Victimization, Perceptions of Crime, and Attitudes to Criminal Justice* (New York: John Wiley).

Spickenheuser, J. L. P. (1982), 'Bevolking en criminaliteit op de Nederlandse Antillen. WODC Ministrie V. Justitie', #34 (Netherlands). (With an English summary.)

Statiska Central Byran (1981), *Offer for Valdsoch Egendombrott: Levnadforhalanden 1978*, Report No.24: Victims of Violence and Property Crimes, 1978 (Stockholm). (With an English summary.)

Sveri, Knut (1982), 'Comparative Analyses of Crime by Means of Victim Surveys: the Scandinavian Experience' in Hans Joachim Schneider (ed.), *The Victim in International Perspective* (Berlin and New York: De Gruyter, 1982) pp.209–19.

UCR (*Uniform Crime Reports*) (1976) United States Federal Bureau of Investigation) (Washington, DC: US Government Printing Office)

Van Dijk, Jan and Steinmetz, Carl (1980a), *The Burden of Crime on Dutch Society 1973–1979*, Report no.XXXVIII (The Hague, Netherlands: Research and Documentation Centre, Ministry of Justice).

Van Dijk, Jan and Steinmetz, Carl (1980b), *The RDC Victim Surveys 1974–1979*, Report no.XXXV (The Hague, Netherlands, Research and Documentation Centre, Ministry of Justice).

Van Dijk, Jan and Vianen, A. C. (1978),. *Criminal Victimization in the Netherlands: Victim Surveys 1974–1977*, Report No.VII (The Hague, Netherlands: Research and Documentation Centre, Ministry of Justice).

# Part I

# On Some Neglected Types of Victimization

# 2 Victims of Abuse of Power: the David/ Goliath Syndrome*

## Ezzat A. Fattah

## PATTERNS AND TRENDS

### The Concept of Power

What is power? What is abuse of power? Although these may seem to be easy questions there is no universal or unanimously agreed upon definition of what power is or of what constitutes abuse of that power. Weber viewed power as the opportunity to fulfil one's own wishes despite the resistance of other participants in the social act in question. Lernell (1979) defines power as the pressure exercised by a person or a group over others so as to influence their actions or their attitudes. For Ottenhof (1980) power is the ability of an individual or of a group to act in such a way as they determine for themselves: I want, so I can.

Distinctions may also be made between various types of power – political power, economic power, social power, religious power, etc. One can even talk about psychic power. The media are full of stories about certain persons who use and abuse the psychic powers with which they are endowed. Another distinction could be made between public power and private power.

In speaking of power, and especially of abuse of power, it is vital to address the question of the *legitimacy* of that power. Consequently, it is not only necessary to distinguish between legitimate and illegitimate power, but also between the abuse of legitimate power and the exercise of an illegitimate power the existence of the latter, by definition, constituting in itself an abuse. Needless to say, such distinctions imply the existence of norms and criteria that make it possible to judge the legitimacy of power. Political power is legitimate, one might say, if it derives from a lawful mandate given by a community to serve the interests of that community. Access to such a power, and the exercise of it take place within a well-defined

29

constitutional and legislative framework. Economic power, on the other hand, may be considered legitimate when it is exercised by industrial or commercial enterprises in conformity with the laws and the best interests of the State in which they operate.

According to the type of economic activity, there is also a need to distinguish between an economic enterprise which was unlawful from the start and a legitimate economic enterprise that deviates from lawfulness in the course of its normal operation. In the former case, one often sees an unlawful, clandestine organization (such as organized crime) penetrating or taking over lawful sectors or fields of activities. The latter is the case of a legitimate organization undertaking, in addition to its normal, lawful activities, criminal, illegal, or shady operations.

### The Concept of Abuse

Etymologically, the word *abuse* comes from the Latin 'abusus' meaning a usage which is bad, excessive or unjust. According to Webster's dictionary, to abuse is to misuse, to use with bad motives or to wrong purposes. Abuse is defined as ill-use, improper treatment, application to a wrong purpose as an abuse of our natural powers, an abuse of civil rights, or of religious privileges . . . a corrupt practice or custom, as the abuses of government.

The concept of *abuse of power* is both vague and too broad. In a general way, the abuse may be just as much in the aims sought by the exercise of power as in the means employed. Acts may be defined as abuse of power when legitimate means are employed to achieve unlawful ends or when illegitimate means are employed to achieve unlawful ends or when illegitimate means are adopted in the pursuit of perfectly legitimate and laudable objectives. Torture is abuse even if it is administered in search of truth and justice. Most of the time, however, abuse of power is constituted by the use of unlawful means to achieve illegitimate ends, the use of violent, fraudulent, or corrupt means to attain dishonest, harmful, or outright unlawful objectives.

The operationalization of the concept of abuse of power requires, therefore, the consideration of three basic elements:

1.  the goals for which the power is exercised;
2.  the means by which the power is exercised;
3.  the limits within which the power should be exercised.

**The Goals**

Abuse of power is often characterized by the unlawfulness of the goals being pursued. A typical case of such abuse is the use of political or economic power to obstruct the normal course of justice either to prevent detection, prosecution, or the imposition of criminal sanctions for crimes committed by persons at the higher echelons of the socio-economic and political structures. Watergate is a perfect example of such abuse. Another example is the use of power to halt or suspend legal proceedings or to halt judgements against malefactors in high positions who are guilty of conventional offences or other breaches of the law.

**The Means**

Abuse of power may be constituted by the pursuit of legitimate goals by illegal and unlawful means. These unlawful means extend from constraint to confinement, from corruption to coercion, from threats to actual torture, from fraud to murder. One may even speak of abuse of power through negligence or carelessness. Furthermore, abuse of power need not be through active acts or commission, it may take the form of omission, or a refusal or unwillingness to act (non-feasance).

**The Limits**

Abuse of power occurs when power is exercised beyond its legal or normative limits. There are international, national, and local rules that regulate the use of power in its various forms and that impose precise and strict limits to such use. For example, the *International Covenant on Civil and Political Rights* has not only been ratified by some countries but many of its provisions have also been incorporated in domestic law thus assigning certain limits upon the exercise of power by governments or their agencies. The same can be said of other conventions such as the *American Convention on Human Rights* and the African Charter on Human and People's Rights.

The introduction of standards in various areas, in particular in the area of corrections, such as the minimum standards developed by the United Nations many years ago, also pose certain limits upon the exercise of power by defining and establishing certain norms, the violation of which may be judged as abuse. These standards usually define and determine the acceptable norms of honest conduct in political, social, or economic life. Other standards might be formulated to protect public health (against the sale and distribution of harmful substances or technological and chemical products), the environment (against pollution, against irreversible or serious harm to the ecology), the consumer (against excessive prices, commercial fraud, misleading advertising, etc.).

It goes without saying that the concept of abuse of power is both normative and relative. It is *normative* because it is closely linked to the system of norms and values and because it derives its content from the political ideology to which people adhere. It follows that the demarcation line between the normal exercise of power and its abusive exercise varies according to the normative model in a given society. Excessive unchecked powers in the hands of the police might be regarded as normal and desirable by those at the right end of the ideological scale and be denounced as oppressive, abusive, and tyrannical by those on the left. That is why abuse of power is *relative* in time and space. What may be regarded as abuse changes continually following political, economic, and social evolution. It also varies from one society to another, according to culture, ideology, political regime, and economic system. Definitions of what constitutes abuse necessarily vary between capitalist and socialist countries, countries with mixed economy and developing countries.

Should the concept of abuse of power be limited to those acts that are in violation of some existing criminal legislation or should it be extended to acts which, although contrary to prevailing norms, are not, or are not yet, made offences by the law? Should the fundamental principle of legality be sacrificed when considering abuse of power. Could we speak of abuse of power even when the 'abuse is not in violation of an existing law or statute'? A legalistic approach to the concept of abuse of power is too restrictive. Many forms of abuse are not currently 'offences' according to existing laws. For example, in the USA only 2% of the sanctions imposed by the courts on large corporations were for violations of a criminal nature (see the report of the inter-Regional Meeting held in New York in July 1979, p.5).

At the Latin American preparatory meeting for the *6th UN Congress on the Prevention of Crime and the Treatment of Offenders* a distinction was made between excess of power and abuse of power: the first consisting of a deplorable overstepping of authority, often circumstantial, by the agents of power, and their lack of co-ordination; the second, involving the deliberate use of power for specific aims that could not be legitimately justified, since they were often for the exclusive benefit of power itself, for the maintenance of a political regime or of an unjust social and economic system (Clark, 1983).

## Patterns of Abuse of Power

Typologies of power are not abundant. However, the literature on abuse of power usually makes a distinction between *political* power and *economic* power. Malinverni (1980) notes that economic power, just like social power, can exist within political power and also be the secondary consequence of it. Similarly, political power may be a secondary corollary of economic and social power and may be found within either of them. He further points out that the autonomy of economic and social power relative to official political power appears not to be very well defined, and in any event is not clear-cut. Malinverni prefers to use 'public' to designate the three basic powers, legislative, executive, and judicial. Against what is 'public' he opposes what is 'private'. Although he recognizes that both economic and social powers have their own characteristics he feels that they must be placed in correlation with the two principal categories of 'public' and 'private'. Malinverni notes that in the regimes which he calls 'regimes of political freedom' the economy, and thereby economic power are mainly or almost totally private. Conversely, in the regimes he calls 'regimes of political subordination' the economy, and thereby economic power, are mainly or almost totally public.

In addition to the visible powers, whether they are public or private, political, or economic, there are hidden powers. They remain in the shade outside or beneath the law and comprise, for instance all sorts of criminal organizations (such as the Mafia). These criminal organizations may command an enormous amount of power and in some cases may have those who hold public positions of power totally under their domination or influence.

A further distinction may be made between the power held by legal organizations such as industrial and commercial corporations and enterprises and illegal organizations such as the Mafia, anti-state groups, terrorist organizations and so on.

Abuse of public power is usually regarded as more serious, and as more far reaching than abuse of private power. In the same vein, abuse of political power is usually seen as having more serious and longer lasting consequences than abuse of economic power. It should be noted, however, that although such distinction is quite important in theory, in practice, its usefulness is often diminished due to the fact that the political, the economic and the social are usually so tied up each with the other that they become indistinguishable, even indivisible. Lejins (1980) draws attention to a specific type of abuse of power where the two types – political and economic – are jointly abused on an international scale. This involves a collusion between economic and political forces which engage in concert in activities which are simultaneously illegal and exploitative. This phenomenon occurs with some frequency in developing countries especially in Africa and Latin America. This collusion between economic and political forces assumes a number of forms. *One* of the models, perhaps the simplest, is that of corruption, where a multinational corporation bribes and suborns the administrators and civil servants so as to secure an immunity from official sanction for its profitable but illegal activities. In some cases, the corporation's influence may even extend to the legislative process. This notably occurs when the corporation succeeds in preventing the legislature from passing laws to ensure the protection of workers or the safety of the workplace. In *another* model of collusion, the multinational corporation is guided not only by its ruthless pursuit of profit but also by its own ideology which leads it to support a particular political party or a given political group subscribing to such ideology in the country where the corporation operates. With the financial assistance of the multinational corporation, this particular group or political party is put in a position from which it can dominate the power structure of the developing country in question or which enables it to overthrow and replace the regime in power. A *third* model broadly resembles the second, but with an additional dimension, namely that the government of the country where the multinational corporation has its registered head office, participates and contributes to the ideological and financial support provided by the corporation in a foreign country to a sector of the population or to a given political group. According to Lejins (1980), the identification of the model has a crucial importance in the choice of remedies and prevention strategies to be followed.

Further distinctions should be made between those forms of abuse of power which currently lie outside the boundaries of criminal law because they have not been criminalized and those forms which are punished but which, for one reason or another, escape detection, prosecution, and conviction.

A final distinction may be made between *crimes of power and crimes of the powerful*. Not every criminal offence committed by a person wielding power would qualify as abuse of power. Some crimes may be committed in a personal capacity and without taking advantage of one's position or power. Abuse of power may then occur in an attempt to cover up, to escape detection, prosecution, or conviction. In other words, the concept of abuse of power should not be extended so as to cover all criminal acts committed by a person in a position of power.

Abuse of power raises an important and intriguing question. How are we to explain the absence of a formal social reaction against certain forms of abuse of power which seriously harm the interests of citizens? There are at least two reasons: either there is a legislative lacuna, or there is administrative default. In the *first* case, there are no legal provisions to control or punish the abuse in question. This absence of legislation may be attributed to historical reasons, public tolerance or indifference, and above all to the influence exercised over the legislature by powerful individuals or groups in whose interest it is to keep the behaviour in question outside the domain of justice, sheltered from penal sanctions. In the *second* case, a law governing the activity in question and punishing the abuse exists but is not applied. Such an administrative deficiency may be explained in various ways: problems of detection, investigation, or prosecution; direct or indirect influence exercised by the malefactors or their associates over the organs of criminal justice either *de facto* or *de jure*. In this last instance, one might cite as an example diplomatic immunity, parliamentary privilege, laxity in relation to ministerial accountability, and doctrines such as 'national security', 'state of war', 'danger of insurrection', etc.

S. C. Versele coined the term *gilded criminals* and the *gilded figure* of criminality to designate the criminal activities of persons wielding public power who exercise it with impunity to the detriment of individuals or the public at large for their own advantage, or who exercise an economic power to the general detriment of society. This involves many different activities which seem to have been immunized by political power or economic strength, often associated for such purposes in skilfully structured and disguised conspiracies. In S. C. Versele's own words:

It is essentially a case of political–economic conspiracies, political–financial collusions, subtle peculations, disguised misappropriations and practical abuses which are assisted by lacunae in the law more or less deliberately engineered, as well as by more or less conscious compliances.

Gilded criminality has not received a great deal of attention from researchers although the wrongs, harm, losses and costs caused by it far exceed those suffered by society from conventional criminality.

**Trends in Abuse of Power**

For obvious reasons, not the least of which is the invisibility or low visibility of several forms of abuse of power and the enormous dificulty of gaining access to the necessary data, there are no reliable statistics or even estimates of the frequency or the extent and scope of abuse of political and economic power. It is, therefore, impossible to follow the trends and patterns of such abuse. Despite the dearth of data, there are reasons to believe that the incidence of abuse is on the increase in various parts of the globe. In addition to the traditional and well-known forms of abuse we are witnessing the emergence of new forms of abuse or at least new varieties of old types. In fact, the forms and modalities of abuse of power seem to be without end.

The most informative source currently available on the systematic abuse of political power is Amnesty International annual reports. Amnesty International, an international non-governmental human rights organization which works for prisoners worldwide, is able, through its broad membership, to gather and document information on human rights violations in a large number of countries.

In one Amnesty International report (1977) as many as 116 countries are mentioned. In most of them serious violations of human rights have been reported. And yet, by Amnesty's own admission the survey is far from complete. It is not only the number of countries where violations have occurred which is alarming. The nature and the extent of the abuse is a cause for grave concern. In his preface to the report, Thomas Hammarberg notes that in some Latin American countries security forces and para-military groups have been used as instruments for a policy of political murder. There, and in other parts of the world, the system of justice no longer functions in practice. Emergency laws have been misused to legalize brutal repression – even when by objective standards there are no emergencies.

Amnesty International reported that government-sanctioned torture is still practised in a horrifying number of states, in spite of the *United Nations declaration against all forms of torture.* In many countries, especially in Asia, a system of long-term detention has been developing. Prisoners are kept in poor prison conditions year after year and the authorities do not grant them the basic right to a trial. This means that innocent people are deprived of their freedom for 5 years, 10 years or even more. In other countries where political trials have taken place the defendants have been denied the opportunity for a proper defence. Amnesty also noted that the laws themselves have in some cases constituted appalling violations of the *Universal Declaration of Human Rights* making a mockery of justice. The trial procedures have been such that they could only serve the interest of the rulers. It further noted that the techniques of repression and the impact of these techniques vary. There are differences not only in the number of victims, but also in methodology, objectives, duration and both short-term and long-term consequences. In some countries regimes allow para-military groups to kidnap, torture, and assassinate political activists; in others, prisoners are kept in detention for years without trial. In some police stations torture is carried out with electric shocks; in others with psychological methods. In some prisons the inmates are refused all communication with their families; in others they are starved.

Amnesty International reported that in spite of the *Universal Declaration of Human Rights* adopted by the United Nations in December 1948, human rights violations exist and persist in a majority of countries all over the world. All major regions, all political or ideological blocs are involved. Although the Declaration states unequivocally that torture is unacceptable, torture persists with the knowledge, and even the support of the governments. The Declaration also affirms the right to life and states that no one shall be subjected to cruel, inhuman, or degrading punishment – and yet more than a hundred countries retain the death penalty (ibid.).

Not only governments, but also certain political organizations outside government control, violate human rights today. Individuals have been taken as prisoners or hostages, torture and executions have been carried out in the name of different political causes. These acts are no less deplorable than repression by governments and their agents (ibid.).

## Few Examples

Amnesty International reported that the South African rule in Namibia is characterized by mass arrests, detention, and the torture of Namibian civilians. Systematic torture was carried out by members of the South African Defence Force and documented by the leaders of the Lutheran, Roman Catholic, and Anglican churches in Namibia. In a *Joint Statement on Torture in Namibia*, the church leaders alleged that the use of torture had reached 'horrifying proportions' and had become 'standard practice' in the interrogation of detainees. The church leaders alleged that the methods of torture most commonly used by South African security police included electric shocks, prolonged solitary confinement, sleep deprivation, burning with cigarettes, beating with fists or rifle butts, and being hung up by the arms, sometimes with a weight added, for long periods.

The situation in South Africa itself was not much different. Hundreds of people, including many women and children, were killed, victims of police shootings. Hundreds of others were detained on political grounds. There were consistent reports of the torture of detainees undergoing interrogation by security police. In addition, hundreds were subjected to partial house arrest and other restrictions under banning orders imposed by the Minister of Justice.

Amnesty International (1977) estimated that 80% of the population of Latin America lives under military rule. A common feature of such regimes pointed out by *The International Commission of Jurists* (ICJ) in a commentary entitled 'Military Regimes in Latin America'[1] is the declaration and implementation of a 'permanent state of emergency'. Such governments regularly invoke special powers which, over a period of time, inevitably lead to the erosion of civil liberties, to the institutionalization of practices such as arbitrary arrest and torture of suspects and dissidents, and to a 'repression which oversteps all constitutional and legal bounds, violating the most elementary standards of humanity'.[2]

According to Amnesty International, one of the most worrying features of repression in Argentina, Chile, and Uruguay has been the acts of terrorism against the population by security forces, who appear to hold both the constitution and the law in contempt. In Argentina, during the period of military rule, thousands of people were abducted by the security forces and taken to secret camps throughout the country, where they were tortured and a countless number were assassinated. The gruesome details of these abductions, torture, and killings are now coming to light following the country's recent return to civilian rule. Similar acts that took place in Chile were documented in a dossier published by Amnesty International to draw world attention to the plight of the 'desaparecidos' and their families. A common typology used in Chile distinguishes between three categories of political prisoners:

1. *Detenidos por el estado de sitio*: those detained under the state of siege legislation, without trial and without any formal charges having been brought against them.
2. *Procesados y condenados*: those detained awaiting trial, pending trial, or serving sentences.
3. *Detenidos desaparecidos*: 'disappeared' prisoners whose detention the authorities refuse to acknowledge. DINA (Dirección Nacional de Inteligencia) is believed to be primarily responsible for these disappearances.

## DYNAMICS OF ACTS LINKED TO ABUSE OF POWER

### The Guise of Legitimacy

One important difference between conventional crime and acts linked to abuses of power is that many of the latter are committed under the guise of legitimacy. Concentration camps are justified by the need to protect internal or external security. Political dissidents are detained in psychiatric hospitals under the pretext that they are mentally unwell and in need of treatment. Police abuse of their power is legitimized as necessary to combat crime, to fight evil with evil and fire with fire. Extra judicial executions are portrayed as acts of self-defence. The use of 'dirty tricks', undemocratic, or outright illegal means, the overt or covert violations of civil liberties are thus rationalized and presented to an unsuspecting or an uninformed public as necessary and legitimate.

The use of terror by individuals or groups is universally condemned while its use by governments is defined as enforcement of the law. The League of Nations *Convention On The Prevention and Punishment of Terrorism* (1937) defined as acts of terrorism 'all criminal acts directed against a state and intended or calculated to create a state of terror in the minds of particular persons, or a group of persons or the general public'. According to the Convention, the category of terrorism includes all acts as well as attempts that cause death or bodily harm to heads of State or Government, their spouses, and public figures, that cause damage to public property; that endanger the lifes of the public; and that deals with arms and ammunition for the commission of any of these offenses in any state (Quereshi, 1976, p.151). The one-sided nature of this definition is self-evident. It defines as terrorist 'all criminal acts directed against the state' but leaves out violent, repressive, and oppressive actions of 'duly constituted' governments. Nor does it apply to atrocities committed by certain political regimes in violation of the *Geneva Convention* such as the killing of civilians or the torture of prisoners. It does not apply to the orchestrated efforts of some governments aimed at intimidating and subjugating minority groups, the members of a particular political party or religious faith, the inhabitants of occupied territories, etc. Even acts of genocide would hardly qualify as terrorist acts under this definition. As Quereshi (1976 p.157) notes:

> The violence of the resister is termed 'terrorist' whereas that of the regime is the enforcment of the law, and what distinguishes one from the other is the condition of legality – as long as the regime observes these conditions its reprisals against the resisters, no matter how harsh, are excluded from the category of terrorism!

Is there a qualitative difference between acts of violence and terror committed by the State and its representatives and those committed by invididuals or groups? Because the State has a monopoly over the use of force, abusing such power should qualify as terror. As Bell (1975, p.14) points out:

> Some regimes also authorize or at least employ techniques to maintain internal order that can be readily recognized by the distant observer as a form of terror: random purges, show trials, torture, internment. In some periods and nations such tactics appear systemic rather than a response to specific provocation.

Many forms of abuse of economic power are also disguised as legitimate activities. According to Schur (1980, p.168) corporate crime is the most glaring example in contemporary American society of systematic immunity from deviance defining by those who commit major social harms:

> As well as showing how concentrated power can help shield wrong-doers from legal control, it illustrates the fact that both stigma and nonstigma outcomes reflect the same basic self-fulfilling mechanism in official deviance processing through which power is confirmed and reinforced.

**The Hidden Nature of Abuse**

Another important characteristic which differentiates abuse of political and economic power from conventional crimes is the low visibility and the hidden nature of the abuse. History has shown that even acts of genocide, the extermination of millions can be shielded from the public eye for years and years. Acts of torture perpetrated in police stations, prisons, institutions and detention camps do not have the same visibility as crimes committed in the streets, in public, or private places. The most common pattern for abductions, kidnapping, and illegal arrests is that they take place in the late night hours, not only under cloak of darkness but when most people are sound asleep.

Even torture can be performed in a manner that makes it difficult for the victim to substantiate his/her claim. Sophisticated torture techniques used by contemporary torturers often leave few, if any, visible traces. In some cases there is no way to detect and document objectively a torture victim's allegations. In other cases this may only be possible through modern scientific research (see Amnesty International Report, 1977, p.38).

During the Stalinist purges of the 1920s and the 1930s the arrests and killings were usually carried out with no public exposure, trials, or announcements. The details remained hidden for years until Nikita Khrushchev released articles, memoirs, and words depicting individual cases of internments and killings.

In many countries, the government has total and absolute control over the means and channels of information. Information on, or linked to, acts of abuse of power is systematically withheld from the public. Furthermore, legal and illegal acts of political repression need not always be overt and violent. They can be perpetrated in subtle, covert, and non-violent ways. For example, political dissent may be suppressed by officially forbidding or by making it very difficult for dissidents to travel, organize public meetings, publish statements, find employment, and so on (Turk, 1982, p.39).

Criminal acts linked to the abuse of economic power are even less visible than those linked to political power. Business offences are not, usually defined as crimes by the general public or by the agents of social control. They are rarely dealt with as part of the crime problem. Schur (1980) notes that in shielding themselves from severe stigma and criminal sanctions, the large corporations have been very successful in sustaining their favoured social definitions of crime and of corporate activity. They have derived benefit from, and have sought to perpetuate, a number of common ideas that together encourage people to feel that corporate crime is not 'real' crime.

The more direct and immediate fears people have of physical violence and other face to face crimes against individuals divert them from the recognition that they are victimized by corporate wrongdoing . . .

Citizen acquiescence in victimization by corporations persists in part because most people see neither the offences nor the offender as posing a personified threat. There is certainly no dearth of victims, even if they themselves don't always realize it or do anything about it . . .

Part of the problem of mobilizing these victims for protest purposes has to do with the hidden and sometimes merely statistical nature of the injury. It is difficult to get people to do something about corporate violations that increase the statistical probability of their eventually dying from cancer, even when this probability may in fact be higher than that of being violently assaulted by a robber. Similarly, with respect to financial victimization, consciousness of the social harm or its full dimensions may remain low.

**Lack of Awareness on the Part of the Victim**

Lack of awareness on the part of the victim is yet another characteristic that differentiates criminal and illegal acts linked to abuse of economic power from common, conventional or ordinary crimes. As Edelhertz (1970, p.23) points out, when a common crime is committed, the victim immediately knows that something has been done to him: he has been assaulted, or robbed, or injured in some clearly definable way. He then has the plain option to report the crime to law enforcement authorities, or to refrain from doing so. This is not necessarily the case with respect to white-collar crimes in which the victim may never learn he has been victimized, or the realization comes too late to do him any good or too late to be of meaningful assistance to law enforcement authorities.

How many families who lost their young children in the developing countries in Africa and Asia realize that the deaths were an indirect result of the milk formula? How many victims become aware of the adulteration in foods and drugs? How many traffic accidents are attributed to the manufacturing of unsafe cars and how many labour accidents are blamed on unsafe conditions in the work place? The health hazards of the pollution of the environment or the dumping of wasteful substances may not be known to the authorities, let alone the victims, for years and years. Edelhertz (1970, p.15) maintains that the white-collar criminal must rely on the ignorance or carelessness of the victim and, in those areas in which regulatory agencies have a statutory mandate to protect the public, the ignorance of the public must be maintained by misleading the agency or circumventing its disclosure requirements. In many instances, corporate crimes are based upon predictable delays in victims' awareness of the fact that they have been victimized. As Edelhertz (1970, p.15) puts it:

Ignorance or carelessness of the victim is crucial to the success of the white collar criminal . . . Ignorance of the victim may be the direct result of a calculated effort to keep in ignorance the regulatory agency whose procedures are designed to protect him . . . In some instances ignorance of the victim is almost a certainty because of the context in which the wrongful actions arise . . . White collar crimes are unique. They generally require the victim to acquiesce in being victimized. In the great majority of cases we are confronted with crimes which require affirmative acts of co-operation by victims before the fraud can be completed. Put another way, victims must help to 'dig their own graves'.

## The Lack of Means of Recourse and Redress

Victims of common conventional crimes have access to the criminal justice system in their attempts to seek justice, to recover their losses, to have the offender punished or removed from circulation. In some cases, victims can claim restitution or compensation through the civil courts, boards of compensation, public, or private insurance. As inadequate as these means and these channels may be, they are better and more accessible than those to which victims of abuse of political and economic power have access. Victims of abuse of political power, in particular, suffer a much sadder lot than that reserved to victims of conventional crime and to victims of abuse of private or economic power. Most of the time, they lack any means of recourse against the perpetrator of abuse. Because the abuser is the government itself or one of its agencies, the victims cannot count on the help or the cooperation of other agencies of government or of normal channels of redress. In some Scandinavian and European countries, and in some Canadian provinces there is an 'Ombudsman' whose duty is to receive, investigate, and deal with citizens' complaints against public agencies or civil servants. In most countries victims of public and political abuse of power are left to suffer in silence and to cope on their own with the physical, psychological, and economic consequences of abuse.

The plight of victims is compounded by a large number of technical obstacles which make the discovery, investigation, prosecution, and punishment of abuse of power extremely difficult. The following are only a few of these obstacles:

1.  The absence of criminal law provisions covering the abuse in question. The criminal codes of most countries are disproportionately slanted towards conventional criminality and the traditional types of delinquency. As a result, several types of abuse of power, as unethical, harmful, or dangerous they may be, have remained, for various reasons, outside the realm of criminalized behaviour.

2.  The existence of explicit legal provisions exempting the government or its agents from responsibility, prohibiting the victims from suing the government, or denying them access to the normal channels of redress.

3.  The complexity or the high technical nature of the laws and regulations covering many areas in which abuse of power may occur. This is particularly the case of the economic and fiscal sectors.

4.  The dispersion of legal texts governing economic and administrative activities.

5.  The ambiguity, imprecision and lack of clarity of texts currently in force, which deal with the behaviours in question. Often the legal provisions covering these areas are vague and susceptible to varying interpretations.

6.  The difficulty of proof: the evidentiary problems in cases of abuse of power can be extremely complex. Quite often, it is much more difficult to document the abuse, to establish guilt and responsibility than it is in the case of conventional crimes.

7.  The skilful, subtle, and sophisticated techniques employed by the guilty parties. In this respect the traditional criminal law often proves to be a rigid and inflexible instrument, too hide-bound by the principle of precedents to be able to face up

to the economic and technological realities which change and develop with great speed.

8. The high political or socio-economic status of the guilty parties and the corruptive influence they may have on the organs of justice. As Schur (1980) points out 'even if we were to assume the complete political independence and impartiality of the judiciary, which assumption may not be fully warranted, the close ties between big business and other major policy makers – both legislative and administrative – would ensure substantial influence on corporate crime policy' (p.172). A similar point is made by Quinney (1974, p.59) when he asserts that the makers of criminal policy are members or representatives of big business and finance, including the legal establishment which is tied to corporate and financial wealth.

9. The fact that the police, the prosecutors, and the courts are too busy combating conventional crimes which preoccupy the public more than abuse of power.

10. The lack of specialized investigators with the necessary expertise in each of the economic sectors in which the abuse occurs.

The prosecution and punishment of those guilty of criminal acts linked to abuse of power is often hampered by the well known phenomenon of *diffuse responsibility*. Schur (1980) notes that

> Obscurity and diffusion of personal responsibility for corporate offenses further limit and undermine the public stigmatizing and official processing of violators. People do not always know precisely whom to blame, and prosecutors may not always be certain who should be prosecuted. The complexities of modern business transactions and also of the corporation's internal and division of labor pose problems in this regard . . .
> Differentiation of tasks and departments within today's large corporations make it very difficult to know which person or unit initiated a given action on whose orders, and with whose knowledge. While it might seem logical to hold top management responsible for systematic criminality of the corporation, more often than not establishing direct responsibility at that level is not easy whether because of intentional actions by management or as a result of organizational structure and procedure.

Conklin (1977, p.65) notes that the delegation of responsibility and unwritten orders keep those at the top of the corporate structure remote from the consequences of their decisions and orders, much as the heads of organized crime families remain 'untouchable' by the law.

Despite the proliferation of corporations, companies, and juridical persons (*personnes morales*) most penal codes continue to place emphasis on the liability of individuals. There is a new tendency to recognize the criminal liability of corporations especially in the field of consumer protection and of environmental protection. France embodied a system of criminal liability for juridical persons in the Draft Bill for the revision of the French Penal Code. Finland is studying proposals to increase the level of criminal liability of large companies, especially in cases where it is difficult to identify the person responsible. German Law has worked out a compromise by admitting a direct liability for juridical persons for crimes, misdemeanours, and infractions they commit. Nevertheless, it only imposes administrative fines to sanction such liabilities.

However, the current imbalance between the criminal liability of corporate bodies and of physical persons remains in most countries and needs to be redressed to provide the victims with more adequate means of recourse against the perpetrators of abuse. One way is to develop a theory of collective liability along with a theory of criminal complicity sufficiently broad to embrace the involvement of collective entities. Another possibility is to extend the field of strict liability so as to include activities and practices which currently lie outside the range of criminal sactions.

### The Abundance of Mechanisms of Concealment and Cover-Up

As mentioned above, many criminal acts linked to abuse of power are by their nature less visible than ordinary, conventional crimes and as such may remain hidden for years or forever. Even when acts of abuse of power become known, those who are guilty usually have enormous resources with which to cover up their guilt, to avoid detection, prosecution, and conviction. When the cover up is elaborate and successful, the abuse of power may never come to light. It is when the cover up fails that the details of the wrong-doings are revealed. The Watergate affair in the United States is a perfect example of a cover-up that failed and it showed to what extent the law itself may be used for the political purpose of hiding or facilitating the abuse. Government ability to control and to withhold information provides abusers of power with a powerful tool to hide or to cover-up their wrong-doing. Theoretically, the *official secrets Act* which exists in many countries is mainly intended to prevent the leaking of information sensitive or vital to the security of the state. In practice, however, these Acts are often used to protect the traditional secrecy of the workings of the state. In many cases disclosure of information attesting to, or documenting the abuse is withheld by invoking the officials secrets Act. 'By this means information is so restructured as to guarantee an ill-informed Parliament, press and people . . .' (Bunyan, 1977, p.11). Bunyan (1977) notes that the *Official Secrets Acts* in Britain have been used more to stop the circulation of government information internally than against the activities of foreign spies and their British-born accomplices. He believes that

The use of three Official Secrets Acts represents the last resort in suppressing public knowledge of the workings of the state. However, there is another method which is occasionally employed – Crown Privilege, which is judge-made law. This gives the Crown (the state) power to withhold documentary evidence from any court.

When the cover up is blown or when the acts of abuse of power are detected then there are several other means by which those in high office can avoid prosecution or escape punishment. Former President Nixon was pardoned by Gerald Ford who succeeded him in office without even being charged with the offences he committed while in office. Spiro Agnew, the Vice-President of the Nixon administration, bartered his office to keep from going to prison. Agnew elicited and accepted bribes while head of the county government in Baltimore. He continued to accept bribes from Maryland contractors after he was installed as Vice-President. Agreeing to resign his office as Vice-President he was allowed to plead *Nolo contendere* to a single charge of income tax violation in exchange for a sentence of unsupervised probation. While Agnew escaped jail, the men who had supplied the information that led to his downfall were sentenced to prison terms of one year and eighteen months (Geis and Meier, 1977, pp.209–10).

Those guilty of abuse of economic power do not fare any less better. Schur (1980, p.179) notes that although it is now widely accepted that corporate crime is one area in which the deterrent effect of severe punishment – especially a convincing threat of imprisonment – is likely to be strong, such punishment is rarely, if ever, imposed, and hence the deterring threat is not credible. According to Schur, the threat of imprisonment does usually remain in the picture, as a kind of background warning, but there is a strong preference for proceeding in most cases under administrative provisions and for imposing administrative sanctions. The preference reflects, along with the general reluctance to brand businessmen as criminals, difficulty in prosecutors establishing criminal intent (Edelhertz, 1970). Schur adds that the close ties that exist between the regulatory agencies and the industries under their jurisdiction are frequently cited as a reason for lack of severity in sanctioning corporate wrong-doing:

> Between the strong tendency of both agencies and prosecutors to accept various types of settlement in lieu of actual trials and the inadequacy of continuous monitoring and controlling procedures, many of the worst corporate abuses persist free of interference. This widespread failure of regulation has been a major reason for the recent growth of public interest organizations, undertaking research, public education, and lobbying in such areas as consumer and environmental protection.

Edelhertz (1970, p.18) notes that concealment is achieved by the design of an organizational structure to frustrate and discourage complaint or pursuit by the victim. Concealment is also achieved by limiting the residue of provable facts, so that there is great difficulty in organizing a case which will meet necessary legal standards for criminal sanctions or civil process.

> Because of the manner in which white-collar crimes are organized and executed it is possible to generalize . . . that in investigating and prosecuting these cases the problem is more one of what the facts bear out than what the facts are. The key question in a prosecution is whether criminal intent is inferable beyond a reasonable doubt from the facts unearthed by the investigation,

that is, was there a crime? If the answer is negative, then the crime is concealed, no matter how deep the wound.

## The David/Goliath Syndrome

Except for the outcome, the victim's situation to the offender in cases of criminal acts linked to abuse of political or economic power is strikingly similar to that of David to Goliath. The David/Goliath syndrome refers to a situation where there is extreme and flagrant disproportion in the powers of the parties involved. The abundance of resources is almost inherent in the concept of power. Thus while the abuser of political or economic power may have at his/her command vast or considerable financial, material, and human resources, the victim of abuse is in many cases entirely on his/her own. Geis and Meier (1977, p.27) note that a person who gains an elective or appointive office acquires with it considerable power to confer favours and to use public resources for personal gain. The office-holder also obtains control of persons and agencies which can be used to engage in illegal activities and to prevent their detection.

Schur (1980, p.172) points out that corporations, because of all the power resources at their command, are in a position of unusual strength in defending themselves against the prospect of being defined as criminal. The unparalleled magnitude and concentration of economic power that corporations hold greatly facilitate the defence of what are essentially economic interests.

The essence of the David/Goliath syndrome is that when it comes to the financial costs involved or the technical expertise needed to seek and to obtain justice and redress, the victims of abuse of political and economic power are clearly at a disadvantage. While their opponents, be it the government, businesses, or corporations, dispose of huge financial and technical resources, the victims can hardly afford the financial burden that litigation is likely to place upon them. And while in many cases the victims may be forced by the shortage of funds or by the circumstances to go through it on their own, the guilty parties are able to hire astute, experienced and tenacious counsel. The counsel's task is to bend every effort, to use every resource and tactic to insulate the clients from indictment, from trial, from conviction, and from the direct or indirect consequences of conviction (Edelhertz, 1970, p.45). Edelhertz notes that counsel will pursue

their objectives by continually seeking conferences with the prosecutor and his supervisors, by interminable motions which are largely
destined for defeat, and by extensive discovery proceedings and
delaying tactics. When and if the case appears to be ready for trial
there will be attempts to dispose of these cases by *nolo contendere*
pleas, or attempts to convince the prosecutor that the defendant
should be permitted to plead to lesser offences which are not even
lesser included offences comprehended within crimes charged in the
indictment (p.46).

What chances does an ordinary consumer or an ordinary citizen
have against General Motors, Ford or Chrysler; against Shell, Exxon
or Gulf; against IBM, Westinghouse or General Electric; against
Nestle, Lilly or Dupont? Could there be any doubt that the balances
of justice are heavily tilted against the victims of abuse?

## IMPACT AND EFFECTS OF ABUSE OF POWER

### Abuse of Political Power

For obvious reasons the impact and effects of acts linked to abuse of
political power are not uniform. Acts of genocide and similar forms
of annihilation and political oppression can claim millions of lives.
Estimates of the number of victims of Nazi holocaust suggest that
between 18 and 35 million were killed in concentration camps
(Bettelheim, 1979). Millions are also believed to have perished
during the Stalinist purges in Russia in the 1920s and the 1930s.
Actual figures may never become known. However, estimates of the
number of those who were interned range from 1 million to 15
million. It is further estimated that a third of those sent to the camps
died, mainly from exhaustion and lack of medical treatment. Conquest (1968) estimates that between 1936 and 1960, 700 000 'legal'
executions took place in Stalinist Russia. There are no accurate
estimates of those who were exterminated by the communist regimes
in China or Cuba, by the Marcos regime in the Philippines or under
Idi Amin in Uganda, to name but a few. The Pot Pol regime in
Kampuchea has been accused of destroying millions of its citizens.

While other forms of abuse of political power may not claim as
many victims, they can have disastrous effects on those victimized,
their families, their communities, and society at large. The traumatic

effects of 'disappearance' on the families of those who vanish are far deeper and much longer lasting than the effects of a loss of one of their members to an act of outright killing or execution. The uncertainty surrounding the fate and the whereabouts of the beloved one amounts to extreme psychological torture. Add the despair and frustration which stem from the inability to find answers, to get information, the feelings of helplessness and anger resulting from the inability to change the course of events or even to trace the person who disappeared. The emotional stress and the mental anguish are compounded by the impossibility, until the corpse is found, to conduct a religious burial or to have a known grave as a memorial place for occasional visits.

Other types of abuse of power such as torture, internment, violations of human and civil rights, while less traumatic, do cause an enormous amount of human pain and suffering. Yet the pain and sufferings of the victims and their families are but one aspect of the total picture. The impact of acts of abuse of power on the social fabric itself can never be over-estimated. The psychological effects of living under conditions of political oppression or under a reign of terror have been all too well described in the literature. In particular, the randomness with which many acts of abuse strike members of racial, religious, or political minorities generates not only feelings of fear, anxiety, and insecurity but outright terror.

The general, long-term effects on society's development, cohesiveness, values, political, and economic stability can never be measured. The frustration, the injustices, the loss of confidence in the ability of the law to protect, the loss of faith in government and in public institutions, and in the impartiality of the justice system, do not lend themselves to quantification or accurate measurement.

The tangible effects of abuse on individual victims or their immediate relatives are easier to observe and to measure than the less tangible effects on the political, social, or economic climates. Several studies have been conducted on survivors of concentration camps and on victims of torture. Psychiatrists report that concentration-camp survivors often display symptoms of 'chronic reactive depression', 'depression due to uprooting', and 'post-concentration camp syndrome'. Many were found to suffer from pervasive depressive moods, morose behaviour, withdrawal, general apathy, angry outbursts, insecurity, lack of initiative and interest, guilt feelings, and self-depreciatory attitudes (Krystal, 1968). Krystal also reports that one of the most predominant complaints among survivors is that they were more likely to fear about something happening to their mates or children when they were out of sight. They also exhibited fears of situations similar to those they have experienced such as being approached by a uniformed officer, or of any other events which awaken their memories. Other complaints reported by Krystal include repetition of nightmares, memory loss, insomnia, and psychosomatic symptoms.

One of the most troublesome sequelae of torture are the psychological, neurological, and mental disturbances displayed by the victims. A Danish study of 32 Chilean refugees in Denmark and 35 former political prisoners held by the Greek Junta's security forces discovered such disturbances in 17 Chileans and 23 Greeks (60%). Objective signs, including neurological findings related to torture, were seen in 21 Chileans and 24 Greeks (67%) (Amnesty International Report, 1977, p.38).

### Abuse of Economic Power

Kapp (1978), quoted by Karunaratne (1983), defines the social costs of corporations as 'all direct and indirect losses sustained by third persons or the general public as a result of unrestrained economic activities'. These may include loss in lives, damage to human health, destruction or deterioration of property values, the pollution of the environment, the premature depletion of natural wealth, or impairment of less tangible values such as the quality of life.

Obviously, no dollar amount can adequately identify the costs of illegal acts linked to abuse of economic power. Many of them are not subject to clear measurement. As Edelhertz (1970) points out:

> How does one set a dollar value on food and drug violations which may permanently disable or kill? What is the true dollar cost of a fraudulent banking operation without valid deposit insurance which destroys the life savings of the elderly and makes them a burden on their children or on the state?
>
> (pp.8–9)

The social and economic costs of tax violations, self-dealing by separate employees and bank officials, adulteration or watering of foods and drugs, charity frauds, insurance frauds, price fixing, frauds arising out of government procurement, and abuses of trust are clearly enormous even though not easily measured.

(p.4)

Several estimates of the financial costs of white-collar crime in the United States have been made. Sutherland and Cressey (1978, p.24) note that the financial losses from fraudulent business transactions are probably many times as great as the financial losses from burglary, robbery, and ordinary larceny. In the late 1960s, the President's Crime Commission acknowledged a range of substantial white-collar crime costs. The Commission said:

> The exact financial loss to the Government caused by tax fraud is difficult to determine but is undoubtedly enormous. Estimates of the amount of reportable income that goes unreported each year range from $25 to $40 billion . . . The financial loss to the public caused by a single conspiracy in restraint of trade may be untold millions in extra costs paid ultimately by the buying public. It is estimated that the cost to the public annually of securities frauds . . . is probably in the $500 million to $1 billion range. A conservative estimate is that nearly $50 million is spent annually on worthless or extravagantly misrepresented drugs and therapeutic devices. Fraudulent and deceptive practices in the home repair and improvement field are said to result in $500 million to $1 billion losses annually; and in the automobile repair field alone, fraudulent practices have been estimated to cost $100 million annually.
>
> (1967, pp.103–6)

Schur (1980) reports that direct and indirect physical costs of corporate violations are also huge although they cannot be easily or adequately documented. Such violations include marketing of inadequately tested drugs, thereby causing illness or even death; unsafe work conditions that lead to injuries and death; environmental pollution producing long-term health hazards; and the marketing of harmful food products. Additional social costs in terms of widespread public cynicism and a generalized hostility among the poor and the exploited, are likewise incalculable (p.174).

Although comprehensive statistics are lacking, it is fair to conclude that lives lost through corporate wrong-doing, criminal, illegal, and shady practices far outnumber those lost as a result of criminal homicide. The potential impact of certain corporate acts or omission such as nuclear plant accidents or industrial pollution are simply enormous. One cannot but be surprised at the sharp discrepancy between the substantial impact of abuse of economic power and the weakness of official responses to it. One reason usually advanced to explain such discrepancy is the non-violent, therefore non-threatening nature of most white-collar crimes. Yet, as Edelhertz (1970, p.9) points out, the impact of white-collar crime on people and on their physical and psychological integrity and security is not so different from that of common crime except that its effects are longer lasting. He writes:

> White-collar crime, like common crime, can have a serious in-fluence on the social fabric, and on the freedom of commercial and interpersonal transactions. Every stock market fraud lessens confidence in the securities market. Every commercial bribe or kick-back debases the level of business competition, often forcing other suppliers to join in the practice if they are to survive. The business which accumulates capital to finance expansion by tax evasion places at a disadvantage the competitor who pays his taxes and is compelled to turn to lenders for operating and expansion capital . . . competitors who join in a conspiracy to freeze out their competition, or to fix prices, may gravely influence the course of the economy, in addition to harming their competitors and customers.

## SELECTED TYPES OF VICTIMIZATION AND VICTIMS

### Human Beings as Guinea Pigs: The Use of Convicted Offenders for Human Experimentation

In 1947, fifteen German doctors were convicted by the Nuremberg war crimes tribunal of criminal responsibility for cruel and frequently murderous 'medical experiments' performed on concentration camp inmates. In their defence, the accused doctors cited comparable experiments carried out on prisoners by American physicians (Mit-ford, 1974, p.151). Mitford reports that since the Nuremberg tribunal there has been a huge expansion of medical research programmes in many prisons in the US sanctioned by federal health agencies and state prison administrators who do not choose to recognize the standards established by the Nuremberg trial as applying to the captives in their custody. In 1961, *the World Medical Association* proposed that prisoners, 'being captive groups, should not be used as the subject of experiments'. However, according to Mitford, the recommendation was never formally adopted, largely because of the opposition of American doctors. She quotes one American scientist as saying 'criminals in our penitentiaries are fine experimental material – and much cheaper than chimpanzees'. She also points out to those large pharmaceutical concerns with huge financial stakes in experimental testing on human subjects because of FDA regulations requiring that all new drugs be tested on humans before being marketed.

In 1963, *Time* magazine reported that the US federal government was using prisoner 'volunteers' for large-scale research, dispensing rewards ranging from a package of cigarettes to $25 cash plus reduction of sentence; that prisoners in Ohio and Illinois were injected with live cancer cells and blood from leukaemia patients to determine whether these diseases could be transmitted; that doctors in Oklahoma were grossing an estimated $300 000 a year from deals with pharmaceutical companies to test out new drugs on prisoners; that the same doctors were paying prisoners $5 a quart for blood which they retailed at $15 (ibid, p.153).

In 1969, the *New York Times* reported that 'the federal government has watched without interference while many people sickened and some died in an extended series of drug tests and blood plasma operations . . . the immediate damage has been done in the penitentiary systems of three states. Hundreds of inmates in "voluntary" programs have been stricken with serious disease. An undetermined number of the victims have died.' (ibid, p.154).

## The Use of Patients for Human Experimentation

Recently, Canadians have awoken to some startling revelations about Canadian psychiatric patients at the Allan Memorial Institute (a renowned psychiatric hospital in Montreal) who in the 1950s were used as guinea pigs in covert psychiatric experiments partly financed by the CIA. According to reports published in the press,[3] the patients' minds were wiped clean using a variety of techniques including: brain electroshock, LSD, curare poison, weeks of drugged sleep, and sensory deprivation extending some times to five weeks. Reduced to a stupor, sometimes with drugs, the patients were then bombarded with tape-recorded messages, designed to programme new patterns of behaviour into their brains. A CIA front organization. The Society for the Investigation of Human Ecology, gave the psychiatrist who conducted the experiments $19 000 a year during the late 1950s and early 1960s to finance the brain washing experiments. In his book *The Search for the Manchurian Candidate* John Marks writes:

> The frequent screams of patients' that echoed through the hospital did not deter (Dr . . . .) or most of his associates in their attempts to 'depattern' their subjects completely.

**The Use of the Poor for Human Experimentation**

In an article on the use of steroids published in *Sports Illustrated*[4] (1 Aug. 1983) the magazine reported a shocking story. It revealed a grandiose plan announced by the founder, president and chief publicist of Nautilis Sports/Medical Industries Inc. at a strength – coaching conference at the University of Virginia. The President declared that

> Next week I am going south of the border to institute a 10 year study using thousands of subjects. Why south of the border? Because we can get the subjects at a price we can afford, and we can get subjects who are motivated, who will train. When you take starving subjects you can motivate them, believe me. We're going to take about 1,000 subjects and give them massive doses of steroids, and we're going to take another 1,000 and give them no steroids. You can't do that in this country. But you can do it down there. When they sign up for this program they will be told in advance, 'Look, what we give you may be a drug, or it may not be. Even if it is you won't know it. The drugs might be dangerous and they might ruin your liver. Now if you don't want to sign up, there's the door, leave!'

On 13 July 1987, the *Vancouver Sun* reported from London that Britain's Ministry of Defence had acknowledged testing nerve gases on human volunteers for the past twenty-five years to assess the possible results of exposure to enemy weapons but said the doses were too small to be dangerous! Volunteers were paid the equivalent of $225 each.

## Acts of Abuse of Power Involving the Deliberate Taking of Human Lives

Nsereko notes that in many African states (and the situation is no different in many other parts of the world) thousands of people die each year, not as a result of natural calamities or pestilences, nor at the hands of common criminals (though these have their share of the death toll) but as a result of the abuse of power by governments or their surrogates. Needless to say, most of these arbitrary deprivations of life go unpunished. By arbitrary deprivation Nsereko means:

> the taking of life by or at the instigation, connivance or condonation of the government or those acting under its authority in a manner that contravenes the principles of natural justice or domestic law or International Human Rights law. Arbitrary deprivation of life generally manifests itself in such practices as summary executions, extrajudicial executions, enforced or involuntary disappearances, law enforcement abuse of power and military excesses.

## Summary Executions

Summary execution is defined by Nsereko as the practice of imposing and carrying out the death penalty in a manner which disregards the rules of natural justice or the due process of law. The proceedings leading to the execution may have a semblance of legality, but they fall far short of the international minimum standards of procedural justice as recognized under the international human rights instruments and under the reasonably developed legal systems of the world. According to Nsereko, the sentence is usually handed down by a special court, a 'people's court', 'revolutionary court' or 'military tribunal', which is not bound up by the ordinary rules of procedure. Such courts are usually set up in times of acute political tension, sometimes following an attempted *coup d'état* or a successful change of government. They were established in Guinea in 1969, Somalia in 1970, Uganda in 1973, in Ethiopia in 1974, in Ghana in 1978, in Liberia in 1980, in Iran in 1979, to name but a few countries. Nsereko notes that even when some procedural safeguards are provided for, the court may disregard them, 'in the interests of revolutionary justice'. The court may condemn an accused to death without formally charging him with any specific offence or giving him a chance to be heard, to adduce evidence in his defence, or after merely examining his file or reading out 'confessions'. Convictions based on confessions extorted from victims by means of torture are also common (ibid., p.7).

At most times the special courts sit in camera, emerge only to announce the sentence or the fact that it has already been carried out. They thus violate a cardinal rule of procedural justice that requires Judicial tribunals to open their proceedings to public scrutiny so that justice is not only done but also manifestly appears to be done . . .

The special courts often do not afford accused persons an opportunity to be assisted by counsel. Even when the right is vouchsafed it may be illusory, since lawyers in the country may feel so intimidated that few may be willing to risk their personal safety by appearing before the special courts on behalf of some accused persons.

The members of the special courts are neither members of the regular judiciary nor trained in the rudiments of the law nor in judicial procedure.

The substantive laws which the special courts apply may sometimes be characterized as despotic and arbitrary. Aimed as they often are at punishing members of an ousted regime or opponents of the incumbent rulers, they usually apply retroactively.

The laws are usually vague and the offences they create incapable of precise definition . . . These laws do oftentime violate substantive human rights recognised under the international human rights instruments . . . the victims are usually not given an opportunity to appeal the conviction or the sentence imposed on them by the special courts, or to petition for pardon or clemency. Even when the right of appeal exists in law it may simply be ignored or it may be illusory. The victims are executed, usually by firing squad, hours after the pronouncement of the sentence (ibid.).

**Extrajudicial Executions**

Nsereko (1983) notes that extra judicial executions and involuntary disappearances are carried out outside the pale of the law. They are acts of murder par excellence, committed by the State against its own inhabitants. They are political in nature, used to eliminate insecure regimes' adversaries, real or imagined, and to cow the population into submission. According to Nsereko, the killings are often directed against targeted individuals such as politicians, professionals like doctors, lawyers and journalists, as well as 'communists', 'capitalists', 'feudalists', 'reactionaries' and 'guerrillas'. They may, however, and often are, directed against entire population groups, be they ethnic, racial, religious or social, sometimes to genocidal proportions (ibid.).

> They are carried out by the army, law enforcement or other government agencies or by paramilitary or political groups acting with the tacit support of the army or the agencies . . .
> Sometimes the killings are carried out publicly during security sweeps by members of the security services . . . It is telling that government agents do not have any qualms over their actions and often make no secret of their role in the killings. Some do however feel a sense of guilt and attempt to conceal their deeds by fabricating such excuses for the killings as: the victim was 'trying to escape' or that he died 'in an encounter' or that he 'committed suicide' or that he was killed by a 'lone assassin'. The killings which take place in detention centres are often preceded by ghoulish acts of torture. Death also often results from the inhuman living conditions in the centres, or from denial of food and water or medical attention (ibid.).

Nsereko adds that terroristic acts are also often employed to kill government opponents in exile. These include assassinations by special liquidation squads or by poisoning, and letter or parcel bombs. Refugee camps are attacked and thousands of refugees massacred by the security forces of their countries of origin or their surrogates. The report on summary and arbitrary executions (E/CN 4/16, 1983) submitted to the *United Nations Commission on Human Rights* by the special rapporteur S. Amos Wako states the number of 'executed' people in the last 15 years in 38 countries (all of them developing except three) as not below 2 million. Even democratic countries are not immune to these extra judicial executions. In Jamaica the number of such executions reached a peak in 1980 during the political turmoil that preceded the elections. Nor are all these extra legal executions politically motivated. Police killings of criminals are common occurrences in many countries. In Jamaica, a country with a total population of slightly over 2 million, 234 citizens were killed by the police in 1980, 252 in 1981, and 150 in 1982. Needless to say, many of these executions are in violation of the

*Universal Declaration of Human Rights.* Article II, Section 1 of the Declaration stipulates that:

> Everyone charged with a penal offence has the right to be presumed innocent until proved guilty according to law in a public trial at which he has had all the guarantees necessary for his defence.

Nor is the case of Jamaica unique. Death squads composed of former or active policemen have been operating in many South American countries for many years. In particular, the Brazilian death squad has gained notoriety for its liquidation of known offenders. On 2 January 1984, Reuter reported that Indonesia's shadowy death squads are continuing their elimination of known criminals. A prominent Jakarta lawyer said that these so called mystery killings may have claimed about 4000 victims. The founder of the Indonesian legal aid institute claimed that the campaign is a joint military – police operation. The bodies of the victims are usually found bullet-riddled and bearing tattoos which are the mark of underworld gangs. The killers strike at night, often operating from jeeps, and shoot from close range. They are believed to be élite special forces units drawn from the para-commandos, working their way down lists of suspects drawn up by the police. Corpses have been found in sacks, rivers, paddy fields, and by the road side; many were ex-convicts. The Government of Indonesia had maintained official silence on the issue since August 1983, when the Indonesian press was banned from detailed reporting of what had already become a controversial issue. The *Regional Council for Human Rights* in Asia condemned the killings after a recent meeting in Jakarta at which members also criticized alleged rights violations in the Philippines, Thailand and Singapore.

**Involuntary or Enforced Disappearances**

The phenomenon of involuntary or enforced disappearances is not a new one. However, it has gained much publicity in recent years following the mass disappearances that took place in Chile and Argentina under the rule of their military governments. Most of those who disappear are killed by Government agents. As Nsereko (1983) notes:

> In cases of disappearances death often occurs after the disappearance of the victim. Government agents masquerading as private

kidnappers, abduct the victim either stealthily at night or out of the sight of third parties, or in open day light in the presence of his relatives, friends, or mere onlookers. They take him into official prison houses or police cells, or into unofficial secret detention centres operated by the various state security agencies. They hold him incommunicado often without any records indicating the fact of his arrest and detention.

In most cases the victim will not be heard of again, and his remains may never be found. He is either buried in secret mass graves, or he is decapitated beyond recognition and either burned to ashes or dumped into the lakes and rivers or in forests.

Disappearances are more tormenting to the families of the victim than overt extrajudicial executions: firstly, because of the uncertainty surrounding the fate of the person who has disappeared, and secondly, because the family is denied the right to conduct a religious burial, or to have the corpse laid into a known grave.

The shocking revelations made recently in Argentina following the ouster of the military regime and the return to democratic rule attests to the seriousness of the phenomenon of disappearances in that country. In January 1984, the Argentinian weekly newspaper *Siete Dias* (Seven Days) reported that more than 1000 prisoners were anaesthetized, tied together, and thrown into the sea from aircraft by Argentina's military authorities during the 'dirty war' against leftist guerrillas in 1975–79. Terrorists or suspected terrorists were kidnapped, tortured, then anaesthetized. As soon as they were asleep, they were undressed, tied together, and thrown out of planes. Injured or dying people were incinerated in large ovens in the basement of a naval mechanics school. The military called it 'roasting'. Torture methods were learnt on the spot, which accounts for a high level of mistakes. Among the 'mistakes' was the death of a young Swedish girl identified as Dagmar Hagelin. Although not connected with the guerrillas she was shot through the head by a military officer.

In a magazine interview publised in *La Semana* (The Week) a former Argentine navy petty officer admitted that he helped kidnap 200 political detainees and witnessed their torture. The detainees had their heads placed under water and received electric shocks. Some were thrown alive out of aircraft into the River Plate after being drugged. The officer was part of a para-military group based in the Navy Mechanics School in Buenos Aires, a notorious secret prison and torture centre in the late 1970s. The group's task was to capture suspected leftist guerrillas who were interrogated and tortured, under the supervision of doctors, before being killed and disposed of secretly. The secret detention centre was set up by former navy chief Emilio Massera in November 1975. It was disbanded in 1978 after the armed forces had virtually annihilated the guerrillas. Up to 3000 people disappeared during the anti-guerrilla campaign.

Sometimes the disappearances and killings extended to whole families. In January 1984, United Press International reported from Buenos Aires that the bodies of three small children were exhumed in the suburb of Boulogne. The children were 6 months old, 4 years old and 5 years old. Cemetery records said the children were shot in the head. The investigation was instigated by Human Rights groups who complained to the authorities that a couple were buried with their three children in 'no name' graves in September 1976 after being shot and killed by security forces. At the time of the shootings a military communique said that 'five subversive delinquents' have been killed in 'a confrontation'.

**The Internment of Civilians**

Another common form of abuse of political power is the internment of civilians, who have committed no offence in concentration camps or in remote isolated areas. A lot has been said and written about the Nazi concentration camps in Europe during the Second World War and about the Siberian labour camps. Amnesty International report (1975) on *Prisoners of Conscience in the U.S.S.R: Their Treatment and Their Conditions* talked not only of internment in labour camps but also of the systematic torture to which the prisoners are subjected.

Again these abuses of power are by no means limited to totalitarian, military, or racist regimes such as the one in South Africa, they do take place occasionally in democratic countries especially during times of external or internal threats. In Canada, recent calls for compensation of victims of acts of abuse of power have prompted the publication of vivid accounts of the injustices to which Canadians of Japanese origin were subjected during the Second World War, their internment, the confiscation, and sale of their property. With Canada's declaration of war on Japan, persecution of Japanese Canadians began. In February 1942 mass evacuation started and by 1943 they had all been transferred from the British Columbia coast-line to the interior of the province. Almost 21 000 Japanese Canadians in British

Columbia were stripped of their farms, businesses, and homes. The properties were sold to the highest bidder (Bohn, 1983). The fate of Japanese-Americans was not much different. 10 000 were removed from Washington State alone – 7000 of them from Seattle. They were sent to camps in Idaho, some with barbed wires and soldiers. The incarceration took over 5 months to complete. Families were given only days to pack belongings and sell homes. They were only allowed to take what they could carry. Before being sent to Idaho, they were ordered to the Puyallup fairgrounds where some stayed in horse stalls. About 4000 from the area found themselves at Camp Harmony at the fairgrounds, where they stayed up to 18 weeks before moving on to the camp at Idaho. In the camp each family was crowded into a single small room. There were no individual bathroom or cooking facilities. When the Japanese-Americans were relocated, the King county Assessor's office in Seattle attempted to add up all the taxes they owed, so they could pay their taxes before they left.[5]

In 1983, the Washington State legislature ordered $5000 in reparation made to each of the state employees who lost their jobs when they were moved to the camps. A congressional study has proposed a $20 000 payment to each Japanese-American interned during the war. Estimates are that half of those interned are still alive. In Canada, it is estimated that 10 000 of those interned are still alive. Compensation to Japanese-Canadian victims along the lines proposed by the congressional study would amount to $20 million. Nothing concrete has yet been done but at least three officials in the federal justice Department in Ottawa are looking at the possible forms of redress.[6]

Another recent example of the deprivation of liberty of innocent civilians in Canada is what happened during the October 1970 crisis which involved the kidnapping of a British diplomat (James Cross) and the kidnapping and subsequent killing of a Quebec Government minister (Pierre Laporte). Once the War Measures Act was passed by the federal Parliament, hundreds of members of the outlawed organization: Fédération de la libération de Québec (FLQ) were rounded up, arrested, and detained. The arrests were made in conjunction with a law that retroactively made the membership in the federation a punishable offence. The law was a clear violation of the fundamental democratic principle of the non-retroactivity of criminal laws.

Another form of internment popular in Russia and in some other countries is the holding of political dissidents in psychiatric hospitals.

A panel of Western experts testifying in September 1983 before a US congressional subcommittee estimated the number of such dissidents held in Russian psychiatric hospitals at 1900. The panel also described what it called 'widespread and systematic abuse of psychiatry' by the Soviet government to punish its critics. According to the panel, the system involves close collaboration between police and selected members of the Soviet psychiatric profession, whose diagnoses are based on 'dubious theories' of mental illness advanced by a leading Moscow psychiatrist.

Peter Brain, a British author of a book on Soviet psychiatric practices, told the subcommittee that over the past 20 years he had documented cases of 500 Soviet individuals against whom politically motivated use of psychiatry was used. According to Brain, this figure represented 5% or fewer of the suspected cases of abuse and did not account for Soviet citizens who have been imprisoned for speaking out against the psychiatric practices.[7]

Psychiatric suppression of politically troublesome or threatening individuals is not uncommon in the United States. According to Turk (1982) such individuals have frequently been neutralized by being treated as mentally incompetent rather than as authentic political resisters. The standard official and public view is that there is of course no 'physical oppression' in a democracy, therefore serious – especially violent – individual or collective political resistance is symptomatic of mental disorder. Turk quotes Kirkham *et al.* (1969) who concluded that

> All those who have assassinated or attempted to assassinate Presidents of the United States (with the possible exception of the Puerto Rican attempt upon President Truman) have been mentally disturbed persons who did not kill to advance any rational political plan.

Turk also cites examples given by Thomas Szasz, himself a psychiatrist, who has vigorously condemned the readiness with which many psychiatrists have facilitated American governmental suppression of political dissidents such as the poet Ezra Pound (who was kept in St Elisabeth's Hospital, Washington, DC, from 1945 to 1958) and general Edwin Walker. Szasz (1965) concludes that the 'strategic purpose' of such psychiatric diversion is always 'to prevent the subject from playing a particular role'. Turk adds that by invoking the imagery of psychological incapacity, authorities can avoid or safely defer legal confrontations on politically embarrassing or dangerous substantive issues. Thus, conventional legal formulas and processes are used by the authorities to inhibit political challenge. Other methods are used to curb legitimate demands for economic and political freedom. The South African dominant whites have elaborated and continue to impose a vast structure of laws to curb the rights of Africans, coloured and Asians. Turk (1982) notes that assembly, education, employment, housing, recreation, residence, taxation, travel, and virtually every other aspect of social life is minutely regulated under an endless stream of legislation, executive proclamations, and administrative judgements.

A major current emphasis in the legal control of Africans is to force them into accepting 'citizenship' in the pseudo-independent states being created in an attempt to divert African political aspirations without relinquishing control of their labor – which is indispensable to the South African economy.

(p.48)

## TYPES OF OFFENDERS

For obvious reasons, typologies of offenders guilty of acts linked to abuse of power are almost impossible at the present time. Although types and forms of abuse can be documented by drawing on various sources, there is so far, as Comfort (1970, p.59) points out, no authoritative study of the personalities of governing individuals, on which we can rely or which is at all comparable with the large number of studies of criminal or mentally deranged delinquents. According to Comfort,

The practical difficulties of verifying any hypothesis about the criminology of power are particularly forbidding. It is relatively easy to study the mentality of any type of delinquent other than the delinquent in office. Lawbreakers in prison, or psychiatric cases referred to clinics, provide material for study which is either relatively docile or relatively defenceless . . . Personal study is, however, one source of information about modern political and executive leaders which the form of society today effectively limits . . . With the politician, it is not only inadequate to base long-range guesses about motivation upon public utterances or policies, but any interpretation of abnormality would be unlikely to fall within the legal definition of privilege or public interest.

The idea that those who commit crimes while holding political office can be classified under specific criminological types is probably false. It is well known that 'power corrupts and absolute power corrupts absolutely'. As Schur (1980, p.175) points out, many people mistakenly believe that only certain kinds of persons can be criminals. In this stereotyped view, crime offenders are then taken to be biologically or psychologically warped in some way, or at the very least, they are pictured as a distinct class of persons set apart socially from the ordinary workings of 'respectable' society. This social stereotype of the alleged criminal was one of the major targets of Sutherland's essay on white-collar crime; yet the tendency he viewed to be unwarranted continues to have strong appeal.

Silberman (1978, p.45) notes that 'well-bred people steal far larger sums than those lost through street crime'. Geis and Meier (1977, p.208) report that after its study of the United States Senate and the House of Representatives, the Ralph Nader investigative group offered the observation that 'it could probably be shown by facts and figures that there is no distinctly American criminal class except Congress'. Geis and Meier add that Americans expect their political leaders to be devious; and the leaders tend not to disappoint them.

Comfort (1970, p.25–7) believes that democratic societies, especially in their centralized form, offer the prospect of entry into public affairs to many aggressive personalities whose ambitions might otherwise be limited to local affairs.

> There is, therefore, in centralized societies, a tendency for the personnel of these occupations . . . to be drawn increasingly from those whose main preoccupation is a desire for authority, for powers of control and of direction over others. In the case of would-be politicians, these impulses may spring from a highly developed political and social sense; they may equally well spring from maladjustment and a deep-seated impulse toward self-assertion and dominance . . . the centralization of power attracts inevitably towards the administrative centre those for whom power is an end in itself.

Comfort (p.29) notes that the suggestion that those who order public fraud, massacre, or deportations must necessarily be criminal or sadistic in their private relationships has no support in theory or in observation. He quotes an essay on *The Moral Implications of the Atom Bomb* in which the author Lewis Mumford (*World Review*, 1949, p.16) wrote that 'the acceptance of genocide as a national "military" policy . . . was made under pressure of war, without public debate of any kind, and it was the work not of moral cretins like Hitler and Goering . . . but of men as conscientious and upright as Secretary Henry L. Stimson' (Comfort, p.61).

Comfort believes that the intense strain and the other incidentals of modern political office have an observable effect in evoking delinquent conduct in persons who would probably not otherwise exhibit it. It is arguable, he writes, whether Hitler would have been actively delinquent had he failed to secure office, in spite of his manifestly abnormal make-up (1970, p.29).

Comfort (1970, p.45) notes that the greatest psychological hazards of parliamentary democracy are probably prejudices, the desire for violence or for suffering, and situation-psychoses sufficiently deep-seated in the personality to appear only under stress, and accompanied by plausibility or force of character.

Decisions taken in private, or personally, as under war conditions, are the most likely to be tainted with such attitudes, occurring in personalities which would probably be adequate in any ordinary context of power – the damage comes from the enormous repercussions which such decisions, made by a minister of modern state, may have.

(p.45)

Comfort (1970, p.46) points out that a considerable number of war crimes have originated in pressure from the executive, often from a single member, backed by expert assurance that they were necessary, even though deplorable.

Addressing himself to specific types of personalities, Comfort (1970, p.46) notes that psychopathic generals may be strikingly successful with their troops – equally psychopathic police officials may achieve great credit for their assiduity in pursuing crime and maintaining the law. The selection of occupation in which coercive power is necessary or tolerated may, according to Comfort (p.52), be a mark of the social delinquent.

Almost four decades ago, Von Hentig (1948) insisted that the police force and ranks of prison officers attract many aberrant characters because they afford legal channels for pain-inflicting, power-wielding behaviour, and because these very positions confer upon their holders a large degree of immunity: this, in turn, causes psychopathic dispositions to grow more and more disorganized. Von Hentig points out that:

> It is often forgotten that many of our legitimate vocations require a lack of emotional sensibility. Prototypes are the executioner, or the officer who applies the lash to a prisoner. Yet those are only the crassest instances, those which cannot be smoothly concealed behind the screen of means justified by the end.

The same killer instincts that motivate acts of criminal homicide committed by ordinary criminals might be behind summary executions and extra-legal executions perpetrated by members of police or military forces.

One technique that facilitates the commission of atrocious crimes against large numbers of helpless and unsuspecting victims is the well-known technique of blaming the victim. The anteriority of the victim's 'guilt', whether this guilt is real or imagined, is apt to rid the potential abuser, almost completely of any sense of culpability. It enables him to legitimize and rationalize the act by denying his own responsibility and by placing the blame on the victim. Blaming the victim is evident in the acts of genocide, where the extermination of a whole minority group is held not only as desirable and useful, but as necessary and justified. Preceding the acts of genocide, the minority group is blamed for all kinds of social or economic ills, so that any compassion for the group is eliminated, and its extermination appears a legitimate and justified act (Fattah, 1976, p.120).

Another technique of rationalization and legitimization is to portray the victim(s) as 'threatening'. Once this is achieved, acts of violence against, or even total extermination of these victims can be justified as necessary acts of self-defence.

These rationalizations and legitimizations might explain why many of those guilty of extreme acts of cruelty and violence may show no sign of guilt or remorse when confronted with crimes they have actually committed or were responsible for. They also enable those responsible for such atrocities to continue their lives and to go on with their daily activities without conceiving of themselves, and without being perceived by others, as criminals. This non-criminal, non-deviant perception those guilty of criminal acts linked to abuse of political and economic power have of themselves, is reinforced by the double standard they share with the public at large *vis-à-vis* conventional crime and white-collar crime, ordinary delinquency and public office delinquency. Geis and Meier (1977, p.207) note that one of the ugliest aspects of the Watergate affair was the contrast between the behaviour of the participants and the public pronouncements of the leading members of the Nixon administration as well as their demands for draconian measures against traditional offenders. And according to Schur (1980, p.168), corporate crime is without doubt the most glaring example in contemporary American society of systematic immunity from deviance-defining by those who commit major social harms:

> As well as showing how concentrated power can help shield wrong-doers from legal control, it illustrates the fact that both stigma and nonstigma outcomes reflect the same basic self-fulfilling mechanism in official deviance processing through which power is confirmed and reinforced. In the legal response to much ordinary street crime, it is low socio-economic power that is reinforced: the already-disadvantaged defendant (who often has a prior criminal record) is deemed a "poor risk" and on that very basis is apt to incur harsh penalties. The same kind of self-propelling cycle is at work (only in reverse) when the "good risk" executive charged with corporate crime escapes negative sanctioning. As one observer comments: lawmakers and judges see businessmen as 'respectable' because they have rarely been convicted of crimes; however, they have rarely been convicted of crimes because they are regarded as respectable.

Since the traditional typologies of criminals and delinquents can only be applied with great difficulty, if at all, to those guilty of criminal acts linked to abuse of power, it would be preferable to develop a different kind of typology. The proposed typology should proceed not from the differential qualities, attributes which characterize the different types, but from the varying attitudes and social reactions *vis-à-vis* the different groups of delinquents. Based on the criteria of social attitudes and social reactions, ordinary, white-collar, corporate, and political delinquents can be classified into four categories:

1.  *The sacrificeables*: these are the poor wretches so well described in Victor Hugo's famous novel *Les Misérables*. They are the scapegoats of society, the poor, the powerless, the underprivileged who commit conventional crimes, who are targeted by the organs of criminal justice system and who form the bulk of those prosecuted, punished and imprisoned.
2.  *The undesirables*: these are the deviants and the marginal types. They are neither dangerous nor harmful in a strict sense. Their real crime is that they have opted for a lifestyle which is deemed immoral, unconventional, or threatening by some other members of society. They are the prostitutes, the pimps, the alcoholics, the drug addicts, the vagrants, the vagabonds and so on.
3.  *The unreachables*: these are the delinquents who cannot be reached by the arm of the law except with great difficulty and in exceptional circumstances. Those who, because of their political power, socio-economic status, remain sheltered from the law and shielded from criminal sanctions. They are the delinquents capable of escaping detection, prosecution, or conviction, thanks to their ability to take advantage of the lacunae which exist in the laws, to obstruct the course of justice, to circumvent the criminal justice process, to avoid the laying of criminal charges, or the administration of penal sanctions.
4.  *The untouchables*: these are the delinquents who are truly above the law, such as the heads of state (Stalin, Hitler, Nixon, Idi Amin, Bokassa, to mention but few examples), and others who enjoy legal immunity from prosecution such as foreign diplomats, and various other categories.

The immunity with which many acts of abuse of power may be committed, acts in certain situations as an incentive. In other situations it acts to check or neutralize whatever internal or external controls may exist to inhibit such abuse.

Comfort (1970, p.11) notes that the egocentric psychopath who swindles in the financial field is punishable – if his activities are political, he enjoys immunity and esteem, and may take part in the determination of laws. He notes that no society based on centralized power has been able to dispense with large groups of people whose make-up is in no way different from that of punishable delinquents. The study of this group today gains urgency from the alarming growth of delinquent acts by states and by organs of power during the last 50 years. Failure to do so can be disastrous because as Comfort reminds us,

It is now possible for a handful of mental patients to terminate human history, and the governments of the atomic powers have repeatedly threatened, and are actively preparing, to do so if they feel their position to be threatened. This is a new situation. It leaves us little time.

(p.13)

**Notes**

*This chapter is based in part on an unpublished report prepared by the author for the United Nations Secretariat.

1. 'Military Regimes in Latin America', *International Commission of Jurists*, no. 17 (Dec. 1976) quoted in AI Report, 1977 p.116.
2. Ibid., p. 116.
3. *The Sun* (Vancouver, 17 Jan. 1984).
4. *Sports Illustrated* (1 Aug. 1983).
5. *The Sun* (Vancouver, 21 Sept. 1983).
6. Ibid.
7. Ibid.

**Bibliography**

Amnesty International (1975, 1977), *Annual Reports.*
Bell, B. J. (1975), *Transnational Terror* (Washington, DC: American Enterprise Institute for Public Policy Research).
Bettelheim, B. (1979), *Surviving and Other Essays* (New York: Alfred A. Knopf).
Bohn, G. (1983), 'Japanese Canadians and the War', *The Sun* (Vancouver, 21 Sept.), p.B1.
Bunyan, T. (1977), *The History and Practice of the Political Police in Britain* (London: Quartet Books).
Clark, R. (1983), 'Crime and the Abuse of power: Offences and Offenders Beyond the Reach of the Law', draft paper prepared for the UN Secretariat.
Comfort, A. (1970), *Authority and Delinquency: a study in the Psychology of Power* (London: Sphere Books).
Conquest, R. (1968), *The Nation Killers* (London: Macmillan).

Conquest, R. (1973), *The Great Purge: Stalin's purge of the 30s* (New York: Macmillan).

Conklin, J. (1977), *Illegal but not Criminal* (Englewood Cliffs, NJ: Prentice Hall).

Edelhertz, H. (1970), *The Nature, Impact and Prosecution of White-Collar Crime* (Washington, DC: US Dept. of Justice, Law Enforcement Assistance Administration).

Fattah, E. A. (1976), 'The Use of the Victim as an Agent of Self-Legitimization', *Victimology*, vol.1 no.1.

Fattah, E. A. (1980), *Crime and the Abuse of Power*, final general report – documents submitted to the 5th Joint Colloquium, Bellagio 21–24 April 1980 (Milan: Centro Nazionale di Prevenzione e Difesa Sociale) pp.69–92.

Fattah, E. A. (1981), 'Terrorist Activities and Terrorist Targets: a Tentative Typology' in Y. Alexander and J. M. Gleason (eds) *Behavioural and Quantitative Perspectives on Terrorism* (New York: Pergamon Press) pp.11–32.

Geis, G. and Meier, R. F. (1977), *White-Collar Crime: Offences in Business, Politics, and the Professions*, rev. ed. (New York: The Free Press).

International Commission of Jurists (1976), 'Military Regimes in Latin America' *ICJ Review*, no.17 (Dec.).

International Council of Churches (n.d.), *Joint Statement on Torture in Namibia.*

Krystal, H. (1968), *Massive Psychic Trauma* (New York: International University Press).

Kirkham *et. al.* (1969) *Assassination and Political Violence*, National Commission on the Causes and Prevention of Violence (Washington, DC: Government Printing Office).

Karunaratne, N. H. A. (1983), *Prevention of Transnational Corporate Abuses and Restitution to Victims Thereof*, paper prepared for the UN Secretariat.

League of Nations (1937), *Convention for the Prevention and Punishment of Terrorism* (Geneva).

Lejins, P. (1980), *Communication* to the 5th Joint Colloquium on Crime and Abuse of Power. Bellagio, 21–24 Apr. (Milan: Centro Nazionale di Prevenzione e Difesa Sociale).

Lernell, L. (1979), *Crime and Abuse of Power*, paper prepared for the UN Secretariat.

Malinverni, A. (1980), *Crime and Abuse of Power*, report presented to the 5th Joint Colloquium on Crime and Abuse of Power. Bellagio, 21–24 Apr. (Milan: Centro Nazionale di Prevenzione e Difesa Sociale), pp. 46–48.

Mitford, J. (1974), *Kind and Usual Punishment – the Prison Business* (New York: Vintage Books).

Mumford, L. (1949), 'The Moral Implications of the Atom Bomb', *World Review*, no.9, p.14.

Nsereko, D. D. N. (1983), *Group Victims of Crime and Other Illegal Acts Linked to Abuse of Public Power with Special Reference to Africa*, paper prepared for the UN Secretariat.

Ottenhof, R (1980), *Crime and Abuse of Power*, report presented to the 5th Joint Colloquium on Crime and Abuse of Power. Bellagio, 21–24 Apr.

(Milan: Centro Nazionale di Prevenzione e Difesa Sociale), pp.4–13.
Parker, L. (1983), 'Internees in US Lost a Way of Life', *The Sun* (Vancouver, 21 Sept.), p.B3.
President's Commission on Law Enforcement and Administration of Justice (1967), Task Force Report, *Crime and Its Impact – an Assessment* (Washington, DC: Government Printing Office).
Quereshi, S. (1976), 'Political Violence in the South Asian Subcontinent' in Y. Alexander (ed.) *International Terrorism: National Regional and Global Perspectives* (New York: Praeger Publications) pp.151–86.
Quinney, R. (1974), *Critique of Legal Order* (Boston: Little Brown).
Schur, E. (1980), *The Politics of Deviance: Stigma Contests and the Uses of Power* (Englewood Cliffs: NJ: Prentice Hall).
Silberman, C. (1978), *Criminal Violence, Criminal Justice* (New York: Random House).
Sutherland, E. and Cressey, D. (1978), *Criminology*, (10th ed.) (Philadelphia: J. B. Lippincott).
Szasz, T. (1965), *Psychiatric Justice* (New York: Macmillan).
Tiedemann, K. (1980), *Crime and Abuse of Power*, report presented to the 5th Joint Colloquium on Crime and Abuse of Power, Bellagio, 21–24 Apr. (Milan: Centro Nazionale di Prevenzione e Difesa Sociale) pp.16–33.
Turk, A. (1982), *Political Criminality: the Defiance and Defense of Authority* (Beverly Hills, CA: Sage Publications).
United Nations, *Report on the Inter & Regional Meeting held in New York* (July 1979) in preparation for the 6th UN Congress on the Prevention of Delinquency and the Treatment of Offenders.
Versele, S. C. (1976), *The Gilded Criminals*, paper prepared for the UN Secretariat.
Von Hentig, H. (1948), *The Criminal and His Victim* (New Haven, Conn.: Yale University Press).
Vjimato, K. V. (1976), 'Prewar and Post War Japanese Community', *Canadian Review of Sociology and Anthropology*, vol.13.

# 3 Victims of Extreme State Terrorism[1]

## Raymond R. Corrado

The intimidation, torture, and murder of citizens by governments for political reasons is a terrifying reality. The common assumption is that governments should protect citizens rather than violate them, yet the 20th century has spawned some of the worst government attacks on individuals. Nazi Germany and the Soviet Union under Joseph Stalin systematically terrorized and eliminated millions of ordinary citizens. The Nazi figures alone are staggering – official and unofficial estimates range from 18 to 35 million people killed in concentration, labour, and extermination camps (Bettelheim, 1979). Unfortunately these events were not historical aberrations. The Pol Pot regime in Kampuchea has been accused of destroying millions of its citizens. Currently military regimes in Brazil, Uruguay, Argentina, and Chile are systematically employing state terrorism to suppress and remove political opposition. Even liberal democratic governments such as those in Canada, the United States and the United Kingdom have been accused of violating basic civil rights and of employing illegal force in dealing with some of their citizens.

Although the degree and extent of violence does vary among countries, the psychological impact on surviving victims of state terrorism can be equally devastating. It is particularly striking that victims appear to undergo common experiences whether in Nazi Germany or in Chile. This chapter will describe the experiences victims have in common and identify the various stages that victims generally go through from arrest to a particular outcome such as escape or release. The emphasis will be on describing the impact, usually psychological, that government acts have on victims in a specific stage. The description of stages and psychological impact generally will be applicable to most cases of state terrorism, however, it should be kept in mind that most of the information about victims is drawn from the extensive reports and research on Nazi concentration camp and Soviet labour camp victims. Far less information is available for more contemporary cases of state terrorism, although

74

autobiographies and Amnesty International reports provide some insight into contemporary victim descriptions.

The range of victim experience with state terrorism is enormous since governments have numerous oppressive techniques available. These techniques can consist of slander, invasion of privacy, use of tax and business penalties, as well as the more directly frightening physical and emotional abuses usually involving some form of detention. The description of victim experiences in this chapter will be limited to the extreme types of state terrorism which begins with arrest and often involves a concentration camp experience.

## ARREST AND INITIAL SHOCK

There is a remarkably consistent pattern in the way persons are apprehended by government agents from most countries that have employed state terrorism. These agents typically rely on surprise in apprehending their victims. A group or squad of government agents act swiftly in disorienting the victim as well as immediately employing verbal or physical abuse. Victims are often interrogated about their political behaviour and the whereabouts of other individuals (Cassidy, 1977; Larreta, 1977). This procedure varied somewhat during the later period of the Nazi regime when the 'final solution' to the European Jews resulted in mass deportation, nonetheless, many of these victims reported an overwhelming sense of disorientation and disbelief (Bettelheim, 1979). The latter feeling is reinforced often by a trip to a police station or military location. During the transportation the victims are blindfolded and driven according to routes that confuse them (Des Pres, 1976; Amalrik, 1970; Amnesty International, 1975). Accordingly, secrecy becomes a paramount concern as the victim is usually not allowed to notify others that he has been apprehended.

The sense of disbelief for various reasons appears to assist the victim through the initial debilitating fear (Alata, 1977). Nazi concentration camp victims suffered such horrendous and often fatal conditions while being transported to sites in Germany and Poland that they remained bewildered and disbelieving that worse horrors could be forthcoming (Des Pres, 1976). Contemporary victims, such as those in Argentina and Chile, were somewhat more fortunate; they often felt that once they had an opportunity to explain themselves to the appropriate government officials, the terrible misunderstanding would be cleared and they would be released (Cassidy, 1977; Valdez, 1975). The disbelief and hope reaction typical of the latter victims would likely be limited to those who knew they were somehow erroneously included as political subversives. There is limited case evidence suggesting that for certain younger male revolutionaries resignation was a response to the inevitable torture and possible death that followed the arrest stage (Larreta, 1977; Valdez, 1975).

## SYSTEMATIC FEAR AND DESPAIR

Victims in initial shock were often too confused to feel a total sense of fear. This reaction often accompanied the stage in which the disorientation and humiliation tactics were systematically and continually applied. Despair was a common reaction as the initial hours of such treatment stretched into days (Des Pres, 1976).

The degree of brutality appears to differ by the particular country and political regime involved in state terrorism, however, the victim's experience typically was one of overwhelming fear and despair. During this stage disorientation tactics often continued such as blindfolding and the prohibiting of any communication other than with an authority. Any violation resulted in immediate physical assault. Extreme physical discomfort would begin when a victim was forced to remain standing or sitting for extended periods. Again violators were punished immediately. Victims would also be placed in cramped cells with little light and noise (Alata, 1977; Utting, 1977; Solzhenitzyn, 1973; Valdez, 1975).

Humiliation tactics were systematic, applied by guards who pushed, shoved, and kicked victims while screaming obscenities. A particularly effective tactic was forcing the victim to suffer extreme anxiety over the need to ask permission to defecate or urinate without knowing whether the request would be granted or refused. The refusal would often be accompanied by a punch, slap, or kick. The most humiliating outcome for many occurred with the guards' denial leading to the victims' inevitable self-soiling. These extreme humiliation tactics were continued in later phases as well (Valdez, 1975; Larreta, 1977).

When subjected to a long and terrifying torture, the victim realizes that his captors are willing to kill him or bring him as close to the pain of death as possible (Timmerman, 1981; Valdez, 1975; Cassidy, 1977;

Amnesty International, 1973). Grotesque physical torture and extreme physical deprivation accomplished this in the Nazi and Stalinist
states while more physically subtle but equally violent techniques are
common today (Amnesty International, 1973). Jacobo Timmerman
(1981, p.35) describes the sensation of the inital systematic torture
that he was subjected to by Argentinian officials:

> A man is shunted so quickly from one world to another that he's
> unable to tap a reserve of energy so as to confront this unbridled
> violence. That is the first phase of torture: to take a man by
> surprise, without allowing him any reflex defense, even psycholo-
> gical. A man's hands are shackled behind him, his eyes blind-
> folded. No one says a word. Blows are showered upon a man. He's
> placed on the ground and someone counts to ten, but he's not
> killed. A man is then led to what may be a canvas bed, or a table,
> stripped, doused with water, tied to the ends of the bed or table,
> hands and legs outstretched. And the application of electric shocks
> begins. The amount of electricity transmitted by the electrodes . . .
> is regulated so that it merely hurts, or burns, or destroys. It's
> impossible to shout – you howl. At the onset of this loud human
> howl, someone with soft hands supervises your heart, someone
> sticks his hand into your mouth and pulls your tongue out of it in
> order to prevent this man from choking. Someone places a piece of
> rubber in the man's mouth to prevent him from biting his tongue or
> destroying his lips. A brief pause. And then it starts all over again
> . . . What does a man feel? The only thing that comes to mind is:
> They're ripping apart my flesh. But they didn't rip apart my flesh.
> Yes, I know that now.
>
> (p.35)

The victim profiles that emerged after these brief stages appears to be
dependent on the particular goals of state terrorism. Where the goal
was simply genocide, then few victims were released at this point.
Similarly mass labour camps usually meant that victims were simply
in transit during the initial systematic fear and despair (shock phase)
stage. Where a political regime or government used terrorism to
suppress a small group of dissidents including political prisoners, then
victims occasionally would be released soon after the initial interrogation and torture sessions. These released victims generally seek exile.
Amnesty International and similar organizations, such as the United

Nations Ad Hoc Working Group on Human Rights, have reported numerous case histories of victims, often foreigners who were released within a week of being apprehended (Amnesty International, 1975). There is very little information available to assess, even in a preliminary manner, what occurs to these victims in terms of physical and mental trauma after their release. Most victims, however, are not released and are moved within days to long-term facilities usually in more remote areas where they are confronted with the terrible option of adapting to a concentration or labour camp existence or dying (Amalrik, 1970; Orlov, 1979).

## INITIAL REACTIONS TO CONCENTRATION CAMP EXPERIENCES

For most victims the introductory phase to concentration camp life is the most dangerous period for survival particularly when the ultimate purpose of state terrorism is either genocide or the physical and psychological suppression of a major segment of its citizens (Des Pres, 1976). The former goal clearly was the policy for the existence of Nazi extermination and concentration camps. The latter goal of suppression was one of the purposes of the Soviet labour camps (Medvedev, 1971). In either situation, massive killing was their desired or accepted political policy.

Survivors from all these camps reported that the inability to adjust quickly to the overwhelming brutality of camp life resulted invariably in death. Similar accounts have been reported for contemporary state terrorism: for example, as implemented under Idi Amin in Uganda and various Latin American regimes (Utting, 1977; Smith, 1980; Grahame, 1980; Timmerman, 1981). The need to adapt immediately was imperative for the victims' survival in overcoming the constant violence meted out by guards and the severe physical and emotional deprivation. Violent harassment was institutionalized. Virtually no social or physical behaviour could be undertaken without permission and all orders had to be strictly obeyed no matter how bizarre or unreasonable (Slanska, 1968). It was impossible to escape the violence since it was impossible for a victim to cope with the whims of the guards instructed to be brutal. In effect, the rules were designed to subject victims to systematic physical violence. If a victim failed to succumb, then the violence was simply escalated until he was killed.

Physical deprivation was also routinized; water and food were below survival levels and health and hygiene were purposefully and entirely ignored. Minimum daily civilized behaviour became impossible (Des Pres, 1976; Bettelheim, 1979; Amalrik, 1970). Stalinist labour camps placed an additional emphasis on overworking victims to death. Also, since permission to do anything was mandatory for victims, it was extremely effective for guards to simply ignore them. As a result, prisoners would remain totally isolated. In the *Gulag Archipelago* (1973, p.564), Solzhenitsyn clearly depicts the labour camp atmosphere:

General-assignment work – that is the main and basic work performed in any given camp. Eighty percent of the prisoners work at it, and they all die off. All. And then they bring new ones in to take their places and they again are sent to general-assignment work. Doing this work, you expend the last of your strength. And you are always hungry. And always wet. And shoeless. And you are given short rations and short everything else. And put in the worst barracks. And they won't give you any treatment when you're ill. The only ones who survive in camps are those who try at any price not to be put on general-assignment work. From the first day.

Similar methods and treatment are even exercised today. Labour camps based upon Stalinist techniques still exist. As late as 1979, dissident groups such as the Moscow Group to Promote the Implementation of the Helsinki Agreement in the USSR, have reported similar morbid conditions (Orlov, 1979).

According to Bruno Bettelheim's (1979) recollections of his experiences through the earlier phase in the evolution of Nazi concentration camps, the highest mortality rate occurred during the initial 3 week adjustment period. The new victims or prisoners attempted to retain the integrity of their personality in the face of the massive assault on their dignity. Part of this struggle focuses on maintaining the distinction between the pre-arrest reality and the unreality of being a victim. Not accepting reality was fatal since it meant such victims would not engage in the appropriate survival behaviour.

A related phenomenon during this 'new prisoner' or adjustment phase which could last up to a year, is the considerable effort in trying to contact outside family. Bribes of all sorts figured in these attempts

(Goldstein, 1949). A difference in contemporary state terrorism, where genocide was not an objective, the outside contact attempts often involved other prisoners who were to be released. In countries such as Argentina and Chile, the hope remained that ouside contacts might lead to legal intervention or external political presure for release (Valdez, 1975; Timmerman, 1981).

The immediate challenge to the new prisoner was to make it beyond the shock or fright reaction to a functional apathy. If the apathy evolved rapidly into severe depression, then the prisoner would often fail to engage in the necessary self-preservation behaviour. Lethargic reactions, visible mourning, and outbursts of temper were all non-adaptive behaviour which brought about brutal and often fatal assaults by guards (Slanska, 1969; Des Pres, 1976). Beyond a one- or two-week period, severe depression and withdrawal became identified as a 'musulman stage'. This stage was characterized by the complete inability to respond, to think, or to feel. These signs were clearly visible in the following behaviour: 'Typically, this stopping of action began when they no longer lifted their legs as they walked, but only shuffled them. When finally even the looking about on their own stopped, they soon died' (Bettelheim, 1979, pp.152–3). These 'walking dead' were overcome before they could adapt themselves to 'the internal knot of laws and prohibitions' which defied any civilized values and the most basic ego needs (Levi, 1966; Solzhenitsyn, 1973; Slanska, 1969).

Certain musulman stage characteristics appear in contemporary state terrorism even though the evidence is not as well documented as with the Nazi and Soviet victims. Case studies from Uganda under Idi Amin, Guinea, and South Africa as well as certain South American regimes reveal persons who appear to give up or to disobey in the face of sure death. In most of these publicly reported instances there is virtually no way of confirming suicide, nonetheless, survivors have reported that suicide is not an uncommon desire. This desire appears, however, in reaction to the boredom and sense of despair as well as representing one of the only methods to cope with the constant humiliation. In such cases, these victim feelings appear not only to be a product of apathy but rather defiance. In effect, suicide is a rebellion against the torture. Whether the prisoner is apathetic or rebellious, he is faced with having to adapt to barbaric conditions in order to survive beyond the initial concentration camp phase (Timmerman, 1981; Valdez, 1975; Alata, 1977).

## ADAPTATION RESPONSES TO PROLONGED DETENTION

A considerable amount of the traumatization of the victims of state terrorism is associated with the arbitrariness and the intensity of the violence that victims are subjected to when they perceive themselves as innocent. Being a Jew, gypsy, social democrat, university student, psychiatrist, or belonging to any broad ethnic, occupational, or non-revolutionary ideological grouping does not justify to any victim why he is reduced to total physical and emotional degradation and fear. Why a government would choose such individuals for such treatment appears largely beyond a victim's comprehension. It appears that once a victim realizes that he is not perceived as an individual but instead as a hated symbol, the adaptation process could resume. Shock and disbelief are replaced by more functional attitudes and behaviour such as distrust, revenge dreams, avoidance of memories, detachment, daydream withdrawal, regression to infantile behaviour, hatred for those on the outside, and identification with the oppressors' values. While some of these reactions are immoral and distasteful in normal contexts, in a concentration camp context they are often adaptative and, on occasion, unavoidable. These harsh attitudes and behaviours are not in any way a complete picture of how victims respond in brutal long-term circumstances. Concentration camp survivors such as psychiatrist Viktor Frankl (1959) and scholars such as Des Pres (1976) have pointed out that humanistic and even heroic behaviour were also part of the daily lives of some concentration camp victims. Des Pres, in particular, has argued that the pathetic view of Nazi concentration camp victims is inaccurate; all such victims were not reduced to a barbaric state of nature where victims and oppressors ultimately became indistinguishable (Kessel, 1972; Gliksman, 1948). Nevertheless, most victim observers such as Bruno Bettelheim and more recently, Jacobo Timmerman, have presented a picture of a survivor dynamic that consists of extremely crude or primordial adjustments to concentration camp life (Cassidy, 1977; Larreta, 1977; Slanska, 1969; Bettelheim, 1979; Des Pres, 1976; Timmerman, 1981; Valdez, 1975; Chodoff, 1966).

Long-term victims accepted that, short of some cataclysmic event, their situation would not change. Omnipresent despair and memory withdrawals accompanied this conclusion. They avoided both the past and the future. Memories and hopes concerning family, friends and occupation or life-style were suppressed (Krystal, 1968). Reminders were unwanted. Also, tenderness, love, and affection were dangerous emotions given the constant threat of betrayal especially from fellow prisoners. Communal punishments added to the distrust; those prisoners who did not adapt to the guard's whims and general camp rules brought about severe communal reprisals.

Detachment and discipline appeared necessary to cope with the constant physical threats and deprivations. To survive anger had to be limited to daydreams and other withdrawal expressions. It was safer to hate the outside world for one's existence rather than to reveal any violent emotions against camp guards. Acting in a submissive and child-like manner towards guards also mitigated their routinely brutal treatment of prisoners. Visible confidence and assertiveness in a victim were unacceptable challenges to the guards' authority (Solzhenitsyn, 1973).

Prisoner acceptance of guard brutality seemed to be as crucial to the guards' survival as it was to the prisoner. According to Franz Stang, a Nazi concentation camp guard, cruelty and humiliation tactics were necessary: 'To condition those who actually had to carry out the [brutal] policies . . . To make it possible for them to do what they did' (Des Pres, 1976; Philips, 1969; Friedrich, 1965).

It is not clear why certain prisoners were able to survive concentration or labour camp experiences. Victim reports and autobiographies indicate that particularly adaptive behaviour was a minimum imperative. As previously noted, total withdrawal or any challenge to authority assured a victim death. And yet, there was no behaviour in particular that precluded a fatal outcome. The physical deprivation and widespread diseases alone were enough to keep mortality rates atrociously high while communal reprisals against victims and totally unpredictable guard behaviour added substantially to the probability of death. This probability, again, is related to the political goals of state terrorism. Nazi state terrorism, for example, explicitly enforced 'the final solution' not only to Jews but also other ethnic groups and ideological enemies. Soviet labour camps also functioned in effecting the massive loss of worker prisoners. In contemporary state terrorism, similar conditions reduced the victims' chances of surviving; in Kampuchea, under the Pol Pot regime, apparently millions of 'unreformed' Cambodians were routinely and brutally murdered or allowed to starve to death. Prisoners in Uganda under the Idi Amin regime were subjected to such extreme physical deprivations and unpredictable violence that death was inevitable for thousands. In

Argentina, Chile and Uruguay, victims who were identified in broad categories, such as radical students, also faced death (Utting, 1977; Smith, 1980; Grahame, 1980; Amnesty International Report, 1982). Victims who survived, therefore, did so despite inhumane and uncontrollable conditions. The survival reaction for some victims included identifying with their aggressors' values and behaviours (Bettelheim, 1979). Taken to the extreme, such victims would become informers, Capos in Nazi concentration camps and other types of 'prisoner-officials'. In certain instances they were even more sadistic toward fellow prisoners than the guards (Krystal, 1968). For some victims, survival routinely involved horrendous decisions about life or death of family, and friends. There was, for example, little choice in Nazi concentration camps when a victim was ordered to participate in sending their parents to crematoriums. In avoiding death or barbaric torture many victims turned into pathological liars who were threatening to fellow prisoners (Bettelheim, 1979). Not all human relations were reduced to abject fear and distrust; in fact, on occasion victims did cooperate and sacrifice for each other. Underground networks even evolved in Nazi concentration and Stalinist labour camps. These groups attempted to deal, though minimally, with the brutality of fellow prisoners and guards (Des Pres, 1976).

Nazi and Stalinist state terrorism are extreme cases, although similar victim behaviour also is evident in more contemporary state terrorism. This is not surprising since many of the Nazi and Stalinist state terrorist techniques were directly copied by political regimes that shared similar ideologies. Soviet satellite countries, for example, have used and continue to use interrogation and intimidation tactics reminiscent of the Stalinist methods (Vidovic, 1977; Pelikan, 1971). The state terrorism procedures followed by the military regimes in Argentina and Chile resemble those routinely used by Nazi officials. Some victims in Argentina reported instances where Hitler's picture was prominently displayed in torture rooms (Timmerman, 1981; Valdez, 1975; Larreta, 1977). Shared tactics were evident in Latin America, since certain victims claimed that Uruguayan officials were operating in Argentina and the latter country also had officials present during state terrorism in Chile (Valdex, 1975).

Whether in Nazi Germany or Chile, victims subjected to extreme and constant physical and emotional abuse by governments appear to react similarly. Clearly, contemporary torture techniques have a devastating effect on victims. The use of electric shock, compromises the integrity, values, and personalities of victims. Few victims are able to withhold confessions and incriminating information about other persons after experiencing even short term terrorist techniques (Valdez, 1975; Cassidy, 1977).

Given the extreme, brutal nature of state terrorism, it is not surprising that the experience inevitably persists even for those who managed to escape or were released (Amnesty International, 1973).

## VICTIM SURVIVOR PROFILES

The preponderance of information concerning surviving victims of state terrorism involves individuals, usually Jews, liberated from Nazi concentration camps and survivors of Stalinist labour camps. Considerably less information is available for survivors of contemporary state terrorism. These data limitations should be kept in mind in the following discussion of the emotional or psychological patterns that characterize survivors. Also much of the more sophisticated attempts to describe these patterns consists of psychiatric case studies and autobiographies. With only these data sources, it is difficult to assess the validity of generalizations made concerning the psychological results of state terrorism, however, there is sufficient evidence that certain behaviour patterns do emerge among survivors.

Bruno Bettelheim (1979) was among the first survivors who described his experiences and observations of the Nazi concentration camps and of the post-release stage. Bettelheim maintains that three broad reactions occurred among survivors: firstly, some suffered serious mental disorders, dissuading their attempts to return to a 'normal' or functional lifestyle; secondly, others simply denied having any difficulty with reintegrating into society or suffering any lasting impact; and thirdly, some successfully reintegrated themselves into society, yet engaged in a life long struggle to consciously incorporate their experiences as a victim. Bettelheim believes that the first reaction is the most tragic while the second reaction is unstable and ultimately inappropriate. In effect, he argues that state terrorism causes varying degrees of damage to its victims and only those who are able to identify this damage may possibly manage to cope with it. But simply recognizing or identifying the damage is insufficient; it is also necessary for a victim to integrate the present in a positive way in dealing with his problem. This, as Bettelheim claims, requires an active commitment to prevent conditions for future state terrorism. Humanistic values and political activism, even violent acts in extreme situations, are essential to preventing state terrorism.

Unfortunately, there is little appropriate evidence to assess the validity of Bettelheim's assertions concerning the adaptive patterns of state terrorist victims. There is, however, clinical evidence that a wide range of mental disorders occurred among certain samples of Nazi concentration camp survivors (see Table 3.1).

One of the few systematic studies of Nazi concentration camp survivors was undertaken by two prominent psychiatrists and university researchers, Henry Krystal and William Niederland. Both psychiatrists specialized in treating concentration camp survivors over a 20-year period. They randomly selected 149 case records for their statistical analysis of the distribution of mental disorders among the survivors. The following is a description of their case information:

> The patients' records were obtained by one or more psychiatric examinations, mostly consisting of anamnesis, review of present symptoms, as well as their development and function since liberation. A special effort was made to obtain a pre-persecution history, both developmental and familial, as well as educational and industrial. We traced the persecutions in detail, trying to identify the exact nature of the traumatic events, and their possible correlation to the post-liberation syndrome. We paid special attention to the patients' reactions to loss of love objects, property, and position, as well as individual characteristics and aspects such as religion, national identity, and other attachments which would be affected by uprooting.
>
> (Krystal, 1968, p.327)

The figures presented in Table 3.1 were compiled from their sample of 149 cases.

Victims who sought psychiatric assistance were described as being in conditions of 'chronic reactive depression' (von Baeyer, 1958), 'depression due to uprooting', and 'post concentration camp syndrome' (Rosenman, 1956). These phrases all were based on the following victim characteristics: pervasive depressive mood, morose behaviour, withdrawal, general apathy, short-lived angry outbursts, helplessness, insecurity, lack of initiative and interest, and self-deprecatory attitudes (Krystal, 1968). According to psychiatrists and physicians such as Bettelheim and Victor Frankel, these attributes evolved as part of the concentration camp routine in coping with extreme brutality and deprivations. These characteristics assisted some victims through harsh conditions. As already mentioned, however, taken to the extreme or musulman state, the chronic depression would be fatal. As a result then, these depressive characteristics were not unexpected given the extreme survival context. Severe and persevering guilt is also common among victim survivors. This characteristic has become more widely known with William Styron's novel and the subsequent movie, *Sophie's Choice*. Styron sensitively described the excruciating and ultimately fatal guilt that tormented the novel's real life central character, Sophie. She was a victim of the main Nazi extermination camp in Auschwitz, Poland. Survival depended upon her choices to curry favour with camp authorities. The most difficult decision was deciding which of her two children had to be sacrificed in order to save the other. Ultimately she remained the only member of her extended Polish Catholic family that survived. As a result, she was never able to overcome her guilt for what she did to survive. Sophie committed suicide both as a commitment to her psychotic Jewish lover and as the solution to her persistent guilt.

In Sophie's case, the guilt was not immediately apparent but was elicited by certain social situations that forced her to confront the past. This pattern is not uncommon; psychiatrists who specialize in treating the post-concentration camp guilt syndrome maintain that there can be a considerable lag before their clients exhibit or recognize their guilt. In effect, victims such as Sophie, appear to avoid their horrific past until an unusual event precipitates a confrontation. How the victim deals with his guilt then largely determines whatever additional problems are likely to occur – such as psychosomatic illness (see Table 3.1).

Psychosomatic illness involving respiratory and cardiovascular problems as well as rheumatic or neurologic pains also appears frequently among surviving victims. Hypochondria is often related to these syndromes. Victims also suffered various states of anxiety and agitation as revealed in insomnia, nightmares, and tremulousness. Fear of further persecution was also noted as certain victims, for example, became agitated when having to deal with uniformed police officers. For many, coping with routine social activities or simply being left alone were difficult (Des Pres, 1976; Krystal, 1968).

Personality or characterological changes occurred particularly among younger victims and adults subjected to extended persecution. For those male victims, changes often focused on defeated masculinity. Phrases such as 'castrated slave role', 'house-boy slave' and 'Lord-Jim' problem reflect related victim experiences involving constant demeaning treatment. These victims were either excessively passive while simultaneously identifying with the aggressor problems, or they needed to perpetually prove to themselves to atone for the previous cowardice and failures (Krystal, 1968).

Psychotic disorders dominated by depressive features are the most serious problems facing victims of prolonged state terrorism. These disorders included 'delusional or semidelusional symtomatology, paranoid formations, morbid brooding, complete inertia, stuporous or agitated behaviour' (Krystal, 1968, p.13). Finally victims who suffered severe physical beatings, and other severe maltreatment especially with organic brain-related damage also exhibited mental disorders.

A. Immediately after liberation: magic expectancies (triumph: reappearance of lost family, etc.)

Symptom-free interval

B. Long-term after-effects: Post-traumatic pathology

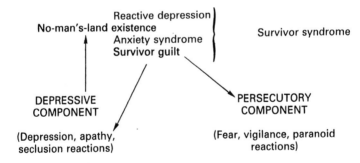

Reactive depression ⎫
No-man's-land existence ⎪
Anxiety syndrome ⎬ Survivor syndrome
Survivor guilt ⎭

DEPRESSIVE
COMPONENT

PERSECUTORY
COMPONENT

(Depression, apathy,
seclusion reactions)

(Fear, vigilance, paranoid
reactions)

Propitiatory and expiatory tendencies
Denial of aggression with masochistic features
Brooding absorption in past and present events
Obsessive–compulsive ruminations
Anxiety dreams and nightmares
Far-reaching personality change
Permanent feeling of loss and sadness
Partial or complete somatization of complaints

Source: Krystal (1968) p. 66.

Fig 3.1   The Post-Release Syndromes

Table 3.1   Survivor Mental Disorders

| Anxiety[a] | | Sleep Disturbances[b] | | | Cognition and Memory Disturbances[c] | | | Chronic Depressive Manifestations[d] | | |
|---|---|---|---|---|---|---|---|---|---|---|
| Degree & Type | % | Degree & Type | Cases | % | Degree & Type | Cases | % | Degree & Type | Cases | % |
| 1. Chronic tendency to worry | 39 | 1. Anxiety dreams & nightmares | 106 | 71 | 1. No disturbances of cognition | 98 | 66 | 1. Establishment of masochistic charactic trait disturbance | 118 | 79 |
| 2. Vigilance & multiple phobias | 77 | 2. Severe nightmares | 61 | 41 | 2. Confusion of past and present under sway of fears or dreams | 12 | 8 | 2. Survivor guilt correl- to loss of mate & children | 151 | 92 |
| 3. Diffuse fears about renewed persecutions | 31 | | | | 3. Hyperamnesia | 12 | 8 | 3. Industrial function & depression (out of 92 men) | 74 | 82 |
| 4.General expectations of catastrophe | 24 | | | | 4. Amnesia alone or with other disturbances of memory | 26 | 19 | related to family lives as wives and mothers: grossly inadequate | 45 | 49 |
| | | | | | 5. Disturbances of orientation: 'lost & bewildered' | 10 | 7 | 4. Clinical syndromes of depression, crying spells, periods of depression, agitated depression, severely psychotic requiring hospitalization | 119 | 80 |
| | | | | | 6. Dreams merging into hallucinations | 6 | 4 | 5. Association of anxiety with depression (patients confusing present with past) | 75 | 53 |
| | | | | | 7. Daytime 'dream-like' experiences in waking states | 4 | 3 | 6. Hallucinations at night (including those who were non-psychotic during the day) | 75 | 53 |

| Object Relations and Schizoid Defences[e] | | | EGO Integrity re Reality Testing and Predisposition to Mental Illness[f] | | | Psychosomatic Disease[g] | | |
|---|---|---|---|---|---|---|---|---|
| Degree & Type | Cases | % | Degree & Type | Cases | % | Degree & Type | Cases | % |
| 1. Disturbance of affectivity in relation to their closed object | 31 | 21 | 1. Depression with paranoid features | 5 | 3.3 | 1. Excessive tenseness, hyperactivity to minor stimuli, startle reactions, including low-grade pain | 70 | 49 |
| 2. Could not relate properly to anyone | 27 | 18 | 2. Loss of faith during the process of persecution | 4 | 2.6 | | | |
| 3. Had *few* friends | 19 | 13 | | | | 2. Syndromes of pain resulting from increased muscle tension | 102 | 81 |
| 4. Had *no* friends | 27 | 18 | | | | 3. Syndromes of headaches– i.e. tension migraine, stabbing headache, characteristic of the survivors | 149 | 100 |
| 5. Could be considered schizoid–socially isolated | 13 | 9 | | | | 4. Allergic-like symptoms | 13 | 9 |
| | | | | | | 5. Anxiety equivalents including: nervousness, palpitations, hyperhidrosis, hyperventilation, various other sympathetic nervous system 'overactivities' | 219 | |
| | | | | | | 6. Parasympathetic symptoms, peptic ulcer -like gastric overactivity | 55 | 37 |

Notes

[a]Total: 142/149 = 97%; [b]Total: 149/149 = 100; [c]Total: 149/149 = 100%; [d]Total: 149/149 = 100%; [e]Total: 149/149 = 100% −poor object relations viewed for overall group; [f]Total: 149/149 = 100%; [g]Total: 149 = 100%.

It is important to reiterate that there are only limited data in the form of clinical evidence and autobiographies providing the basis for the above victim survivor profiles (for example see Table 3.1). Nevertheless it appears that at least some victims appear to pass through various stages or phases afterwards (see Figure 3.1). Again, for many contemporary survivors of state terrorism it is not possible to assess the validity of the victim profiles from solely Nazi victim experiences. Not only is there little available information, but also insufficient time to assess long-term victim impacts.

It should also be noted that there are contradictory data and assertions about victims of Nazi concentration camps, i.e. they did not suffer any abnormally high incidences of mental disorders. Serious validity issues were raised about these conclusions reached by Kral (1951), since they are based on aggregate data sources that are not appropriate for clinical diagnoses (Krystal, 1968). There is, however, more recent information presented by a developmental psychologist, Sarah Moskovitz (1983), in her book *Love Despite Hate* offering a similar viewpoint on the long term impact of state terrorism with regard to some of its youngest victims. In her very limited sample of 20 survivors from Nazi concentration camps, only one person appears to have suffered a serious mental disorder while all the other survivors developed stable family relationships.

While the debate continues about the long-term impact of state terrorism, there is complete agreement that it is one of the most dreaded victimization experiences. It is not only the scope and fury of its physical human destructiveness, but also the apocalyptic sense of despair it creates among its victims as well as the rest of civilization.

**Note**

1.   I would like to thank Annamarie Oliverio, Steve McCartney, and Stefan Karlberg for their assistance in researching material for this chapter.

**Bibliography**

Aguilera, Peralta (1980), 'Terror and Violence as Weapons of Counter-insurgency in Guatemala', *Latin American Perspective*, vol.8, no.2, pp.91–112.

Alata, Jean-Paul (1977), 'African Prison', *Index on Censorship*, vol.6, no.8, pp.13–18.

Amalrik, Andrei (1970), *Involuntary Journey to Siberia* (New York: Harcourt Brace Javanovich).

Amnesty International (1973), *Report on Torture* (London: Gerald Duckworth).

Amnesty International Report (1975), *Prisoners of Conscience in the USSR: Their Treatment and Conditions* (London: Russell Press).

Amnesty International (1975), *Mission to the Republic of the Philippines* (London: Amnesty International Publications).

Amnesty International Report (1982), *A Survey of Political Imprisonment, Torture and Executions* (London: Amnesty International Publications).

Babington, Anthony (1968), *The Power to Silence* (London: Robert Maxwell).

von Baeyer, W. (1958), 'Erlebnisreaktive Stoerungen und ihre Bedeutung fuer die Begutachtung', *Deutsch. med. Wochenschr.*, vol.82, pp.2317–21.

Bettelheim, Bruno (1979), *Surviving and Other Essays* (New York: Alfred A. Knopf).

Bizzarro, Salvatore (1978), 'Rigidity and Restraint in Chile', *Current History*, vol.74, pp.68–83.

Bukovsky, Vladimir *et al.*, 'A Manual on Psychiatry for Dissidents', *Survey*, vol.21, no.1(2), pp.180–99.

Cassidy, Sheila (1977), 'Tortured in Chile', *Index on Censorship*, vol.5, no.2, pp.67–73.

Chodoff, Paul (1966), 'Effects of Extreme Coercive and Oppressive Forces: Brainwashing and Concentration Camps', *American Handbook of Psychiatry*, 3, Arieti, Silvano (ed.) (New York: Basic Books).

Dallin, Alexander *et al.* (1970), *Political Terror in Communist Systems* (Stanford University Press).

Des Pres, Terrence 91976), *The Survivor* (new York: Oxford University Press).

Frankl, Viktor E., *From Death-Camp to Existentialism* (Boston: Beacon, 1959).

Friedrich, Carl J. *et al.* (1965), *Totalitarian Dictatorship and Autocracy* (Cambridge: Harvard University Press).

Gliksman, Jerzy (1948), *Tell the West* (New York: Gresham).

Goldstein, Bernard (1949), *The Stars Bear Witness* (London: Victor Gollancz).

Grahame, Iain (1980), *Amin and Uganda: a Personal Memoir* (Toronto: Granada Publishing).

Hildebrand, George (1976), *Cambodia: Starvation and Revolution* (New York: Monthly Review Press).

Hinkle, Lawrence E. (1961), *The Manipulation of Human Behaviour* (New York: John Wiley).

Kessel, Sihn (1972), *Hanged at Auschwitz* (London: Talmy Franklin).

Korczak, Janusz (1978), *Ghetto Diary* (New York: Holocaust Library).

Kral, V. A. (1951), 'Psychiatric Observations Under Severe Chronic Stress', *American Journal of Psychiatry*, vol.108, pp.185–95.

Krystal, Henry (ed.) (1968), *Massive Psychic Trauma* (New York: International University Press).

Larreta, Enrique Rodriguez (1977), 'Kidnapped in Buenos Aires', *Index on Censorship*, vol.4, pp.22–9.

Levi, Primo (1966), *Survival in Auschwitz: the Nazi Assault on Humanity – If This Is a Man* (New York: Collier).

Lifton, Robert Jay (1961), *Thought Reform and the Psychology of Totalism* (New York: W. W. Norton).

London, Artur Gerard (1970), *The Confession* (New York: Morrow).

Medvedev, Roy A. (1971), *Let History Judge* (New York: Alfred A. Knopf).

Moskovitz, Sarah (1983), *Love Despite Hate* (New York: Schocken Books).

Orlov, Yurii (1979), 'On Prisoners in Soviet Camps', *Survey*, vo.24, no.2, pp.67–83.

Pelikan, Jiri (ed.) (1971), *The Czechoslovak Political Trials* (Stanford University Press).

Philips, Walt (1969), *The Tragedy of Nazi Germany* (New York: Praeger).

Piacentini, Pablo (1977), 'Terror in Argentina', *Index on Censorship*, vol.6, no.2, pp.3–7.

Rosenman, S. (1956), 'The Paradox of Guilt in Disaster Victim Populations', *Psychiatric Quarterly Supp.*, vol.30, pp.181–221.

Sarkisian, E. K. *et al.* (1965), *Vital Issues in Modern Armenian History* (Massachusetts: Library of Armenian Studies).

Scheflin, Alan W. (1978), *The Mind Manipulators* (New York: Paddington).

Schein, Edgar H. (1961), *Coercive Persuasion* (New York: W. W. Norton).

Slanska, Josefa (1969), *Report on My Husband* (London: Hutchinson).

Smith, George Ivan (1980), *Ghosts of Kampala* (London: Weidenfeld & Nicolson).

Solzhenitsyn, Aleksandr I. (1973), *The Gulag Archipelago* (New York: Harper & Row).

Soviet Prisons (1975), 'Interview with Prisoners from Perm Camp no. 35', *Survey*, vol.21, no.4, pp.195–216.

Styron, William (1979), *Sophie's Choice* (New York: Random House).

Timmerman, Jacobo (1981), *Prisoner without a Name, Cell without a Number* (New York: Alfred A. Knopf).

Utting, Gerald (1977), 'Uganda Prison from the Inside', *The Sun*, (Vancouver, 15 July).

Valdez, Herman (1975), *Diary of a Chilean Concentration Camp* (London: Victor Gollancz).

Vidovic, Mirko (1977), 'Inside a Yugoslav Jail', *Index on Censorship*, no.5, pp.52–7.

Walker, Christopher J. (1980), *Armenia* (London: Croom Helm).

# 4 Victims of Terrorism: Dimensions of the Victim Experience

## Edith E. Flynn

Modern society has come to experience terrorism in a variety of ways:

1. as a form of political expression or action by political dissidents striving to overturn an existing government;
2. as a cataclysmic way of seeking redress for real or imagined grievances;
3. as a method of gaining publicity for causes or grievances;
4. as surrogate warfare against governmental entities;
5. as a means for gaining local, national, or international leverage for causes or issues; and
6. as a novel rationalization for the commission of essentially apolitical, ordinary crimes.

Terrorism purposively uses fear as a means to attain particular ends. Terrorism is by nature coercive, dehumanizing, a theatre of the absurd, and designed to manipulate its victims, and through them, a larger audience. Definitions of terrorism are notoriously difficult and imprecise. A nosology includes:

1. *non-political terrorism*, defined as the deliberate creation of fear for coercive purposes with an end goal of collective or individual gain, or terrorism engendered by seriously mentally disturbed individuals;
2. *quasi-terrorism*, defined as the application of terroristic techniques in situations that do not involve terroristic crimes as such. Examples of this type abound and include the taking of hostages in derailed bank robberies or prison riots as bargaining leverage to secure freedom or concessions;
3. *limited political terrorism*, which involves ideologically or politically motivated terroristic acts, such as assassinations or the

93

bombing of public buildings, but which fall short of seeking to overthrow established governments;

4. *official or state terrorism*, defined as governmental rule based on fear, oppression and persecution; and finally,

5. *political terrorism*, defined as violent, criminal behaviour designed to create fear in a society – or in a substantial segment of it – for political purposes.[1] When fully developed, political terrorism is revolutionary in character and seeks to subvert or overthrow an existing government.

Even though the data on the incidence and severity of terrorism, in all its forms, are sketchy, fragmented and, therefore, suspect, it appears that terrorist activity is rising the world over, that there is a trend toward more lethal incidents and injuries compared to years past, and that US citizens (diplomats, the military, and business personnel) and US property are being increasingly targeted.[2] The October 1983 suicide bomb attack that killed 241 US marines in Lebanon is but an example of the growing risk of terrorism and its increasing costs. Given these trends, an increasing number of officials and private citizens will find themselves involved in terroristic crime, as victims of abductions and hostage-holding incidents, or as targets for destruction. Some victims are deliberately targeted on the basis of their personal or professional characteristics or because they symbolize whatever has become the object of terrorist hate and annihilation. Other victims are chosen randomly and become victims strictly by chance.

There is a growing body of literature on the subject of terrorism and its victims, but it is scattered and reflects many points of view, as well as many disciplines.[3] The diversity of research methodologies used, such as retrospective studies of hostage experiences or laboratory studies of stress and sensory deprivation, presents major problems for generalizing from the information we do have. In the absence of epidemiological studies and base line data, it is difficult to chart psychological, social, or physiological changes, much less predict future effects of terrorization on the victims of these crimes. Given the complexity of the issues, starting with the acute trauma surrounding the terrorist event, the peculiar interrelationship that may develop between the terrorist and his victim, the variety of psychological and physiological response mechanisms that are involved, it is obvious that any holistic understanding of the victim experience can only be derived from an interdisciplinary perspective.

It is the purpose of this chapter to synthesize and critically assess our knowledge of the victim experience in terrorism. Drawing on the contributions of the disciplines of medicine, psychology, psychiatry, and sociology, general principles are identified to further the understanding of the phenomenon, aid in the preparation for the experience of victimization of persons at risk, and to assist in the development of an improved system response to victims.

## THE EFFECTS OF TERRORISM ON SOCIETY

Any examination of recent history clearly shows democracy's peculiar vulnerability to terrorism. Bound by the rule of law and due process, a democratic regime cannot resort to the same bloody methods used against it in combating terrorist crime. It is surely no accident that we do not hear much of revolutionary violence in totalitarian countries, where autocracies with limitless powers terrorize ethnic, religious, or racial groups, and sometimes brutally subject entire populations. Terrorism is by definition anti-democratic for at least two reasons. Firstly, sustained incidents of terrorism will inevitably produce governmental counter-measures for the purpose of self-defence. These, in turn, can also become oppressive, thereby alienating the population from their government. Secondly, terrorist movements are clearly élitist, in spite of their alleged glorification of and identification with the masses. By seeking to coerce duly elected governments into concessions or even abdication, terrorists exert great stress on a country's institutionalized legal mechanisms and wholly circumvent the democratic process established to bring about orderly social and/or political change. While there are no systematic studies of the effect of terrorism on the quality of life in nations experiencing sustained and serious assaults, there is growing evidence of encroachments on the civil liberties in such nations. Great Britain, for example, one of the oldest and more stable democracies in the world, in its struggle with sectarianism and periodic armed insurrection in Northern Ireland, has instituted such basically undemocratic measures as internment, interrogation-in-depth, as well as arrests, searches and seizures without the benefit of warrants. There is also censorship. There has even been a relaxation of the rules of criminal procedure, such as trials without juries, the admission of hearsay evidence, a shift in the burden of proof from government to defendant, as well as an increase in penalties for activities classified as terrorism. West Germany and Italy, under sustained assault, have made comparatively benign procedural changes but have also significantly increased the penalties for terrorist-related crimes. Government counter-measures such as these, are not only understandable as mechanisms for self-defence, but are also demanded by the public. No form of political authority can long expect to survive continued, serious assaults on its institutions, and people, under the long-recognized concept of 'social contract' do have a right to protection. Public outrage and demand for harsh action against terrorists seems to be the norm in nations experiencing serious problems with terrorism. Jenkins, commenting on public opinion polls conducted in Western Europe during the 1970s, notes that a majority of people polled supported military reprisals, the killing of terrorist leaders, capital punishment for offenders, and summary executions, even if these measures seriously violated civil liberties or endangered innocent civilians.[4] European nations are not alone in terms of public resentment of terrorism and in succumbing to questionable control mechanisms. When in the early 1970s the city of San Franciso experienced the so-called 'Zebra' killings, in which white persons were randomly shot on the streets by a small band of profoundly disturbed blacks, public fear led to public approval of search and seizure tactics that were clearly in violation of the probable cause requirements of the US Constitution. In addition, states and federal governments, perennially resort to military force to quell domestic violence, whenever they deem it necessary. These and similar developments justifiably raise serious questions as to the future of democracies as democracies.[5] How does one properly balance the protection of the public with the requirements of constitutionally guaranteed civil liberties? The collective evidence clearly points to an erosion of these liberties, whenever counter-terrorist controls are applied, and to a public only too willing to trade its freedoms for a modicum of law and order. It can, therefore, be stated that to the degree that terrorism succeeds in changing a democracy into a facsimile of a garrison state and thereby into a totalitarian regime, the foremost victim of terrorism is democracy itself.

## THE EFFECTS OF TERRORISM ON THE QUALITY OF LIFE

Looking at the impact of terrorism on invididual citizens in countries that have consistently borne the brunt of terrorism, such as Italy, Northern Ireland, Spain, and West Germany in Europe; Egypt, Israel, and Lebanon in the Middle East; Turkey; and Argentina, El Salvador, Nicaragua, and Uruguay in Latin America, one notes a serious erosion in the quality of life of those affected. Terrorism is exacting a heavy toll on international diplomacy and on the life styles and work habits of political leaders, diplomats, and business executives the world over. Political assassinations disrupt the conduct of governmental affairs and can overthrow existing state authorities; international relations are strained when diplomats are killed or imprisoned and their embassies sacked; officials and representatives of criminal justice systems must carry out their work under well-advertised death threats; and corporate executives cannot operate their businesses without persistent threats of kidnappings, bomb threats, extortion attempts, and similar terrorist activities.

Concerns for personal safety are affecting a widening circle of people the world over. For example, air travel is encumbered through the scanning and frisking procedures for travellers who must endure a serious invasion of their privacy. Sally-ports and waiting areas separate passengers from family and friends. The transport and sorting of luggage is increasingly difficult. Airports, banks, industrial complexes, private and public institutions, and even penitentiaries have been affected by terroristic actions. The fear generated by terrorism and by the possibility of victimization in an ever widening arena are raising the social costs of the problem, in addition to the economic costs. They do so by weakening the social and political fabric of affected countries and by diverting scarce economic and criminal justice resources from other vital areas.

## THE EFFECT OF TERRORISM ON ITS VICTIMS

### Setting the Stage

The circumstances under which individuals may become victims of terrorist acts are as varied as the causes of terrorism and depend upon the particular objectives and targeting tactics of the terrorists. Victims may be chosen selectively or at random. In selective terrorism, specific groups, such as police, judges, soldiers, or prison personnel are targeted. In randomized terrorism, victims are chosen indiscriminately, a method guaranteed to instill maximum fear among the public. Variations in the objectives of terrorists affect the degree of threat posed to the victim. As a result, victims may be killed, maimed or injured. They may also be taken prisoner or hostage. Further, the specific form of terrorist victimization also varies widely. There may be face to face contact, such as during state-sanctioned torturing of prisoners or concentration camp inmates, the brainwashing of prisoners of war, skyjackings, or other hostage-taking events. There may also be anonymity between victims and terrorists. Letter bombings, car bombings, or similar explosive devices, randomly or purposively placed, fall into this category. Some incidents may be brief ranging from minutes to a few hours, while others may be of long duration, lasting weeks, months, and sometimes years. As seen earlier, some incidents may involve political hostage takings and others may be instigated by criminal or mentally deranged persons. Yet, in spite of the formidable diversity of the circumstances and form terrorist incidents can take, there is evidence of similarities in the effect of victimization.[6] These similarities persist to a considerable degree, even when unexpected terrorist captivity is compared with victim experience of natural disasters.[7] Given this evidence, exploration of that experience is warranted, independent of its causes and forms. The exclusive focus on victims is merited, both for its own sake, and because a cumulative systematic assessment and evaluation of the victim's knowledge and experience can increase the effectiveness of treatment, improve society's responses and thereby reduce the harm to victims of future events, and finally, to the small degree that it may be possible, facilititate prevention.

Before proceeding with the detailed analysis of the victim experience, it is useful to note that our knowledge of this subject is based on a gradually accumulating body of information about the pathology connected with trauma-induced stress. It includes retrospective studies of torture victims, concentration camp survivors, and information on such psychologically coercive techniques as the 'brainwashing' of prisoners of war in North Korea, first collected during the 1950s and 1960s.[8] Szu-hsiang kai-tsao, also known as Chinese thought reform or ideological remoulding is also included in this genre, since it exploits so-called brainwashing techniques on a mass scale. Since these earlier years, more data have been added by studies of former prisoners of war in Viet Nam and by the examination of torture and other abusive treatment of political prisoners in Northern Ireland, Portugal, Greece, South Africa, and several Latin American nations, to name a few.[9] The most recent efforts have examined hostage experiences in Ireland, Iran, Canada, and the United States.[10] While much empirical research remains to be done, the cumulative effect of this knowledge base is helpful in defining the parameters of the issue and in pinpointing critical areas where more data will be needed.

## The Social Psychology of the Terroristic Experience: Key Elements of the Process

Regardless of the objectives and format of terrorization, its basic process involves an unpredictable, powerful force, threatening the victim with annihilation. The experience is immensely stressful and generates in the victim feelings of anomia, total helplessness, and powerlessness. Terrorization denies the victim's ability to control his behaviour. Psychological and physical shock, characteristic of any severe trauma, follow. The degree of horror involved is perhaps best described by Weiss, who coined the term idiocide.[11] It means 'death of self', and constitutes an almost universal crime characterized by many degrees. Weiss defines the term as a crime, committed against an individual, which 'reduces, extinguishes, or precludes the presence or exercise of vital human powers'. Idiocide contains two elements: denial of status and denial of stature:

> There is a denial of status when an individual is brought down or kept from the position he normally or rightfully occupies, turning him into a victim, a hostage, a prisoner, a neglected or alienated member of society, cut off from the opportunity to survive, to maintain a level already achieved, or even to grow – thereby making his promise meaningless . . . Where a loss in status precludes the carrying out of some role, a loss in stature affects an individual as a single unit. Starvation, torture, and murder have it as an inescapable consequence. Indeed, every means of human destruction, from genocide to war, no matter what the occasion, excuse, explanation, or benefit, is inevitably idiocidal, radically reducing the stature of an individual, making him less than a human can be and should be.[12]

Ochberg, on the basis of systematic hostage interviews, offers a more operational, yet remarkably parallel definition of terrorist victimization: '. . . when somebody who is bigger and stronger or better-armed than I am assaults and damages me, and as a result of that aggression I feel less powerful, more fearful, in essence knocked down a couple of rungs on a dominance hierarchy, then I've been victimized'.[13]

Since the choice of victims in many terrorist attacks (as well as in most criminal assaults) is determined by chance, they can neither anticipate nor control the event. The victim's experiential repertoire contains little, if anything, to prepare him for such an incident, on the basis of which he can try to predict what may happen next or how he should best conduct himself. The multiple threats to life, security, bodily integrity, and self-esteem, precipitate in most victims a crisis reaction in which the emotions and behaviour of the threatened person are significantly disrupted.[14] A victim suddenly faced with the very real possibility of imminent death, finds himself unable to muster the necessary physical and mental resources to rise against the assault on his person. Such feelings of impotence shatter the self-image, dissolve the self-confidence and set in motion sequelae of complex and interrelated social-psychological and physiological response mechanisms. Some of these involve conscious efforts on the part of the victim, others are deeply submerged in the subconscious. The primary purpose of these efforts is to assure the survival of the victim. The remainder of this chapter focuses, in detail, on these response mechanisms, to see how they may be affected by the crisis situation and modified by the victim's life experiences and character traits.

**Experiencing Terrorism: Acute Victim Response**

*The Psychodynamics of Experiencing Terrorism*
In his informative work on victimization, Symonds identifies four distinct phases of psychological responses of victims to violent crimes.[15] While the duration and intensity of each phase varies according to the nature and quality of contact between the criminal and his victim, the responses seem to hold for such diverse victimizations as kidnapping, hostage takings, rape, robbery, and even burglary, where there is no contact with the criminal at all. The first two phases constitute the acute victim response, the last two the delayed victim response.

The first phase of the victim response to terrorization is concerned with the immediate situation and its experience. It consists of shock, disbelief, denial, and delusion. It is characterized by a paralysis of action and the denial of sensory impressions.[16] Only when the victim begins to perceive the reality of the situation and feels hopelessly entrapped, the second phase begins. It is characterized by a paralysis of affect. Symonds calls this terror-induced, pseudo-calm, noticeably detached behaviour 'frozen fright'. Trapped in a life-threatening situation, there is often a brief period of delusion of imminent reprieve. Unrealistically, victims expect that authorities will rescue them within minutes or at least within a few hours. While such imaginings are usually not grounded in facts, this phase is generally thought to reflect a growing acceptance by the victim of his or her predicament. If unresolved, a period of adaptation sets in, which the literature invariably describes as 'coping'. It includes such activities as writing, reading, counting, handcrafts (if possible), or similar 'busy work', and for most victims, an embarking on a review and reflection upon one's past life. Strentz, after interviewing many former hostages of skyjacking events, notes that he has never interviewed anyone who did not take stock of his life, or vowed to change for the better, should he be given a second chance after the horrifying experience.[17]

If victims are not rescued during this period of initial adaptation – a period that can last from a few hours to one or two days – the pressures of the situation and terror combine to overwhelm most victims and produce a state of *traumatic psychological infantilism* in the majority of the victims.[18] Individuals in this condition lose their ability to function as adults and begin to respond instead with adaptive behaviour first learned in early childhood. Thus, behaviour exhibited under the phenomenon of traumatic psychological infantilism includes appeasement, compliance, submission, and ingratiation. Even cooperation and wholly voluntary acts are often noted, which tend to confound rescuing authorities, the public, and even the victims themselves. Persons experiencing this syndrome will empathize and sympathize with their victimizer. They may even come to his aid and contravene the efforts of their rescuers. If the situation is not resolved within a relatively short period of time and the terror continues unabated, the traumatized victim tends to attribute his continuing survival to the good will of the offender. At this point, many victims experience profound and lasting attitudinal as well as behavioural changes. Symonds calls this latest development *pathological transference*.[19] It tends to occur when a victim's life has initially been threatened by someone who later decides (perhaps only temporarily) not to kill. Given these conditions, victims no longer focus on the actual death threat but begin to feel that they have been given their very lives by the offender. These changes in victim perceptions are particularly acute and reinforced in criminal or political terrorist hostage takings, where their instrumentality is obvious to all concerned. Victims will quickly delude themselves that their captors will not harm them, if only the intended victim – the one who has the power to meet the demands of the terrorists – acceded to their demands. It should be noted that the fact that police guns and other weapons are trained on terrorists and victims alike, is not lost on the latter. It further reinforces their delusions that if the terrorists got what they wanted, and the police retreated, the matter would be resolved with no one being hurt. Pathological transference is said to be complete when the victims begin to perceive their release as being contingent upon the offender's realization of his goals. This perceptual merging of the victim's hopes for freedom with the purposes of the terrorists has led some to speculate that we may be dealing with a variant of yet another psychological phenomenon, the *identification of the victim with the aggressor*.[20] It is a psychoanalytic concept and refers to the well-known socialization processes of early childhood, during which children learn to identify with their parental role models. In normal childhood situations, this process describes a positive development. If, on the other hand, the parent-figure is excessively punitive and inconsistent, the child may incorporate the parent's punitive and aggressive traits, in an effort to adapt to highly stressful and often intolerable situations. The concept of identification with the aggressor is related to the notion of conversion and has been useful in explaining instances where prisoners of concentration or similar death camps assume the character of their keepers and begin to torture fellow prisoners, in an unconscious, last ditch effort to save themselves. The chief motivational factors in these instances are hate (not love) for their enemy and the primordial desire to survive.[21] As helpful as this concept has been in explaining the otherwise unexplainable, it is of doubtful theoretical value in illuminating the psychodynamics of most terrorist episodes. The literature records no recent event during which victims of terrorism either abused or tortured their fellow victims. The few instances where at least some elements of conversion may apply, are those where a victim, after being subjected to traumatic stress, joins the cause of the captors and actively participates in subsequent terrorist operations. A highly dramatic case in the recent past fitting this category involves the kidnapping of Patricia Hearst in 1974. Donald 'Cinque' DeFreeze, self-proclaimed leader of the 'Symbionese Liberation Army', a small pseudo-revolutionary band of former prisoners and radicalized youths from the University of California at Berkeley, had been an inmate at the California Medical Facility at Vacaville from 1968 to 1972.[22] At Vacaville, DeFreeze underwent chemotherapy, aversive conditioning, and similar experimental treatment techniques designed to rehabilitate or 'convert' seriously disturbed criminal offenders. It appears that DeFreeze subjected Patricia Hearst to a mixture of violence and drugs, as well as to variations of the same conversion techniques that had been applied to him. The rest is history. Patty joined the gang, denounced her parents, posed in a fetching battledress complete with submachine gun in front of the seven-headed Cobra symbol of the SLA, assisted in a bank robbery in San Francisco, robbed a store, and went on the lam. Until her capture in September 1975, she managed to lead the Nation's law enforcement apparatus on an embarrassingly fruitless chase. When the government finally did catch up with her and tried her, she took the Fifth Amendment to the Constitution to avoid self-incrimination no less than 42 times.[23] Fields, analysing the case, likens Hearst's experience to those of adolescents in Northern Ireland, who, when subjected to traumatic stress, are less able than adults to withstand assaults on their ego and notes:

> She was terrorized, and she converted to terrorism. Had she been less isolated from the support systems of the larger society, and had she experienced a shorter captivity, it is probable that she would never have assumed the role of a fugitive bank robber. The case of Patty Hearst epitomizes the dynamic relationship between victim and terrorist because of its singularity in combining the features evident in other cases: i.e. psychological and psychotechnological forces operating in a social context that exacerbates stress through denial of institutional supports, prolonged threat to life, identity, and bodily integrity, occurring in a circumstance of powerlessness, helplessness, and unpredictability.[24]

While the Hearst kidnapping appears to be a classic example of the phenomena of identification with the aggressor and conversion, we must look elsewhere to explain what has fittingly been described as an 'unholy alliance between terrorist and captive, involving fear, distrust, or anger toward the authorities on the outside'.[25] As will be seen, the theoretical formulations describing the *Stockholm Syndrome* provide a better fit.

*The Stockholm Syndrome*

Traumatic psychological infantilism and pathological transference are two critical components of what has come to be recognized as the Stockholm Syndrome.[26] It is named for the unexpected positive feelings developed by captives for their captors, during a prolonged hostage taking at the Sveriges Kreditbank in Stockholm, Sweden, in 1973.[27] During the incident, 4 bank employees were held hostage in the bank's vault for 131 hours by an escaped prisoner. The group was later joined by another convict and former cellmate of the would-be bank robber, who had demanded his release from prison. Once the Syndrome is manifest, it tends to last for the duration of the crisis and beyond. In fact, it may continue for years. Strenz reports that positive or negative bonds tend to develop between captors and captives with the passage of time.[28] In essence, if perpetrators do not abuse their victims, that is if there is no serious physical abuse, assault, battery or rape, a positive bond (the Stockholm Syndrome) is likely to develop between them. However, if victims are seriously and persistently abused, the Syndrome is not likely to develop. But even in situations of abuse, exceptions are noted, as when victims, injured or assaulted during the initial rush of capture, come to identify with the offender and his cause during subsequent phases of their captivity. In these cases, victims rationalize initial abuse and/or injury as having been necessary for the offenders to gain control, and more often than not, blame themselves for their victimization. Only when victims closely identify with their government, or when there has been at least some training or preparation for the ordeal of captivity, does the Stockholm Syndrome not tend to develop. The annals of terrorism reflect some outstanding examples of such instances. In the 1970s, British Ambassador to Uruguay Geoffrey Jackson was captured and held hostage by Tupamaro terrorists for 244 days.[29] Maintaining his distance and dignity under the most difficult of circumstances, he won the grudging admiration of his captors without ever succumbing to the Stockholm Syndrome. The same applies to American agronomist Claude Fly, also held by the Tupamaros for 208 days. Similarly, military records bear witness to many instances where American prisoners of war in Korea and Viet Nam survived unspeakable horrors of captivity without ever approaching an alliance of identification with the captors.

While the Stockholm Syndrome is a relatively new phenomenon for law enforcement and the public, the fields of psychology, psychophysiology, and psychosomatic medicine have long recognized its basic element of 'regression' as one of several defence mechanisms available to victims of inordinate psycho-social stress. Next to regression, the remaining defence mechanisms include the previously discussed conversion syndrome, repression, rationalization, and sublimation. Even though these concepts are well-accepted by researchers and theorists of stress disorders, they leave us with many unanswered questions.[30] For example, we know little about the processes involved in selecting and elaborating a particular defence mechanism. Also, what is the nature of interaction between unconscious cognitive activity of victims and their conscious awareness of the situation? What internal factors are at work that enable the unconscious to accept the success or failure of a particular defence strategy? In the absence of answers and unifying concepts in this area (and pending future research), we must be content with the conjecture that the processes of regression and the Stockholm Syndrome are probably functional for most victims of terrorist attacks. Given the trauma of sudden life-threatening events that characterize most incidents, the alternative ego defence mechanisms would hardly do. Thus, the victim's return to the adaptive patterns of infancy has substantial surface validity, since it provides him with behavioural modes that have worked before, when he was totally dependent upon a caring adult in terms of sustenance and life. As such, this adaptation speaks volumes not just about the horror of the teroristic victimization but also about the apparent terror inherent in the ordinary childhood experience.

It is important to note that the Stockholm Syndrome goes beyond victim identification with and sympathy for the offender, which may last far beyond the actual period captivity. It also involves the development of the captive's negative feelings and distrust towards police in particular and governmental authorities in general. These feelings are exacerbated the longer captivity and/or negotiations last. After all, the victim wants to survive. And survival is tied to release. Therefore, anything that delays his release will be interpreted as a rejection of the captive's needs, as cold-blooded indifference to his plight and as an outright expression of hostility toward the hostage who is facing a life-threatening situation.

The final component of the Stockholm Syndrome often involves the development of reciprocal positive feelings on the part of the terrorists toward their captives. It is this aspect of the Syndrome that is of major significance to law enforcement, since it can aid immeasurably in the successful resolution of the situation. Beyond these basic elements of the Stockholm Syndrome, it is best understood as an automatic, at least partly unconscious adaptation mechanism for the survival of exceedingly traumatic and highly lethal situations. Factors which seem to promote the Syndrome are (a) the quality and intensity of the victimization experience, (b) the passage of time, (c) the degree of dependence of the captive on the captor for survival, and (d) the psychological distance of the captive from his or her government.[31] It seems that no particular age group is exempt from the Syndrome. Males and females succumb to it equally. As noted before, this remarkable phenomenon does not develop immediately upon seizure but requires time to evolve. But if it takes hold at all, it will be well established by the third day.[32]

The Stockholm Syndrome occurs with sufficient frequency during kidnappings, hostage takings, and similar victimization that highly organized terrorist groups have begun to apply tactics to prevent its occurrence. For example, hostages may be kept in total isolation. They may have hoods placed over their heads to prevent any contact whatsoever with their captors. They may be bound and forced to lie face down to prevent eye contact with anyone. They may be permitted to have only one spokesman and guards may be changed frequently during prolonged captivity to interdict the development of any relationships between hostages and terrorists. Any such development, if known to law enforcement, adds special urgency to rescue efforts because of the added risks to the lives of the hostages.

Given the obvious advantages to the hostages of a fully developed Stockholm Syndrome, law enforcement agents should foster its growth to the degree that it may be possible. As a result, any activity which may require captor and captives to work together for the common good should be encouraged. For example, food preparation, distribution of blankets or clothing etc. are ways in which joint activity and cooperation can be engendered.

Finally, given any extended exposure of captives to hostage-takers, law enforcement should never count on the assistance of the victims, when they communicate and deal with them during rescue efforts. Otherwise, police may find, much to their dismay, some of the victims counteracting their rescue efforts. Similarly, prosecutors should expect considerable difficulty in gaining victim cooperation during subsequent prosecution of the offenders. The star witness for the prosecution too frequently turns into the star witness for the defence. And governmental authorities should prepare to hear bitter complaints from released hostages who tend to judge official responses to their plight as inadequate, bungling, and grossly inept. Up to this point, this analysis of the sequelae of victim responses to terrorism has been limited to the psychodynamics of the acute victim response. As important as these responses are to our understanding of the victim experience, the picture remains incomplete. The terroristic experience includes physiological and psychosomatic damage as well. Its impact reaches far beyond the actual event and is the subject of the section below.

*The Physiology of Experiencing Terrorism*
The physiological response of victims to highly threatening situations is best understood by examining stress and stress reactions. Stress, in the words of its foremost researcher Hans Selye is the 'non-specific response of the body to any demand made upon it'.[33] Of importance is that stress is not the 'precipitating incident', but rather the condition of the human organism as it responds to the event. Recent researchers have modified Selye's definition by emphasizing that stress results from three interrelated elements: (a) stimulus, (b) response, and (c) a combination of stimulus-response reactions.[34] Thus, stress is seen as disrupting a person's psychological and physiological condition such that he or she is forced to deviate from normal functioning.[35]

Even though the timing of the stress response varies considerably from person to person, the response does involve three distinct stages: the initial stage involves alarm, followed by resistance. If stress continues unabated, the body's resources become exhausted and the victim's defence mechanisms will break down. Selye labelled this adaptation pattern GAS, or *General Adaptation Syndrome*. The alarm stage consists of two phases: during the 'shock' phase the body's resistance is lowered, while physiological defences are mobilized during the 'countershock' phase. Surging adrenalin triggers the release of glycogen from the liver, increases the rate of respiration and heart, and shifts the blood flow away from the skin and digestive tract toward the muscles and brain. All this leads to the resistance stage, during which the body will show maximum adaptation to stress. An individual faced with a terrifying situation will now be able to perform at peak output, and, if possible, will either fight or engage in flight. If stress continues, the body's reserves will be depleted. The third stage involving exhaustion will last until the body's resources have been replenished.

Unalleviated stress is increasingly tied to symptoms of physical and mental illness. As such, stress will interact with the individual to disrupt psychophysiological homeostasis and may lead to psychosomatic disorders.[36]

Recent research findings in such diverse disciplines as psycho-neuro-endocrinology and psycho-neuro-immunology on the subject of stress add special poignancy to victimization by terror. It is not the stress itself that is dangerous to individuals but rather their inability to cope with it that is significant. Whether a person eventually succumbs to physical or mental illness, and whether that illness will be serious or fatal, seems to revolve around the individual's ability to do something about the situation and proactively change his or her predicament. And since the essence of terrorization involves the negation of the victim's capacity for willing his behaviour, it must be seen as one of the most damaging stressors that can be inflicted on humans.

It is now known that prolonged stress affects at least five basic response systems: 1. the skeletal-muscular system, leading to muscular pain and tension headaches; 2. the parasympathetic nervous system, leading to gastro-intestinal distress, such as ulcerative colitis or ulcers; 3. the sympathetic nervous system, leading to hypertension, arrhythmia, palpitation, sodium and fluid retention; 4. the endocrine system, responsible for the overall integration of skeletal-muscular, parasympathetic, and sympathetic nervous systems; and 5. the immune system, responsible for the body's complex infection-fighting mechanisms.[37]

Current research has begun to tease out the exact processes of stress responses. Upon perception of a serious threat, neurons in the brain tissue stimulate the hypothalamus which regulates all essential life-support systems. The hypothalamus then stimulates the pituitary gland of the endocrine system and triggers the sympathetic branch of the autonomic nervous system. The pituitary gland, in turn, releases a series of hormones: Beta-endorphin and adrenocortico-tropin (ACTH), the most important and best known hormones in the stress response. The ACTH travels to the adrenal glands (located near the anterior medial border of the kidney), which in turn release corticosteroids. The latter chemicals exert positive as well as negative effects on the body. While corticosteroids function to reduce inflammation in the body, they can also depress the body's immune system, when stress continues unresolved. The adrenal glands also secrete epinephrine and norepinephrine (better known as adrenalin and noradrenalin), which are substances designed to serve the goal of preparing the organism to meet threatening situations involving fear, rage, or pain.[38]

In sum, epidemiological research on stress has come to recognize the hormonal secretion accompanying the stress response not only assists the body in coping with stress, but also can cause direct and indirect damage. Direct damage can occur during the alarm stage of the General Adaptation Syndrome through ulceration of the gastro-intestinal tract,[39] and indirect damage can occur through the shrinkage of the thymus gland and the reduction in the number of lymphocytes in the blood. The latter phenomenon weakens the immune system's capacity to resist infection, and thereby increases the likelihood of illness.[40]

These findings, coupled with a growing body of research analysing the long-term effects of highly stressful situations on humans (and animals), all point to far-reaching consequences for the victim's state of health. As a result, the psychological shocks and trauma of the terroristic incident pall when compared with the long-range damage inflicted on victims.

A final aspect of the stress response to be discussed here has major significance for law enforcement. Judging from the results of physiological and psychological measurements of stress reactions, mind and body are not activated simultaneously as has previously been thought.[41] Rather, a victim's ability to think and act is not only modified under stress, but mind and body are also activated separately. First, the relationship between activation and performance under stress is best described by an inverted 'U', where performance is optimal for many activities at an intermediate level of activation, and where either too much or too little activation produces a decrease in performance. Second, mind and body are activated independently of each other. Under the concept of *dissociation of arousal* a victim's (or terrorist's) ability to think clearly and rationally may be at maximum output, while the autonomic system may be on low, or vice versa. The relevance of these findings for hostage management situations is clear. A highly aroused victim may bungle a rescue operation, if complex tasks are expected of him. Nor is it prudent nor productive to withhold food and/or water (or otherwise manipulate such stressors as heat or cold and lack of sleep), if the result is a reduction of the terrorist's or hostage's capacity to think rationally, while disinhibiting their visceral and autonomic nervous systems. The result of such action could easily be a 'finely tuned animal, unfettered by reason (and) dangerously coiled and ready to spring'.[42]

### Experiencing Terrorism: The Delayed Victim Response

As noted earlier, there is considerable and growing evidence from long-range case studies and laboratory research that victims of terrorism suffer serious and long-lasting damage to their physical, mental, and emotional health. Even brief events can produce major problems, years after they have occurred.[43] In this respect, these victims are not very different from any other victims of trauma and violence. Unfortunately, these findings have yet to enter the public's mind. Nor are they reflected in the criminal justice system in terms of compensatory and punitive damages awarded to victims. The same is applicable to sentencing practices because punishment, in most instances, is not commensurate with the harm done to victims.

The last two phases of victim responses to terror tend to occur long after the horrific incident has passed.[44] Phase three consists of an array of psycho-physiological reactions. Phase four involves victim adaptation and formulation of new resolve. Both are the subject of the ensuing discussion.

Post-traumatic psychological reactions tend to involve the following response patterns.[45] Closely following an incident, victims tend to exhibit a wide variety of anxiety syndromes, ranging from intense anxiety to free-floating anxiety, to phobias. Victims will report insomnia, startle reactions, nightmares and nightsweats, inability to concentrate, memory lapses, sexual problems, and interpersonal difficulties with spouses or significant alters. Obsessive reviews of the terroristic incident lead to much self-recrimination, self-blame, and circular spells of anger, apathy, depression, hostility, rage, reclusiveness, resentment, and resignation. The motivation for these alternating responses is based on the absolutely devastating effects of depersonalization, helplessness, powerlessness, and humiliation victims experience during the incidents. Depression, a mental state characterized by feelings of dejection, lack of hope, and alienation, may last long after the traumatic event. Less frequent reactions include feelings of paranoia, with victims exhibiting abnormal sensitivity, suspicion, brooding, excessive self-consciousness, and fixed ideas that may include systematized delusions of persecution.[46]

A reinforcing circle between psychological and physiological effects of terror emerges when insomnia, dietary changes and self-imposed restrictions affect the victim's gastro-intestinal and circulatory systems which in turn can lead to further mental and physical impairments.

Still longer after the incident, physical and psychophysiological damage can bring about significant pathological changes in victims.[47] Hypertension, for example, has consistently been identified as a major contributing factor in the development of cerebral vascular accidents, the genesis of congestive heart failure, coronary thrombosis, atherosclerosis, and kidney failure.[48] The previously discussed suppression of the body's immune system may lead to a plethora of illnesses, including cancer.

*Differential Victim Responses*
Even though victim response patterns reflect remarkable similarity, it should be clear that stress responses do not produce identical psycho-physiological reactions in everyone. Roth identifies at least five sources of variability in stress responses:[49]

1. *stimulus-response specificity*, referring to specific kinds of stressors eliciting specific kinds of physiological responses;
2. *response specificity*, reflecting idiosyncratic differences in patterns of reactivity based on genetic and learned response differences;
3. *personality specificity*, attributable to differences in personality characteristics leading to differences in response patterns;
4. *emotional specificity*, assignable to differences in victim reactions to stressors; and
5. *conflict specificity*, traceable to differences in intrapsychic impedimenta victims bring into a stress situation.

Assessing delayed victim responses, differences emerge along a number of variables. Availability of treatment to the victim and his or her family appears to be a major factor affecting the extent of trauma and damage. System response can greatly ameliorate or aggravate the victim's feelings.[50] In addition, after-effects of traumatic experiences are inversely related to (a) previous experiences of a similar nature; (b) the age of the victim (maturity and a well-developed sense of identity lessen the traumatic effect); (c) the degree of humiliation and ego threat experienced by the victim; and (d) the degree of psychological and social isolation experienced by the victim.[51]

*Delayed Victim Response – Final Phase*

During the final phase of the victim response, a resolution of sorts is worked out, which integrates the victim's experiences into a new set of behavioural patterns. This involves regaining some feelings of control over his or her life, shoring up of self-respect, and the development of new patterns of alertness and defence mechanisms. Those looking for encouraging evidence of victims returning to a state of normalcy will not find it in the literature. Even though there are many degrees of adjustment, the accumulated evidence suggests that the scarring of the experience of terror is so damaging to mind and body that victims will never be as they were before.[52] With time, most arrive at a *modus vivendi*, characterized by revised values and attitudes towards life, government, faith, criminal justice, people, and material possessions. In sum, the trauma sustained by victims of terrorism appears to be of such magnitude that it is not an exaggeration to analogize the experience to an interstellar catastrophe during which planets are forever forced off their trajectory.

The foregoing sections have analysed the victim experience using a multi-disciplinary perspective. The remaining and final sections of this chapter present a synopsis of adaptation or 'coping' mechanisms that have previously been proven to be helpful in withstanding traumatic experiences;[53] and some suggestions for improving society's response to victims of terrorism.

## Successful Adaptation Strategies to the Terrorist Experience

The analysis of a wide variety of victim experiences of stressful situations reveals a number of coping strategies,[54] all of them geared toward

1. bringing the crisis situation to a quick resolution with a minimum of loss in terms of life and limb;
2. keeping one's anxiety level within tolerable limits to remain alert and functional;
3. maintaining one's self-esteem in spite of frequently dehumanizing and degrading experiences;
4. preservation of one's relationships with fellow victims; and
5. establishing some linkage with the terrorists (to the degree that it may be possible) without ingratiation.

Once caught up in the crisis situation, the following repertoire of coping mechanisms appears to produce positive results:[55]

1. assuming a familiar role, if possible, by engaging in such varied activities as writing, handcraft, counting, etc.;
2. adjusting one's expectations to the reality of the situation;
3. learning from successful coping behaviour of fellow victims; and
4. accepting constructive criticism without losing one's sense of self-worth and self-esteem.

**Improving Institutional Support Systems for the Victims of Terrorism**

Given the documented deleterious effects of terrorism on its victims and the fact that the United States is now at a greater risk of terrorism than ever before, it is critically important to develop effective strategies for counteracting acts of terrorism and for assisting its victims. There is an urgent need to develop a thoroughly coordinated national policy to fight terrorism. Given the peculiar and inefficient structure of law enforcement in this country, most terrorist incidents come under the control of local law enforcement agencies, with national organizations standing by or offering assistance. The net result is a veritable maze of too many agencies with little or no coordination between them. If terrorism is to be effectively controlled, we will have to have a totally integrated command, control, communications, and intelligence system.

Looking at institutional support systems for victims, there is an equally critical need to develop an integrated and comprehensive system response. Embassy personnel, members of the military, airline staff, business executives (including midlevel managers) abroad and at home are fast becoming attractive potential victims. As a result, comprehensive security measures, defensive strategies and tactics, as well as training for seizure and captivity are urgently required. While some hostage training has been undertaken for embassy staff since the Iranian Embassy débâcle, such efforts need to be systematized and extended to all persons at risk. At a minimum, business executives of US multinational firms overseas should be provided such training.

In addition, the scores of private firms offering an array of protection services, which have mushroomed in the face of rising anti-American terrorism the world over, should be scrutinized by government agencies to protect the consumers. The uncontrolled growth of these businesses cries out for objective evaluation of services and the development of at least some guiding principles and regulations. On the individual level, law enforcement agencies and emergency personnel responding to victims of terrorism need to make sure they do not inflict secondary damage to the victims. Given their experience of dehumanization and feelings of helplessness, care needs to be taken to act in a nurturing and patient manner. Symonds writes of the victims' 'silent expectations' that rescuers will help restore their self-esteem and injured pride.[56] If victims are met with indifference, detachment, emotional insulation so characteristic of professionals, their silent expectations will go unmet. Their feelings of helplessness and rejection will be reinforced and a 'second injury' will have been inflicted by the system. In sum, victims of terrorism require much reassurance, comfort, a willingness to listen and much support, not only from law enforcement and emergency personnel, but from the entire criminal justice system, friends, family, the community and society as a whole. In this respect, current system responses are wholly inadequate. And yet, the necessary remedies are the easiest to procure. Other nations are doing a much better job in responding to their hostages:[57] Israel looks at victims of terrorism as heroes. England includes former hostages in training seminars for police negotiators and most Western nations provide compensatory damages and treatment for their victims. Is it not time to do justice to the victims on these shores?

**Notes**

1.  *Disorders and Terrorism*, Report of the Task Force on Disorders and Terrorism (Washington, DC: US Government Printing Office, 1976) pp.3–6.
2.  Ibid., pp.7–8; Brian M. Jenkins, 'Statements about Terrorism', *The Annals*, vol.463 (Sept. 1982) pp.11–23.
3.  *Terrorism*, National Institute of Justice, Selected Library in Microfiche (1982 ed.)
4.  Brian M. Jenkins, op.cit., p.18.
5.  Irving Louis Horowitz, 'Can Democracy Cope with Terrorism?', *The Civil Liberties Review* (May/June 1977) pp.29–37.

6. Rona M. Fields, 'Victims of Terrorism: the effects of prolonged stress', *Evaluation and Change*, Special Issue (1980) pp.76–83.
7. Calvin J. Frederick, 'Effects of Natural vs. Human-Induced Violence Upon Victims', *Evaluation and Change*, Special Issue (1980) pp.71–75.
8. Robert J. Lifton, *Thought Reform and the Psychology of Totalism* (New York: W. W. Norton, 1961).
9. Leo Eitinger and Axel Strom, *Mortality and Morbidity after Excessive Stress* (New York: Humanities Press, 1973).
10. Jenkins, op.cit.; Eleanor S. Wainstein, *The Cross and Laporte Kidnappings, Montreal, October 1970*, Rand Paper R-1986/1-DOS/ARPA (Santa Monica, CA: The Rand Corporation, Feb. 1977); *Mobilization I: The Iranian Crisis*, The Task Force on Families of Catastrophe, The Family Research Institute, Final Report (West Lafayette, IN: Purdue University, Feb. 1980).
11. Paul Weiss, 'Idiocide', *Evaluation and Change*, Special Issue (1980) p.3.
12. Ibid., p.3.
13. Susan Salasin, 'Evaluation as a Tool for Restoring the Mental Health of Victims: An Interview with Frank Ochberg', *Evaluation and Change*, Special Issue (1980).
14. Morton Bard and Dawn Sangrey, 'Things Fall Apart: Victims in Crisis', *Evaluation and Change*, Special Issue (1980) pp.28–35; Gerald Caplan, *Principles of Preventive Psychiatry* (New York: Basic Books, 1964) p.39; Leo Eitinger in Roland D. Creslinsten (ed.), 'The Stress in Captivity', *Dimensions of Victimization in the Context of Terroristic Acts*, Centre International de Criminologie Comparée, Université de Montréal (Montréal, Sept. 1977).
15. Martin Symonds, 'The "Second Injury" to Victims', and 'Acute Responses of Victims to Terror', *Evaluation and Change*, Special Issue (1980) pp.36–41.
16. Ibid. p.36.
17. Thomas Strentz, 'Law Enforcement Policy and Ego Defenses of the Hostage', *FBI Law Enforcement Bulletin* (Apr. 1979) p.8.
18. Symonds, p.36.
19. Ibid, p.36.
20. Strentz, p.4.
21. Calvin S. Hall, *A Primer of Freudian Psychology* (New York: The World Publishing Co., 1954) p.78.
22. Albert Parry, *Terrorism from Robespierre to Arafat* (New York: The Vanguard Press, 1976) pp.342–64.
23. Ibid., pp.342–64.
24. Fields, p.80.
25. Frank Ochberg, 'The Victim of Terrorism: Psychiatric Considerations', *Terrorism*, vol.1 no.2 (1978) pp.147–68.
26. Ibid., pp.160–2.
27. An exact account of the bank robbery incident is given by Strenz, p.2.
28. Ibid., pp.6–10.
29. Geoffrey Jackson, *Surviving the Long Night* (New York: Vanguard, 1973).

30. Barbara B. Brown, 'Perspectives on Social Stress', in Hans Selye (ed.), *Selye's Guide to Stress Research*, vol.1 (New York: Van Nostrand Co., 1980) pp.21–45.

31. Ochberg, op.cit., pp.160–2.

32. Ibid., pp.160–2.

33. Hans Selye, *The Stress of Life* (New York: McGraw-Hill, 1956).

34. R. S. Lazarus, *Psychological Stress and the Coping Process* (New York: McGraw-Hill, 1966); J. E. McGrath, 'Stress and behavior in organizations' in M. D. Dunnette (ed.), *Handbook of Industrial and Organizational Psychology* (Chicago: Rand-McNally, 1976); and C. N. Coffer, and M. H. Appley, *Motivation: Theory and Research* (New York: John Wiley, 1964).

35. T. A. Beehr, and J. E. Newman, 'Job Stress, employee health, and organizational effectiveness: A facet analysis, model and literature review', *Personnel Psychology*, vol. 31 (1978).

36. Ibid.

37. Joseph P. Buckley, 'Present Status of Stress Research Related to the Development of Cardiovascular Diseases' in Hans Selye (ed.), *Selye's Guide to Stress Research*, vol.2 (New York: Van Nostrand Reinhold Co. Inc., 1983) pp.363–74; Sally K. Severino, 'Renal Failure and Stress in Hans Selye (ed.), *Selye's Guide to Stress Research*, vol.3 (New York: Von Nostrand Reinhold Co. Inc., 1983) pp.128–35; and Kathleen C. Light, John P. Koepke. Paul A. Obrist and Park W. Willis IV, 'Psychological Stress Induces Sodium and Fluid Retention in Men at High Risk for Hypertension', *Science* (22 Apr. 1983) pp.429–31.

38. Marianne Frankenaeuser, 'Psychoneuroendocrine Approaches to the Study of Stressful Person–Environment Transactions in Hans Selye (ed.), *Selye's Guide to Stress Research*, vol.1 (New York: Van Nostrand Reinhold Co. Inc., 1980) pp.46–70.

39. Hans Selye, *The Stress of Life* (New York: McGraw-Hill, 1956; rev. ed. 1976).

40. J. Cassel, 'The Contribution of the Social Environment to Host Resistance', *American Journal of Epidemiology*, vol. 104 (1976) pp.107–23.

41. W. Roth, 'Psychosomatic Implications of Confinement by Terrorists', in Ronald D. Crelinsten (ed.), *Dimensions of Victimization in the Context of Terrorist Acts*, Centre International de Criminologie Comparée, Université de Montréal (Montreal: Canada, Sept. 1977).

42. Ochberg, op.cit., p.156.

43. Symonds, op.cit., p.39; Stan G. Sommers, 'Ex-Hostages & POWs: Serious Emotional Problems Develop-Later', *Behavior Today*, vol.11, no.43 (3 Nov. 1980).

44. Symonds, op.cit., pp.36–8.

45. Ochberg, op.cit.,Roth,op.cit.,Fields, op.cit.

46. Ochberg, op.cit., pp.162–4.

47. A. M. Ostfeld, 'The Interaction of Biological and Social Variables in Cardiovascular Disease', *Milbank Memorial Fund Quarterly*, 45 (1967) pp.13–8.

48. Joseph P. Buckley, 'Present Status of Stress Research Related to the

Development of Cardiovascular Diseases', in Hans Selye (ed.), *Selye's Guide to Stress Research*, vol 2 (New York: Van Nostrand Reinhold Co. Inc., 1983) pp.372.

49. Roth, op.cit.
50. Symonds, op.cit.
51. Fields, op.cit.
52. Mortimer Appley and Richard Trumbull (eds), *Psychological Stress* (New York: Appleton-Crofts, 1967); Alan Monat and Richard S. Lazarus (eds), *Stress and Coping: An Anthology* (New York: Columbia University Press, 1977); Fields, op.cit.
53. Ochberg, op.cit.; Monat and Lazarus, op.cit.
54. Ochberg, op.cit.; Jared R. Tinklenberg, Peggy Murphy, and Patricia Murphy, 'Adaptive Behavior of Victims of Terrorism', in Roland D. Crelinsten (ed.), *Dimensions of Victimization in the Context of Terroristic Acts*, Centre International de Criminologie Comparée, Université de Montréal (Montreal: Canada, Sept. 1977).
55. Ochberg, op.cit.; Tinklenberg *et al.*, op.cit.
56. Symonds, op.cit., pp.36–8.
57. Ochberg, op.cit., p.160.

# 5 Victimization of Canada's Natives: the Consequences of Socio-Structural Deprivation

Curt T. Griffiths, J. Colin Yerbury and Linda F. Weafer

Tell us in fact how a people die and we can tell you how a people
live . . .

(Alan Fry, 1970)

## INTRODUCTION

The involvement of natives in crime and delinquency and at various stages of the criminal justice system has received increasing attention from social-science researchers in recent years (Morse, 1976; Lautt, 1979; Verdun-Jones and Muirhead, 1980; May, 1982). This increased concern is a consequence of the high rates of arrest and incarceration of natives in many jurisdictions. Research inquiries suggest such patterns are due in large measure to a mutual hostility and distrust which exists between natives and agents of the white criminal justice system. Further, there is considerable evidence that natives often do not understand the criminal justice process and that many criminal justice personnel have little knowledge of native customs and life-styles (Alberta Board of Review, 1978; Hylton *et al.*, 1979; Parnell, 1979).

In an attempt to address the difficulties experienced by natives in the criminal justice system, several initiatives have been undertaken in the area of native policing, native court-worker programmes, and in other areas at the federal and provincial level (Jolly, 1980; Van Dyke and Jamont, 1980).

Despite these recent initiatives in the delivery of criminal justice services, there has been little consideration of either the aetiology of native crime and delinquency or of native victimization. As Verdun-Jones and Muirhead (1980, p.18) argue:

> Very few attempts have been made to develop any general theory capable of furnishing explanations for the nature of native criminality and the societal response to it . . . The majority of studies have focused upon a number of decision making points in the criminal justice process without making any effort to relate the findings to the broader context of native peoples in Canadian society.

At present, there exist few published studies in the areas of native criminality and victimization and, as a consequence, no conceptual framework has been developed within which the victimization of natives can be studied (see LaPrairie and Griffiths, 1982).

The present study was designed as a preliminary inquiry into the victimization of Canada's natives and examines data on registered Indians and the general population in Canada and the province of British Columbia. It will be argued that any attempt to understand the victimization of natives must consider their socio-structural condition and that the consequences of the minority position that natives occupy in Canadian society are high infant mortality rates and high rates of violent death. The conceptual framework adopted by the inquiry moves beyond the level of the specific offender–victim relationship to consider natives as the victims of structural arrangements in society and of a majority/minority relationship. Further, a major premise of the paper is that in order to develop and implement policies and programmes that meet the needs of native victims, not only must their socio-structural position be understood, but consideration must also be given to the cultural and linguistic diversity and the relative geographic isolation of Canada's native population.

## NATIVE VICTIMIZATION: A CONCEPTUAL FRAMEWORK

> *victim*: "Someone or something killed, destroyed, injured or otherwise harmed by, or suffering from, some act, condition, agency, or circumstance" . . .
> 
> (*Websters New 20th Century Dictionary*, 1978)

The lack of published research on native victimization is due in large measure to the failure of social scientists generally, and victimologists in particular, to develop viable conceptual frameworks for such inquiries.

Social scientists have generally been inclined to use an 'acculturation/assimilation' model in their study of North American natives that defines and attempts to measure stages or levels of acculturation somewhere between native traditional norms and the norms of the white superordinate group (see Yerbury, 1980). This model has had important implications for the study of native victimization.

The underlying assumption in acculturation studies, according to Jorgensen (1971, p.68), '. . . is that the direction change takes is from a primitive, under-developed society – i.e. a society with low economic output and low standard of living – to a civilized, developed society that becomes fully integrated into the dominant white society'. From this perspective, it is assumed that precontact native cultures were 'under-developed' and that there is no need, therefore, to analyse '. . . why Indians are as they are today'. The poverty, high mortality rates, levels of victimization are assumed to be due to the inability of natives to adapt to the culture of the superordinate group.

The acculturation/assimilation model has been criticized by several observers in Canada. Verdun-Jones and Muirhead (1980, p.18) contend that the involvement of natives in the Canadian criminal justice system '. . . must be viewed in the light of the history of their colonial status vis-a-vis the dominant white society and their present socio-economic situation'. This conceptual approach was initially employed by Reasons (1975). In his discussion of native offenders in the criminal justice process, Reasons argued that the history of natives in Canada must be viewed in terms of their subjugation by a colonial power. Verdun-Jones and Muirhead (1980, p.5) pointed out that this socio-structural explanation has gained increasing credibility in recent years:

> These structural explanations assert that a dependency relationship between any unskilled minority group and an industrialized economic social order is the basis for these conflicts. Poverty ensures social and economic dependence and this dependence perpetuates a cycle of poverty.

Neither has the field of victimology provided conceptual frameworks useful for examining native victimization, traditionally focusing on the victim(s) of crime and the relationships between victim(s) and offender(s). Investigations that have been conducted on the victimization of minority group members have generally emphasized criminal–victim relationships as well. Hans von Hentig (1948), for example, used psychological, social, and biological factors to construct a typology of victims that included the category of minority victims, arguing that a lack of social and legal equality with the dominant population increased the chances of victimization. According to von Hentig, racial prejudice and discrimination placed the minority person in a position of powerlessness that increased the likelihood of victimization by criminals.

While von Hentig identified minorities as a potential category of victims, and thus provided a useful guideline for research, he and other victimologists have not considered minorities as victims of a more inanimate offender – the structural arrangements of society. Further, von Hentig's typology was developed in the absence of systematic empirical observations and without a supporting conceptual framework. As several observers in the field of victimology have noted, limiting the scope of victimology to the study of the victims of criminal acts and offences instead of all victims is to subordinate the discipline within criminology (see Mendelsohn, 1974; Separovic, 1974).

In recent years, several observers have argued that the field of victimology should expand its focus beyond the offender–victim relationship. Separovic (1974, p.16) has argued that a criminological classification of victims is not sufficient, since there are non-crime victims, such as the victims of accidents: '. . . the focus of victimology must be broader, since there are crime and non-crime victims'. To this end, Separovic (1974, p.17) proposed that a victim be considered as '. . . anyone, physical or moral person, who suffers either as a result of ruthless design, or accidently', thus introducing the notion of victim-risk or victim proneness (1974, pp.18–9):

. . . individuals possess varying amounts of this factor and are more or less accident prone . . . people differ very much in their potential for crime or accident risk and these differences represent a continuum from 'very bad' to 'very good'.

Elaborating on this view, Dadrian (1976: p.42) suggests that victim proneness may be the consequence of structural arrangements in society:

. . . to the extent that many types of victimization are residual in the institutional arrangements of a given society and are supported by sets of values and related interest groups, removing or obviating such types of victimization will require structural changes.

In short, the development of the field of victimology has been characterized by a focus on the victim–offender relationship within a specific setting and pattern of interaction. Recently, observers have argued that this focus must be expanded to include certain groups within society that are more prone to accidents and crime as a consequence of their structural position. Victimological inquiries, therefore, should be holistic and include as a victim anyone who experiences physical or mental suffering or death as a result of cruel intention, self-infliction, accident, or socio-political subordination. In addition, the structural conditions in which minority groups such as natives exist should be considered as a causal factor in their victimization.

## THE NATIVE CONDITION IN CANADA

The findings of numerous inquiries document a consistent pattern of pervasive socio-structural deprivation and economic and psychological dependency among registered Indians in Canada, particularly in relation to their home environment, educational achievement, and employment opportunities.

A recent Federal report, *Indian Conditions: a Survey* (DIAND, 1980, p.31), found that in 1977, fewer than 40% of registered Indians' homes had running water, sewage disposal, and indoor plumbing, as compared to more than 60% of all Canadian rural households. The report (1980, p.36) further stated: 'Poor quality of housing, crowding and lack of services (particularly in remote communities) are probably contributing to high respiratory, digestive and infective diseases as well as to high fire deaths among Indians.'

Conditions of deprivation are also apparent in Indian families DIAND, p.9). The strength and stability of family units appear to be eroding, as evidenced by increasing divorce rates, births outside marriage, children in care, adoptions of Indian children by non-Indians, and juvenile delinquency. In noting the high percentage of registered Indian children in care in the province of British Columbia, W. T. Stanbury (1975, p.213) concluded that '...the principal reason for admission into care is the "inability of parents to provide necessary care" '. Poor social conditions and economic opportunities both on reserves and off reserves tend to perpetuate all these features of deprivation.

On the national level, the report (pp.28–9) found that the use of social assistance and welfare among the nation's registered Indian population had increased from slightly more than one-third to slightly more than one-half in the last 10 to 15 years. The report concluded that the '. . . increased use of social assistance among Indians reflects poor social conditions and economic opportunities on reserves and may perpetuate a sense of dependence among Indians' (1980, p.29).

In the Province of British Columbia, Stanbury (1975, p.193) reported that the overall unemployment rate among British Columbian Indians living off reserves in 1971 was 47%, as compared to approximately 6% for the total British Columbian labour force. Stanbury (1975, p.208) provides 1971 census figures that indicate, as a result of this lack of employment and income: 'the poverty rate (the proportion of all families below the poverty line) of BC Indians living off reserves in 1970 was two and one-half times the rate for all Canadians'. Information from the 1976 census indicates that the average wages and income for Indians, even while employed, were still well below national levels (p.62). It is highly likely that the current economic recession will result in further deterioration of family and socio-economic conditions among Canada's natives.

This brief review suggests that a conceptual framework that considers the role of socio-structural conditions of registered Indians in Canadian society is most useful for examining the victimization of natives. In the following section, national data on infant mortality and violent death for Canada's registered Indian population and registered Indians in the Province of British Columbia are presented.

## THE CONSEQUENCES OF SOCIO-STRUCTURAL DEPRIVATION

Data for the study were drawn from national sources and from the Province of British Columbia.[1] It should be noted that there are numerous difficulties associated with collecting and analysing data on natives in Canada. Data collected by federal and provincial agencies classify natives either on the basis of legal status or band affiliation.[2] Generally, statistical information is available only on status or registered Indians, thus excluding large numbers of non-status Indians, Metis, and Inuit.[3]

Nevertheless, these data do provide the opportunity to consider the patterns of native victimization and to initiate the development of a conceptual framework that could be utilized for future research on natives and other minorities.

**The National Data**

Nationwide Canadian data indicate that the socio-structural condition of registered Indians in Canada results in the extensive victimization of native peoples, as manifested by poverty, high infant mortality rates, a lower life expectancy, high rates of accidents, poisoning and violence, high suicide rates, and alcoholism.[4] The data also provide insight into the causes of violent death among the country's registered Indian population in comparison with the national rate among Canadians.

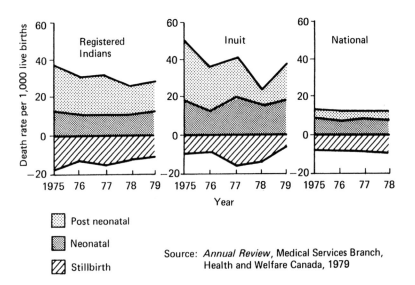

Source: *Annual Review*, Medical Services Branch, Health and Welfare Canada, 1979

Fig. 5.1   *Infant Mortality Rates among Registered Indians, Inuit, and the National Population, 1975–79*

## Infant Mortality

It is revealing that both the registered Indian population and the Inuit evidence rates of still births, neonatal deaths, and post-neonatal deaths that are nearly three times that of the general Canadian population. Further, these rates have remained fairly constant over the 1975–79 period for the Canadian population at approximately 18 per 1000 live births and less than 10 per 1000 total births for still births. Among the Inuit, the rate of neonatal and post-neonatal deaths (with the exception of 1978) has been near or over 40 per 1000 live births. This is twice the national rate. For registered Indians, the rate of neonatal infant deaths remained constant during the 1975–79 period, and was only somewhat higher than the rate for the national population. However, the rate of post-neonatal infant deaths, while declining somewhat from the 1975 rates of nearly 40 per 1000 live births, remained at a high level.

The disparity in the infant mortality rates of the Canadian population and natives is similar to that which exists between underdeveloped and developed countries. For instance, developing countries such as the Dominican Republic and Mexico had an infant mortality rate in 1973 of 64 and 69 respectively, while developed countries like Japan and France had rates of 13 and 15 (Harris, 1975, p.431).

## Accidents, Poisoning, and Violence

Data on the crude death rates per 100 000 population by age for accidents, poisonings, and violence indicate considerable differences between Indians and the general population. Among the registered Indian population, deaths from accidents, poisonings, and violence accounted for 35% of all deaths, compared to only 9% among the Canadian population as a whole. Among the registered Indians, the crude death rate from accidents, poisonings, and violence is over 250 per 100 000 population in the 0–1 age range, compared to a rate of under 50 per 100 000 for this age group among the general Canadian population. While the crude death rates for both registered Indians and the general population declines during the years 1–14, it then increases through ages 15–24, for both populations. The national population remains fairly constant at approximately 60 per 100 000 until age 65, while the rate for registered Indians escalates to 300 per 100 000, dropping off only after age 64.

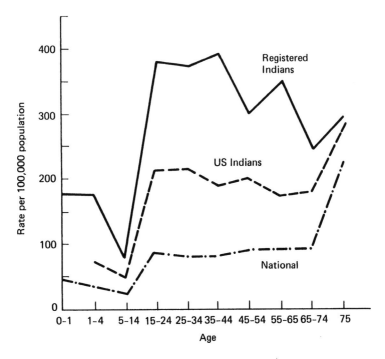

Sources:
(1) *Annual Report*, Medical Services Branch, Health and
    Welfare Canada, 1978
(2) Statistics Canada, 1976
(3) Trajectory of Indian Health Care, US Department of
    Health, Education and Welfare 1977
(4) Department of Indian Affairs and Northern
    Development, 1980.

Fig.5.2   *Deaths by Accident, Poisoning, and Violence among Registered
          Indians, US Indians, and the National Canadian Population*

The violent death rate for Canadian registered Indians from
accidents, poisonings, and violence is not only significantly higher
than the national rate, but also higher than the rate per 100 000 for
US Indians. It is also important to note that while the rates are
significantly higher for Canadian Indians, the increase in violent
deaths during the 15–24 age range and subsequent changes in rates
across the different age groups are mirrored by US Indians, albeit at a
much lower rate. It is only in the 75+ age category that US Indian

rates for violent death approximate those of Canada's registered Indians, which remain at nearly four times the rate of US Indians across the various age groups.

The rates of violent death per 100 000 population for natives and the national population for six selected categories of death are also revealing.

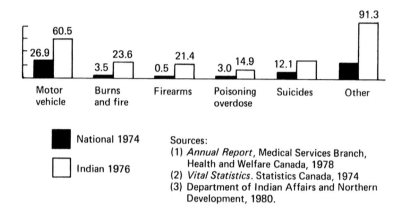

**Fig.5.3**  *Violent Deaths among Registered Indians and the National Population per 100 000 Population*

National data from 1974 and data from 1976 on the registered Indian population indicate that for motor vehicle deaths, burns and fires, firearms, poisonings and overdose, and suicides, Indians evidence higher rates than the national population. The Indian death rate per 100 000 from motor vehicle accidents is more than two times the national rate, while it is nearly eight times higher for Indians from burns and fires, and nearly three times higher for suicides.

The suicide rate per 100 000 for registered Indians is nearly three times the national rate with an alarming increase in the number of suicides in the 15–24 age category. In fact, statistics indicate that suicides account for a staggering 35% of the accidental deaths for the 15–24 age group and approximately 21% of the accidental deaths for the 25–34 age group.

In sum, the data presented reveal high rates of infant mortality and suicides as well as high rates of violent death from firearms among

Canada's registered Indian population. Most alarming are the extremely high rates of infant mortality in the first year of life, and high rates of violent death among young Indians in the 15–24 age range.

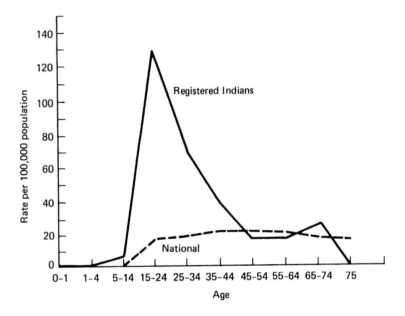

Sources:
(1) *Annual Report* Medical Services Branch, Health and Welfare Canada, 1978
(2) Department of Indian and Northern Affairs, 1977 (Indian Population)
(3) Statistics Canada, 1976 (National Population)
(4) *Indian Conditions: a Survey*, Department of Indian and Northern Affairs, 1980

Fig.5.4   *Suicides by Age Group among Registered Indians and the National Population, 1977*

## Violent Death Among Registered Indians in British Columbia

Data collected in the province of British Columbia on the causes of death among the registered Indian population and the general population provide further insights into the victimization of Canadian natives.

**Infant Mortality**

For Indians in British Columbia, the infant death rate per 100 000 live births is two to three times higher than for the general population for the five-year period, 1975–79.[5]

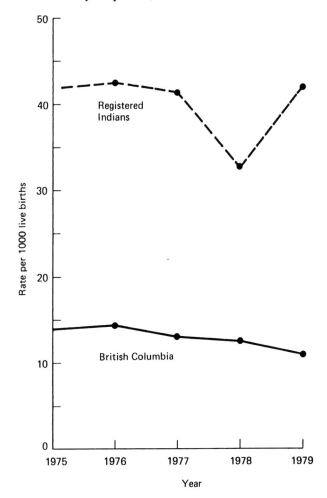

Source: *Vital Statistics.* Ministry of Health,
Province of British Columbia, 1980

Fig.5.5   *Infant Deaths among Registered Indians and the British Columbia Population, 1975–79*

Accidents account for the higher number of deaths among Indian infants annually, while pneumonia and influenza are other leading causes of infant death. Figure 5.5 also reveals that while the rates of infant mortality were for the British Columbian population declining over the period 1975–79 (with the exception of 1978), the rates for natives remained high and were increasing in 1979.

**Major Causes of Death**

Data on the ten major causes of death among registered Indians in British Columbia indicate that accidents accounted for the largest percentage of total deaths in 1980.

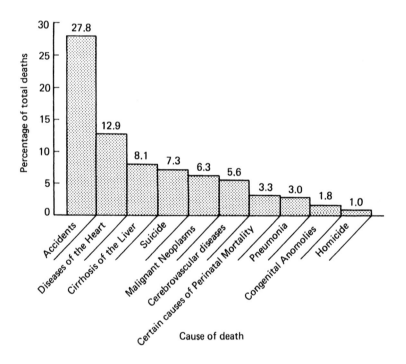

Source: *Vital Statistics*. Ministry of Health, Province of British Columbia, 1980

Fig.5.6   *Deaths from 10 Main Causes among Registered Indians and the British Columbia Population, as Percentage of Total Deaths, 1980*

The category of 'accidents' includes motor vehicle and transport deaths, poisoning, falls, accidental fires, drowning involving small boats, firearms, missiles, and inhalation deaths. The accident death rate for Indians in British Columbia was 194.1 per 100 000 in 1980 compared to a rate of 60.8 for the general population in the province.[6]

In addition, the rates for cirrhosis of the liver, suicide, pneumonia, and accidents are two to four times higher for Indians than the general population.

## Accidents

The accident rate per 100 000 population for British Columbian Indians is over three times the rate for the general population.

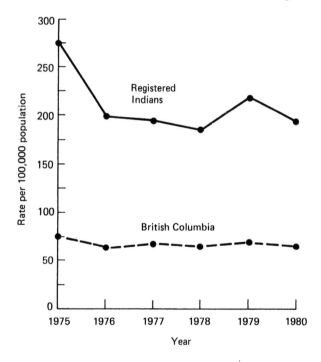

Source: *Vital Statistics.* Reports of the Ministry of Health, Province of British Columbia, 1975–1980

Fig.5.7 *Accidents among Registered Indians and the British Columbia Population, 1975–80*

Although there has been a general decrease in the accident rate for
Indians over the period 1975–80, it was not significant – 219.4 per
100 000 to 194.1. On the other hand, the accident rate for the general
population has ranged from a high of 76.6 per 100 000 in 1975 to 60.8
in 1980.

**Suicides**

For the 6-year period 1975–80, the suicide rate for Indians in British
Columbia was two to four times higher than that of the general
population.

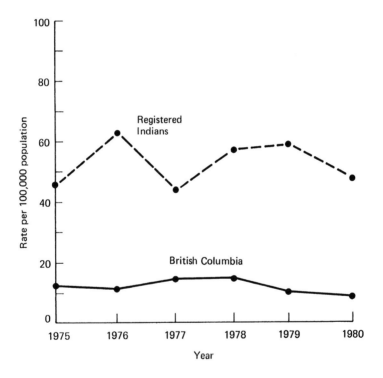

Source: *Vital Statistics.* Ministry of Health,
Province of British Columbia, 1980

Fig.5.8   *Suicides among Registered Indians and the British Columbia
Population, 1975–1980*

Although the suicide rate decreased from 61.2 in 1979 to 51.2 in 1980, the rate for the general population declined from 16.3 per 100 000 to 15.0 during these years. Further, the percentage of total deaths of Indians attributed to suicide were significantly higher than for the general population.

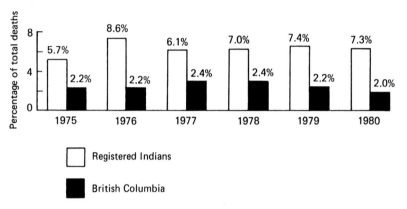

Source: *Vital Statistics.* Ministry of Health, Province of British Columbia, 1980

Fig.5.9   *Suicide as a Percentage of Total Deaths for Registered Indians and the British Columbia Population, 1975–80*

For the general population, suicides remained at a little over 2% of the total deaths, while for Indians, suicides ranged from a low of 5.7% of total deaths to a high of 8.6%. The data also indicate that the 15–19 age group is the most vulnerable to suicides, accounting for a total of 85 Indian deaths during the period 1975–80. In fact, suicides were the leading cause of death for this age group, followed by motor vehicle deaths that accounted for 80 deaths over this time period. It is also becoming apparent that suicide among young adults between 20 and 29 years is increasing. These deaths are, no doubt, correlated with the lack of opportunity and with the social distress, uncertainty, and confusion experienced among the province's native peoples.

**Cirrhosis of the Liver**

The most widely used measure of alcoholism as a cause of death among populations are rates of cirrhosis of the liver. Figure 5.10 indicates that, over the 6-year period from 1975–80, death rates from cirrhosis of the liver for Indians have been two to five times those of the general population in the province of British Columbia.

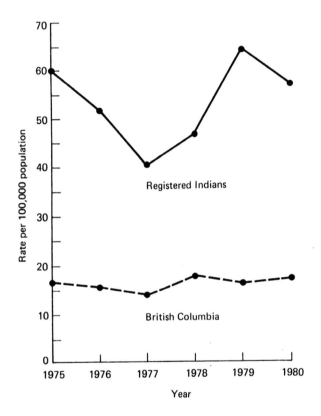

Source: *Vital Statistics.* Reports of Ministry of Health, Province of British Columbia, 1975-1980

Fig.5.10   *Cirrhosis of the Liver among Registered Indians and the British Columbia Population, 1975–80*

These statistics suggest high rates of alcohol abuse among Indians in the province, ranging from a high of 64.7 deaths per 100 000 from cirrhosis of the liver in 1979 to a low of 40.6 cirrhosis deaths per 100 000 population in 1977. In comparison, the rates of the general population have ranged from 14.8 deaths from cirrhosis of the liver per 100 000 in 1977 to 18.4 per 100 000 in 1978. It has also been estimated that alcohol abuse was a contributing factor in 80% of all deaths from accidents (Health and Welfare Canada, *Annual Report*, 1978, p.6; 1979, p.6).

In summary, an examination of infant mortality rates, several categories of violent death, and the rates of cirrhosis of the liver among registered Indians in the province of British Columbia reveal patterns consistent with those found in the national data. Both the provincial data and the nationwide data provide conclusive evidence of high rates of death of natives related to the socio-structural condition within which they they live and indicate that these 'death styles' of natives are different from those of the general population.

## IMPLICATIONS

The data presented on the death rates of registered Indians in Canada and in the province of British Columbia have significant implications for the study of minority groups in the field of victimology and for the development and implementation of policies and programmes for native victims at the federal, and community levels.

On a conceptual level, the data establish conclusively the high rates of victimization of natives, particularly from violent deaths, and suggest a strong correlation between victimization and the subordinate position of natives in Canadian society. To gain an understanding of the aetiology of native victimization, victimologists must shift their focus to allow consideration of the socio-structural determinants of victimization. More specifically, future research should focus on the victimization of status and non-status Indians as well as of the Metis and Inuit populations. In such inquiries, an attempt should be made to ascertain the impact of cultural and linguistic differences, differences in personal and community resources of native communities and bands, and of the rural and northern environment on both rates of victimization and the specific forms of victimization that occur. Of considerable interest would be a determination of the factors – social, economic, political, cultural, and linguistic – on the proneness of natives to victimization.

The findings also have programmatic implications. The development of intervention strategies to address the high rates of victimization of natives must consider the rural and often isolated location of the people involved, the wide differences among native communities and bands in terms of their cultural and linguistic heritage, and their personal and community resources. Such differences necessitate modification of victim and witness assistance programmes and restitution programmes that have been developed primarily for urban areas of the country where communities are predominantly white. For example, it is highly unlikely that restitution programmes and victim–offender reconciliation programmes, designed and implemented in the 'southern' population areas of Canada, would operate successfully in Inuit communities. It is quite possible that programmes developed in the more urbanized areas of the country for non-natives are not relevant to the needs and requirements of native peoples in more rural and northern areas of the country. Such initiatives must be undertaken by natives themselves, utilizing strategies that are appropriate for each particular band and the community in which they live. Increased attention must also be given to developing and improving community based prevention and assistance programmes.

Further, it will be impossible to develop a uniform set of initiatives designed to address the needs of native victims that are applicable to all native groups. Given the diversity among bands in Canada in terms of personal and community resources, cultural and linguistic attributes and socio-political organization, it is likely that initiatives that are appropriate for one band in a particular setting may be inappropriate for another band, even though both are geographically similar in their location. In sum, policy initiatives must avoid the mistakes and overgeneralizations that have often characterized other criminal justice initiatives involving native Indians in Canada (see Griffiths and Yerbury, 1984). By treating native peoples as a homogenous group, critical differences have been ignored that may substantially affect programme effectiveness.

### Notes

1. There is no exact figure on the number of natives in Canada. There are just over 300 000 registered Indians in Canada, belonging to 573 bands, the exact number of non-status Indians, which includes non-registered Indians and Metis, is unknown. Estimates range from 260 000 to 850 000. The Inuit population is estimated to be about 22 000. A 'guesstimate' is that there are about 1 million native people residing in Canada.

2. A native band may be (a) a group of Indians who share the use and benefit of reserve lands; (b) a group of Indians who share monies held

by the Department of Indian Affairs; (c) a group of Indians that the Department of Indian Affairs has identified as a band. A reserve is a tract of land that is owned by the government but that has been set apart by the government for the use and benefit of a band of Indian people.

3. The *Indian Act of Canada* defines an 'Indian' as 'a person who pursuant of this Act is registered as an Indian or is entitled to be registered as an Indian'.

4. Generally, data on these and other types of deaths among natives are available only for the registered Indian population. Further, there is no standardized data collection procedure that results in the same types of data being gathered. Data are generally not available for non-status Indians or Inuit, except in certain selected instances. Further, there is no standardization of data between the federal government and the provinces. Given these limitations, the statistical materials utilized for the present paper must necessarily be viewed as only illustrative and suggestive rather than conclusive. The statistics that are available, however, do provide a fairly consistent picture of the general socio-structural condition of registered Indians in Canadian society and of the rates of violent death, accidents, and mortality.

5. Statistics compiled in British Columbia include Indians as part of the general population as well as separating Indians as a separate category. Thus, the rates for British Columbia population would be even lower if Indians were excluded from the vital statistics data.

6. The categories of the major causes of death for registered Indians are similar to those for the general population, with the exception of congenital abnormalities and homicide that were included in the ten major causes of death for the general population in 1980.

## References

Alberta Board of Review: Provincial Courts. 1978. *Native People in the Administration of Justice in the Provincial Courts of Alberta.* Edmonton: Solicitor General of Alberta.

Dadrian, V. N. 1976. 'The Victimization of the American Indian', *Victimology*, vol.1, pp.517–37.

Fry, A. 1970. *How a People Die.* Toronto: Doubleday Canada.

Griffiths, C. T. and Yerbury, J. C.1984. 'Natives and Criminal Justice Policy: The Case of Native Policing' *Canadian J. of Criminology*, vol. 26(2), pp.147–60.

Harris, M. 1975. *Culture, People, Nature.* New York: Thomas Y. Crowell.

Health and Welfare Canada, 1978 and 1979, *Annual Reports* (Ottawa: Medical Services Branch).

Hylton, J. H., Mantonovich, R., Varro, J. and Thakker, B. 1979. *Job Satisfaction in the Regina Police Department.* Regina: Regina Police Department.

*DIAND* (Department of Indian Affairs and Northern Department), *Indian Conditions: A Survey.* 1980. Ottawa.

Jolly, S. 1980. *A Review of the Ontario Native Courtworker Program.* Toronto; Ontario Native Council on Justice.

Jorgensen, J. 1971. 'Indians and the Metropolis', in *The American Indian in Urban Society*, J. Waddell and M. Watson (eds), Boston: Little, Brown, pp.66–113.

Laprairie, C. P. and Griffiths, C. T. 1982. 'Native Indian Juvenile Delinquency: A Review of Recent Findings'. *Canadian Legal Aid Bulletin* (Special Issue, 'Native People and Justice in Canada), pp.34–46.

Lautt, M. 1979. 'Natives and Justice: A Topic Requiring Research Priority?' in D. M. Hepworth (ed.) *Explorations in Prairie Justice Research.* Regina: Canadian Plains Research Centre, pp.55–155.

May, P. A. 1982. 'Contemporary Crime and the American Indian: A Survey and Analysis of the Literature' *Plains Anthropologist*, vol.27, pp.225–38.

*Medical Services Annual Report*, Pacific Region, 1978.

Mendelsohn, O. B. 1974. 'The Origins of the Doctrine of Victimology' in *Victimology*, I. Drapkin and E. Viano (eds), Toronto: Lexington Books, pp.3–11.

Morse, B. W. 1976. 'Native People and Legal Services in Canada' *McGill Law Journal*, vol.2, pp.504–40.

Parnell, J. 1979. *We Mean no Harm – Yukon Indian Police Relations: A Preliminary Survey of Attitudes.* Whitehorse: Yukon Association of Non-Status Indians.

Reasons, C. E. 1975. 'Native Offenders and Correctional Policy'. *Crime et/and Justice.* vol.4, pp.255–67.

Separovic, Z. P. 1974. 'Victimology: A New Approach in the Social Services', Chapter 3 in *Victims and Society.* E. Viano (ed.), Washington, DC: Visage Press, pp.15–24.

Stanbury, W. T. 1975. *Success and Failure: Indians in Urban Society.* Vancouver: University of British Columbia Press.

Verdun-Jones, S. N. and Muirhead, G. 1980. 'Native Indians in the Canadian Criminal Justice System: An Overview'. *Crime et/and Justice*, 7/8:3.21.

Van Dyke, E. W. and Jamont, K. C. 1980. *Through Indian Eyes: Perspectives of Indian Special Constables on the 3b Program in "F" Division.* Regina: "F" Division, Royal Canadian Mounted Police.

von Hentig, H. 1948. *The Criminal and His Victim.* New Haven: Yale University Press.

Yerbury, J. C. 1980. 'British Columbia Native Nations in Transition: The Urbanization Process'. *Urban Anthropology.* vol.9, pp.319–39.

# Part II

# On Women and Children as Victims

# 6 Women as Victims

## Laurie Vaughan-Evans and Diane Wood

### INTRODUCTION

When attempting to research and document a topic such as 'women as victims', the magnitude and complexity of the task is, at the outset, an overwhelming consideration. This issue is comprised of numerous facets which each merit serious scrutiny by those who are concerned with the right of all individuals to a life free of abuse, harassment, and coercion.

Unlike other victims in our society who may find themselves targets of crime through negligence or chance, there are too many situations in which women are victimized by their vulnerability and dependence on the very persons to whom they look for respect, protection, and support, both in family and business relationships.

In many instances, women are victimized because they are women, and have been socialized to play a role established and perpetuated by a society which appears to condone this victimization through a refusal to acknowledge the existence and severity of the victimization women experience in many areas of their day-to-day life.

This chapter attempts a review of some of the cases of women's victimization and some of the specific crimes to which women predominantly fall victim. While there are many areas where women are the predominant victims, we are choosing the following specific areas of victimization of women for inclusion in this chapter: incest, sexual harassment, wife battering, and abuse of the elderly. In most of these areas, women are not the only victims, but after reviewing the current research on these topics, it is evident that the overwhelming majority of victims in the above-mentioned instances are female, and that the nature of their victimization is relative to the fact that they are female.

## BACKGROUND

While this chapter presents a primarily Canadian perspective, it should be noted that these problems are not solely a North American phenomenon. The declaration by the United Nations of 1975–85 as the Decade for Women: Equality, Development and Peace, was to draw attention to the fact that in different countries, with varying degrees of severity depending on political, social, and cultural differences, the exploitation of women is a grave concern.

The World Programme of Action, developed in 1975, and to which Canada responded with its own National Plan of Action on the Status of Women, put forth numerous recommendations to improve the condition of women, and was intended to lead to the re-evaluation of the roles of women and men in all the member countries of the United Nations. Canada's Plan of Action for initiatives at the federal level made a strong connection between attitudes and women's position.

In 1980, a world conference was held in Copenhagen, to study the advances made during the first half of the UN Decade for Women and to determine new strategies and areas for action for the second half of the decade.

It is worth noting that the objectives outlined under Health considerations in the Programme of Action for the Second Half of the UN Decade for Women included:

> The development of policies and programmes aimed at the elimination of all forms of violence against women and children and the protection of women of all ages from physical and mental abuse resulting from domestic violence, sexual assault, sexual exploitation and any other form of abuses.[1]

Promotion of research, provision of victims services, and the elimination of the glorification of the sexual exploitation of women were included under priority areas for action during the following five years.[2]

Under our National Plan of Action, the federal government agreed to review the Criminal Code as it pertains to sexual offences, examine the issue of sexual harassment in the work place, establish a national clearinghouse on family violence, and establish guidelines for the elimination of sex-role stereotyping in the Canadian media. It is gratifying to see that major inroads have been accomplished in all these areas to date.

Another major advancement at the International level, was Canada's ratification of the United Nations' Convention on the Elimination of All Forms of Discrimination Against Women. This was ratified on 10 December, 1981 with the consent of all the provinces and territories.

Article 5 (a) of this Convention states that signatories shall take all appropriate measures:

> . . . to modify the social and cultural patterns of conduct of men and women, with a view to achieving the elimination of prejudices and customary and all other practices which are based on the idea of the inferiority or the superiority of either of the sexes or on stereotyped roles for men and women . . . [3]

Article 11 of this Convention also stipulates that appropriate measures should be taken to eliminate discrimination against women in employment settings.[4]

While the specifics of the many situations in which women are victimized are quite diverse, it becomes clearer that the values and roles men and women adopt as they mature, seriously undermine the equality of women and men and contribute to the victimization of women in our society.


## AREAS OF VICTIMIZATION

This section outlines the specific areas of victimization as indicated in the introduction. One should keep in mind that certain topics, such as sexual assault, are specifically excluded because they are being dealt with elsewhere.


### Incest

*The Problem*
The sexual abuse of children within the nuclear or extended family betrays that important bond of trust between an adult and a child. In spite of the abhorrence society feels for it, incest is always a closely

guarded secret, while sexual abuse of children outside the family is considered a matter of community concern.

In her *Handbook of Clinical Intervention in Child Sexual Abuse*, Suzanne Sgroi describes child sexual abuse as:

. . . a sexual act imposed on a child who lacks emotional, maturational and cognitive development. The ability to lure a child into a sexual relationship is based upon the all powerful and dominant position of the adult . . . which is in sharp contrast to the child's age, dependency and subordinate position. Authority and power enable the perpetrator, implicitly or directly, to coerce the child into sexual compliance.[5]

In cases of incest, this coercion is facilitated, and seen to be all the more distasteful, because of the role of guardianship of the adult and the degree of vulnerability, dependency, love, and trust in the relationship between this adult and the child.

A legal handbook published in London, Ontario presents a statistical picture on the incidence of incest in this country. It is estimated that 10% of our population are victims of incestuous relationships and that 97% of offenders are male (with fathers/stepfathers being the most common) and that 90% of the victims are female.[6]

The Canada Law Reform Commission studied conviction rates for incest cases between the years 1917 and 1967 and it was found that there was an average of 53 charges and 40 convictions per year.[7] This finding is alarmingly low when compared to estimated incidence rates. Vancouver, British Columbia, has an incest hotline which received 600 legitimate calls in 1980.[8] Incest calls to a Calgary Sexual Assault Centre rose 104% from 1980 to 1981.[9] Comparisons based on studies undertaken in the United States, would result in conservative estimates of 1500 cases of incest per year for a city the size of Vancouver or 2800 cases per year in cities such as Toronto and Montreal. On a national scale, this would mean the possibility of approximately 23 869 cases in one year.[10] It is figures such as these which lead specialists in the area to conclude that incest could very well be considered a major public health problem.

The dynamics of an incestuous relationship are such that the victim is emotionally and often physically scarred. The majority of cases involve a male adult and a female child. Studies dealing with victims of incest after the end of a relationship outline the many physical and psychological consequences of an adult/child relationship. These include self-hypnosis, mentally induced rational anesthesia,[11] self-mutilation, sexual dysfunction in later life, and low self-esteem.[12] Unfortunately, the very nature of incest precludes discovery and the relationships may go undetected for years. In fact, some families conspire to suppress knowledge of the incest because it permits certain other family dynamics to remain unchallenged.

The discovery of an incestuous relationship relies on factors such as chance, the observations of others or the ability of the child to communicate her problems. This ability to communicate may be impeded by the age, isolation, degree of fear, or loyalty of the child, and the willingness of the listener to believe and act in the child's interest.

The issue of loyalty becomes a key factor as well after a disclosure has taken place. In many instances of father/daughter abuse, the mother will choose to support the offender in order to preserve the family unit or because she is financially dependent on her spouse and would lose her security upon a separation or the imposition of a jail sentence.[13]

In cases where the offender is a parent or relative, the victim is often pressured by other family members to retract the charge. Even when a child does testify in court, she may be an ambivalent witness due to her natural affinity for the offender.[14]

Those who interact with children, such as teachers, day care staff, doctors, nurses, and relatives, should be aware of some of the non-verbal cues that a child is being sexually abused or a victim of incest. Several of these symptoms are: crying with no apparent reason; fear of the dark or sleeping in own room; resistance to certain persons; change in eating habits; aggressive behaviour; drawings of a sexual nature or advanced knowledge of sex for child's age; venereal disease; persistent illness or absence from school; regression; nightmares; overt seductive behaviour; poor self-image; suicide attempts; and promiscuity or the extreme opposite.[15]

*Treatment and Prevention*
There seem to be no family stereotypes or patterns in offenders (except that the majority are men).[16]

Offenders do, however, show a lack of impulse control and a marked confusion in roles. They often have a poor relationship with their wife and children, and tend to be domineering and restrictive. This exertion of power in the family setting may result from low self-esteem and lack of power in other facets of day to day life, such as at work. Offenders rarely acknowledge responsibility for their actions and may tend to minimize the damage to the child or even blame the child for the seduction.[17]

Interventionists must deal with the whole family as a unit, or treat the child and perhaps other family members in isolation should the offender be removed from the family unit.

The education of children from a young age to respect their own bodies and to voice objection to physical contact which is offensive from *any* person is a key element in preventing abuse by coercion. As well, children should be believed and action taken on complaints of unwanted attention.

Parents, as well, need more information on their roles in child raising and should be informed of the adverse effect of a break in the trust of a parent/child relationship and the short and long-term side effects of child sexual abuse.

*Criminal Code*
Incest, as defined by S.150 of the Criminal Code of Canada is 'sexual intercourse between two people who by blood relationship are either parent and child, brother and sister, half-brother and half-sister or grandparent and grandchild' and carries a maximum penalty of 14 years imprisonment.[18]

The shortcomings of this definition are clear in that not all abuse includes sexual intercourse and not all abusers are blood relatives (i.e. stepfathers). As well, one may question incarceration of the offender as the best remedy to an incestuous relationship. Depending on the length and extent of the abuse, victim and family counselling with a view to reconciliation may be a more viable alternative.

A major factor to consider is that recidivism in incest is rare when properly handled at the time of disclosure and that it is possible, with the help of proper controls, to keep the offender in the community or return him to the family after counselling, without fear of incest recurring.[19]

As the criminal law and criminal process have considerable problems in dealing with family matters,[20] a future emphasis on community and counselling services for victims of incest would be a very desirable trend.

**Sexual Harassment**

*The Problem*

Sexual harassment can take many forms ranging from cat calls on the street, to obscene phone calls, lewd jokes, unwanted physical contact, and coercion to take part in sexual acts.

In Canada recently, the primary focus for this issue has been on sexual harassment in the work place. While the awareness of this problem is relatively new, this does not mean that sexual harassment is a new employment problem.

A recent survey conducted in Quebec of 2465 women revealed that 64% of these women had experienced sexual harassment by a colleague or supervisor and an overwhelming 89% felt that sexual harassment at work is a serious problem.[21]

Two factors have increased our realization of the extent of this problem: the large increase of women in the paid labour force (40%),[22] and the growing organization of women through the women's movement which has drawn attention to many inequities between men and women of which sexual harassment in the workplace is just one.

For the purposes of this chapter, sexual harassment in the workplace is defined as: any persistent conduct, comment, gesture, or contact of a sexual nature, which might reasonably be perceived by an employee as being a condition of employment, or any persistent conduct, comment, gesture, display of literature, or contact of a sexual nature which is likely to cause offence, embarrassment, or humiliation to an employee.[23]

One of the key factors to consider is the quality of persistence. Harmless, normal male/female interaction in any setting is not to be confused with sexual harassment which is not a mutually acceptable interaction and usually continues to thrive regardless of its one-sided nature and contains some element of threat.

Sexual harassment has been viewed by some as a social problem, based on learned stereotypical roles played by women and men. It is viewed as an expression of power and is not sexually motivated behaviour.[24] Another very serious consideration of this type of behaviour, is one of economic survival.

The impact of sexual harassment is very serious for women. Of all women 40% are self-supporting[25] with much lower job status than men. They earn less money than men (60%)[26] and are less often protected by a union. Even those who are fortunate enough to be unionized (27%),[27] belong to a union whose membership is male dominated. In this instance, the union may develop policy or make decisions based on or affected by majority membership.

All of these factors, place women in a very vulnerable position and make them dependent on their employers or co-workers for their financial security. In more serious occurrences the harasser is in a superior position in the workplace hierarchy, and has the ability to fire an individual who would not comply with his requests for sexual favours.

A victim, upon rejecting harassing advances, may begin to receive poor job evaluations which may eventually lead to dismissal, and which means the harasser is protected. The trauma experienced by the victim can be severe enough as to hamper her work performance, because she cannot deal effectively on a professional level with, or in the presence of, the individual who has harassed her. Therefore, a woman's health, job performance, and economic security are threatened when she becomes a victim of sexual harassment.[28]

*Treatment and Prevention*
In addition to an employer losing a valuable employee, there can be a loss of productivity due to increased absenteeism, and when employees cease to function up to par. The financial cost in decreased productivity has been a cause for concern. Employers, unions, and all levels of government are beginning to develop policy in this area.[29]

Sexual harassment is covered by all provincial and federal human rights legislation (as a subsection under discrimination on the basis of sex). At the federal level, Labour Canada has proposed amendments to the Canada Labour Code which concern sexual harassment in the workplace, and the Canadian Human Rights Commission is developing a more definitive policy on this issue. Treasury Board has issued a set of guidelines on the problem of sexual harassment for public service employees.

Primary responsibility for ensuring that sexual harassment does not exist or thrive in the workplace rests with the employer. In fact, however, the responsibility for rectifying the situation rests with the victim who must bring the incident to the attention of the proper authorities. Increasing sexual harassment seminars in employment settings by either the employer, union, or Human Rights Commissions, would result in all employees being aware of the causes, and effects of such behaviour, and the punitive measures which could be taken by the employer to ensure the quality of working life for all employees. The development of personnel policy on this matter by individual employers is integral to the elimination of this type of victimization. While human rights tribunals and the courts can address individual cases, work place policies affect larger numbers and alleviate the burden on victims of attempting to remedy an intolerable situation.

## Wife Battering

*The Problem*
Abuse of women by their husbands or partners is a complex and widespread problem in Canada.

An estimated 1 in 10 women are battered[30] physically and/or verbally by their husbands. In 1982, the House of Commons Standing Committee on Health, Welfare and Social Affairs, released a report on wife abuse in Canada which indicated that wife battering is rarely a one-time occurrence and is very frequently severe.[31] In 1975, of 107 reported murders in immediate families, the wife was killed by her husband in 49 cases.[32]

In examining the dynamics of wife abuse, one must consider the historical basis for marriage. We go back to the time when a woman's legal identity merged with that of her husband upon marriage. As recently as 1840 a husband could beat his wife or have her imprisoned if she refused to cohabit with him. In 1891, both of these rights were abolished. However, we still have not put in place adequate structures or legal remedies to prohibit such behaviour. The vestiges of these laws remain in our attitudes. The notion of the sanctity of marriage and family unit and the privacy of the home serve to protect batterers and at times may perpetuate violence in the home. With the changes to family and matrimonial property laws in the late 1970s and the 1982 amendments to the Criminal Code of Canada to include as an offence the sexual assault (rape) of a wife by her husband, there has been some attempt to address the problems women face. In fact the Criminal Code has never excluded the wife as a possible victim of assault. Wife battering is a crime; it has only rarely been treated as one.

While legislation has given the woman a legal identity independent of her spouse, socialization and societal standards still prevail which keep many women in potentially life threatening situations.

The dynamics of wife battering are extremely intricate, as many recent studies and reports have indicated.

The socialization of women as being passive and of men as being dominant sets the stage for the battering relationship. The conscious or subconscious fostering of dependence in a relationship increases a woman's vulnerability to abuse. This vulnerability can be characterized in many ways, such as physical and emotional isolation from family and friends, low self-esteem, limited resources, young children, and fear.[33] Wife-abuse is both a symptom and a generator of women's vulnerability.[34]

Dependency as a key factor leading to abuse is further exemplified by the high rate of abuse during pregnancy, a time when women are extremely reliant on their spouses, and social isolation may be heightened.[35] A recent study of five separate Canada samples indicated that, in one sample, 46.3% of the women who had been battered stated that they had been assaulted during their pregnancy.[36]

In examining what determines why certain relationships are abusive, several common factors become evident. A survey of transition houses across Canada (MacLeod, 1980) revealed that 50% of the husbands of women interviewed had been beaten as children.[37] This characteristic is referred to as the 'cycle of violence' and was noticed as well in the results of an Ontario Study (Kincaid, 1982) which showed that, in an Interval House sample, 63.8% of the husbands of residents had been abused as a child and/or had witnessed parents assaulting each other, while 45% of the residents themselves had not experienced previous family violence.[38] While these results indicate that violence may be cyclical, learned behaviour, there is not sufficient extensive research to isolate this as the sole cause of wife abuse.[39] It is equally certain that not all men who batter have been abused as children.

Other factors sometimes described as contributing to violence in the family are financial status, low job satisfaction, alcohol consumption, stress,[40] natural male aggression, and mental illness.[41] These should be classed in the category of 'myths' surrounding this issues. Such theories cannot be used to excuse the use of life-threatening violence.

Once violence has occurred in a family setting, an important question arises as to why the wife remains in the home to tolerate this treatment, or returns to a violent relationship after having left on any number of occasions.

A primary factor to consider, as mentioned previously is the degree to which the wife is dependent on the husband.

Psychological dependency frequently results from low self-esteem and lack of self worth, feelings of guilt and of having deserved the punishment, and fear of retaliation.[42]

Practical dependency is characterized by isolation, lack of information on remedies, dependent children,[43] and most importantly financial dependence.

Often the women simply have nowhere to go. In 1980, 45% of Canadians lived in areas without access to shelters and if the woman has suffered isolation from family and friends she may not see any alternative to her present situation.[44] Even if the woman is fortunate to live in a community which has a shelter, these homes are sorely overcrowded and must turn people away.[45]

What many women experience could be described as a double victimization. Not only are they abused in their homes, but often police, clergy, medical, and legal representatives will attempt to encourage the woman to preserve her marriage and remain in a violent situation.

While policies are changing, police have often hesitated to intervene in cases of domestic violence, leaving the onus on the victim to press charges against her spouse.[46] The reasons for this are many.

Many religions believe strongly in the sanctity of marriage, the family, the subordinate role of the woman in the family, and do not support a battered wife in seeking outside help.

Medical staff are not required and have never been trained to probe the causes of injuries brought to their attention. Often women are prescribed tranquillizers to cope with anxiety. This is a practice which may provide temporary relief, but no long-term cure. It may lull a woman into remaining in a violent situation rather than actively seeking help.

A United States study showed that, contrary to the belief that women's psychological problems lead to abuse, these psychological problems developed as a result of women's violent experiences.[47]

Legal barriers faced by battered women consist of inability to secure and/or have enforced restraint or peace-keeping orders against their husbands.[48] Women also may experience difficulties obtaining maintenance or alimony payments, especially if they flee from the provincial jurisdiction in which the husband lives. Access to children is also a serious consideration for battered wives who have left violent husbands.

There are many battered women who work actively to change their situation. However, the fact that it is so difficult is primarily a function of the blocks created by institutional structures.[49] It is the responsibility of the social services and the criminal justice system to provide every assistance to battered women.

*Treatment and Prevention*
There has been an increased focus on wife battering recently in Canada. In May 1982, House of Commons Standing Committee on Health, Welfare and Social Affairs released a report on wife battering which has resulted in a more concerted government effort to initiate new policies and programmes to address the problems of battered women. The following are some of the federal initiatives:

1.   150 social housing units allocated for transition homes as well as a financial assistance programme – CMHC.
2.   Review of police procedures and establishment of training related to family violence – Solicitor General.
3.   Staff-training programmes as well as recent amendments to the Criminal Code of Canada – Justice.

As well, the Ontario Government has just released a similar report on wife battering which outlines provincial concerns and proposals regarding wife abuse.

Many municipalities, such as Vancouver, St. John's, Restigouche, Campbellton, Burlington, Hamilton, London, Edmonton, Victoria, and Toronto, have established family violence assistance programmes which complement the local police departments.[50]

**Elderly**

Recently, in the realm of research on the victims of crime, certain subgroups have been identified as possessing characteristics that might indicate more likelihood of being victimized: 'Groups which run a high risk of victimization are comparatively defenceless persons such as the young and the old, females and drunks'.[51]

While the elderly of both sexes may be more vulnerable to crime, the vast majority of the elderly in Canada are women. Therefore, this may doubly affect the probability of their becoming victimized.

## The Problem

It has been asserted that the elderly are more 'victim prone' as a result of their physical, situational, and social vulnerability.[52]

When examining women as a separate group, physical vulnerability is not only a characteristic of old age, but a socialization and physiological factor as well. Women are generally not as strong as men, young or old, and have learned non-aggressive and non-assertive behaviour over a lifetime.

Even if the individual does not perceive herself as weak, the perpetrator may attribute these stereotypical characteristics to an elderly woman by virtue of her sex and thereby attempt to commit a crime against her on that basis.

The elderly are situationally vulnerable as limited resources may force them to live in high crime areas.[53] This is especially true for elderly women who, more often than men, are living in poverty in their old age. 'To be old and female, is the best combination to ensure being poor in Canada.'[54]

Women do not have equal access to pensions and benefits because many have worked in the home and have had little control over family finances until their spouse's death. In most cases, this is too late to ensure a comfortable life style for the elderly woman.

Women of all ages are socially vulnerable as discriminatory attitudes towards women still prevail in 1983. Elderly women are doubly vulnerable as the factors of sex and age come into play in establishing social status: 'Sex and age discrimination are a poisonous combination.'[55]

The report *Violence et personnes âgées* presented to the Quebec Ministry of Justice by L'Association Québecoise de Gérontologie points out that, of every three victims of abuse, two are female.[56]

There has been a recent emergence of media articles on abuse of the elderly within their own homes or the homes of their children.

This abuse, referred to as 'granny-bashing' or 'gram-slamming', goes largely undetected and unmeasured in our society.[57] Betty Havens, a researcher for the Manitoba Department of Health, estimates that only 10% of cases of abuse of the elderly are detected.[58]

The previously mentioned Québec study found that one of the highest percentages of the elderly who were abused were victimized in their own homes[59] by their children or their children's spouses[60]. This category was second only to abuse of the elderly taking place in institutional settings.

Abuse of the elderly can take many forms: physical, psychological, and financial. A national study conducted in the United States indicated that the victimization of elderly women reflected the victimization pattern of all females whereas the victimization of the elderly men did not.[61] This underscores the fact that the victimization of elderly women is not as contingent on the age of the person as on the sex.

Another American study on victims concluded that one of the single most important factors affecting fear of victimization was sex,[62] pointing out that more women than men feared being victimized.

This feeling of vulnerability can seriously affect an individual's behaviour and sense of freedom, thereby lessening the quality of life.

Fear of victimization in the elderly is almost as serious a factor as the actual victimization. Cases have been documented which illustrate the adverse affects of self-imposed isolation on mental and physical health.

*Future Trends*

The increased focus on the elderly through the federal pension review and national studies such as the recent NDP survey of the elderly in Canada, will serve to heighten awareness of the rights of the elderly to live securely in their later years. Further research on the victimization of the elderly is the first step to determining how society can best ensure adequate quality of life for our senior citizens.

Educational programmes and an increase in community support services would assist the elderly in functioning independently without fear of threat to their financial, physical and mental well-being.

**CONCLUSION**

Through history, civilizations have been founded, to a greater or lesser degree, upon the institutionalization of force or its threat through their legal systems. Violence was once regularly employed by courts and prisons, masters, the church and civil authorities as a legitimate means of social control . . . as an instrument of intimidation of those at the bottom of the hierarchy.[63] As has been demonstrated throughout this paper, women are victimized by individuals who perceive them to be at the 'bottom of the hierarchy' and see the use of force as a viable means of ensuring the status quo. Women are not only victims of crime, but they are also victims of an age-old power struggle.

Women's victimization belongs in the same category as systemic discrimination and there are a number of reasons why this type of victimization can be viewed as separate from the problems of victims in general. These reasons are: women and men are taught attitudes about women and their role in society from an early age; women's place in the hierarchical structure of the family, the workplace and society in general is very low; the legal, medical, and religious institutions persist in tacitly or overtly reinforcing the above two points.

The double victimization women suffer has been outlined throughout this paper: the abused child faces apathy or disbelief by parents and professionals; the harassed worker must initiate her own remedies often facing the prospect of threat to employment/financial security; the battered wife is not adequately supported by the police, the courts, the medical profession; and the fearful elderly woman often lives in isolation with little family or community support and with few financial resources during her last years.

The law, particularly Criminal Law, has been more concerned of late with offenders, than victims, and as a result, it is the victim's credibility as a witness which determines, to a large degree, their right to the due process of law. While this pragmatic treatment of evidence facilitates the decision to proceed to court, it does little to reinforce a victim's sense of worth and 'hardly places the helping agencies of society in a state of readiness to meet the victim half way'.[64] Female victims need to be reassured that the legal system exists for all Canadians.

Victims' services and social agencies need to focus on the non-legal short, medium and long-term effects of female victimization: such as changes caused to personal relationships, health, lifestyle, and earning capacity, as well as offering advocacy to the victim during her experience with the criminal justice system.

Education of the public from instruction of children starting in elementary school to research on the various areas of victimization of women should be non-sexist.

One of the major aspects in sexist literature and research is the prevalence of a male perspective. This expresses itself not only in what is researched, and how the research is conducted, but also in what is *not* researched.[65]

Reliable, current, Canadian research on wife battering and incest is conspicuous by its absence: 'There has never been a representative study of the real extent of wife battering . . . there has never been a representative study of the extent of incest in Canada, which tends to be a crime committed by adult males on female children.'[66]

As a society, Canada has not yet reached its goal of equality between women and men and therefore, researchers still operate within a social context of which *one* important aspect is male–female relations based on inequality.[67]

To the degree that public money is spent on research, the products should be free from sex bias; to be otherwise, is slight to 52% of the Canadian population and unjust to female victims who deserve recognition of the unique characteristics of their problems.

**Notes**

1.  *Programme of Action for the Second Half of the United Nations Decade for Women: Equality, Development and Peace* (New York: United Nations, 1980) p.31.
2.  Ibid, p.32.
3.  *Convention on the Elimination of All Forms of Discrimination Against Women* (New York: United Nations, n.d.), p.6.
4.  Ibid, pp.8–9.
5.  As paraphrased in 'Perspectives on Child Sexual Abuse Intervention' in *Response to Family Violence and Sexual Assault*, vol 5, no.3 (Washington: Center for Women Policy Studies, 1982) p.10.
6.  Cochrane, Rosemary and Hipfner, Eileen. *Incest: a London Legal Handbook* (London: UWO Graphic Services, 1981) p.1.
7.  Grescoe, Audrey, 'Nowhere to Run' in *Homemaker's* (Toronto: Comac Communications, Apr. 1981) p.38.
8.  Ibid, p.42.
9.  'Alberta Incest Cases Overload Services, Say Social Workers' in *Behaviour Today*. (New York: Atcom Editorial Staff Publication, July 1982) p.3.
10. Grescoe, *op. cit.*, p.38.
11. Ibid, p.34.
12. Cochrane *et al, op. cit.*, pp.3–4.
13. Hebert, Carol P., 'Sexual Abuse of Children' in *Canadian Family*

*Physician*, vol.28 (Willowdale: College of Family Physicians of Canada, June 1982) p.1174.

14. Burgess, Ann Wolbert, Holmstrom, Lynda Lytle, and McCausland, Maureen P., 'Divided Loyalty in Incest Cases' in *Sexual Assault of Children and Adolescents* (Toronto: Lexington Books, 1978) p.116.
15. Cochrane *et al, op. cit.*, pp.3–4.
16. Burgess *et al, op. cit.*, pp.173–74.
17. Ibid, p.174.
18. *Criminal Law: Sexual Offenses, Working Paper 22* (Ottawa: Law Reform Commission of Canada, 1978) p.30.
19. Cooper, Ingrid K., 'Decriminalization of Incest – New Legal-Clinical Responses' in *Family Violence: an International and Interdisciplinary Study* (Toronto: Butterworths, 1978) p.523.
20. *Law Reform Commission of Canada, 1978*, p.31.
21. Vallée, Evelyne, 'Le harcèlement sexuel au travail' in *Communiqu'elles*, vol.8, no.9 (Montreal; Les Editions Communiqu'elles, Dec. 1982) p.8.
22. *Labour Force Survey – 1981 Annual Averages*, table 57 (Ottawa: Statistics Canada, 1982) p.80.
23. *Report No. 16, Administration, Policy and Priorities Committee*, (Ottawa: Office of Equal Opportunities for Women, City Hall, 15 June 1981).
24. Backhouse, Constance and Cohen, Leah, *The Secret Oppression: Sexual Harassment of Working Women* (Toronto: Macmillan of Canada, 1978) p.38.
25. Attenborough, Susan, *Sexual Harassment at Work* (Ottawa: National Union of Provincial Government Employees, 1980) p.7.
26. *Income Distributions by Size in Canada – 1979*, table 72 (Ottawa: Statistics Canada, 1981) p.135.
27. White, Julie, *Women and Unions* (Ottawa: The Canadian Advisory Council on the Status of Women, 1980) p.21.
28. Attenborough, *op. cit.*, p.6.
29. Chart, *Definitions of Sexual Harassment* (Ottawa: Canadian Human Rights Commission).
30. MacLeod, Linda, *Wife Battering In Canada: the Vicious Circle* (Ottawa: The Canadian Advisory Council on the Status of Women, 1980) p.21.
31. *Report on Violence in the Family: Wife Battering* (Ottawa: House of Commons Standing Committee on Health, Welfare and Social Affairs, 1982) p.10.
32. MacLeod, *op. cit.*, p.10.
33. Paltiel, Freda L., *Conceptualization Towards a Breakthrough* in Symposium on Inter-Spousal Violence (Ottawa: Canadian Association of Social Workers, 1981) p.63.
34. Ibid, p.62.
35. MacLeod, *op. cit.*, p.30.
36. Kincaid, Pat J., *The Omitted Reality: Husband–Wife Violence in Ontario and Policy Implications for Education* (Maple: Publishing and Printing Services, 1982) p.132.

37. MacLeod, *op. cit.*, p.31.
38. Kincaid, *op. cit.*, p.110.
39. Ibid, p.141.
40. Paltiel, *op. cit.*, p.63.
41. MacLeod, *op. cit.*, p.23.
42. Dixon, Jean, *Domestic Violence: the Tip of the Iceberg* (Charlottetown: Department of Justice, 1980) pp.26–27.
43. Barnsley, Jan, *'Battered and Blamed' – a report on Wife Assault from the Perspective of Battered Women* (Vancouver Transition House and Women's Research Centre, 1980) p.69.
44. Lewis, Debra J., *A Brief on Wife Battering with Proposals for Federal Action* (Ottawa: Canadian Advisory Council on the Status of Women, 1982) p.7.
45. Ibid, p.5.
46. Dutton, Donald G., *The Criminal Justice Response to Wife Assault* (Ottawa: Solicitor General of Canada, 1981) p.6.
47. As paraphrased in Lewis, *op. cit.*, p.2.
48. Dutton, *op. cit.*, p.6.
49. Lewis, *op. cit.*, p.2.
50. Norquay, Geoff and Weiler, Richard, *Services to Victims and Witnesses of Crime in Canada* (Ottawa: Solicitor General of Canada, 1981) pp.129–144.
51. Jayewardene, C. H. S., Juliani, T. J., and Talbot, C. K., *The Elderly as Victims of Crime* (Ottawa: Department of Justice, 1982) p.2.
52. Ibid, p.10.
53. Ibid, p.10.
54. Dulude, Louise, *Women and Aging: a Report on the Rest of Our Lives* (Ottawa: Canadian Advisory Council on the Status of Women, 1978) p.38.
55. Ibid, p.11.
56. Bélanger, Lise, *Violence et personnes âgées* (Québec: Ministère de la Justice, 1981) p.22.
57. Whiteway, Doug, *The Sins Against the Elderly* (Winnipeg Free Press, 21 Sept. 1982) p.21.
58. Ibid, p.21.
59. Bélanger, p.24.
60. Ibid, p.26.
61. As reported in Jayewardene *et al, op. cit.*, p.34.
62. Ibid, p.45.
63. Goldman, Pearl, *Violence Against Women in the Family* (Jan. 1978) p.1.
64. Paltiel, Freda L., *Battered Women: Concepts, Prospects and Practices*, notes for an address for the workshop for Social Workers on Battered Women (1 Dec. 1981) p.1.
65. Eichler, Margrit, *Towards a Strategy for Non-Sexist Research: a Position Paper* (Toronto: Ontario Institute for Studies in Education, 1981) p.18.
66. Ibid, p.19.
67. Ibid, p.5.

**Bibliography**

'Alberta Incest Cases Overload Services, Say Social Workers' (1982), *Behaviour Today* (New York: Atcom Editorial Staff Publication (July).

Attenborough, Susan (1980), *Sexual Harassment at Work* (Ottawa: National Union of Public Employees).

Backhouse, Constance and Cohen, Leah (1978), *The Secret Oppression: Sexual Harassment of Working Women* (Toronto: Macmillan of Canada).

Barnsley, Jan, (1980), *'Battered and Blamed'- A Report on Wife Assault from the Perspective of Battered Women* (Vancouver Transition House and The Women's Research Centre).

Bélanger, Lise (1981), *Violence et personnes âgées* (Québec: Ministère de la Justice).

Burgess, Ann Wolbert, Holmstrom, Lynda Lytle and McClausland, Maureen P. (1978), *Divided Loyalty in Incest Cases; Sexual Assault of Children and Adolescents* (Toronto: Lexington Books).

Cochrane, Rosemary and Hipfner, Eileen (1981), *Incest: a London Legal Handbook* (London: UWO Graphic Services).

*Convention on the Elimination of all Forms of Discrimination Against Women* (nd), (New York: United Nations).

Cooper, Ingrid K. (1978), *Decriminalization of Incest – New Legal–Clinical Responses, Family Violence: an International and Interdisciplinary Study* (Toronto: Butterworths).

*Criminal Law: Sexual Offenses, Working Paper 22* (1978), (Ottawa: Law Reform Commission of Canada).

*Definitions of Sexual Harassment* (Chart) n.d., (Ottawa: Canadian Human Rights Commission).

Dixon, Jean (1980), *Domestic Violence: the Tip of the Iceberg* (Charlottetown: Department of Justice).

Dulude, Louise (1978), *Women and Aging: a Report on the Rest of Our Lives* (Ottawa: Canadian Advisory Council on the Status of Women).

Dutton, Donald G. (1981), *The Criminal Justice Response to Wife Assault* (Ottawa: Solicitor General of Canada).

Eichler, Margrit (1981), *Towards a Strategy for Non-Sexist Research: a Position Paper* (Toronto: Ontario Institute for Studies in Education).

Goldman, Pearl (1978) *Violence Against Women in the Family*, Master of Laws Thesis, McGill University, Jan.

Grescoe, Audrey (1981), 'Nowhere to Run', *Homemaker's* (Toronto: Comac Communications, Apr).

Hebert, Carol P. (1982), 'Sexual Abuse of Children', *Canadian Family Physician*, vol.28 (Willowdale: College of Family Physicians of Canada, June).

*Income Distributions by Size in Canada – 1979* (1981), (Ottawa: Statistics Canada).

Jayewardene, C. H. S., Juliani, T. J. and Talbot, C. K. (1982), *The Elderly as Victims of Crime* (Ottawa: Department of Justice).

Kincaid, Pat. J. (1982), *The Omitted Reality: Husband–Wife Violence in Ontario and Policy Implications for Education* (Maple: Publishing and Printing Services).

*Labour Force Survey – 1981 Annual Averages* (1982), (Ottawa: Statistics Canada).

Lewis, Debra J. (1982) *A Brief on Wife Battering with Proposals for Federal Action* (Ottawa: Canadian Advisory Council on the Status of Women).

MacLeod, Linda (1980) *Wife Battering in Canada: the Vicious Circle* (Ottawa: Canadian Advisory Council on the Status of Women).

Norquay, Geoff and Weiler, Richard (1981), *Services to Victims and Witnesses of Crime in Canada* (Ottawa: Solicitor General of Canada).

Paltiel, Freda L. (1981) *Battered Women: Concepts, Prospects and Practices*, notes for an address for the Workshop for Social Workers on Battered Women (Ottawa: Health and Welfare Canada, Dec).

Paltiel, Freda L. (1981), *Conceptualization Towards a Breakthrough*, Symposium on Inter-Spousal Violence (Ottawa: Canadian Association of Social Workers).

'Perspectives on Child Sexual Abuse Intervention', (1982), *Response to Family Violence and Sexual Assault*, vol.5, no.3 (Washington: Center for Women Policy Studies).

*Programme of Action for the Second Half of the United Nations Decade for Women: Equality, Development and Peace* (1980), (New York: United Nations).

*Report No. 16* (1981), Administration, Policy, and Priorities Committee, Office of Equal Opportunities for Women (Ottawa: City Hall).

*Report on Violence in the Family: Wife Battering* (1982), (Ottawa: House of Commons Standing Committee on Health, Welfare and Social Affairs).

Vallée, Evelyne (1982), *Le harcèlement sexuel au travail*, Communiqu'elles, vol.8, no.9 (Montréal: Éditions Communiqu'elles, Dec).

White, Julie (1980), *Women and Unions* (Ottawa: Canadian Advisory Council on the Status of Women).

Whiteway, Doug (1982), *The Sins Against the Elderly* (Winnipeg Free Press, 21 Sep).

# 7    The Victimhood of Battered Women: Psychological and Criminal Justice Perspectives

Donald G. Dutton

Let me begin this chapter with the following questions: 1. what are reasonable expectations that societies should have of their citizens regarding the reporting of crimes committed against them in private locations? 2. How can we balance state intervention on behalf of those citizens with protection of citizen's privacy from state surveillance – a growing problem as we move into the age of a computer technology that appears ready to record and register our daily transactions? Let me suggest that this dilemma is enormously complex with severe consequences for a policy error in either direction. If states maximize the rights of citizen privacy within the home, problems associated with families in isolation, such as child abuse, wife assault, incest, and other issues of 'family dysfunction' are not amenable to correction by outside influence. If states maximize their ability to detect and intervene in such problems, then the risk of 'Big Brother' appears to be upon us, coincidently, arriving as 1984 approaches.

At the time of writing this chapter, the tension between opposing social forces bearing on this dilemma is increasing. Political pressure, mainly by women's groups, has raised the national consciousness about the high incidence and grave nature of abuse in families.[1-4] At the same time, we see evidence of a growing concern about intrusions by the state into family privacy.[5] Recent changes in the laws governing the reporting of suspected child abuse in British Columbia, led to lists of 'suspected child abusers' and then to a reaction against the maintenance of lists of names of people accused of unsubstantiated crimes.[6] Child abuse presents one example of the policy dilemma presented above. Wife assault presents another. Although

161

battered women would seem to have, by virtue of their adulthood, a greater capability of reporting crimes committed against them in private, they rarely do (only about 17% of wife assaults are reported to police[4]) and even when reported, the charges are often not pursued.[7] I intend to describe the psychological consequences of wife assault for the victim and will argue that these consequences make difficult the requirements of the criminal justice system for the reporting and carrying through of charges by battered women. A cautious extrapolation of these arguments for child victims of sexual and physical abuse broadens the issue to the entire question of state intervention into 'private (i.e. family) crimes'.

My research on the dynamics of wife assault has included in-depth analyses of police procedures for handling 'domestic disturbances',[8] a review of criminal justice system policy and practice in proceeding with wife assault charges,[9] the development of a theoretical system for explaining male violence,[10-12] and an examination of the emotional and cognitive processes which lead women into battering relationships, and serve to keep them there.[13,14] It is toward this latter area of research that I now turn.

I want to preface with a caveat; research on populations where a large 'chiffre noir' exists (e.g. rapists, and rape victims, wife assaulters, and victims) can never pretend to represent entire populations of aggressors and victims. Samples from the criminal justice system are less and less representative the further into the system the sample is taken. Victim surveys indicate that report rates for wife assault (to the police) may be as low as 17%*.[8] Given that a report to police and a request for assistance have been made, police attendance is not guaranteed,[8] and even if police do attend, they write reports of the incident in only about 1 in 5 cases.[8] Charges are laid in about 10% of cases written up,[8] and in most jurisdictions, attrition rates for cases coming before a judge are high.[9,15,16] These sampling problems make certain 'conclusions' in the literature suspect. We do not have empirical evidence bearing on the question of whether many women leave their husband after simply one assault. Frequency counts for violence are not recorded on divorce petitons and cohabitators who are not legally married could separate without so much as an archival trace. Hospital emergency rooms rarely ask questions about the basis for injuries and readily accept plausible stories of accidental misfortunes.[61] Those reports which do come to the attention of the police[17]

---

* Based on Straus Conflict Tactics scale items N (kicked, bitten, or hit with fist) to R (used a knife or fired a gun).

tend, on retrospective examination, to show prolonged periods of violence escalating in seriousness.

Empirical studies of battered women[13,18–20] typically draw their samples from transition houses or shelters and hospitals. These studies support the notion that for cases which come to institutional attention violence was both recurrent and escalating and that despite this violence women in all reported studies[13,17–20] stayed with their husbands until they were either hospitalized through battering or else feared for their lives and the safety of their children.[20] As Rounsaville (1978) stated:

> The most striking phenomenon that arose in the interviews and in treatment with battered women was the tenacity of both partners to the relationship in the face of severe abuse sustained by many of the women. Even those who had divorced or separated stayed in contact with the partner beyond ordinary activities such as visitation of children.
>
> (op.cit, pp.20–21)

In my own research both police[8] and transition house-workers[14] have reported a tendency of battered women to drop charges and/or return to a relationship where the risk of violence has not diminished. This has led to my usage of the term 'traumatic bonding' to describe the powerful emotional attachments formed under conditions of intermittent abuse.[13] Since, in the case of battered women, the abuse is one type of private crime which we described above, and with which governments must deal, it may be helpful to understand some of the dynamics involved in traumatic bonding. Why, in effect, do some women get into and stay in, relationships that are both physically and psychologically dangerous?

There is some evidence to suggest that exposure to violence in one's family of origin is correlated with the likelihood of either being violent[21,22] or the victim of violence[4,22–5] in one's own relationship. Straus (1977),[23] for example, found that as frequency of violence personally experienced in a woman's family of origin increased, the likelihood of violence in her marriage increased. A victim survey of 1793 women in Kentucky supported this finding.[4] A variety of mechanisms could support this correlation; the most frequently cited being the model of marriage or role expectations created by violence in the family of origin. Such an explanation assumes that battered women developed, in their family of origin, the expectation that violence was 'part of marriage'. One viewpoint on wife assault is that it is supported by norms in the broader culture and claims that 'a marriage licence is a hitting licence'.[26] This perspective views wife assault as widespread to the point of being normative. In my view, this analysis is wrong, although it represents some of the current mythology about wife assault. It exaggerates the incidence of wife assault by lumping survey counts of couples who self-report 'pushes and slaps' together with couples who report more serious forms of violence. While I believe that 'pushes and slaps' can escalate into something worse, they do not contribute to a norm for 'battering'. The oft-cited survey question by Stark and McEvoy (1970)[27] 'would you approve of slapping your spouse under appropriate circumstances?' received a 20% rate of agreement despite being worded so as to solicit agreement (i.e. the circumstances are described as 'appropriate'). This study has been cited as supported a 'norm' for wife assault but 20% of men and women approving of slapping one's spouse under 'appropriate circumstances' in no way suggests a societal norm that condones vicious assaults. If we take as a definition of assault, any case where a man kicked, or bit a woman, or hit her with his fist or an object, beat her up, threatened her with a weapon or actually used a weapon on her, the incidence estimates based on two broad surveys,[4,62] is that less than 10% of women are assaulted during their lifetime: I suggest that this is a large enough percentage to constitute a major social problem but not large enough to constitute a 'norm' for wife assault.

An alternative view is that many wife assaults are not normative, that when they first occur in a relationship, they surprise and upset both parties but are viewed as anomalies that 'will not recur'. The man's behaviour is viewed as an aberration caused by stress, the woman determines that she will be loyal, and will support her mate through *his* 'rough time'.

The socialization of women into accepting responsibility for the success of relationships certainly contributes to this response but it does not mean that if that same woman saw a future of repeated violence at that point in the relationship she would stay. Platt[29] describes 'social traps' where immediate payoffs obscure our awareness of long-term negative effects. I suggest that battered women represent one form of a social trap. Since battering usually starts early in the relationship,[20,30] it often appears as an aberration,[13] and coupled with the 'calm respite' that follows,[18] seems unlikely to recur. In fact, it may not recur for some time if we can believe the retrospective analyses that provide most of our data base.[4,14,17,31] During this time between violent episodes, a more positive interaction between husband and wife frequently occurs[13,18] and the resulting pattern of positive treatment punctuated by violence sets up an intermittent reinforcement schedule, the strongest schedule for the development of emotional attachments known to research psychology.[13,32-4]

I have described these processes in detail elsewhere.[13] They appear to fit the 'cycle theory' of violence described by Walker and are consistent with retrospective reports given by battered women.[13,14,18,35] My view is that assaults occurring early in a relationship, while appearing to be anomalous and therefore not sufficient to warrant leaving, contribute in ways unknown to the victims, to their emotional bonding to the aggressor. By the time that the violence has recurred a sufficient number of times for the woman to realize it is not anomalous, the emotional bond is already firmly established, and leaving becomes extremely difficult. Even when some women do leave for short term stays in shelters, and appear to progress toward independence, they occasionally 'snap' back to the relationship. This snapping is metaphorically similar to an elastic band, which, as it stretches, increases the pull or tension toward homeostasis. If we conceive of an emotional bond that represents unmet needs as having that property of elasticity and homeostasis, then departures from the relationship (even an abusive one) will be accompanied by increasing emotional pressure to return. At some point, the attachment will begin to weaken and the pressure relents. Huge individual differences appear to exist in the dissolution of attachments.[13,14] Such bonds are not particular to battered women, but seem to develop in all upper primates when intermittent abuse occurs,[32-4] and in many human relationships characterized by extreme power imbalances.[36-8] For example, similar phenomena are reported for dogs[32] and monkeys,[33] victims of hostage takings[38] and other prisoners,[36] incest victims,[37] and members of authoritarian 'cults'.[67] The effects, not being particular to battered women, should not therefore be attributed to a defect in the battered woman's character or personality, or to some unsubstantiated label such as 'masochism'.

Apart from the emotional attachment, intermittent abuse produces accompanying cognitive 'coping mechanisms' which include the tendency of victims to blame themselves for the violence.[14] This tendency to self-blame seems common whenever recurrent, uncontrollable violence is directed at victims who feel powerless to control the violence,[14,36,37] Bruno Bettleheim described similar responses amongst prisoners at Buchenwald.[36] Psychoanalytically oriented writers call this phenomenon 'identification with the aggressor'; literally the adopting of the aggressor's viewpoint as a last ditch effort to save one's life. Stretz (1979) invokes it to account for the positive reactions of hostages to their captors. Another view[37] attributes 'self-blame' to the need to believe in a just world. When uncontrollable, aversive events befall an innocent victim, both third-party observers and victims themselves attribute blame to the victim. Even cancer victims[40] or car accident victims[41] (who were hit when stopped at a red-light) blame themselves for their plight, as do battered women.[14] The alternative, it seems, is to accept a universe where aversive events occur unpredictably and capriciously, a premise that we apparently cannot accept.[37] Blame is thus internalized because it offers a shred of hope that one will be able to avoid future recurrences of the aversive event by viewing it as being under one's control, even when it is not. One develops in other words, what Becker (1973)[63] called a 'necessary illusion', one that conveys a sense of meaning and temporary relief from anxiety.

In cases of private crimes, these processes are often amplified by a power imbalance that develops when an aggressor uses violence to create and sustain a power advantage in a relationship. The use of violence in battering relationships is frequently accompanied by a variety of forms of psychological abuse; ranging from complete control of a woman's use of her time, her isolation from social contact and the annihilation of any possible basis for her self-esteem. In this sense, it closely resembles the techniques and processes used against prisoners in the Korean war[68] which we have come to term 'brainwashing'. One could argue that the effects of 'brainwashing' are more devastating when they come from a lover than from an expected enemy, since the breakdown of personal identity, crucial to the phenomenon, would be accelerated in romantic relationships. The psychological effect in any case is to create a feeling of powerlessness, helplessness, self-blame, guilt, and shame, coupled with a powerful attachment to one's tormentor. One consequence is that battered women often attempt to cover up the crimes committed against them, to hide their injuries, and to protect their tormentor. They appear, to an outside observer, as apathetic, withdrawn, and extremely distracted. The distraction appears to stem from deficits in attention and concentration associated with post-traumatic stress.[64] The most severe effects of post-battering stress are immediate, although they can last for weeks.[14,31] As they begin to dissipate, heightened pressure to return to the relationship develops as a consequence of traumatic bonding. Clearly this is a victim in need of extraordinary support and advocacy. However, as we shall see, it is at this very point that the criminal justice system demands responsible, persistent and assertive action from a battered woman.

A battered woman's first contact with the criminal justice system may often come through calling the police for protection,[4,8] although one victim survey showed that only 9% of assaults were reported to police. The likelihood of calling police decreases as the victim's education increases[4] (college educated victims only call the police 3% of the time). In a study of police response to 'domestic dispute' calls, Levens and Dutton (1980) found that about 59% of husband–wife fights were reported by the victim, 39% by a neighbour who heard the fight, and the remaining 2% by the husband. At the time of that study (1975), police in the jurisdiction studied were not empowered to arrest for common assault unless it happened in their presence. Consequently, the responsibility for deciding the outcome of the police intervention was often left to the woman. She could charge her husband with assault, allow the case to be referred (to social work – counselling services) or do nothing. Levens and Dutton (1980) found that referrals were the most typical (56.3%) outcome of police calls reported (although the police reports represented only 18% of husband–wife calls attended and are probably not a representative sample). Since social work and crisis counsellors at that time had no specific expertise in treating wife assault as a behaviour disorder, referrals were probably not an effective way of preventing repeat violence. The frequency of arrests by police varies greatly with jurisdiction, with estimates ranging from 41%[4] to 14%.[8] Many of these arrests however, were made simply to remove the husband for the evening. They did not involve assault charges being laid. The Levens and Dutton research led to the question of which route (arrest, referral outside and criminal justice system, etc.) would be the most effective at preventing recidivism. However, a long-term tracking study of recidivism as a function of conflict resolution decisions proved impossible to implement at that time, so the data required to evaluate various forms of dispute resolution do not exist. To this day, we have no empirical basis for our criminal justice policy on resolution of family violence (see, for example, Dutton, 1981).[9]

From the perspective of gaining protection for a woman who has been beaten by her husband, several problems exist in following many present legal avenues. Divorce and civil actions are lengthy processes. Single assaults are rarely grounds for cruelty. The divorce act seeks to preserve marriage. Husbands have tortial immunity from their wives in most jurisdictions. Even where they don't have this immunity, torts are a largely ineffective means of seeking redress.[45] Protection orders don't remove the husband from the home (so the victim has to leave), are not strongly enforced,[43,44] and are simply too easy to violate, since the husband can violate them and avoid police detection by leaving before the police arrive.[43] Assault charges carry their own set of problems. Assaults against women, have been treated in most jurisdictions as summary offences which meant the police were not empowered to lay charges except in cases of extremely serious injuries, in which case an indictable offence was deemed to have occurred. This left responsibility for laying an information with the victim. As we have seen from the above analysis of the emotional state of victims, this expected responsibility may be unwarranted. It assumes first of all that a battered woman who was assaulted without witnesses will blame her husband and decide not to protect him.) While 'common sense' tells us that victims should blame their aggressors, the special dynamics of battering relationships as decribed above make many victims of battering likely to blame themselves for the battering,[14,40] as unlikely as that might seem to a 'rational' outside observer. The result is a peculiar problem for criminal justice: a victim who colludes to protect the aggressor.

Furthermore, the criminal justice system expects this victim to take responsibility for laying charges even though this may require persistence and cognitive clarity in order to deal both with bureaucratic requirements and skepticism or indifference from a Justice of the Peace. A study of Justices of the Peace[45] found them generally reluctant to accept information from battered women, refusing to do so in some cases until a 'cooling down period' had ensued and a police report had been filed. However, Levens and Dutton (1980) found that police attended only half the cases where their presence was requested and filed reports in only 18% of the cases attended. We can assume some bias toward attending and reporting more serious cases, nevertheless, our research raises the question of whether the police themselves always satisfy this requirement of a Justice of the Peace. If not, the criminal justice system is putting a woman in an impossible situation. Bard and Zacker (1974),[65] in an observational study of police practice, reported assaults occurring in about 33% of the dispute calls police attended. Although their research was carried out in a different jurisdiction from Levens and Dutton, it raises the question of whether some assaults are not being written up in police reports, since their observed figure is much higher than the 18% report rate obtained by Levens and Dutton. If they are not being written up, requiring such a report represents an impossible bureaucratic 'double bind' for a battered woman.

It is important to note that both police and Justices of the Peace justify their inaction on the basis that the woman 'will only drop the charges anyway',[8,45] yet in jurisdictions where women are encouraged to cooperate with the state on charges laid by the state, dropped charges occur from only 8% of the time (Santa Barbara) to 22% of the time (Seattle).[46] Victim cooperation is essential to successful prosecution however. In Seattle, a 45% conviction rate (9% acquittal) when the victim testified, became a 12% conviction rate (34% acquittal) when they did not.[46] Clearly, the law in most jurisdictions expects the victim to take some responsibility for prosecution. In my opinion, erecting barriers to prosecution before a victim who has been traumatized in the manner described, is an unreasonable expectation by the state. As we see in jurisdictions where the state proceeds with charges and educates, encourages and supports a victim as to the advantages in her cooperation with the state, victim cooperation is high. One wonders then, if practices of the criminal justice system itself contribute to high rates of dropped charges in other jurisdictions. If this is so, then attributing the case of dropped charges to the battered woman herself constitutes a form of 'blaming the victim'.[69]

Furthermore, for those women who did overcome initial barriers to prosecution, the law itself can present special difficulties in cases of assaults in private. To satisfy the criteria of admissible evidence (the Doctrine of *Res Gestae*) statements made by a battered woman must be 'spontaneous exclamations' made to a third party.[43] That is, there must be some temporal contiguity between the attack and disclosure to a third party so as to avoid the possibility of fabrication. In cases of wife assault where a woman sought solitary refuge after the danger had ceased, or resisted admitting to being battered out of a combination of shame and self-blame, statements explaining the origin of her injuries or her need for refuge could not be adduced into evidence[43] (see *Ratten* v *The Queen*, 1971, *R*. v *McMahon* (1889), *R*. v *Goodard* (1882) cited in Goldman. p.81). The legal basis for admission of evidence is that the physical shock of an assault is likely to produce the truth when the declaration is made within such time as to deny the victim the opportunity to misrepresent the facts.[43,47] Some legal experts have argued that the Doctrine of Recent Complaint (where statements made at the first reasonable opportunity are admissible), be extended to cases of wife assault.[43] It seems on the basis of our research with battered women, that circumstances immediately following an assault by their husband are such, that 'spontaneous exclamations' may not always occur. The severe confusion surrounding what happened, tendencies to blame oneself rather than the assaulter, concerns about the outcome of prosecution, and the shame and guilt that battered women feel may operate against 'spontaneous exclamation' as required under *Res Gestae*. I do not suggest an easy answer to this problem, only that psychological and legal expertise recognize the issues involved in considering the possible reforms for admissible evidence in cases of 'private crime'.

One other legal issue is relevant here. Similar fact evidence requires that similar acts be connected to the alleged crime by 'proximity in time, in method or in circumstance' (*R. v Bond*, 1906)[43] to be admissible as evidence against the argument that the alleged crime was accidental. This requirement is based on the legal requirement that an accused person may not be convicted on the basis of prior conduct which merely tends to deepen the suspicion of their guilt in the offence charged.[43] Clearly this can create an additional problem for a battered woman; while she may be seeking relief from a repeated crime against her, the court is considering the single assault which is the subject of the charge. While this assault, viewed in isolation may not seem to warrant a severe sentence, or even mandatory treatment, recognition of its existence as part of continuing acts of violence and intimidation is crucial for the victim. Discussions of the legal issues involved in the use of similar fact evidence may be found elsewhere,[43,48] suffice it to say for present purposes that the 'reality' constructed by what is admissible in court may bear little resemblance to that experienced by the battered victim.

Legal concepts of responsibility have tended to focus on the *actus reus* and the *mens rea*[49–51] and to emphasize those conditions deemed necessary for the occurrence of an event. Such conditions are said to be 'abnormal' in that they represent a departure from the ordinary and reasonably expected course of events. Complex legal theories dealing with a defendant's level of responsibility have evolved which can modify the interpretation of the defendant's actions and serve as defenses for an otherwise criminal act. These include (1) factors justifying the act (e.g. self-defence), (2) factors leading to diminished criminal capacity on the part of the defendant (e.g. decreased mental responsibility) and (3) situational circumstances modifying responsibility (e.g. coercion to perform an action by threats which 'a person of reasonable firmness in this situation would have been unable to resist').[52]

I am arguing that the legal criteria for criminal responsibility, if applied to a battered woman's responsibility to report and proceed with the laying of an information would suggest an instance of diminished responsibility. A post-battering stress syndrome, in my opinion, suggests 'decreased mental responsibility'. The acute arousal and anxiety commonly reported after experiencing violence from a spouse creates attentional deficits,[53,54] an amotivational state of 'learned helplessness'[18,55] and emotional ego-protective responses such as 'identification with the aggressor'[56] with the consequent cognitive tendency to blame oneself for 'causing' the violence.[14,41] In short, the research on battered women suggests an acute reaction to the battering that would diminish their capability for taking 'responsible' action as defined by law. To a certain extent, legal and social science explanations for behaviour represent a 'paradigm clash'.[70] The law focuses on predispositional determinants of behaviour and recognizes situational determinants only when they are extreme and vivid (e.g. threat and coercion). Social science focuses on the interaction of predispositional determinants with far more subtle situational determinants. Hence, social traps, reinforcement schedules, information control, and power dynamics are given more weight by social science than by legal explanations of behaviour. In my view, we must move toward a reconciliation of legal concepts of responsibility with contemporary social science notions of situational determinism. Such a reconciliation will be difficult, anything less may be unjust.

We see in the battered woman a diminished capability for taking responsible, resourceful, persistent action as is currently required by the criminal justice system policy in many jurisdictions.

When this diminished capability is combined with a response from police or a Justice of the Peace that is intended to discourage legal action, or when subsequent legal issues concerning admissible evidence manifest themselves, situational factors and diminished capacity combine to lessen the likelihood of a battered woman proceeding with charges.

If the victim's responsibility for proceeding with charges is diminished it is no great surprise that many women drop charges in jurisdictions where criminal justice policy discourages such charges and places a victim in a legal maze. One consequence of such policy is that cases of more severe battering (unless detected by police on the basis of calls from neighbours) would be less likely to be successfully prosecuted than would less severe cases. In my opinion, a reason for this is that the victim of the more severe battering is less capable of crossing criminal justice hurdles. Some evidence for this contention comes from an assessment of violent men performed by one of my graduate students for his dissertation.[11] Taking a sample of men who had been convicted of wife assault and court-ordered to mandatory therapy by the courts, he compared them for degree of prior violence to a group of men who had voluntarily referred themselves to another treatment programme for wife assault in the same jurisdiction. The average level of prior violence towards wives was higher for the self-referred group. Some men in the court-ordered group had been assaultive only once and the assault did not resemble the type of severe battering that leaves a victim psychologically unable to proceed. Those more serious batterings are less likely to be detected by a criminal justice system that places primary responsibility for proceeding on the victim of the battering.

Some changes are beginning to improve this situation. Wife assault is now a 'dual offence' which gives police more power to charge under the Criminal Code of Canada. (They no longer have to witness the assault.) More needs to be done with Justices of the Peace, Judges, and emergency ward doctors and nurses,[66] to inform them of the issues of wife assault and improve their ability to detect the problem and serious consideration needs to be given to some form of advocacy for battered women. Increased prosecution probably will not act as a general deterrent so long as wife assault is an impulsive act and prosecution and 'punishment' remain improbable.[57, 58] However, there is initial reason to believe that increased prosecution, if coupled with effective therapeutic intervention, can serve as a specific deterrent. The case for specific deterrence looks promising based on the work of new treatment programmes,[59, 60] yet the definitive evaluation of these programmes remains to be done as does the basic research needed for a stronger theoretical base.[71]. Perhaps the strongest reasons for increased prosecution lie in the state's moral obligation to protect women and in the didactic value served by law. That is, the state must not appear to condone wife assault through a lack of aggressive prosecution. The state has a moral obligation to label any activity that threatens the welfare of any group or category of its citizens as '*mala in se*'. If however, a policy of aggressive prosecution is to be implemented, it must be supported by treatment programmes which are both effective and properly evaluated. At present, this process of change has begun. Only time will tell if it will be successfully completed.

### References

1. Roy, M., *Battered Women: a Psychosocial Study of Domestic Violence* (New York: Van Nostrand, 1977).
2. Macleod, L., *Wife Battering in Canada: the Vicious Circle* The Canadian Advisory Council on the Status of Women (Canadian Govt. Publishing Centre, 1980).
3. Straus, M., Gelles, R. J. and Steinmetz, S., *Behind Closed Doors: Violence in the American Family* (New York: Anchor Press, Doubleday, 1980).
4. Schulman, M., *A Survey of Spousal Violence Against Women in Kentucky*, (US Dept. of Justice, Law Enforcement Assistance Administration, 1979).
5. Margulis, S., 'Privacy as a Behavioral Phenomenon', *Journal of Social Issues, 33*(3) (1977).
6. See *Vancouver Province* (11 Feb. 1983).
7. Field, M. and Field, H., *Marital Violence and the Criminal Process: Neither Justice nor Peace, Social Service Review* (June 1973).
8. Levens, B. R. and Dutton, D. G., *The Social Service Role of Police: Domestic Crisis Intervention* (Ottawa: Solicitor General of Canada, 1980).
9. Dutton, D., *The Criminal Justice System Response to Wife Assault* (Ottawa: Solicitor-General of Canada, 1981).
10. Dutton, D. G., 'A Nested Ecological Theory of Male Violence Towards Intimates' *International Journal of Women Studies*, vol. 8, no. 4, pp.404–13, 1985.
11. Dutton, D. and Browning, J., *Towards a Profile of the Wife Assaulter* (UBC, 1982).
12. Dutton, D. G., Fehr, B. and McEwen, H. 'Severe Wife Battering as Deindividuated Violence', *Victimology,* vol. 7, nos 1–4, pp. 13–23, 1982.
13. Dutton, D. G. and Painter, S. L., 'Traumatic Bonding: the Development of Emotional Attachments in Battered Women and Other Relationships of Intermittent Abuse', *Victimology,* vol. 6, nos 1–4, pp. 139–51, 1981.
14. Porter, C., *Blame, Depression and Coping in Battered Women* (UBC, Dept. of Psychology, 1983).
15. Fields, M., 'Wife Beating: Government Intervention Policies and Practices' in *Battered Women: Issues of Public Policy* (Washington DC, US Civil Rights Commission, 1978).

16. Parnas, R. I., 'Prosecutional and Judicial Handling of Family Violence', *Criminal Law Bulletin*, vol.9(1973) p.733.
17. Wilt, G. M. and Breedlove, R. K., *Domestic Violence and the Police: Studies in Detroit and Kansas City* (Washington: Police Foundation, 1977).
18. Walker, L., *The Battered Woman* (New York: Harper & Row, 1979)
19. Rosenbaum, A. and O'Leary, K. D., 'Marital Violence: Characteristics of Abusive Couples', *Journal of Consulting and Clinical Psychology*, vol.41 (1981) p.63.
20. Rounsaville, B., 'Theories of Marital Violence: Evidence from a Study of Battered Women', *Victimology*, vol.3 (1978) pp.11–31.
21. *San Francisco Family Violence Project Handbook* (San Francisco, 1980).
22. Baker-Fleming, J., *Stopping Wife Abuse* (Garden City, NJ: Anchor Books, 1979).
23. Straus, M., 'Sociological Perspective on the Prevention and Treatment of Wife Beating', in M. Roy (ed.), *Battered Women: a Psychosocial Study of Domestic Violence* (New York: Van Nostrand, 1977).
24. Gelles, R. J., *The Violent Home: a Study of Physical Aggression Between Husbands and Wives* (Beverly Hills: Sage Publishers, 1974).
25. Hilberman, E., and Munson, K., 'Sixty Battered Women', *Victimology*, vol.2 (1977–78) pp.460–70.
26. Straus, M., 'A General Systems Theory Approach to a Theory of Violence Between Family Members', *Social Science Information*, vol.12 (1973) pp.105–125.
27. Stark, R. and McEvoy, J., 'Middle Class Violence', *Psychology Today*, vol.4(6) (1970) pp.107–112.
28. Straus, M., 'Violence in the Family: How Widespread, Why It Occurs and Some Thoughts on Prevention', in *Family Violence: Proceedings from Symposium* (United Way of Greater Vancouver, Mar. 1977).
29. Platt, J., 'Social Traps', *American Psychologist*, vol.28 (1973) pp.641–51.
30. Gelles, R. J., 'Abused Wives: Why Do They Stay?', *Journal of Marriage and the Family*, vol.38 (1976) pp.26-33.
31. Dutton, D. and Painter, S. L., *Male Domestic Violence and Its Effects on the Victim* (Ottawa: Health and Welfare Canada, 1980).
32. Scott, J. P., 'The Process of Primary Socialization in Canine and Human Infants', *Monographs of the Society for Research in Child Development*, vol.28 (1963).
33. Harlow, H. and Harlow, M., 'Psychopathology in Monkeys' in H. K. Kimmel (ed.), *Experimental Psychopathology* (New York: Academic Press, 1971).
34. Rajecki, P., Lamb, M. and Obsmacher, P., 'Toward a General Theory of Infantile Attachment: a Comparative Review of Aspects of the Social Bond', *Behavioral and Brain Sciences*, vol.3 (1978) pp.417–64.
35. Martin, D., *Battered Wives* (New York: Kangaroo Paperbacks, 1977).
36. Bettleheim, B., 'Individual and Mass Behavior in Extreme Situations', *Journal of Abnormal and Social Psychology*, vol.38 (1943) pp.417–52.
37. Zingaro, L., *Victims of Incest*, Lecture (UBC, 1983).

38. Strentz, T., 'Law Enforcement Policy and Ego Defenses of the Hostage', *FBI Law Enforcement Bulletin* (Apr. 1979) p.2.
39. Lerner, M. J., Miller, D. T. and Holmes, J. G., 'Deserving and the Emergence of Forms of Justice', in L. Berkowitz and E. Walster (eds), *Advances in Experimental Social Psychology*, vol.9 (New York: Harcourt, Brace Janovitch, 1976).
40. Wortman, C., 'Causal Attributions and Personal Control', *New Directions in Attribution Research*, vol.1 (1976) pp.23–52.
41. Op. cit.
42. Linden, A., 'Restitution, Compensation for Victims of Crime and Canadian Criminal Law', *Canadian Journal of Criminology*, vol.19 (1977) p.9.
43. Goldman, P., *Violence Against Women in the Family* (McGill University, Faculty of Law, 1978).
44. See Reference 2.
45. Hogarth, J., *Battered Wives and the Justice System* (UBC, Faculty of Law, 1979).
46. Lehrman, L., *Prosecution of Spouse Abuse: Innovations in Criminal Justice Response* (Washington DC: Centre for Women Policy Studies, 1981).
47. Hutchins, R. and Slesinger, D., 'Some Observations on the Law of Evidence', *Columbia Law Review*, vol.432 (1928) p.433.
48. Sklar, R., 'Similar Fact Evidence – Catch Words and Cartwheels', *McGill Law Journal*, vol.23 (1977) p.62.
49. Fincham, F. and Jaspars, J., 'Attribution of Responsibility: From Man the Scientist to Man as Lawyer', *Advances in Experimental Social Psychology*, vol.13 (1980) pp.81–138.
50. McGillis, D., 'Attribution and the Law: Convergences Between Legal and Psychological Concepts', *Law and Human Behavior*, vol.2(4) (1978) pp.289–300.
51. Hart, H. and Honore, A., *Causation in the Law* (London: Oxford University Press 1959).
52. *Model Penal Code* (Philadelphia: American Law Institute 1962).
53. Meninger, K., 'Regulatory Mechanisms of the Ego under Stress' in A. Monat and R. Lazarus (eds), *Stress and coping* (New York: Columbia University Press, 1977).
54. Easterbrook, J., 'The Effect of Emotion on the Utilization and Organization of Behavior', *Psychological Review*, vol.66 (1959) pp.88–201.
55. Walker, L., 'Battered Women and Learned Helplessness', *Victimology: an International Journal*, vol.2(3–4) (1977–78) pp.525–34.
56. Freud, A., *The Ego and the Mechanisms of Defense*, rev. edn (New York: International Universities Press, 1942).
57. Fattah, E., 'Fear of Punishment: Deterrence Law Reform Commission of Canada: 1976' (Ministry of Supply and Services).
58. Zimbring, F. E. and Hawkins, G. J., *Deterrence: the Legal Threat in Crime Control* (University of Chicago Press, 1973).
59. Novaco, R., *Anger Control: the Development and Evaluation of an Experimental Program* (Lexington Books, 1975).

60. Ganley, A., *Court Mandated Therapy for Wife Assaulters* (Washington DC: Center for Women Policy Studies, 1981).
61. Stark, E., Flitcraft, A. and Frazier, W., 'Medicine and Patriarchal Violence: the Social Construction of a Private Event', *International Journal of Health Services*, vol.9(3) (1979) pp.461–93.
62. Steinmetz, S. and Straus, M., (eds), *Violence in the Family* (New York: Harper & Row, 1974).
63. Becker, E., *The Denial of Death* (Glencoe: Free Press, 1973).
64. *Diagnostic and Statistical Manual of the Mental Disorders* (Washington, DC: American Psychiatric Association, 1980) p.236.
65. Bard, M. and Zacker, J., 'Assaultiveness and Alcohol Use in Family Disputes: Police Perceptions', *Criminology*, vol.12(3) (1974) pp.281–92.
66. Grantham, P., *Violence in the Family* (UBC, Faculty of Medicine, 1980).
67. Conway, F. and Siegleman, J., *Snapping* (New York: Delta, 1978).
68. Schein, E., *Coercive Persuasion* (New York: Norton, 1971).
69. Ryan, W., *Blaming the Victim* (New York: Vintage, 1971).
70. Kuhn, T., *The Structure of Scientific Revolutions* (University of Chicago Press 1970).
71. Berkowitz, L., 'Aversive Conditions as Stimuli to Aggression', *Advances in Experimental Social Psychology*, vol.15 (1982) pp.249–88.

# 8   The Child as Victim: Victimological Aspects of Child Abuse*

Ezzat A. Fattah

## THE VICTIMIZATION OF CHILDREN

Children are easy victims. They are weak, frail, and extremely vulnerable. Under certain age, they are incapable of defending themselves, retaliating or even complaining and constitute, therefore, ideal targets for victimization. Victimization of children is as old as mankind itself. Infanticide was probably one of the earliest crimes. It is the ultimate victimization; the annihilation of a helpless, unaware and unsuspecting victim. This horrible, primitive crime has not yet disappeared and probably never will. It is still practised with relative frequency in some illiterate and underdeveloped communities though its incidence has sharply declined in modern, technological societies as a result of the widespread practices of abortion and birth control. Abortion renders infanticide unnecessary by making it possible for the mother to get rid of the baby before it is born. Though infanticide is probably the most serious crime to be committed against a child, it is but one single form of child victimization. Throughout history and until the present day children have been and are being subjected to a wide variety of abuses, neglect and maltreatments. Bakan (1971) reminds us that:

> Children have been whipped, beaten, starved, drowned, smashed against walls and floors, held in ice water baths, exposed to extremes of outdoor temperatures, burned with hot irons and steam pipes. Children have been tied and kept in upright positions for long periods. They have been systematically exposed to electric shock; forced to swallow pepper, soil, feces, urine, vinegar, alcohol, and other odious material; buried alive; had scalding water poured over genitals; had their limbs held in open fire; placed in roadways where automobiles would run over them;

177

placed on roofs and fire escapes in such manner as to fall off;
bitten, knifed, and shot; had their eyes gouged out.

(Bakan, 1971, p.4)

Despite the well-documented fact that beating and torturing of
children have taken place throughout the ages, the last two decades
have witnessed a growing awareness of, and mounting interest in,
child victimization and the emergence of child abuse as a major social
issue. In a 4 year period beginning in 1962, the legislatures of all fifty
American states passed statutes against the caretaker's abuse of
children (Pfohl, 1977, p.310). Concern for the beaten and neglected
child increased dramatically during the last years of the 1950s and in
1962, Dr Henry Kempe coined the now widely used term the
'battered child syndrome' and published with others an article in the
*Journal of the American Medical Association* bearing that title. The
big publicity given to the phenomenon of child abuse in the mass
media and the lack of accurate figures about its true incidence
resulted in the currently widespread belief that child abuse is a major
social problem of staggering proportions the incidence of which is
rapidly escalating.

Pfohl (1977) suggests that the labelling of child abuse as deviance
and the speedy, universal enactment of criminal legislation that
followed was a result of efforts of certain organized medical interests
whose concern in the discovery of the 'battered child syndrome'
contributed to the advance of humanitarian pursuits while covertly
rewarding members of the medical profession.

Labelling was generated by powerful medical interests and perpetuated by organized media, professional and upper-middle class
concerns. Its success was enlarged by the relative powerlessness
and isolation of abusers, which prevented the possibility of organized resistance to the labelling.

p.321

## CHILD ABUSE: THE PROBLEM OF DEFINITION

Despite growing concern over child abuse among the medical and
helping professions and within the public at large, there is no
satisfactory definition of what constitutes abuse. Current definitions

of 'abuse' and 'neglect' are vague and ambiguous. And it is even more difficult to adequately define terms such as 'emotional injury' or 'emotional deprivation'. Gil (1970) feels that one important reason for the difficulties is that many investigators constructed definitions of child abuse in terms of the observed effects of an attack on a child, such as injuries sustained by him, rather than in terms of the motivation and behaviour of the attacking person. Gil observes that such definitions disregard the motivational and behavioural dynamics of perpetrators and result in vagueness, since the outcomes of violent, abusive acts depend not only on the perpetrator's behaviour, but also on the victim's reaction to the perpetrator's behaviour, and on environmental and chance circumstances (p.5). Gil proposes the following definition:

> Physical abuse of children is the intentional, non-accidental use of physical force, or intentional, non-accidental acts of omission, on the part of a parent or caretaker interacting with a child in his care, aimed at hurting, injuring or destroying that child.

Gil's definition is more restrictive than the one used by the US National Committee for Prevention of Child Abuse. The Committee, established in 1972 defines child abuse as 'non-accidental physical injury, gross neglect, emotional or sexual abuse'. This definition is vague and unsatisfactory. It does not explain what 'gross neglect' and 'emotional abuse' are. It considers 'non-accidental injury' to be synonymous with 'intentional injury' and extends the definition beyond physical abuse to include emotional and sexual abuses as well. Some authors are in favour of limiting the definition of 'child abuse' to the 'battered child syndrome' thus excluding all forms of neglect, non-violent sexual molestation, sexual exploitation, and infanticide. Because these latter forms of victimization are dealt with separately by the criminal law, they are seen as distinct phenomena and are excluded by some authors from the domain of child abuse. Gil (1970) expresses this view noting that perpetrators of sexual abuse are motivated differently from perpetrators of physical abuse. The former seem to seek primarily sexual self-gratification while the latter seem primarily intent on hurting the child. Gil concludes that the two phenomena are likely to differ in their dynamics and should, therefore, be studied apart from each other (p.7).

Although sexual abuse and sexual exploitation may be aetiologically distinct from physical abuse, they still share with the latter phenomenon certain common denominators which warrant their treatment under the general rubric of 'child abuse'. On the other hand, infanticide is in many ways different from other forms of abuse or neglect even when these latter behaviours lead to the death of the victim. The elimination of the newly born baby which is the primary or the sole motive for infanticide is usually absent from the list of motives which drive certain parents or other caretakers to neglect or to abuse the children under their care.

Divergence of opinion can also be observed in regard to active and passive abuse. Some authors, see assault and neglect as two facets of the same phenomenon and point to empirical evidence indicating that in many cases they occur concurrently. Other authors believe that the two are symptomatically, if not aetiologically, distinguishable. Giovannoni (1971), for example, observes that 'neglect appears to be more closely associated with those stresses emanating directly from poverty' while abuse appears to be 'associated with interpersonal and intrapsychic kinds of stress' (p.650).

Obviously, serious cases of torture, mutilation, or molestation do not pose any major definitional problem. Definition, however, is a real problem in those minor cases where it is difficult to draw the line between permissible disciplinary action by parents in the process of rearing their children and cruel, abusive behaviour. Where does discipline stop and abuse begin? There is no easy answer. The matter is complicated further by the fact that in many cultures physical punishment of children for misbehaviour is considered not only an appropriate means of socialization but a necessity. 'Spare the rod and spoil the child' is a dictum in which many parents and educators firmly believe. In 1975, The Supreme Court of the United States ruled that corporal punishment in schools is permissible unless it can be proven that the physical contact between the hitter (teacher, principal, or educator), and the hittee (student or pupil, under the age of eighteen), was so severe as to constitute cruel and unusual punishment. Needless to say, that judging the severity of the inflicted punishment, and deciding whether it is within or beyond acceptable boundaries is a discretionary matter on which opinions are likely to differ widely.

Another issue related to the definitional problems of child abuse, whether physical or sexual, is the problem of the upper age limit beyond which the victim is no longer considered a child. At what age should physical assault no longer be regarded as 'child beating' or 'child battering'? At what age may adolescents and teenagers be considered as capable of freely consenting to sexual experiences with adults? Till what age should the criminal law govern the sexual behaviour and sexual activities of young people? At what age should adults' sexual experience with children no longer be regarded as 'sexual abuse' or 'sexual exploitation'?

The upper age limit varies greatly from one country to the other. And in countries where there are several provinces (such as Canada), or several states (such as the United States) the age of a child up to which injuries are reportable may vary from one province to the other or from one state to the other. American reporting laws have used varying age limits in their definition of the children coming under the protection of reporting laws. Four states (Colorado, Georgia, Missouri, Oregon) limit reporting to children under age 12, the state of Wyoming extend the reporting requirement to age 19 while the other states have opted for ages in between (see American Humane Association, 1966, pp.7–8).

The age at which the criminal law considers the child to be able to freely and knowingly consent to sexual activities is also subject to wide geographical, cultural, and gender variations. The age of consent to heterosexual relations is set in some countries as low as 12 or 13 years while in others it is set as high as 18 or 21 years. The age of consent to homosexual practices is usually set somewhat higher with the majority of jurisdictions adopting 18 or 21 years as the minimum age. Some countries (such as Holland) have recently lowered the age of consent to homosexual practices to make it identical to that of heterosexual activities.

## EPIDEMIOLOGY OF CHILD ABUSE

The victimization of children is a universal phenomenon. It is not limited to certain types of societies or to certain cultures. However, the frequency with which such victimization occurs varies greatly from one society to the other and from one culture to the other. It is difficult, in fact it is impossible, to obtain accurate figures of actual incidents of child abuse. It is a well-known fact that the dark figure for child victimization is very high. Because child abuse typically (though not exclusively) takes place within the home and is perpetrated by those who are responsible for the care and welfare of the child, a large number of cases escape detection. Many cases are never brought to the attention of authorities. Others are not identified and recorded as such. Until recently, children who suffered serious injuries at the hands of their parents were not diagnosed as abused children. Pfohl (1977) cites four factors which supposedly have impeded the recognition of abuse by clinicians and hospital physicians. First, doctors in emergency room settings were simply unaware of the possibilities of abuse as a diagnosis. Second, many doctors were simply psychologically unwilling to believe that parents would inflict such atrocities on their own children. The third obstacle to a diagnosis of abuse seems to have been the possibility of legal liability for violating the confidentiality of the physician-parent relationship with physicians primarily viewing the parent, rather than the child, as their real patient. A final deterrent, to the physician's 'seeing' abuse is the reluctance of doctors to become involved in a criminal justice process that would take both their time and ability to guide the consequences of a particular diagnosis (Pfohl, 1977, p.316). There are also reasons to believe that the dark figure for sexual victimization is higher than that for physical abuse.

As a result of a heightened awareness of child abuse in recent years there has been a dramatic increase in the reporting of incidents. The increasing number of cases being identified or reported, the attention given to such cases and the wide coverage they get in the media have created the impression that the incidence of child abuse is rapidly increasing and that child battering is occurring at an ever accelerating rate. This has led some quarters to view the problem as one of staggering dimensions which has reached crisis proportions. Consequently, there is an evergrowing demand that more financial and human resources be made available to deal with the problem. Yet there is no convincing empirical evidence to substantiate such fears, to support these widely held beliefs, or to prove that these impressions are well founded.

Some authors such as Smith (1975) speculate that there is an increase in child abuse and that this increase is associated with the documented increase in illegitimacy and teenage parenthood. It is much more likely, however, that the higher figures of recent years are simply a reflection of an increase in reporting and not an increase in the actual incidence of abuse. This view is shared by Maden and Wrench (1977) who note that

Given the recent increasing interest in the child abuse problem resulting in comprehensive reporting statutes and a higher index of suspicion, it is more likely that incremental incidence rates reflect the fact that a larger proportion of the child abuse population is identified.

(p.198)

Needless to say that official figures of child abuse went up quite dramatically after various American states passed laws requiring mandatory reporting of actual or suspected child abuse and neglect. The State of Massachusetts is a good case in point and illustrates well what happened following the passing of mandatory reporting laws. In 1974, a new state law went into effect in Massachusetts mandating the reporting of child abuse by physicians, medical interns, medical examiners, dentists, nurses, public or private school teachers, eductional administrators, guidance and family counsellors, probation officers, and police. In addition, reporting is authorized but not mandated, by any person aware of harm to a child. The type of injury to be reported was expanded to include emotional injury and injury caused by neglect and sexual abuse. Along with passage of the law, a publicity campaign was launched drawing attention to the new law and to the problem of child abuse. The effects were, to say the least, dramatic. The yearly reporting of injury to children in Massachusetts (with a population of just under 6 million people) under the Abused Children Statute was 101 in 1965, 175 in 1970, 195 in 1973, 700 in 1974 (the year of the new law), 2238 in 1975, and approximately 4000 in 1976 (Rolde, 1977).

The extent of hidden victimization simply means that official data on child abuse are neither accurate nor reliable. In the absence of reliable data one can only try to estimate the true incidence of the phenomenon. Extrapolations have to be made using reports that suffer from variations in the definition, interpretation and administration of widely varying reporting statutes. In 1970, Kempe (1971) estimated the incidence of the extended battered child syndrome in the USA to be as common as 6 in 1000 live births. He noted that reported cases in Denver and New York range between 175 to 225 reports per million population per year. Provided these figures are representative, the annual number of cases in the USA would be somewhat between 30 000 and 50 000 with the true frequency undoubtedly higher than those figures. Cohen and Sussman (1975) estimated the extent of child abuse in the USA by extrapolating the number of confirmed reports of child abuse from the ten largest states and yielded a national projection of 41 105 cases (see Maden and

Wrench, 1977, p.198). More recently, Gelles (1977) interviewed a national probability sample of 1146 families with children between the ages of 3 and 17. On the basis of extrapolated frequencies, the study estimated that between 1.2 and 1.7 million children were kicked, hit, or punched and between 460 000 and 750 000 children were beaten up in 1975. The study estimated generally that in 1975 between 1.4 and 1.9 million children 'were vulnerable to physical injury from violence', (ibid; p.198). The accuracy and validity of all these estimates are, of course, open to serious questions.

Some estimates are also available for countries other than the USA. In his Windermere lecture, delivered in 1970 and published in 1971, Dr Kempe estimated that for 500 000 new babies born yearly in Great Britain there may be 3000 cases half of which will be significantly injured and the other half seriously deprived. In the early 1950s, Chesser (1952) studied child abuse in England and reported that between 6 and 7% of all children were 'so neglected or ill-treated or become so maladjusted' as to come to the attention of the National Society for the Prevention of Cruelty to Children.

Some information on the situation in West Germany is provided by Kaiser (1977). Kaiser reports that in 1973 police in W. Germany published for the first time data on victims of certain offences of bodily injury. According to the data, 1795 (88.3%) of the victims of crimes committed in violation of section 223 of the German Penal Code were children under 14 years of age; among them 1038 (57.8%) were boys. A decrease of 7.7% was recorded in 1974 with 1656 victims (95.4%) under 14 years of age (among them 894 or 54% were boys) (p.297).

One of the dangers of the various estimates and extrapolations is their potential for creating false impressions about the real extent of child abuse. Gil, who is to be given credit for conducting one of the first epidemiological studies of child abuse, cautions against overestimating the true incidence of the phenomenon. In an article published in the journal *Pediatrics* in 1969 Gil writes:

Although no claim can be made that the nationwide survey uncovered the true incidence rate of physical abuse of children, it seems clear nevertheless, that the magnitude of the phenomenon has been exaggerated. Six thousand reported cases of physical abuse per year in a nation of 200 million, in spite of under reporting, do not constitute a major social problem, at least in relative terms, tragic as every single incident may be. If then the

6000 reported cases represent as a group the more severe segment of the physical abuse spectrum, it follows that in qualitative terms, physical abuse is by and large not very serious as reflected by the data on the extent and types of injury suffered by the children in the study cohort. The classical 'battered child' syndrome is a relatively infrequent occurrence. Even if allowance is made for the gross under reporting of fatalities, physical abuse cannot be considered a major killer and maimer of children.

## NATURE AND TYPES OF ABUSIVE BEHAVIOUR

Abuse of children is not a uniform phenomenon. It takes various forms which differ in motivations, aetiology, dynamics, and contexts. Obviously, a taxonomy of abuse is necessary if the different manifestations are to be classified in more or less homogeneous units for the sake of study and comparison. A simple typology of abuse may divide the various types into three broad categories: physical, mental, and sexual with each type divided, in turn, into several sub-types.

**Physical abuse**

Most literature on violence against children deals with intentional, non-accidental physical abuse resulting in injury or bodily harm with special attention given to the battered child syndrome. Physical abuse may be divided into active abuse (maltreatment) and passive abuse (neglect). Active abuse includes all deliberate acts aimed at the infliction of physical pain and bodily suffering on the child such as assault, battery, beating, burning, physical torture, mutilation, isolation, restriction of the freedom to move, etc. Physical assaults on children do not have to result in minor or serious injury in order to qualify as active abuse. Serious abuse, however, often leads to different kinds of visible or invisible injuries. Among the frequent types of injury resulting from physical abuse are bruises, abrasions, burns, lacerations, visceral injuries (such as gastric or intestinal perforations; liver, spleen, and kidney lacerations or ruptures, etc.), ocular damage, neurological and head injuries (such as skull fractures or subdural haematoma). Passive abuse or neglect can equally take various forms of derelictions and deprivations the most common of which are those depriving the child of food, clothing, shelter, or sanitation.

Another form of abuse which could be related to physical abuse is the commercial, non-sexual exploitation of children. Child servitude and child labour are among the most common forms of exploitation of children. Moreover, children are frequently used to push illegal goods such as illicit drugs so that the adult may not be caught in possession of the forbidden substance.

**Mental abuse**

Mental abuse of children may also be divided into active and passive abuse. Active abuse may take the form of verbally assaultive, abusive, and threatening behaviour, intentional mental torment, deliberate instillation of fear, anguish and anxiety in the mind of the child, as well as acts aimed at the wilful humiliation or degradation of the child. Passive forms of mental abuse are more common. They include the withholding of affection and the deprivation of parental love. Mental abuse may also take other forms including intellectual and educational deprivation.

**Sexual abuse**

Sexual abuse of children may be perpetrated with or without violence, with or without coercion. The use of threats is a common form of coercing the child into agreeing to the normal or deviant sexual demands of the adult. In many cases, however, especially when the child is too young to understand the nature of the acts being performed on him/her by the adult, the use of force, coercion, or threats is unnecessary. Yet, even when the child or the minor is aware of the sexual nature of the adult's exigencies, he/she can often be made to consent through seduction, persuasion, or enticement. Not infrequently, the child's craving for affection and his natural curiosity make enticement easy or even unnecessary.

Like physical abuse, sexual misuse of children may take various forms. Incest, rape and statutory rape, sexual assault, and sexual molestation are probably the most common forms. In addition to these sexual behaviours in which the child is used for the sexual gratification of the adult, there are other ways in which children may be sexually exploited. They can be pushed into (or led to) prostituting themselves to provide money for the parent, the guardian, or the pimp. The use of children in pictorial pornographic material (movies, magazines) constitutes both sexual and commercial exploitation.

## FAMILY ABUSE AND INSTITUTIONAL ABUSE

Abuse may be classified, according to the social context in which it takes place, into family abuse and institutional abuse. Family abuse, usually perpetrated by natural, step- or foster-parents, by parent substitutes, or by guardians, occurs mainly in the home and is contextually different from institutional abuse directed against children placed in institutional care (orphanages, institutions for mentally defective or retarded children, training schools, correctional institutions for juveniles, etc.) and from abuse perpetrated by school teachers or principals against their pupils. Those two types of abuse are likely to be different in their motivation, psycho- and socio-dynamics and need, therefore, to be analysed independently from one another.

Gil (1977) notes that child abuse, viewed as inflicted waste of children's intrinsic potential, is endemic in most existing institutional settings for children, since these settings usually do not facilitate the full actualization of the human potential of all the children in their care.

A second level at which child abuse occurs is the institutional level, such settings as day care centers, schools, courts, child care agencies, welfare departments, correctional and other residential child care settings, etc. In these settings, acts and policies which inhibit, or insufficiently promote, the development of children, or which deprive children of or fail to provide them with, material, emotional and symbolic means needed for their optimal development, constitute abusive acts or conditions . . . In the same way as in the home, abusive acts and conditions in institutional settings may result from supposedly constructive, or from negative and hostile attitudes toward children, and they may be one-time or occasional events or regular patterns.

(Gil, 1977, pp.187–8)

For obvious reasons, institutional violence did not receive as much attention from researchers as did family violence. Yet, it is a well-known fact that victimization and exploitation of inmates (or residents if one is to use the modern euphemism) is a common feature of everyday life in juvenile and adult institutions alike. One of the few studies that examined institutional victimization of juveniles was carried out by Bartollas, Miller and Dinitz (1976). The authors undertook their research in a maximum security 'training school' for 'hard core' adolescent offenders in Columbus, Ohio. The picture they depict of the institution is that of a world in which the exploitation of the weak by the strong is pervasive and endemic. Further studies of juvenile victimization and exploitation in correctional and other institutions need to be done and are likely to reveal conditions not too different from those found by Bartollas and his colleagues in the training school they studied.

In his book, *Weeping in the Playtime of Others* Wooden (1976) points out that 50% of the children in detention centres have committed no crime. Of those imprisoned, half have violated no criminal law; they are incarcerated for status offences: truancy, 'incorrigibility', running away. Others are detained because they are dependent or neglected children for whom the state has no other facility. In the institutions, the children's nutritional, medical, educational, and recreational needs are too often ignored or neglected. Some are placed in solitary confinement even for minor disciplinary offences. Many are beaten, kicked, punched, and sexually assaulted either by fellow inmates or by members of the staff. Wooden notes that some children are whipped, subjected to 'GI scrubs' with wire brushes, made to stand motionless for hours, given enormous doses of tranquillizers, sedatives, and hypnotics, sometimes followed by 'a shot of alcohol to sting'.

**The Circumstances of Abuse**

On the basis of responses concerning 1380 cases of the sample cohort, Gil (1970) developed a crude typology of circumstances in which physical abuse occurs. The typology comprises 14 different 'constellations' some of which are more frequent than others. In the majority of cases incidents of abuse seem to develop out of disciplinary action taken by caretakers who respond in uncontrolled anger to real or perceived misconduct of the child. Other incidents seem to derive from a general attitude of resentment and rejection of the perpetrator toward a child with specific acts of the child precipitating the acting out of such attitudes. Persistent behavioural atypicality of the child, e.g. hyperactivity, high annoyance potential, etc. is also inducive to abuse. Among other circumstances cited by Gil are those developing out of a quarrel between the caretakers of the child, physical abuse coinciding with a perpetrator's sexual attack on a child or motivated by the perpetrator's search for sadistic gratification, the marked mental and/or emotional deviation of the perpetrator, his/her alcoholic intoxication at the time of the abusive act, mounting stress on perpetrator due to life circumstances, the temporary absence of the mother or substitute during which the child is cared for and abused by a boyfriend, or other male or by a female babysitter. Gil admits that his typology is quite crude and will require further exploration, testing, and refinement (pp.126–30).

## PERPETRATOR–CHILD RELATIONSHIP

Family abuse of children is characterized by the specific relationship that binds the victim to the victimizer. The aetiology of child abuse need to be examined and analysed within the dynamic context of this specific bond. This family relationship is quite often responsible for generating the motives for abuse. Because of this relationship the child is accessible to the adult as a target for hostility projection and abuse. As will be noted later on, the dependence of the child on the adult for the satisfaction of his material and affective needs and his inability to engage in meaningful social interaction are two features of the relationship that play an important part in initiating or triggering abuse.

In the large majority of cases, the child is abused by his natural parents, by a stepmother, or by a foster parent. Mothers seem to be more abusive prone than the fathers. In the typical household the mother spends more time with the child than the father does and carries the responsibility of looking after the child's nutritional and sanitation needs. Moreover, in many households the father is absent as a result of divorce, separation, abandonment, etc. This may explain why global figures show a higher percentage of abusing mothers.

Gil (1970) found that in 47.6% of the sample cohort the child was abused by his mother or mother substitute, in 39.2% by his father or father substitute. Thus in 86.8% the perpetrator was a parent/substitute with whom the child had been living. In 12.1% the perpetrator was another relative, and in 1.1% the relationship of the perpetrator to the child was unknown. Gil notes that 29.5% of the children were living in fatherless homes. Fathers and substitutes were involved as perpetrators in nearly two-thirds of the incidents occurring in homes that did have fathers or father substitutes, and mothers or substitutes were involved in slightly fewer than one half the incidents occurring in homes that did have a mother or mother substitute:

> Thus the involvement rate of fathers was actually higher than of mothers. It is also noteworthy that about one third of the fathers or substitutes who were involved as perpetrators were not biological fathers but stepfathers.

(Gil, 1970, pp.116–7)

## CHARACTERISTICS OF THE BATTERED CHILD

### Age

As will be mentioned below, physical abuse of children is more likely to occur under specific circumstances and in crisis situations in which the adult caring for the child reacts violently to some irritating behaviour of the latter such as prolonged and repreated crying episodes, bedwetting, defecation in bed, soiling clothes, etc. If such behaviour does play an important role in triggering abuse and battery, then it is understandable that infants and very young children are in greater danger of being abused than other age categories. Clinical studies, in particular, seem to indicate that abuse is most common among children under 3 years of age and that children in this particular age group are at highest risk and constitute the primary target for abuse. Epidemiological studies, on the other hand, tend to reflect a somewhat different picture and produce a more even age distribution. How can these differences be explained? Maden and Wrench (1977) note that clinical studies often arbitrarily restrict the age of the sample or rely on case records from pediatric services that exclude older children, whereas surveys include reports from sources that have contact with older children and adolescents. Also, abuse in young children is more likely to be detected and less likely to be confused with accidental injury. The authors point out that despite these biases, the evidence does support the conclusion that abuse victims more often fall into the younger age categories. They quote three surveys (Gil, 1970; Fergusson *et al.*, 1972; Johnson, 1974) all of which reported that the majority of abused children were younger than six. They further note that surveys which include older children and adolescents run the risk of incorporating sexual molestation reports. This is likely to be the case since all three cited surveys report higher percentages of abused females in age categories over ten.

Gil (1970) conducted two cohort studies in 1967 (N = 5993) and 1968 (N = 6617) and found that one-third of the victims of abuse were under the age of three and that slightly over 53% were under 6 years of age. The first year of life was the highest risk year with little more than 13% of all abuse cases occurring during the 12 months following birth. Gil further found that 16–17% of the abused children reported in the two cohorts were over 12 years of age (pp.104–5).

Findings of European studies summarized by Kaiser (1977) also reveal somewhat different results regarding the frequency of child abuse within the various age groups. For instance Schaible-Fink (1968) found that children between 3 and 4 years are the most frequently battered, followed by babies of up to one year. Bauer (1969) came to similar results and ascertained – in contrast to the investigations of Mende and Kirsch (1968) – a decrease of child abuse around the 6th–7th year of age. The latter investigators came to the conclusion that 7–9 year old boys are most exposed to child abuse, a finding similar to the Danish results reported by Christiansen (1970). Kaiser (1977) has two-way explanation for the high frequency of abuse among children 6–7 years old: the high detection rate among children of school age and the increased probability of behavioural problems requiring disciplinary action in this particular age group.

> The frequency of abuse among the seven to eight years old can probably be explained by the greater visibility of such cases. This might be similar with abuses in baby-age. If a high number of such cases is reported, it is because physicians are more frequently consulted after babies have been battered since with babies the effect of the blow is more serious than with older children. Therefore, babies are not necessarily beaten more violently, but in their case the 'negative success' is bigger than with older children. First real educational difficulties occur with toddlers learning and perfecting their motor skills. The child tries to assert himself/ herself. He is in the age of obstinacy and will break many objects by his attempt to walk and tighten his grip. Parents intensify their attempts to train the child. Many of these attempts probably lead to abuse.
>
> (pp.297–8)

Gelles (1973) pinpoints three interrelated factors which result in the 3 month to 3 year old child being particularly vulnerable to parental abuse. First, the small infant or toddler lacks the physical durability to withstand much physical punishment or force. While an older child might absorb a great deal of physical punishment, the 3 month to 3 year old is likely to be severely damaged or even killed by the same type of force. Thus, since the younger child is more likely to be harmed, he is more easily abused. Secondly, the fact that the infant is not capable of much meaningful social interaction may create a great deal of frustration for the parent, who is trying to interact with the child. Because the parent cannot 'reason' with the infant, he may feel his only course of action is physical punishment. Thirdly, the new or infant child may create stress for the parent by his birth. He may create economic hardship for the family, or may interfere with professional, occupational, education, or other plans of the parents. Thus, the new child may create structural stress for his parents, which is responded to by abuse.

**Sex**

Gil (1970) found that slightly more than half the children in both study cohorts were boys, 52.6% in 1967 and 51.2% in 1968. Analysis of the sex distribution of different age groups revealed, however, that although boys outnumbered girls in every age group below age 12, they were outnumbered by girls among the teenaged victims of child abuse, 63.3% as against 36.7% in 1967 and 63.8% as against 36.2% in 1968.

Gil (1971) is of the opinion that changes in sex distribution of victims of child abuse during different stages of childhood and adolescence reflect culturally determined child-rearing attitudes. He noted that girls tend to be viewed as more conforming than boys throughout childhood, and physical force tends to be used less frequently in rearing them. However, during stages of sexual maturation parental anxieties concerning their daughters' heterosexual relationships lead to increasing restrictions, intensified conflicts, and increasing use of physical force in asserting parental control. With respect to boys the pattern seems different. Physical force tends to be used more readily throughout childhood to assure conformity. During adolescence, however, as the physical strength of boys increases and often matches or even surpasses their parents' strength, the use of physical force in disciplining boys tends to diminish. Gil's explanation is not universally accepted. Maden and Wrench (1977) point to evidence refuting Gil's arguments provided by Elmer (1967) and Straus (1971). The former reported that girls were more frequently punished at an earlier age, and tentatively, disciplined with greater severity. The latter found that among a sample of college students recalling high school experiences, boys had been punished as frequently or severely as girls.

There is some evidence suggesting that female abuse victims run a higher risk of death as a result of the sustained injuries than their male counterparts (Thomsen *et al.*, 1971; Scott, 1973; Lauer *et al.*, 1974; and Johnson, 1974). It has also been known for a long time that in primitive societies, infanticide is committed with much greater frequency against female infants.

**Ordinal position**

Researchers report conflicting findings regarding the ordinal position of the abuse victim in the sibship. Several studies found that older, especially first-born, children were more frequently abused, while other studies indicated that the youngest child was more susceptible (see Maden and Wrench, 1977, p.199). The conflicting findings may be due in part to the fact that most studies failed to control for family size. Smith (1975) found that 'when birth order is properly related to family size, the suggestion that a child's particular ordinal position carries more risk of battering does not hold' (p.206). Authors like Steele and Pollock (1968) who feel that the most important factor in the genesis of parental abuse is 'the lack of mothering skills' would probably be inclined to view the first born as being in the greatest danger of parental abuse.

A number of authors observed that in multiple-children families quite often, only one child is subjected to abuse. For example, Thomsen *et al.*, (1971) found that one specific child was the target of abuse in 88% of the 376 cases they studied. Other studies, however, reported that siblings were also mistreated. Maden and Wrench (1977) cite two studies which used relatively complete data on sibling abuse (Skinner and Castle, 1969; Baldwin and Oliver, 1975). Both indicate that when first-born children are abused, subsequent children carry significant risk as well.

There seems to be a positive correlation between large family size and a low level of child-care. Larger families also seem to have a higher incidence of abuse than smaller ones. Justice and Justice

(1976) cite evidence from several studies in the USA, England and New Zealand indicating that 'the average family size for asbusing families substantially exceeds the national average'. Gil's epidemiological study (1970) revealed that the proportion of families with four or more children was nearly twice as high for the sample cohort as a whole as for all families in the US population, and the proportion of small families was much larger in the US population than in the sample cohort.

## PRONENESS TO VICTIMIZATION

### General Vulnerability Related to Childhood

Infants' and children's vulnerability to victimization is too obvious to be discussed in great detail. The relative lack of viability of the human infant, the helplessness and defencelessness of young children make them easy targets for attack, abuse, and destruction. Already in 1948, Von Hentig drew attention to this extreme vulnerability of children and youth when he wrote:

> Youth is the most dangerous period of life. Young creatures under natural conditions are the ideal prey, weak and easy to catch and savory.
>
> (p.404)

Several factors contribute to making the child an easy prey. The helplessness of infants and the very young, their underdeveloped defensive mechanisms, their inability to resist or to oppose the attacker, to retaliate or even to complain, their inability to communicate, to express their wishes and explain their needs, their total dependability on adults for the satisfaction of their needs, their accessibility as ready targets for the projection of anger, frustration and hostility or for the satisfaction of sexual desires act, no doubt, in many cases as stimulus for adults to engage in physical and sexual abuse.

As mentioned above, proneness to pysical abuse seems to be at its peak from birth until the age of 3 or 4. Vulnerability is also at its highest point during that critical age when the child's irritating behaviour (incessant crying, wet and dirty habits, temper-abrading and eroding activities, etc.) combined with the parent's lack of rearing skills and of self-control are likely to elicit violent and aggressive responses from the adult against the child.

While male children seem to be slightly more prone to physical abuse than their female counterparts, the latter's vulnerability to sexual abuse is by far higher than that of boys. Moreover, vulnerability to sexual abuse follows a different age distribution. The most criticial age for sexual abuse is understandably higher than that for physical abuse with girls in the pre and early adolescent years constituting the most prone age group. Vulnerability seems to increase at the beginning and with the progress of sexual maturity.

In his study of incest, Maisch (1973) discovered that the average age of the female incest victim in his survey group is 12.3 years and the most represented age is the (completed) 13th year. Roughly two-thirds were between their tenth and sixteenth years of life (9 years to 15.6 years). The youngest girl was 6 at the start of incest and the oldest 19. Comparable surveys in Germany, Sweden, and the USA quoted by Maisch report similar results (p.102).

While incestuous relationships with girls before the (completed) seventh year of life and after the age of 19 seem to be rare, non-incestuous heterosexual offences and cases of rape on girls under seven do not seem to be quite infrequent (see Maisch, 1973, p.102). Mohr *et al.*, (1962) established that the vulnerability age for victims of non-incestuous heterosexual sexual offences lay between 6 and 11.

In a research on sexual victimization of children conducted in New York in 1967 and 1968 (De Francis, 1969), the median age for child victims in the study sample was found to be 11.65 years. Almost one-third of the children were in the age range 7 to 10, and about one-third in the bracket 13 to 15 years of age. 87% of the victims in the study sample were girls, 13% were boys.

**Specific Vulnerability Related to Particular Attributes of the Child**

Qualitative differences are likely to be found not only between abusive and non-abusive parents but also between abused and non-abused children. The findings of many studies seem to leave little doubt that some children because of specific attributes or due to some particular qualities have a higher than average potential for being abused. Justice and Justice (1976) use the term 'high risk children' to describe those particular children who are especially prone to abuse (p.248). Gil (1970) refers to the findings of many investigators who have observed that some children, because of unusual congenital or acquired characteristics may occasionally be more prone to provoke abusing attacks against themselves than other, more 'normal children' (p.3).

Who are these children that are particularly disposed to victimization? Among them, according to Kempe (1971) are the hyperactive and precocious, the premature, the adopted, and the step-child, the child who from the earliest day seems to be singularly unrewarding to the mother no matter how hard she tries, though it is not easy to know in a given situation whether the primary problem lies mostly with the baby or with the mother. Kempe sees the act of battering as resulting from a triad: (a) the potential for abuse, (b) the characteristics of the particular child as seen by the particular parent, and (c) there must be a crisis (p.33).

Flynn (1970) describes what he calls the 'obnoxious child' whom he sees as a natural stimulus for abuse. Bishop (1971) identifies six groups of children who are in specific risk of abuse: (a) illegitimate children, (b) premature babies, (c) congenitally malformed babies, (d) twins, (e) children conceived during the mother's depressive illness, and (f) children of mothers with frequent pregnancies and excessive work loads. The percentage of illegitimate children among those who are abused varies from one study to the other. On the basis of their limited sample (35 abusing parents), Justice and Justice (1976) report that 17% of the abused children were illegitimate. On the other hand, Zalba (1971) reported that 50% of the abused children in Massachusetts were conceived out of wedlock.

Justice and Justice quote a study undertaken by Leonoski (1973) in which he examined 674 cases of abuse. Lenoski found that 22% involved children who had been premature babies. This compared with 10% of 500 control cases. In the abused group 30% had been delivered by Caesarian section (compared with 3.2% in the control group) and 9% had complicated deliveries (compared with 4.2% in the control group).

Friedrich and Boriskin (1977) point to mounting evidence which demonstrates that any perception of the child as strange, different, damaged, or abnormal increases the risk of its being subjected to abusive treatment:

Prematurity and low birth weight are important factors, as are mental retardation and physical handicaps. In effect, therefore, the child is victimized twice over, bearing both a physical burden of deprivation or damage and the anger this provokes in those responsible for its care.

(p.405)

To the above-mentioned categories of children who are especially prone to abuse and victimization we have to add those babies and children who are particularly difficult, aggravating, and hard to handle. Kempe and Kempe (1978) report that at least a quarter of the young who have been abused (and probably more of the older ones) are negative, aggressive, and often hyperactive as well. They write:

These children seem veritable demons, who have responded to the experience of aggression with almost manic activity. They move constantly, unable to sit still or attend more than briefly, and are almost completely incapable of playing acceptably with other children. This behaviour may be an imitation of the aggression they have experienced, but it is socially so insufferable that they may constantly be rejected in nursery school or any other play group unless a specific effort is made to modify their behaviour. These are very difficult children to manage, not listening to directions, impervious apparently to disapproval, and forever hitting out at other children. The only attention they seem to try for is negative, and their language is often even more aggressive than their behaviour.

(pp.34–5)

As mentioned earlier, sometimes it is difficult to ascertain whether the mental and behavioural symptoms observed in abused children are the reason or the consequence of abuse.

Justice and Justice (1976) offer several explanations for the high risk to which certain children are exposed. Regarding the disproportionate number of premature or low birth-weight babies among abused children, they note that prematurity predisposes a baby to anoxia, which in turn causes irritability and fussiness. Another explanation is that babies who weigh less than 5.5 lb at birth may have subtle dysfunctions of the central nervous system which result in restlessness and distractibility. Low birth-weight babies also are unlikely to be picked up as often as normal-weight infants, and this factor possibly has an unfortunate influence on the neonate's development, resulting in unresponsive behaviour. Another theory is that because premature infants are separated from their parents for the first several weeks of life, the establishment of the child–caretaker bond is delayed, which in turn adversely affects the interaction between baby and mother – especially the mother's response to the infant. Discussing the higher incidence of and the high risk potential for abuse which have been reported for illegitimate children, Justice and Justice point to the mother's rejection of the child resulting from her unwanting him or being ashamed because of him.

Furthermore, the baby's behaviour may contribute to her rejecting or abusive behaviour. Illegitimate and unwanted babies are especially prone to be irritable and colicky . . . Even if the mother does want the baby, his different behaviour can make her feel inadequate and resentful. And if her stress continues or if she looks to the baby for love, abusive behaviour may be triggered. The unwed mother sometimes seeks a symbiotic relationship with her child, not for the child's well-being but for her own. If she feels rejected by the child's father, she may view the child as her last chance to obtain the love and nurturing she never received from her own parents or from boyfriends. When the child fails to provide this love and nurturing, abuse may occur.

(p.251)

## THE DYNAMICS OF CHILD ABUSE

### The Reactive and Interactive Nature of Child Abuse

Earlier explanations of child abuse tended to stress the psychopathological traits of the abusing parents, their family background, their lack of rearing skills, their stressful environment and their low socio-economic status. Current explanations, on the other hand, are emphasizing more and more the interpersonal dynamics of abuse and the interactive character of the relationship between the abuser and the child. Clearly a dynamic, interactionist model is needed to explain why abuse occurs in specific situations under specific circumstances, why certain children are battered but not others, and why in multi-child families it is usually one child who is the target of abuse. Etiological studies of child abuse have been dominated by the search for those psychological, sociological or cultural factors that predispose some parents to use violence against their children or that may be responsible for turning some parents into child abusers. They overlook the fact that it is only the conjunction of predisposing and triggering factors which creates the crisis situation in which abuse is likely to occur. Milowe, quoted by Gil (1970), summarizes the dynamic cycle of events that leads to abuse as follows:

The parent's childhood loads the gun; present life conflicts cause the parent to raise it; the child's phase-specific needs help pull the trigger.

(p.29)

Neither the personality traits of the parent nor the particularities of the child can explain by themselves why abuse occurs or why it occurs under certain circumstances but not under others, why it takes place at certain developmental stages more frequently than at others. Justice and Justice (1976) developed a psycho-social system model of child abuse in which the child and the stressful behaviour or conditions he embodies are considered the agent that precipitates abuse. They emphasize that abuse results from a system of multiple interactions between parent and child, husband and wife, adult and environment, child and environment, and culture and parent. All play a part, but the child is most commonly the immediate source of external stress for the abusive parent. The child's very proximity makes him an easy target for the parent whose frustrations spill over into physical aggression (p.59).

The following explanation of how abuse occurs, given by Kempe and Kempe (1978), is an excellent illustration of the interactive nature of child abuse:

When the baby is difficult to feed, rejecting the bottle or spitting up, an insecure mother may overract, as if the baby's problems were a deliberate attempt to frustrate her. Toilet-training accidents are probably the second highest immediate cause of abuse attacks, and along with other normal autonomous behaviour, seem to produce the greatest frustration in the parent who feels he can't maintain control. It is the feeling of helpless lack of control that so often leads to rage and striking out.

(p.28)

Milowe, quoted by Gil (1970), also notes that some batterings occur only when specific developmental stages in the child trigger specific conflicts in the parent and not at earlier or later times (p.30).

Only a dynamic, interactionist model of child abuse can explain why in multi-child families only one child will be singled out as a target of parental wrath and physical violence or why certain children get battered in sequential foster home placements where no other has ever been battered.

In many cases, abuse can be traced to the child's failure to meet the parent's expectations or to satisfy their needs. According to Morris and Gould (1964) an abusing parent view his victim not as the child he really is but as his own parent, who has failed, hurt, and frustrated him. The abuse is intended for that 'absent parent' but is displaced and acted out against the helpless present child. The child in such cases is expected by the parent to meet his (the parent's) complex emotional needs, rather than having his needs met by the parent: when the child fails to do so, the frustrated parent attacks, injures, and at times destroys the child (Gil, 1970, p.23). Speaking of abusive parents, Justice and Justice (1976) note that they have unrealistic expectations concerning their children. They seek satisfaction of unmet needs for comfort and nurture from their own child. When the child fails to deliver, the parent interprets this failure as a rejection and his anger and frustration mount (p.94).

Another interactive aspect of child abuse relates to the distorted perception many parents have of their children. They do not perceive the infant as an infant, but as an organized human being capable of sensing the parent's needs and meeting them. And when the child fails to perform or to behave in a way that satisfies the parent's need or make the parent feel good, frustration, anger, resentment, hostility are aroused in the parent and prepare the ground for physical abuse. Steele and Pollock (1968) found that the parents in their study groups treated their children as adults capable of providing grown-up comfort and love. And Galdston (1965) notes the following revealing observation about abusive parents:

> In the extreme of their ambivalence these parents perceive the child they assault as a hostile, persecutory adult. The child, by its presence alone, evokes affects in the parents which they find to be intolerable.
>
> (p.442)

Child abuse is a typical 'relationship crime' or to use the German term 'ein Beziehungsverbrechen'. It cannot be understood unless it is analysed within the context of the specific relationship that binds the victim to the victimizer, their interdependence and their mutual reliance on each other for the satisfaction of certain material and affective needs. The potential for abuse is no doubt present in many parent–child relationships but it is enhanced tremendously by certain personality constellations and by the frequent incompatibility of the temperamental characteristics of the parent and the child. The potential for abuse is low when only one of the protagonists in the relationship is particularly disposed to become a victim or a victimizer. It is low when a difficult child is born to loving, understanding, and emotionally stable parents or when a quiet, docile baby is born to inexperienced parents lacking in mothering and rearing skills. On the other hand, the potential for abuse is extremely high when an irritating baby is born to an irritable mother or a hard to manage child is born to unstable and temperamental parents. It is the 'mismatch' or the incompatibility that greatly increases the risk of abuse. Justice and Justice (1976) point out that the match between baby and parent is important. A difficult child can be a problem to almost any parent, but this type of child is at even greater risk if his mother or father, because of his or her temperament and characteristics, expects or demands docile, compliant behaviour from the child. Martin and Beezley (1974) found that even if the child is not especially difficult or does not have an unpredictable temperament, there still may be a:

> disparity between characteristics of the infant and the parent's capability and capacity to parent that type of child. The characteristics of the infant and child need not be abnormalities, but rather idiosyncratic traits within a spectrum of normalcy . . . Assessing variations in infants' behaviour repertoires may prove extremely helpful in preventing abuse by identifying those parent-child matches which need intervention.

(p.74)

**The Victim's Triggering Behaviour**

In the great majority of cases, child abuse is a reactive behaviour. It is a reaction, rather an overraction, to a stressful situation created by a stress-producing environment and triggered by the child's irritating or provoking behaviour. Triggering behaviour of the child does not require or imply conscious, deliberate acts or irritating or provoking nature. In many cases, the child is too young to wilfully provoke or even to communicate. But some temperamental characteristics, some attitudinal and behavioural patterns may serve as a stimulus that elicits abuse from a parent suffering from a permanent or temporary lack of self-control.

A dynamic model of child abuse cannot ignore or overlook the triggering behaviour of the victim. The child is not physically abused all the time. Beating or battering is likely to take place only under those specific circumstances which Gil (1977) call 'triggering contexts'. It tends to be triggered by the condition of the parent and the behaviour of the child. On the part of the abuser, stress and frustration may cause a reduction in self-control and may increase the irritability of the adult and the likelihood of a violent reaction to the child's behaviour. On the part of the child, it is usually the intractable crying, messy feeding, soiling which are the most frequent irritants. Kempe and Kempe (1978) express the view that when a child is abused, it is always at a point of crisis, often an apparently trivial one, such as the infant's interruption of its parents' sexual intercourse by protracted crying. Justice and Justice (1976) also note that parents who seek nurturing and comfort from their children may be provoked to anger and violence if the child responds with crying or agitated behaviour. When the child makes unusually great demands or represents an exceptional stress, he is in even greater danger of being physically abused.

Referring to the child's irritating, provoking, or triggering behaviour does not imply an assignment of blame or an attribution of guilt. It is not an attempt to excuse or exonerate the abusive parent. It is simply a recognition of the fact that child abuse is a dynamic phenomenon that cannot be understood or explained unless the interactions of the abuser and the child are analysed. In many cases, it would be impossible to understand and explain the parent's loss of control, his violent reaction, his abusive behaviour without taking into account the whole set of circumstances that trigger that aggressive behaviour. Gil (1970) quotes Henry Makover of the Albert Einstein College of Medicine and a psychiatric consultant of the Family Court of New York as saying:

. . . I have seen a few cases in which it would be difficult to deny the provocative behaviour of the child as being responsible for the event. Such children, themselves disturbed, may evoke severe parental punishment and the interaction between parent and child would, perhaps, be the most fruitful avenue of research.

(p.34)

Schaible-Fink (1968) analysed 172 cases of child abuse and concluded that the triggering behaviour is primarily bedwetting and defecation in bed, followed by stubbornness and obstinacy. Other triggering behaviours are refusal to accept food, lies, stealing, weak efforts in school, playing with genitals, etc.

Gil (1966) notes that some children may be more provocative than others in their behaviour towards adults and that such children may play a contributing role in their own physical abuse. The same author (1970) found that about a quarter of all reported cases of child abuse represent cases of 'persistent behavioural atypicality of child, e.g. hyperactivity, high annoyance potential, etc. that is cases which could be regarded as 'child-initiated or child-provoked abuse' (see Kaiser, 1977, p.298).

Barbara Bender (1976) reports that in working with two boys aged 8 and 10 who had been battered as young children, she was strongly impressed by a behaviour pattern in both that seemed directly related to the abusive treatment they had received from their parents. Both had a compulsive need to provoke punishment from everyone they came in contact with, both peers and adults. Bender describes the two boys as 'self-chosen victims' and their provoking behaviour as 'scapegoating behaviour'. While in some cases it may be clear that the child's provoking or irritating behaviour has been influential in triggering the adult's abusive behaviour, in other cases it may be difficult to establish whether the irritating behaviour has preceded or succeeded the abuse, whether it has triggered the assault or resulted from it, whether it was responsible for the battery or whether it was produced by the battery.

Needless to say that the parent's physical abuse of the child may be triggered by factors other than the child's behaviour. The mere presence of the child may in certain cases elicit aggressive or eliminating impulses from one or both parents. The behaviour of the child hardly plays any role in the traditional act of infanticide. Here, to quote Bakan (1971), ' . . . the critical factor is that children may constitute a burden and a threat, and thus they elicit the impulse to remove them from being' (p.15). Psychiatrists have known for a long time that aggressive impulses toward the child may develop during pregnancy and may intensify with the birth of the child:

Thus the experience of childbirth may well arouse aggressive impulses in the mother toward the child. This aggression may not be unique either to very painful and exhausting deliveries or to young mothers, although these factors may enhance the aggression.

(Bakan, 1971, p.96)

Feelings of hatred and the wish to kill or to harm the baby may be particularly acute shortly after the delivery during the depressive phase known as 'the post-partum psychosis' a state from which some mothers may suffer after giving birth to a child. Furthermore, not every child arouses feelings of love, tenderness, and affection in his parents or those in whose care he is placed. Some may create stress or anxiety to their parents by their birth, they may evoke feelings of hatred, jealousy, guilt, or shame. This is particularly the case of children conceived in an incestuous relationship or as a result of rape. It is not uncommon in the case of children born out of wedlock, unwanted children in general, and those bearing strong resemblance to a detested partner.

According to Bakan (1971) the very helplessness of the child may be the stimulus that evokes abuse and even infanticide:

Babies are naturally helpless, inept, weak and irregular in excretion, and their needfulness may create unpleasantness for others. The child urinates and defecates. He throws up. He cannot feed himself, and when he tries to, he makes a mess of things. He cries and wimpers and asks for attention. When he is not given attention, he may even develop neurotic mechanisms to irritate others into giving him the attention he is not otherwise able to get.

(p.104)

### The Repetitive Nature of Child Battering

There is a strong empirical evidence pointing to the repetitive nature of child abuse and battering. Not only do battered children tend to be repeatedly victimized but they also tend when they grow up to abuse their own young ones. The latter phenomenon has been called 'the intergenerational cycle of abuse'.

Repetitive abuse of the same child has been reported by many researchers. Gil (1970) found that at least half the children of the sample cohort had been victims of physical abuse prior to the incident reported in 1967. Since this item was checked as 'unknown' for nearly a quarter of the sample cohort, Gil believes that over 60% of the children had a history of prior abuse. His data for the 1967 and 1968 study cohorts suggest the same proportion of prior abuse. Gil comments that his findings suggest that physical abuse of children is more often than not an indication of a prevailing pattern of caretaker-child interaction in a giving home rather than of an isolated incident (p.108). In another study, Brandon (1976) reports that three out of every five children returning home after treatment for an injury were subsequently reinjured.

Two main reasons seem to be responsible for the recurrence of abuse: first, adult–child interaction patterns that lead to abusive incidents tend to be repetitive. The characteristics, the peculiarities and the behaviour disorders of the child which may have triggered the first incident of abuse or may have acted as a stimulus eliciting parental violence are likely, in the absence of effective intervention, to result in repeated or continued abuse. In fact, abuse is likely to aggravate the child's emotional or behavioural disorders which in turn produce a vicious circle: crying, abuse, further crying, further abuse or punishment, deteriorating relationship, frustration, and further punishment. Secondly, the abuse of a child seems to create a child who invites abuse. As Bakan (1971) points out

> Furthermore, children who are abused tend to develop character-istics which make them even more unlovable. The well taken care of child attracts positive responses. The child who is abused and neglected becomes ugly in appearance and behaviour and invites further abuse and neglect . . . The very stifling of development prolongs the helplessness of the child, which continues to be the provocation for further assault or neglect.
>
> (p.109)

It is well known that persons who engage in violence tend to have been victims of violence. It comes therefore as no surprise to learn from studies of abusive parents that a large percentage had been abused children themselves. Chesser (1952), studying child abuse in England, observed that cruelty toward children was related to deep-seated psychological deviations of the perpetrators which could often be traced to physical and mental cruelty inflicted upon them during childhood by their own parents. Gil (1970) cites several studies the findings of which suggest that many abusive parents had been abused by their own parents during childhood. This finding is identical to that of Kempe and Kempe (1978) who reported that the most consistent feature of the histories of abusive families is the repetition, from one generation to the next, of a pattern of abuse, neglect, and parental loss or deprivation.

Parents tend to use the same rearing patterns they themselves had learned from their own parents and through this learning process violence is usually transmitted from generation to generation. Every time the child's undesirable behaviour is punished by the use of violence he is being taught that the use of violence is a proper mode of curbing undesirable behaviour. He grows up believing that the use of violence in the process of upbringing is right, legitimate, and justified. Child abuse provides the future generation of parents with the necessary justifications and rationalizations to use violence against their own children. The process is well described by Bakan (1971):

> Because child abuse victims learn to abuse children in this manner quite directly, they are filled with a sense of the moral righteousness of what they are doing. The internal injunction in an abusive parent has a kind of moral imperative associated with it which is hard to match. His sense of the righteousness and justice of the act derives from the fact that he himself was so punished in his childhood, and developing the sense that such punishment is legitimate and even righteous was the only way in which he could accept it. One of the greatest obstacles in dealing with a child-abusing parent is this feeling that the actions were justified.
>
> (p.116)

That a large percentage of abusive parents had been themselves victims of abuse can be explained through the processes of learning and imitation and by the general tendency of children to internalize the behavioural models to which they are exposed. More difficult is to ascertain a causal link between the abuse endured during childhood and the later deviant or delinquent behaviour of the child. Some recent studies report that a good number of abused children are later reported to family or juvenile courts as delinquent or ungovernable. In an attempt to establish the relationship between child abuse and neglect and later socially deviant behaviour, Alfaro (1978) examined records of courts and social agencies in eight New York counties for the years 1959–72. His findings indicated that as many as

50% of the families reported for child abuse had at least one child who was later taken to court for delinquent behaviour, that a significant number of children who were reported abused were later reported to a court as delinquent or ungovernable, and that delinquent children who were reported as abused or neglected tended to be more violent than other delinquents. Reference to two unpublished studies is made by Bolton *et al.* (1977). In the first of these Weston interviewed 100 juvenile offenders and found that 82 of these juveniles could recall significant child abuse in their lives. In the second study, Steele interviewed 200 juveniles and had corroborative evidence for 100 of the cases. Steele found that 92 of the documented cases had been bruised, lacerated, or fractured by their parents within 18 months prior to their arrest. Of the remaining 100 cases, without documentation, 72 reported having been abused. None of these studies provides conclusive evidence of a relationship between abuse, maltreatment, and juvenile delinquency. Even if such link is unequivocally established, it will be extremely difficult to assess it in terms of causality or to conclude that abuse leads to future delinquent behaviour. It may well be that the behavioural problems or disorders which led to the abuse are the ones responsible for the later socially deviant behaviour. It may also be that the same environmental conditions which create the potential for abuse contribute to the future delinquency of those brought up in such conditions.

## CONCLUSION

These few victimological considerations on child abuse do have far reaching practical implications. First, it seems evident that a punitive approach using criminal sanctions as a deterrent is not likely to be effective in eliminating or even in reducing the incidence of abuse. Typically, child abuse is not the kind of rational behaviour that may be curbed or influenced by the threat of punishment. The causes of, and motives for, abuse appear to be far beyond the reach of the criminal law. Second, treatment and preventive models centered upon the abusing parent, his particularities, his psychopathology, and aimed at strengthening his self-control, or at changing his behaviour are not likely to solve by themselves the problem of child abuse.

What is needed is a new approach that takes into account the specificity of the relationship between the abuser and the child, the dynamics of the situation in which abuse is likely to occur, and that pays equal attention to both the predisposing and the triggering factors. What is further needed, is a radical change in current rearing practices and the methods of child upbringing. Physical or corporal punishment has to disappear from the home, the school and from institutions. The mentality of the rod has to be changed and replaced by a reward system, by the deprivation of privileges, and by the withholding and/or withdrawal of affection.

Penal law might still be used to ensure an adequate reporting of abuse cases and to sanction the failure of those who are required to report but do not do so. But to expect the criminal law to solve the problem of child abuse or any other social problem is nothing more than an utopian dream.

**Note**
* This chapter is a reprint of an article published in the *Revue Internationale de Droit Pénal*, vol.50, nos 3 and 4, 1979.

**Bibliography**

Alfaro, J. D. (1978), *Relationship Between Child Abuse and Neglect and Later Socially Deviant Behaviour* (New York State Assembly-Select Committee on Child Abuse, New York Division of Criminal Justice Services).

Bakan, D. (1971), *Slaughter of the Innocents: a Study of the Battered Child Phenomenon* (Toronto: Canadian Broadcasting Corporation).

Baldwin, J. A. and Oliver, J. E. (1975), 'Epidemiology and Family Characteristics of Severely Abused Children', *British Journal of Preventive Social Medicine*, vol.29(4) pp.205–21.

Bartollas, C., Miller, S. J. and Dinitz, S. (1976), *Juvenile Victimization: the Institutional Paradox* (New York: Halsted Press, J. Wiley,) pp.324.

Bauer, G. (1969), *Die Kindersmisshandlung Ein Beitrag Zur Kriminologie und Kriminalistik sowie zur Anwendung des 223b St Gb* (Lubeck).

Bender, B. (1976), 'Self-Chosen Victims: Scapegoating Behavior Sequential to Battering', *Child Welfare*, vol.2 55(6), pp.417–22.

Bennie, E. H. and Sclare, A. B. (1969), 'The Battered Child Syndrome', *American Journal of Psychiatry*, vol.125(7), pp.975–9.

Bishop, R. I. (1971), 'Children at Risk', *Medical Journal of Australia*, vol.1, pp.623–8.

Bolton, F. G., Reich, J. W. and Gutierres, S. E. (1977), 'Delinquency Patterns in Maltreated Children and Siblings', *Victimology*, vol.2, pp.249–357.

Brandon, S. (1976), 'Physical Violence in the Family – an Overview'in Marie Borland (ed.), *Violence in the Family* (Atlantic Highlands: Humanities Press).

Chesser, E. (1952), *Cruelty to Children* (New York: The Philosophical Library).

Christiansen, W. F. (1970), 'The Battered Child: Danish Data', *Excerpta Criminologica*, vol.10, pp.79.

Cohen, S. and Sussmann, A. (1975), 'The Incidence of Child Abuse in the United States', *Child Welfare*, vol.54(6), pp.432–43.

De Francis, V. (1966), *Child Abuse Legislation. Analysis of Reporting Laws in the United States* (Denver: Children's Division. The American Humane Association).

De Francis, V. (1969), *Protecting the child Victim of Sex Crimes Committed by Adults: Final Report* (Denver: The American Humane Association Children's Division).

Elmer, E. (1967), *Children in Jeopardy: a Study of Abused Minors and Their Families* (University of Pittsburgh Press).

Fergusson, D. M., Fleming, J. and O. Neill, D. (1972), *Child Abuse in New Zealand* (Wellington: Research Division Department of Social Work).

Flynn, W. R. (1970), 'Frontier Justice: a Contribution to the Theory of Child Battery' *American Journal of Orthopsychiatry*, vol.46(4),pp.580. A Summary is published in *Victimology*, vol.2(2), pp.405–6.

Galdston, R. (1965), 'Observations on Children Who Have Been Physically Abused and Their Parents', *American Journal of Psychiatry*, vol.122(4), pp.440–3.

Gelles, R. J. (1973), 'Child Abuse as Psychopatology: a Sociological Critique and Reformulation', *American Journal of Orthopsychiatry*, vol.43(4), pp.611–21. Reprinted in S. K. Steinmetz and M. A. Straus (eds), *Violence in the Family* (New York Harper & Row, 1974), pp.190–204.

Gelles, R. J. (1977), *Violence Towards Children in the United States*, paper presented at the meeting of the American Association for the Advancement of Science, Denver, Colorado (quoted in Maden and Wrench, 1977).

Gil, D. G. (1969), 'Physical Abuse of Children: Findings and Implications of a Nationwide Survey', *Pediatrics* (Supplement), vol.44, pp.857–64.

Gil, D. G. (1969), *A Nationwide Epidemiologic Study of Child Abuse Progress Report*, Presented at the National Conference on Social Welfare (Chicago, June).

Gil, D. G. (1970), *Violence Against Children: Physical Child Abuse in the United States* (Cambridge, Mass: Harvard University Press) 204.pp

Gil, D. G. (1971), 'Violence Against Children', *Journal of Marriage and the Family*, vol.33(4) (Nov.) pp.637–47.

Gil, D. G. (1977), 'Child Abuse: Levels of Manifestation, Causal Dimensions, and Primary Prevention', *Victimology*, vol.2(2), pp.186–94.

Giovannoni, J. M. (1971), 'Parental Mistreatment: Perpetrators and Victims', *Journal of Marriage and the Family*, vol.33(4), pp.649–57.

Helfer, R. E. and Kempe, C. H. (1968) (eds), *The Battered Child* (University of Chicago Press) pp.268.

Hentig, H. von (1948), *The Criminal and His Victim* (New Haven, Conn.: Yale University Press).

Johnson, C. L. (1974), *Child Abuse in the Southeast: an Analysis of 1172 Reported Cases* (Georgia University, Athens, Welfare Research).

Justice, B. and Justice, R. (1976), *The Abusing Family* (New York: Human

Sciences Press) 288.pp

Kaiser, G. (1977), 'Child Abuse in West Germany', *Victimology*, vol.2(2) pp.294–306.

Kempe, C. H. and Silverman, F. N. *et al.* (1962), 'The Battered Child Syndrome', *Journal of the American Medical Assocaition*, vol.181(1), pp.17–24.

Kempe, C. H. (1971) 'Pediatric Implications of the Battered Baby Syndrome', (The Windermere Lecture 1970), *Archives of Diseases in Childhood*, vol.1(46), pp.28–37.

Kempe, R. S. and Kempe, C. H. (1978), *Child Abuse* (Cambridge, Mass: Harvard University Press) pp.136.

Lauer, B. *et al.* (1974), 'Battered Child Syndrome: Review of 130 Patients with Controls', *Pediatrics*, vol.54(1), pp.67–70.

Lenoski, E. F. (1973), 'Translating injury data into preventive services – physical child abuse', unpublished paper, Division of Emergency Medicine. University of Southern California Medical Center, Los Angeles (quoted in Justice and Justice, 1976).

Maden, M. F., and Wrench, D. F. (1977), 'Significant Findings in Child Abuse Research', *Victimology*, vol.2(2), pp.196–224.

Maisch, H. (1973), *Incest* (London: Andre Deutsch). First published in German under the title *Inzest*.

Martin, H., Beezley, P., Conway E. F. and Kempe, C. H. (1976), 'The Development of Abused Children', *Advances in Pediatrics*, vol.21, pp.25–73.

Mende, U., Kirsch, H. (1968), *Beobachtungen zum Problem der Kindesmisshandlung* (München).

Mohr, J. H. *et al*, (1962) 'The Pedophiliacs: Their Clinical, Social and Legal Implications', *Canadian Psychiatric Association Journal*, vol.7, pp.255–60.

Morris, M. and Gould, R. (1964), 'Role Reversal: a Necessary Concept in Dealing with the Battered Child Syndrome', *American Journal of Orthopsychiatry*, vol.33, pp.298–9.

Pfohl, S. J. (1977), 'The "Discovery" of Child Abuse', *Social Problems*, vol.24(3), pp.310–323.

Rolde, E. J. (1977), 'Negative Effects of Child Abuse Legislation', *Child Abuse and Neglect*, vol.1(1), pp.167–71.

Schaible-Fink, B. (1968), *Das Delikt der Körperlichen Kindesmisshandlung: Literatur, Statistik, Kasuistik* (Hamburg: Kriminalistik Verlag).

Scott, P. D. (1973), 'Fatal Battered-Baby Cases', *Medical Science and Law*, vol.13(3), pp.197–206.

Skinner, A. and Castle, R. (1969), *Seventy-Eight Battered Children: a Retrospective Study* (London: National Society for the Prevention of Cruelty to Children (NSPCC)).

Smith, S. M. (1975), *The Battered Child Syndrome* (London: Butterworths) pp.292.

Steele, B. F. and Pollock, C. B. (1968), 'A Psychiatric Study of Parents Who Abuse Infants and Small Children' in Helfer, R. and Kempe, C. H. (eds), *The Battered Child* (Chicago University Press, 1968) pp.280.

Straus, M. A. (1971), 'Some Social Antecedents of Physical Punishment: a Linkage Theory Interpretation', *Journal of Marriage and the Family*, pp.658–63.

Thomsen, E. M. *et al* (1971), *Child Abuse: a Community Challenge* (East Aurora, New York: Henry Skewart).

Wooden, K. (1976), *Weeping in the Playtime of Others* (New York: McGraw Hill) pp.264.

Zalba, S. R. (1966), 'The Abused Child: I. A. Survey of the problem', *Social Work*, vol.11(4), pp.3–16.

Zalba, S. R. (1967), 'The Abused Child: II. A Typology for Classification and Treatment', *Social Work*, vol.12(1), pp.70–9.

Zalba, S. R. (1971), 'Battered Children', *Trans-action*, vol.8(9/10), pp.58–61.

# 9 Child Abuse and the Courts: Finnish and Swedish Experiences*

## Marja Korpilahti

Until recently, child abuse has been regarded primarily as a medical problem (Kempe and Kempe, 1980). Also in Finland it was the physicians who first paid attention to the phenomenon (Tornudd, 1948). This has determined the main emphasis on cases of physical assault, which were at times presented in a sensationalist manner. As a result, people have found it easy to regard these cases as the results of the acts of pathological parents. The logical connection with corporal punishment has remained hidden.

There has recently been a tendency to consider child abuse rather as a social than a medical problem. The social-welfare authorities presumably bear the greatest burden for developing this view. This new view has brought about an expansion of the concept of child abuse to include even slight cases of assault as well as mental abuse. This change is also gradually reflected in legislation.

This chapter deals with the legislation and criminal justice system practice in regard to child abuse in Finland and Sweden. Data on court cases have been gathered in the cities of Helsinki and Turku in Finland, and Stockholm and Uppsala in Sweden.

The concept of the child refers to persons under 15 years of age. The data include cases of mental and sexual abuse. Since the data are gathered from court cases, the offences must have been proven to the extent that the police have turned the cases over to a prosecutor.

## PREVIOUS STUDIES AND REPORTS

In Finland the idea of physical inviolability of children has not been discussed much before the 1970s, and even today there are not many studies on the subject. The Mannerheim League for Child Welfare published a report in 1974 based mainly on foreign studies. Santasalo and Santasalo (1979) studied the abused children brought to Aurora Children's Hospital in Helsinki in 1970–76. Korpilahti (1981) studied child abuse cases dealt with by the courts. The attitudes towards corporal punishment were surveyed in 1978 and 1981 (Peltoniemi, 1983a).

In Finland, the major private organizations which deal with children's rights are the Central Union of Child Welfare, the Mannerheim League for Child Welfare, and the First Homes' Federation of Finland.

In 1981, the Central Union for Child Welfare in Finland launched a campaign against child abuse. The organization published a translation of *Child Abuse* by Ruth and Henry Kempe in 1982. The National Board of Social Welfare and the National Board of Health produced a booklet (Taskinen, 1982) for professionals who encounter child abuse in their work. Child abuse problems were also discussed in a study of Finnish shelters (Peltoniemi, 1981), and in other studies concerning family violence (Peltoniemi, 1980; Peltoniemi and Honkavaara, 1981).

In Sweden, publications on child abuse are more frequent than in Finland (e.g. Pierre, 1971; Lagerberg, 1982). *Child Abuse* by Kempe and Kempe was published in Sweden in 1979.

The first Swedish study on child abuse was carried out by the National Board of Welfare in 1969 (Socialstyrelsen, 1969). Later on, the same administration carried out a new study including psychological and sexual child abuse (Socialstyrelsen, 1975). An active research group, the PRU project in Uppsala (PRU-Gruppen, 1979), has been financed by the 'Rädda Barnen' organization. This group has surveyed the attitudes towards corporal punishment in Sweden (SIFO, 1981).

In addition to the public authorities there are two organizations devoted to the prevention of child abuse in Sweden: 'Rädda Barnen' distributes information and material, aids in opinion-forming activities, and functions through the Children's Ombudsman. The organization is also active in the developing countries. Yearly, about 150 child-abuse cases are reported to 'Rädda Barnen'.

BRIS (Children's Rights in the Society) was founded in 1971. BRIS works partly as a lobbyist to improve children's legal status and life conditions in Sweden. Annually, about 200 child abuse cases are reported to BRIS.

## A COMPARISON BETWEEN FINLAND AND SWEDEN

In an international perspective, the child protection legislation of Finland and Sweden is considered progressive, especially compared to the legislation in most of the Anglo-Saxon countries. Even so, there are some important differences between the legislation in the two countries. Child battering was considered a social problem in Sweden earlier than it was in Finland. This is evidenced by the considerably greater amount of publications on the subject in Sweden as mentioned above.

According to a 1981 survey, 47% of the Finns approved of corporal punishment at least in exceptional cases (Peltoniemi, 1983a). This opinion was shared by only 26% of the Swedes. This approval rate is considerably lower than in 1965: at that time, 53% of the Swedes approved of corporal punishment (SIFO, 1981). This declining support for corporal punishment has existed in Sweden for a longer period than in Finland even though the approval of corporal punishment has decreased in both countries.

The rapid development in public opinion and the accompanying view that a child is an independent individual whose inviolability must be respected provide insight into the banning of all corporal punishment and other ill-treatment of children in Sweden in 1979, and in Finland a few years later, in 1984.

According to the child-welfare legislation of Finland, the State may intervene if a child is assaulted at home or if his health, life, or morals is in danger. Each year, child welfare measures include over 8000 new cases. The number of reported cases of child abuse has increased from about 20 per year during the 1930s to over 100 per year during the 1970s. The number of cases of child neglect has increased from about 400 per year during the 1950s to over 1500 per year during the 1970s. The figure for 1978 corresponds to about 30 cases of child neglect per 100 000 inhabitants. However, the statistics alone do not indicate whether or not child abuse or neglect has actually increased. It may be that the statistics reflect the increasing resources available to the child welfare authorities and the easier detection of cases as a result of, for example, urbanization and the change in the attitudes of the general population.

During 1978, 1247 children were the subjects of child-welfare measures due to child abuse or child neglect in Sweden. The number of cases has steadily increased since the beginning of the 1970s. It is remarkable, however, that there are more cases of child abuse in

Finland than in Sweden, despite Finland's smaller population (1699 cases were reported in Finland during 1978). Even so, it is obvious that the number of reported cases reflects the praxis of the authorities rather than any real differences in incidence.

## LEGISLATION

### Finland

The Act of the Care and Visiting Rights of Children and an amendment of the Guardianship Act became effective in the beginning of 1984. The objective of the legislation is to allow more attention to the child's own needs, wishes, and interests when making decisions affecting the well-being of the child. The Act emphasizes the child's need for safety and care provided by the parents. This is reflected in a provision banning the use of corporal punishment: 'The child shall be raised in such a way that he receives understanding, safety, and affection. The child shall not be oppressed, corporally punished, or ill-treated in any way' (Savolainen *et al.*, 1981.)

Another objective of the law is to stress that the provider has no right to use corporal punishment when raising the child. The definition of petty assault is also being applied in cases where a child is hit on purpose.

The Penal Code of Finland includes three types of assault: petty assault, 'ordinary' assault, and aggravated assault. The penalty for petty assault is a fine; for ordinary assault, imprisonment for up to 2 years or a fine; and for aggravated assault, imprisonment for 6 months to 10 years.

When the Penal Code was amended in 1969, a section permitting corporal punishment of a child was repealed. In the public debate, this step was understood in two somewhat contradictory ways. One school of thought held that the repeal was not to be understood as a prohibition against reasonable corporal punishment, while the other school of thought advocated that the reform completely prohibited any corporal punishment of children.

In general, however, the reform has been interpreted to mean that corporal punishment is punishable if it meets the definition of petty assault. Thus, it can be argued that the present Penal Code does not *specifically* prohibit the corporal punishment of children. However, it is apparent that the reform was certainly not intended to extend the scope of permissible corporal punishment; it only removed the explicit right of parents to inflict corporal punishment from the Penal Code, thus depriving parents of legal justification.

## Sweden

A new section was added to the Swedish Parenthood and Guardianship Code in 1979, prohibiting corporal punishment: 'A child shall not be exposed to corporal punishment or any form of ill-treatment' (SOU 1978:10).

The Parenthood and Guardianship Code thus prohibits the inflicting of bodily injury or pain on a child. Hitting a child, pulling his hair, pinching him, etc., are prohibited even if the force used would be slight or the pain temporary. The reform is not to be understood as a prohibition against all use of force. For example, the use of force is acceptable to prevent a child from harming himself; a child can thus be forcibly removed from the vicinity of a hot stove.

A child is not to be exposed to any form of ill-treatment. Examples of such ill-treatment are the shutting of a child in a cupboard or closet, or threatening to leave a child.

The provisions in the Swedish Penal Code on assault are applicable to child-abuse cases. There are three forms of assault mentioned in the Code. 'Ordinary' assault is punishable by a maximum of 2 years' imprisonment. Petty assault may result in a fine. Aggravated assault leads to imprisonment for 1 to 10 years.

When the Parenthood and Guardianship Code was amended, no special sanctions were introduced for corporal punishment. Thus, in practice, minor acts of physical punishment will not lead to a sentence. This was done with the understanding that the investigation and court hearing of minor cases of punishment might in itself cause harm to the child.

## THE DATA

The Finnish data are part of a larger study of family violence (Peltoniemi, 1983b). The Helsinki cases were collected from the court records of assault cases during 1979. The Turku cases were gathered from court records and the records of the criminal police and the uniformed police covering 1977 to 1980. The Uppsala cases were gathered from the court records of assault cases from 1978 to

1980. Finally, the Stockholm cases were gathered by sending a letter to the judges of the courts, asking them for copies of child abuse cases. The letters resulted in data on only 3 child abuse cases over a 5 month period, despite the fact that some 25–35 cases are reported to the Stockholm police each year. All of these cases, however, are not brought to court.

Most of the cases involved inter-spouse violence. Of all the family violence cases in Helsinki, Turku, and Uppsala 8% involved violence directed at a child. In 8 cases (4%) both an adult and a child were assaulted. These two types of assault appear to form a distinct group. Peltoniemi (1980, 1981) reports similar results from studies carried out on Finnish shelters and the cases reported to the police.

There were 7 child abuse cases in Helsinki, 17 in Turku, 2 in Uppsala, and 3 in Stockholm. Totally, the 29 court cases of child abuse involved 30 victims and 30 offenders: one case in Turku had 2 children as victims, and another case in Turku had 2 offenders.

## THE OFFENCE, THE OFFENDERS, AND THE VICTIMS

In general, the court cases did not involve exceptional violence. Two cases led to fractures and one to a burn. The most common forms of violence were slapping or the pulling of hair. The most common injury (15 cases) was a bruise. In most of the other cases, the injury was even slighter.

The cases involving a father and child were the most typical (17). There were 5 such cases in Helsinki, 11 in Turku, and one each in Stockholm and Uppsala. There were 5 cases involving a mother and a child. There were 7 cases where the offender was the mother's boyfriend or common-law spouse.

The average age of the offenders was 35 years in Helsinki and Turku and 34 years in Stockholm and Uppsala. The youngest offender was 23 years old, the oldest 60 years old. The average age of the victims was 10 years in Helsinki and Turku and 5 years in Stockholm and Uppsala. The youngest victim was 1-year-old and the oldest was 15 (the cut-off point of the data). A study of child abuse cases dealt with in Aurora Hospital in Finland revealed an average age of 5 years (Santasalo and Santasalo, 1979).

In the majority of cases (84%), the offender was a man. This was true of all of the Helsinki cases. In Turku, there were 16 male offenders and 2 female offenders. In Sweden, there were 2 male offenders and 3 female offenders. The victims were roughly equally distributed as to sex: 52% were boys and 48% were girls. The Swedish victims included 3 boys and 2 girls.

There does not appear to be any correlation between the sex of the offender and of the victim. The strong dominance of men in the data (84%) is rather surprising in light of the results of some foreign studies. These studies indicate that men are offenders more often than women (see Maden and Wrench, 1977), but the prevalence of male abusers was not as great. According to Santasalo and Santasalo (1979), 59% of the abusers in Helsinki were men and 41% were women. A Swedish study (Partanen, 1981) placed the share of women at 75%. It is possible that the strong dominance of men in the present study is due to the source of the data; perhaps the child-abuse cases handled by the social welfare and health authorities are different, and primarily cases involving male offenders are selected for court action.

In the Swedish cases, three out of five involved an immigrant family. Two families were Turkish and one was Greek. Similar overrepresentation of immigrants in child abuse families has been reported by Bergstrand *et al.* (1976) as well as Partanen (1981) in Sweden. Only one case in the Finnish data involved a non-Scandinavian family.

There was a strong concentration of abusers belonging to the lower social strata. Santasalo and Santasalo (1979) reported similar results in Finland, and observed that the offenders were largely unskilled workers. The same was shown in Partanen's study (1981) in Sweden. These findings are similar to those of many foreign studies (see Maden and Wrench, 1977). However, it must be kept in mind that the reported cases may not give a representative picture of reality: it may be that child abuse in upper-class families more seldom comes to the attention of a hospital or a court.

## THE CHILD ABUSE SITUATION

In general, the child abuse took place at home. Only three cases took place elsewhere. Usually there were other persons present in addition to the offender and the victim: this was true of two-thirds of the cases.

This 'outside person' was usually the other parent or a sibling who often tried to intervene in the situation, for example, by preventing the abuse or by sending someone to get help.

The offenders' use of alcohol often influenced the initiation of the abuse. A drunken offender often loses his temper and hits the child. The offender was drunk in every other case. There were six drunken offenders in the Helsinki data, eight in Turku, and one in Sweden. However, the role of alcohol in this study is less prominent than what has been found in family violence studies in general (see, e.g. Peltoniemi, 1982). In the Finnish study carried out by Santasalo and Santasalo (1979), the offender was drunk in 68% of the cases. The corresponding figure for the Swedish study undertaken by Partanen (1981) was 73%.

## THE BACKGROUND OF THE CHILD ABUSE SITUATION

There were a variety of underlying problems in the child abuse cases. Problems at work, quarrels between the spouses, and the children's misbehaviour were cited. Some of the offenses were intentional while others seemed more accidental. Commonly, corporal punishment and child abuse were mixed. Table 9.1 summarizes the motives cited in the cases.

Table 9.1 The Motive for Child Abuse Cases in Helsinki, Turku, Uppsala, and Stockholm

| | *Helsinki 1979* | *Turku 1977–80* | *Uppsala and Stockholm 1978–80* | *Total* |
|---|---|---|---|---|
| Corporal punishment | 2 | 8 | 4 | 14 |
| Loss of temper | 1 | 3 | 1 | 5 |
| Protection | 2 | 2 | – | 4 |
| Sexual motive | 1 | 1 | – | 2 |
| Accident | – | 1 | – | 1 |
| Other reason | 1 | 2 | – | 3 |
| Total | 7 | 17 | 5 | 29 |

## CORPORAL PUNISHMENT

Nearly half of the child abuse cases (14) began or were carried out as corporal punishment. This group of motives was also emphasized in the Finnish study by Santasalo and Santasalo (1979). Corporal punishment was accepted as a method of raising children, and the offenders did not believe themselves to be guilty of an offence:

> I only hit him to teach him. I know that the boy has done all kinds of bad things which his mother and I so far have chosen to ignore.

The mother in one case thought that the father was guilty of child abuse 'because such things go beyond normal corporal punishment, which is part of raising a child' (Turku).

According to a survey, 68% of the Finnish population have themselves experienced corporal punishment as children (Peltoniemi, 1983a). This is also reflected in the offender's attitudes and in the motives cited:

> I emphatically deny that it was a question of assault; as far as I can see, it was quite normal corporal punishment, which has long been used in raising children in Finland. Compared with the old-fashioned corporal punishment that I received as a child, this was almost nothing.
>
> (Turku)

The line between child abuse and corporal punishment is not clear. It could have been that the purpose of the offender was to punish the child, but his anger led him to treat the child more severely than he intended:

> It wasn't my purpose to start assaulting the boy; I was carried away by temporary anger. I didn't mean to give any further punishment, just talk the matter over.
>
> (Turku)

In general, corporal punishment was regarded as an effective way of raising children. An extreme example of this is the case where the father decided to beat up his son so that the boy would stop beating up other people:

I thought that once my son is given a proper beating and feels pain, he might learn.

(Turku)

## OTHER REASONS

In five cases, it is difficult to understand the abuse other than as the result of a loss of temper. In these cases, the incident began as a quarrel between adults.

In four cases, the child was beaten in connection with quarrels between adults when the child tried to help the other parent. In one case, the child was hit by accident in connection with a fight between spouses.

The data included two sexual abuse cases. In three other cases, it was difficult to determine the motive.

## THE COMPLAINANT

Most often, the mother reported the case to the police (11 cases). In three cases the abuse was reported by a relative. The abused child reported the incident in two cases. In one case, the mother had urged the child to report. Neighbours or eye-witnesses reported three of the cases:

> The mother beat her four-year-old son in a store when the child had been naughty and asked for candy. Two women who saw what happened followed the mother home and then reported to the police.
>
> (Stockholm)

In two cases, the matter was reported by a physician, in one by the child welfare board, and in three by the police. In four cases, the reporter is not identified.

## THE CHARGE

In every other case (15), the offender was charged with 'ordinary' assault (Table 9.2). In two cases, the charge was petty assault. One of these cases involved a father who had thrown his child against a cupboard, and the other involved a father who had slapped his child in the face – the child was not yet 2-years-old.

Table 9.2    The Charge in the Child Abuse Cases in Helsinki, Turku, Uppsala, and Stockholm

|  | Helsinki 1979 | Turku 1977–80 | Uppsala and Stockholm 1978–80 | Total |
|---|---|---|---|---|
| Petty assault | 1 | 1 | – | 2 |
| Assault | 3 | 7 | 5 | 15 |
| Deprivation of liberty | – | 1 | – | 1 |
| Kidnapping | 1 | – | – | 1 |
| Sexual abuse | 1 | 1 | – | 2 |
| Charge withdrawn | – | 1 | – | 1 |
| No charge | 1 | 4 | – | 5 |
| No data available | – | 2 | – | 2 |
| Total | 7 | 17 | 5 | 29 |

A father who tied his daughter to the foot of a bed in order to teach her a lesson was charged with deprivation of freedom. There were also two sexual offenders.

In one case where the charges were withdrawn the reason was the death of the offender. In five cases, no charges were laid, because of lack of evidence. The problems inherent in these cases are demonstrated by the case in Finland involving a foreign-born person in an academic profession suspected of abusing his sons. According to a physician's records, there were repeated 'signs of external injuries' on the children. The physician who observed the injuries strongly demanded that the father be prosecuted. The physician also reported the case to the prosecutor. The father, however, explained that the injuries were caused by the children's strenuous play. As other witnesses testified that the father treated his children well, the prosecutor decided that there was no evidence of assault.

## THE VERDICT AND THE SENTENCE

There does not seem to be any discrepancy between the charges and the final verdict of the court. In one case where a father was charged with slapping his 2-year-old child the judge did not find sufficient evidence for conviction. One case in Sweden was appealed in the Court of Appeals. This case involved an immigrant mother who allegedly had burned her 3-year-old on the arm, hand, and buttocks with a hot knife. The lower court rejected the assault charge, but the Court of Appeal found her guilty and placed her on probation. In all other cases, the offender was found guilty in accordance with the charge.

In one case, the court waived punishment. The offender had thrown his girlfriend's child on the floor and pulled the child's hair, tearing some out in the process. The court declared that the offence was slight and that 'the act, with due regard to the circumstances was pardonable and due to thoughtlessness, and that the public interest did not call for a sentence'.

The most common penalty was the imposition of a fine. There were 4 such fines in Helsinki, 6 in Turku, and 1 in Sweden. The fines ranged from 160 to 880 Marks. The lowest fine was set for a father who had slapped his daughter and thrown her against the edge of a bathtub. The highest fine was given an offender who had beaten her son with a belt buckle so severely that the boy had to be taken to the hospital for 3 days. Four offenders were sentenced to jail, and six were sentenced to parole. The sentences of imprisonment varied from 1 to 7 months, and the average term was 3 months (Table 9.3).

## DISCUSSION

A comparison of the data on child abuse in Finland and Sweden provides a picture of many parallels. The differences today are especially evident in the attitudes toward corporal punishment, but also in the attitudes toward assault. In 1981, as many as 47% of the Finns, but only 26% of the Swedes supported corporal punishment of children.

A direct comparison of the sentences given in child abuse cases is difficult because of the small number of Swedish cases. The Finnish cases were usually petty offences that started out as corporal punishment. The Swedish cases were closer to what can be called 'typical'

Table 9.3  Probationary and Unconditional Imprisonment Sentences Given in Child Abuse Cases in Helsinki, Turku, Uppsala, and Stockholm

| Case | Description | Offence | Sentence |
|---|---|---|---|
| Turku | A father tied his teenage daughter to the foot af a bed | deprivation of freedom | probationary imprisonment for 1 month |
| | A father slapped his 14 year-old son in the face and attempted to strangle him | assault | probationary imprisonment for 2 months plus 800 marks in day-fines |
| | A father whipped his 10 year-old son with an electric cable | assault | probationary imprisonment for 1 month |
| | A father impregnated his daughter | unchastity with a child and incest | unconditional imprisonment for 1 year and 10 months |
| Helsinki | A father abused his 13-year-old daughter sexually and assaulted her with his fist and by spanking her | assault and aggravated unchastity with a child | unconditional imprisonment for 4 years and 8 months |
| | A father kidnapped his 3-year-old son | kidnapping | probationary imprisonment for 7 months |
| Sweden | A common-law spouse assaulted a 4-year-old boy by tearing his hair and hitting him | assault | probation* |
| | A mother slapped her 4-year-old child for being naughty | assault | probation |

| A mother burned her 3-year-old daughter's arm and buttocks with a hot knife | assault | Charges rejected by the lower court but the Court of Appeal sentenced her to probation for 1 year and 6 months |
| A father spanked his 10-year-old daughter and hit her head against the wall | assault (against the child) and aggravated assault (against the mother) | Probationary imprisonment for 1 year and 6 months |

*In Sweden, the probationary sentence (villkorlig dom) does not establish the actual length of the sentence. The sentence is for a trial period of 2 years.

child abuse cases. There were also slight differences in the sex distribution: in Finland, the offender was usually the father, but in Sweden, the mother was more often the abuser.

The legal systems in Finland and Sweden appear to differ primarily in respect to what is considered the most important element: the society, the family, or the child. In Sweden, the interests of the child have received strong emphasis, while in Finland, the emphasis has been on the family. The relative lack of data makes it difficult to evaluate whether this difference in emphasis parallels the attitudes towards corporal punishment, or is rooted in more basic ideological differences between Finland and Sweden.

In half the cases the offender claimed that he was only using well-deserved corporal punishment. In general, corporal punishment and child abuse can be seen as different degrees of the same phenomenon. This lack of distinct definition of the difference is also reflected in the attitudes of the general population. The hazy borderline between corporal punishment and child abuse can be clarified – at least to some extent – by legislation, as the development of changed attitudes towards corporal punishment in Finland and Sweden shows. The legislation must – of course – be customized to fit the cultural climate of the society.

## Note

* This is the revised version of a research report presented at the Fourth International Congress on Child Abuse and Neglect in Paris, 6–11 Sept, 1982. Ms Korpilahti's research was supported by a grant from the National Swedish Council for Crime Prevention and the Finnish Research Institute of Legal Policy.

## References

Bergstrand, C. G. and Forslund, M. and Stibner, I–B, (1976) 'Barnmisshandelsfall in Malmö 1967–1974' (Child Abuse Cases in Malmö, 1967–1974), (Läkartidningen, Stockholm) vol.73(33), pp.2671–7.

Kempe, Ruth and Kempe, C. Henry (1980), *Child Abuse* (London: Fontana, 1980).

Korpilahti, Marja (1981), *Barnmisshandel i Finland och Sverige* (Child Abuse in Finland and Sweden), Research Institute of Legal Policy, publication no.50 (Helsinki).

Lagerberg, Dagmar (1982), *Du skall icke slö. Om fysisk och psykisk misshandel av barn* (Do Not Hit the Child. About physical and psychological child abuse) (Liber, Helsingborg).

Maden, Marc F. and Wrench, David F, (1977), 'Significant Findings in Child Abuse Research', *Victimology*, vol.2(2), pp.196–224.

Mannerheim League for Child Welfare (1974), *Lasten pahoinpitely* (Child Abuse), Report A18 (Espoo, 1974).

Partanen, Pirjo (1981) *Skadlig behandling av bar i Botkyrka kommun, 1975 och 1979* (Ill-treatment of Children in Municipality of Botkyrka, 1975 and 1979), mimeograph (Institute of Sociology, University of Stockholm).

Peltoniemi, Teuvo (1980), 'Family violence: Police House Calls in Helsinki, Finland in 1977', *Victimology*, vol.5(2-4), pp.213–224.

Peltoniemi, Teuvo (1981), 'The First 12 months of the Finnish Shelters', *Victimology*, vol.6(1–4), pp.198–211.

Peltoniemi, Teuvo (1982), 'Alcohol and Family Violence' in *28th International Institute on the Prevention and Treatment of Alcoholism, Munchen 5–9, 7,1982*, Proceedings, International Council on Alcohol and Alcoholism, pp.562–76 (Lausanne).

Peltoniemi, Teuvo (1983a), 'Child Abuse and Physical Punishment of Children in Finland', *Child Abuse and Neglect*, vol.7(1), pp.33–6.

Peltoniemi, Teuvo (1983b), Familjevald i Finland och Sverige – omfattning och attityder (English Summary: Family Violence in Finland and Sweden – Prevalence and Attitudes), Research Institute of Legal Policy, publication no. 5 (Helsinki).

Peltoniemi, Teuvo and Honkavaara, Pirjo (1981), *A Bibliography of Family Violence and Child Battering* (Helsinki: Central Union for Child Welfare in Finland, 1981).

Pierre, Birgitta (1971), *Det misshandlade barnet* (The battered child) (Zindermans, Halmstad).

Pru-Gruppen (1979) *Vilsebarn i välfärdsland* (A lost child in the welfare society) (Stockholm – Helsingborg 1979).

Santasalo, Maija and Santasalo, Martti, Liber, (1979), *Lasten pahoinpitelyn tausta* (The Background of Child Battering), Mannerheim League for Child Welfare, publication no.B36 (Helsinki).

Savolainen, Matti and Cantell, Ilkka and Halminen-Kauranen, Ritva and Jaakkola, Risto (1981), (Proposal of the working group on the reform of guardianship legislation). Ministry of Justice Law Drafting Department publication no.4/1981 (Helsinki).

SIFO (1981) (Corporal Punishment of Children and Child Battering) (Mimeograph) (Stockholm).

Socialstyrelsen (1969), *En utredning om barnmisshandel* (A Report about Child Abuse) (Stockholm: The National Board of Social Welfare).

Socialsytrelsen (1975), *Barnsom far illa: En undersökning om barnmisshandel och skadlig uppväxtmiljö (ill-treated children)*. A Study of Child Abuse and Harmful Neighbourhood). Stockholm: The National Board of Social Welfare.

SOU 1978:10 (1978) *Barnets ratt 1. Om förbud mot aga* (The Rights of the Child, 1. Regarding the Prohibition of Corporal Punishment)(Official Government Reports (Stockholm).

Taskinen, Sirpa (1982), *Lasten pahoinpitely ja hoidon laimnnlyonti* (Child Abuse and Neglect). The National Board of Social Welfare, Publication 1. (Helsinki).

Tornudd, Margit (1948) '*Misshandel av barn*' (Child Battering), *Barnavard och ungdomsskydd*, vol.23, (Helsinki) pp.18–21.

# Part III

# On Response to, and Consequences of, Victimization

# 10 Victim–Offender Dynamics in Stranger to Stranger Violence: Robbery and Rape

Richard Block

## THE CRIMINAL EVENT

Violent crime like most social behaviour involves at least two actors and their interaction. The target of violent crime is the intended victim. Not all targets become victims. Many do not. Offenders are those who intend to commit a crime. While target and offender can be clearly differentiated in stranger-to-stranger robbery and rape, in many violent crimes, especially assaults, it is difficult to tell the target from the offender. Target–offender interaction is the sequence of resistance and attack occurring during a crime event. This triad, target, offender, and their interaction, together with its setting will be called the crime event.[1]

The crime event is one incident surrounded by social relationships, physical structures, neighbourhoods and communities, ideas of violence, self-defence, social class, and segregation. The two actos, target and offender, interact with and are affected by these structures, but they retain individuality; their behaviour can never be fully predicted.

The outcome of the crime event is often affected by the interaction of target and offender. Outcome affects the target's decision to call on the criminal justice system, and the decisions of the police and court to process and prosecute the crime event. The criminal event and its interaction are the sparks that light the entire criminal processing system. These relationships are outlined in Fig.10.1.

The environment of the crime event is the physical, social, and economic structure of the community in which it occurs. Some communities are structured with a wide availability of targets for criminal attack. There may be tourists in one neighbourhood or many

231

History and culture

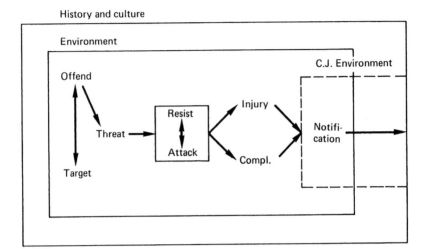

Fig.10.1    *The Violent Crime Event*

homes which are unoccupied during the daytime in another. Other neighbourhoods may have fewer obvious targets. Some communities have many opportunities for legitimate behaviour; others have few. Some communities may expose potential targets to many risks. Others may expose them to few risks. The environment of criminal behaviour is also the immediate network of events and structures surrounding the crime. It is the relationship of target and offender, relative, known, or stranger. It is the location of a crime, at home, in a bar, or on the street.

As can be seen in Fig. 10.1, the environments of crime and the criminal justice system overlap. Still, they are not congruent. Much of the environment of crime is largely irrelevant to the criminal justice system and the criminal processing environment has little effect on criminal behaviour. Much of the criminal justice system's environment is defined by structural capabilities and capacities – how many cases and what types can it handle.

If this model is correct, research which uses data gathered by the criminal justice system to analyse victimization may be greatly distorted as also may be victim surveys of the criminal justice system. The perspective of the victim and offender is lost in the environment of the police. While victims may react to police treatment, they have little knowledge of the constraints on police work.

Within its environment the crime event is the initiator of outcomes and actions. Thus, the interaction of target and offender largely determine whether the crime is a rape or an attempt and often determines the seriousness of injuries. To a large extent, the outcome of a violent crime predicts whether or not the police will be notified. It is generally believed that the police are far more likely to be notified of a homicide than an assault (Zimring *et al.*, 1976). They are more likely to be notified of a completed robbery than an attempt (Block and Block, 1981; Skogan, 1981). Notification is the bridge between the victim and the criminal justice system. Factors which influence the decision to inform the police of a crime, degree of injury, or outcome, are also factors which affect the police decision to investigate.

Given the importance of the crime event for its target, it is unsurprising that much of the early research in victimology was concerned with victim–offender interaction. Once the study of victims went beyond descriptions of the spatial and demographic depiction of events the first topics addressed were victim–offender relationship and the victim as a generator of victimization (von Hentig, 1948: Mendelsohn, 1956). Mendelsohn developed a typology of six types of victims, varying from those who were more guilty than the offender and those who were solely guilty to those who were guiltless (Schafer, 1977). Von Hentig also developed a typology of victims and discussed a victim–offender duet (1948). Wolfgang and his students carried on this tradition in studies of various categories of crime (Wolfgang, 1958; Normandeau, 1968).

These studies utilized police and court records. Thus, victim-precipitated homicides or rapes were those perceived that way by the police, courts, medical examiner, or coroner. The data greatly affected theses studying the data source. Before a crime is officially recorded, it must pass through several filters. If these filters randomly select events, then descriptions from police records should be quite similar to those from victim surveys. However, the crimes that are reported to the police are not a random sample of all crimes. First, the victim or observer must decide that the benefits of reporting or the moral imperative are sufficiently great to require police notification. Then, the police must decide that they have the resources and interest to respond to the crime.

As I have shown, both target and police decisions are affected by the crime event, especially its outcome (Block and Block, 1980). Crimes which succeed are more likely to be reported to the police than attempts. The criminal justice system records far different events than do surveys of victims, and the outcome of crime as reported in victim surveys is far different than that reported in official records. Criminal Justice system records are highly appropriate to study the effect of victim characteristics or victim–offender dynamics on police, prosecution, and court decisions (see Williams, 1978). They are not appropriate to study the background of criminal events, the relationship of target and offender, or the dynamics of their interaction. To study these, knowledge of the victim's perspective and environment is most appropriate. These can only be collected through a victim survey.

## AN EXAMPLE, ROBBERY AND RAPE

For this presentation, I will analyse stranger to stranger robbery and rape as examples of victim–offender interaction in violent crime. These motivated but seemingly random confrontations are among the most feared of crimes in modern societies. In 1980, 550 000 robberies and 82 000 rapes were recorded in the Uniform Crime Reports (UCR) (p.41) in the United States. However, the police were not told of many robberies and rapes and did not record others.

The National Crime Survey (NCS) was designed as an alternative measure of crime which could describe and estimate the dark figure of crimes not recorded by the police. Rape: forced sexual intercourse; and robbery: theft by force or threat of force, are two crimes which the NCS was designed to count and describe.[2]

The data for this report are taken from the continuing NCS panel survey of a random sample of the US population. It is not based upon police reports. While the NCS panel is massive with more than 135 000 interviews each 6 months, and its published reports estimate large numbers of crime, robbery and rape are relatively rare phenomena. The actual number of these crimes detected by the NCS is not large. Consolidating 7 years of the NCS (1973–79), 4270 stranger-to-stranger robbery events and 503 stranger-to-stranger rape events were recorded.[3] These are the data analysed in this chapter.

Analysis of the NCS permits description of crimes in far more detail than the UCR which, except for homicides, is based upon police summary statistics rather than reports of individual crimes.

Using the NCS, we can study details of target and offender characteristics and the dynamics of the crime event with far more specificity than using data collected for the UCR.

Some robbery and rape events are not included in the analysis. Fatal violence is obviously excluded by the method of the victim survey, which did not have a technique for interviewing the dead. Most commercial crimes including robberies of stores and banks are also excluded from the NCS panel survey. In addition, we have excluded robbery and rape events in which the victim was acquainted with or at least recognized the offender. Previous research has shown that these may not be as well reported as stranger-to-stranger violence. Our own preliminary analysis indicates that non-stranger robbery and rape were different from stranger-to-stranger crimes.

While there are many similarities between robbery and rape events, there are also important differences.[4] Most important of these is the object of the crime. The object of most robbery events is money or valuables, not injury to the victim. The object of most rape events is the target herself. Thus a completed robbery need not include attack or injury to the victim. The rapist's success requires attack. A victim might hope to avoid injury by giving in to the robber's demands. The woman who gives in to the rapist's demands is, by definition attacked, and can only hope to avoid additional injuries.

Summarizing, the purpose of this example is to describe and analyse non-fatal robbery and rape events from the target's perspective. We will examine the dynamic of target–offender interaction – the inter-relationship between the offender's attack and the target's resistance. We will consider this interaction outcome as measured by the crime's completion and the injuries sustained by the target. Finally, we will picture the interrelationship of the crime's outcome, the target's resistance, and notification of the police.

At least three important limitations of this data set prohibit definitive conclusions. Most importantly, we cannot analyse robbery and rape events which end in the death of the target. This most serious outcome of criminal violence remains undescribed. Previous research based upon police records indicates that there may be significant differences between fatal and non-fatal crimes. Secondly, targets were not asked to sequence the crime event. The researcher cannot know if resistance followed attack or attack followed resistance. Thirdly, while it is presumed that almost every robbery or rape must begin with some threat, only targets who were not physically attacked are asked how they were threatened. In a crime which included both threats and attacks, we would only know of the attacks.

## DYNAMIC CHARACTERISTICS OF ROBBERY AND RAPE

### Threat

Almost all stranger-to-stranger violence begins with a threat. While in many cases the data does not allow analysis of this threat, all targets were asked whether or not the offender had a gun, a knife, or some other weapon during the confrontation. Most did not. Half of the robbers were not armed as were 70% of the rapists. Of the confrontations with weapons, guns and knives were equally likely to be present. Other weapons, such as clubs, were less likely to be present. A few crimes involved the presence of more than one weapon.

The robber's weapon choice is apparently related to a perception of the target's potential strengths. While women were only slightly less likely to be robbed with a gun than men, teenagers (13% gun presence) and targets over 60 (16% gun presence) were less likely to be threatened with a gun than persons 20–59 (25%). Whites (18%) were much less likely to be confronted with a gun than blacks (31%). This may mean that offenders believe black targets are more likely to be armed than white targets, or, as some criminologists believe, acts which approximate robbery are so common in some black neighbourhoods, that only the more serious ones are likely to be remembered and reported to the interviewer.

The rapist's weapon choice is less strongly related to characteristics of the target. Most importantly, because there is much less variation in target characteristics. Most rape targets are quite young. Most are confronted while alone, and all are women. As in robbery, rapists of black women were much more likely to confront their target with a gun (33%) then were those of white women (9%).

Fortunately, the weapons that were present were rarely used. For both crimes, a gun was fired in only about 10% of the incidents in which they were present. A knife was used in 17% of the robberies where it was present and 8% of the rapes. Given the small percentage of crimes which included the presence of a knife or gun, the actual use of gun or knife is rare. The actual use of a gun was involved in 7% of robberies and 3% of rapes, including both those that hit or missed the target. A far greater percentage of targets were attacked in some other way; 53% of robberies and 65% of rape targets were physically attacked. The remainder were only threatened. As in many other studies of robbery, there is a strong relationship between an offender's weapon choice and the likelihood the target will be attacked. The target was physically attacked in 28% of the robberies in which a gun was present and 40% of those in which the offender had a knife. However, the target was attacked in 67% of the robberies without a weapon. Apparently, the offender's threat in a weaponless robbery often includes a physical attack. Further, as we shall demonstrate, the robber's weapon choice is strongly related to the target's decision to resist. A gun is such an efficient threat that few targets resist, and, therefore, the robber is less frequently required to attack the target to gain compliance.

**Resistance**

Most targets of robbery (55.5%) and rape (83.2%) resist. However, rape targets are much more likely to resist than robbery targets. For this analysis, we define two forms of resistance, non-forcible and forcible. Non-forcible resistance includes reasoning or verbally threatening the offender, yelling for help, or running away. Forcible resistance include physical attack with or without a weapon. Robbery targets were only slightly more likely to use non-forcible than forcible resistance (30% vs. 25%). Among rape targets, non-forcible resistance is much more common (51%) than forcible resistance (32%).

The target's decision to resist a robber is related to both the target's age and sex. From the twenties to old age, the percentage of targets who do not resist increases linearly from 37% to 64%. Of those who do resist, the percentage who resist forcibly declines with age from 51% among targets in their twenties to 29% of those who are older than seventy.

Blacks were less likely to resist a robber than whites; 58% of blacks offered no resistance as compared to 41% of whites. Blacks, however, were more likely to be robbed with a gun than whites, and fewer people are willing to resist a gun threat than one with another weapon. Still, holding constant the offender's weapon threat, blacks remain less likely to resist than whites; 36% of white targets and 28% of black targets of gun robberies resisted.

A woman's decision to resist a rape is related to the environment of the crime. Women who were confronted at home were less likely to resist than other women. The target's age was less strongly related to resistance to rape than to robbery. Black women were less likely to resist a rapist (30%) than were white women (14%). Part, but not all, of this difference is related to the far greater likelihood that a black woman will be attacked with a gun. However, regardless of the offender's choice of weapon, black women are less likely to resist than white women.

By resisting, the target hopes to foil the offender's attack. In the next sections, we consider the offender's likelihood of success, the target's risk of injury, and their relationship to resistance.

## THE OUTCOME OF ROBBERY AND RAPE EVENTS

Many of the possible effects of stranger-to-stranger violence are not measured by the NCS. Rape and robbery may have long term psychological and social consequences which go wholly unmeasured in the victim survey. The rape victim may lose trust in all men – the robbery victim may move or change jobs to prevent future crimes. These long term consequences and death of the target are unmeasured in the NCS. The survey measures short term physical and economic outcomes of crimes. Was something stolen? How much was the loss? Was the victim injured? Was medical attention required?

Of all robbery events 60% resulted in property loss. If anything was stolen, the median dollar loss was $30. About half of all rape attempts were completed. While most women who were robbed were not raped, the two crimes overlap. In almost all rape events during which the woman was robbed, she was also raped. However, most women who were raped were not robbed.

About one-third of the robbery targets and one-half of the rape targets were injured. Of the injured rape targets, 56% suffered some injury in addition to rape. Of those who were injured, 39% of robbery targets and 48% of rape targets required some medical attention; however, in both cases, less than 10% of the injured required an overnight hospital stay. Thus, while some injury is likely in these crimes, the risk of serious injury is not high. *Remember, that crimes with fatal outcomes are excluded from analysis.*

These outcomes are not random events. They are related to characteristics of the target(s) and offender(s) and to the environment of the crime. More importantly, they are related to the interaction – the dynamics of target and offender during the crime event.

## RESISTANCE, INJURY, AND COMPLETION

### Robbery

The object of most robberies is the target's property. The single factor which most affects the robber's chance for success is the target's resistance (Table 10.1).[5] Something is stolen from 85% of the targets who do not resist, but from only 43% of the targets who resist non-forcibly and 37% of those who forcibly resist. The average non-resisting target loses $58. The average non-forcible resister loses $19, and the average forcible resister loses $14. Thus, resistance greatly affects the probability a robbery will succeed, but the type of resistance has a much smaller effect.

Table 10.1  Robbery: Target's Resistance and Outcome

| | N | % attacked | % injured | % overnight hospital | % something stolen |
|---|---|---|---|---|---|
| No resistance | 1915 | 47.1 | 29.8 | 3.3 | 84.7 |
| Non-forceful resistance | 1278 | 48.2 | 29.1 | 1.7 | 42.5 |
| Forceful resistance | 1076 | 69.21 | 44.1 | 6.8 | 36.8 |

Non-forcible resistance has little effect on the probability a target will be attacked or injured during a robbery. Forcible resistance is strongly related to the probability that the target will be attacked and injured and to the probability that the injury will be serious enough to require hospitalization. However, from the data available, it is not possible to determine whether forcible resistance provoked the robber's physical attack or the robber's attack resulted in the target's decision to resist. Thus, it is not possible to analyse forcible and nonforcible resistance tactics as if they were alternatives in similar situations. They probably were not.

While not included in the current analysis, non-forcible resisters were more likely to be injured than non-resisters in robberies with a weapon. However, they were less likely to be injured than forcible resisters.

Figure 10.2 illustrates the interrelationship of resistance, injury, and property loss during robbery events. The figure is a three-dimensional diagram of the frequency of events with particular characteristics. The horizontal dimension represents the target's resistance. The vertical dimension is the degree of injury. The height of each column represents the number of cases with each combination of injury and resistance. The shaded area of each column represents the number of events in which property was lost.

The most common scenario for a robbery event is loss of property without injury or resistance. Resistance, with or without force, decreases the likelihood that something will be stolen, but forcible resistance is associated with an increased risk of serious injury.

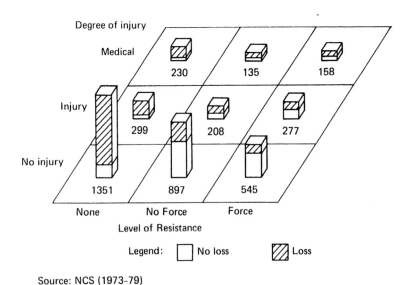

Source: NCS (1973-79)

Fig.10.2    *Frequency Block Chart*

Remember, however, that the sequence of forcible resistance and attack is not clear in the victim survey. It is possible that many people who forcibly resisted did so because they were being forcibly attacked.

## Rape

While the dynamics of target–offender interaction in rape are in some ways quite similar to those just described for robbery, they are in other ways, quite different. The usual object of robbery is property. A successful robbery does not require attack. The object of rape is the target herself. Rape requires a physical assault. A woman who successfully resists a rapist may still be attacked or injured, but a woman who is raped can only hope to avoid further injury or attack.

Table 10.2   Rape: Target's Resistance and Outcome

| | N | %<br>attacked | %<br>raped | %<br>injured | %<br>something<br>stolen |
|---|---|---|---|---|---|
| No resistance | 85 | 69.1 | 57.7 | 30.4 | 31.4 |
| Non-forceful resistance | 257 | 52.1 | 19.2 | 27.1 | 14.8 |
| Forceful resistance | 162 | 84.5 | 32.7 | 54.4 | 10.5 |

Table 10.2 and Fig. 10.3 examine the relationship between resistance and crime outcome for rape. While resistance to rape is more likely than resistance to robbery, the overall relationship between resistance and completion is the same. Women who resist their confronter, either forcibly or non-forcibly, are less likely to be raped than women who offer no resistance. However, only 58% of women who do not resist are raped as compared to nearly 90% of non-resisted robberies which are completed. Perhaps, a third party intervened to stop the crime, or, perhaps, the lack of clarity in the NCS questions on rape allowed some women to define an act as attempted rape which other women did not. The reasons for the failures of these attempted rapes with no resistance cannot be analysed using the NCS.

Women who resisted without force were least likely to be raped and non-forcible resistance had little effect on the risk of other injury.

Both forms of resistance reduced the probability that a woman would be robbed during a rape attempt. However, women who forcibly resisted were 24% more likely than those who offered no resistance to be injured. As with robbery, the direction of this relationship can not be examined in the NCS.

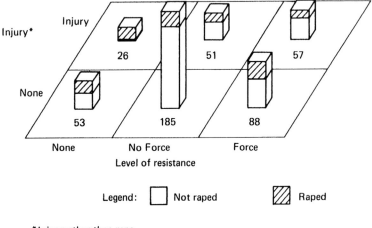

Injury*

Injury

None

26    51    57

53    185    88

None    No Force    Force

Level of resistance

Legend:    ☐ Not raped    ▨ Raped

*Injury other than rape

Fig.10.3   *Frequency Block Chart*

Figure 10.3 portrays the interrelationship of resistance, rape, and other injuries. Similar to Fig. 10.2, the horizontal dimension represents resistance, the vertical dimension injury other than rape, and the shading of columns represents the number of women who were raped.

If we consider completion of the rape plus other injuries to be the worst outcome of the event and failure of the attack and no injury to be the most favourable outcome from the victim's viewpoint, then non-resistance has the highest probability of the worst outcome. Non-forcible resistance has the highest likelihood of the most favourable outcome; 19% of women who non-forcibly resisted were raped and 27% were injured.

Overall, resistance seemed to reduce the likelihood of negative outcomes of a rape event. Women who resisted nonforcibly were less likely to be raped, attacked, injured, or robbed. Women who resisted forcibly were more likely to be attacked and injured, but less likely to be raped than women who did not resist. The probability of injury is higher for forcible resisters than non resisters. The reduction in probability of rape is much less than for non-forcible resisters. However, the sequence of forcible resistance, injury, and rape is not clear in the NCS. Forcible resistance may be a woman's last desperate attempt to stop a rape, or it may be a provocation to further attack and injury. Such attacks are excluded from our analysis.

The NCS does not allow analysis of the sequence of attack and resistance. Without knowledge of this sequence in non-fatal attacks, or any knowledge of resistance in fatal attack, it is not possible to recommend actions to the woman who is threatened with rape, except to say, non-forcible resistance is, where possible, a good tactic.

## NOTIFICATION, RESISTANCE, AND OUTCOME

As Fig. 10.1 indicates, the two factors that most affect the decision to notify the police are the level of injury to the victim and the crime's completion.[6] Figures 10.4 and 10.5 picture these relationships. As we saw in Fig. 10.2, loss without injury is the most common outcome of a robbery event. These crimes are more likely to be reported than those without loss, but less likely to be reported than those with injury. In robbery events, injury and loss seem to be independent positive determinants of police notification. Those rape events with neither rape nor other injury are most common, but they are the least likely to be reported to the police. However, women who are both raped and injured are less likely to notify the police than those who are either injured or raped.

The relationship between resistance and police notification is only indirect, through the effect of resistance on the outcome of crime. As we have shown, crimes during which the victim resisted are less likely to be completed than those without resistance.

Completed crimes are more likely to be reported to the police than attempts. They were notified of 37% of robbery events in which nothing was stolen and 64% of completed robberies. The police were notified of 55% of attempted and 64% of completed rapes, One of the most important factors determining whether or not a crime event is completed is resistance; therefore, any relationship between resistance and notification should be fully accounted for by the relationship between resistance and outcome. In other words, Fig. 10.1

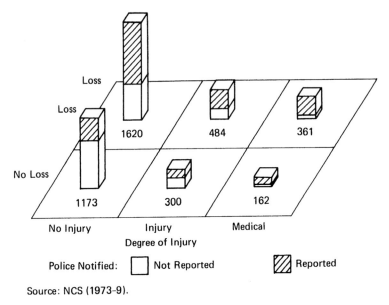

Police Notified: ☐ Not Reported ▨ Reported

Source: NCS (1973-9).

Fig.10.4　*Frequency Block Chart*

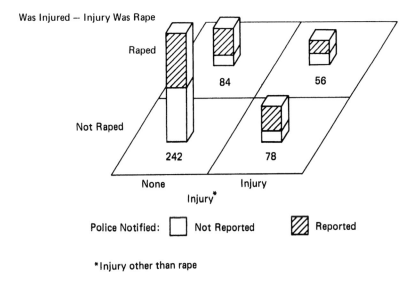

Police Notified: ☐ Not Reported ▨ Reported

*Injury other than rape

Fig.10.5　*Frequency Block Chart*

describes the outcome of a crime event as an intervening variable which explains a negative relationship between resistance and notification of the police. This description holds true only for robbery. The mild negative relationship between resistance and notification (gamma=0.16, significant at 0.001) disappears when loss is held constant (loss=0.01, no loss=0.06). In this data, there is little relationship between resistance during rape events and notification of the police.

**FIGURE 10.1 OPERATIONALIZED: THE ROBBERY EVENT**

Figure 10.1 is a hypothetical model of victim–offender dynamics during violent crime events. In Fig. 10.6, I have operationalized this model for stranger-to-stranger robbery events. Yule's Q or its extension, Gamma, are measures of zero order relationship. All associations above 0.10 are significant above the 0.01 level. The operationalization of variables is as follows:

Target and offender characteristics → race, black, other
Threat → presence of a gun, yes, no
Attack → physical attack, yes, no
Resistance → non-forcible, none
Injury → medical attention, injury, no injury
Completion → loss, no loss
Notification → reported to the police, yes, no

As illustrated in Figure 10.6, all the predicted relations exist in stranger to stranger robbery except for one, the relationship between attack and non-forcible resistance.[7]

Non-forcible resisters are no more likely to be attacked than those who do not resist. Most other predicted relations are quite strong. For example, black offenders are much more likely to choose black than white targets. Targets who are threatened with a gun are much less likely to resist than those threatened in some other way, and the police are much more likely to learn about a completed than an attempted crime.

Two unexpected zero order relations occurred: a strong negative relationship between victim's race and resistance (which remained even in a multivariate analysis), and a positive relationship between

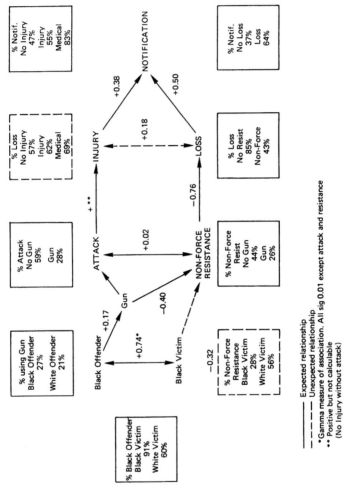

Fig.10.6  *An Example of the Violent Crime Event: Stranger to Stranger Robbery*

injury and loss. At the level of simple two variable analysis this model fits the data quite well.

A log-linear multivariate analysis also fits this model quite well. The best fit model of the relationship of guns/loss/injury and resistance included three-way interactions between injury/resistance and guns and injury/resistance and loss and a two-way interaction between guns and loss. The three-way interactions are predicted by the model. The bivariate relationship of gun/threat and loss indicates that in addition to the indirect relationships between guns and loss, there is a direct relationship. The offender's gun threat seems to increase the likelihood that the crime will be completed regardless of the victim's resistance.[8]

The log-linear analysis of the relationship of loss, injury, resistance, and notification of the police also indicates a good fit to Fig. 10.6. The best fit model includes three-way interactions between injury, resistance and loss, and between injury, loss, and notification of the police. The model does not include a relationship between resistance and police notification. This is precisely the model predicted in Fig. 10.1 and 10.6.

Thus, the model proposed in Fig. 10.1 and operationalized in Fig. 10.6 provides a good fit with reports of stranger-to-stranger robberies as collected in the National crime Survey. This model provides for a logical and dynamic relationship between threat and resistance, injury and loss, and notification. While the model also provides a good fit for rape events to explain injury and completion of the rape, it predicts a much stronger than observed relationship between outcome and notification of the police.

## CONCLUSIONS

In this presentation, I have considered the relationship between target–offender interaction during the stranger-to-stranger violent crimes and characteristics of the event's environment and actors. I have also demonstrated the relationship between target–offender interaction, the crime's outcome, and notification of the police. It has been shown that resistance has a strong negative relationship to the completion of a robbery or rape. Targets who resist are less likely to be robbed or raped than those who do not. Little relationship was found between non-forcible resistance and injury to the target;

however, targets who forcibly resisted were more likely to be injured than those who did not.

Both injury and loss were found to be independently related to the likelihood that the police would be notified of a robbery event. The police were most likely to be notified of robberies with both injury and loss. The relationship between the outcome of rape events and police notification is not so clear. The police were least likely to be notified of attempted crimes with no injuries, but they were most likely to be notified of crimes with completion or injury but not both.

Conclusions from this analysis must be made cautiously. They are limited by the structure of the NCS, most importantly:

1. Crimes during which the victim died are excluded by the victim survey method.
2. The sequence of attack and resistance is not recoverable from the victim survey. We cannot tell if attack followed or preceded resistance.

Victim surveys are moving away from the estimation of crime prevalence or incidence to consideration of behavioural characteristics which differentiate targets and non-targets. These studies consider crime prevention and the precipitation of crime. When crime prevention fails, target–offender interaction begins. Studies of this interaction demonstrate that actions of the target may affect the crime's final outcome and, at least, the initial actions of the police.

### Notes

1. While the concept of the crime event is useful for describing crimes with a clear beginning and end, it is much less appropriate for describing continuous crimes (for example, many white-collar crimes), or in describing crime without a victim or with a willing victim.
2. Respondents to the screening portion of the NCS were asked if they had been targets of robbery or attempted robbery. They were not asked if they were targets of rape. A (person in some years) woman who responded that she had been threatened or attacked was then asked if she had been a victim of rape or attempted rape. Along with 503 women, 47 men responded positively to this question. The males are generally excluded from this analysis.
3. Published reports of the NCS generate estimates of the number of crimes for the US population age 12 or older. For these reports, a

relatively small number of cases are reweighed to represent the US population. Incidents weights are frequently over 1000. In addition, these reports generally exclude 'series' victimizations those which are so frequent as to be undifferentiateable in the victims' memory. For this analysis reweighing is used only to reflect sampling procedures. The incident weight is divided by the mean for all crimes. Series crimes are counted as a single crime.

4. Although we will treat the two crimes as if there was no overlap, about 20% of the rape events (107) also included a robbery, attempted, or completed. These will be included in both analyses. We have no way of knowing for these events, whether the criminal's original intent was rape or robbery or both.

5. To simplify this section, we consider only the target's resistance and its relationship to outcome. Remember, however, that the resistance is related both to the offender's threat and attack.

6. The police may be notified of a crime by someone other than the victim; however, except for crimes with very serious injury, type of notification was not strongly related to the variables analysed in this example.

7. No value could be placed on the relationship between attack and injury. In almost all cases, attack must precede injury.

8. In addition, the mean loss is higher for robbery events with a gun ($70) than with other weapons ($26), and this difference is still substantial if only incidents in which something was stolen are analysed ($115 vs. $71).

**Bibliography**

Amir, Menachem (1971), *Patterns of Forcible Rape* (University of Chicago Press).

Block, Richard (1981), 'Victim–Offender Dynamics in Violent Crime', *Journal of Criminal Law and Criminology*, vol.72,no.2, pp.743–61.

Block, Richard, and Block, Carolyn R. (1980), 'Decisions and Data: the Transformation of Robbery Incidents into Official Robbery Statistics', *Journal of Criminal Law and Criminology*, vol.71 (winter) pp.622–36.

Brownmiller, Susan (1975), *Against Our Will: Men, Women and Rape* (New York: Simon & Schuster).

Bureau of Justice Statistics (1982), 'Violent Crime by Strangers', *Bureau of Justice Statistics Bulletin* (Washington, DC: US Dept. of Justice, Apr.).

Bureau of Justice Statistics (1981), *Criminal Victimization in the United States, 1979* (Washington, DC: US Dept. of Justice).

Chappell, Duncan, *et al.* (1977), 'A Comparative Study of Forcible Rape Offenses Known to the Police in Boston & Los Angeles' in Duncan Chappel, Robley Geis and Gilbert Geis (eds), *Forcible Rape: the Crime; the Victim & the Offender* (New York: Columbia University Press).

Chappell, Duncan and Singer, Susan (1977), 'Rape in New York City: a

Study of Material in the Police Files and Its Meaning' in Duncan Chappell, Robley Geis and Gilbert Geis (eds), *Forcible Rape: the Crime, the Victim, and the Offender* (New York: Columbia University Press) pp.245–72.

Chappell, Duncan and Fogarty, Faith (1978), *Forcible Rape* (Washington, DC: Law Enforcement Assistance Administration).

Conklin, John E. (1972), *Robbers and the Criminal Justice System* (Philadelphia: J. P. Lippincott).

*Criminal Victimization in the United States: 1973–79 Trends* (1981) (Washington, DC: Bureau of Justice Statistics).

*Criminal Victimization in the United States, 1979* (1981), Bureau of Justice Statistics (Washington, DC: US Department of Justice).

Director, Federal Bureau of Investigation (published annually), *Uniform Crime Reports for the United States* (Washington, DC: US Dept. of Justice).

Dunn, Christopher (1976), *Patterns of Robbery Characteristics: Analytic Report*, 15. (Washington, DC: Law Enforcement Assistance Administration, US Dept. of Justice).

Einstadter, Werner J. (1969), 'The Social Organization of Armed Robbers', *Social Problems*, vol.17,no.1 (summer).

Galton, Eric R. (1975–76), 'Police Processing of Rape Complaints: a Case Study', *American Journal of Criminal Law*, vol.4(1), pp.15–30.

Garofalo, James and Hindelang, Michael J. (1977), *An Introduction to the National Crime Survey* (Washington, DC: National Criminal Justice Information and Statistics Service, Law Enforcement Assistance Administration, US Dept. of Justice).

Griffin, Brenda, S. and Griffin, Charles T. (1978), 'Targeting & Aiding the Population at Risk', paper presented at Southwestern Political Science Association, Houston, Texas, 1978.

Griffin, Susan (1977), 'Rape: The All-American Crime' in Duncan Chappell, Robley Geis, and Gilbert Geis (eds), *Forcible Rape: the Crime, the Victim and the Offender* (New York: Columbia University Press) pp.47–67.

Groth, Nicholas A., Burgess, Ann Wolbert, and Holmstrom, Lyn (1977), 'Rape, Power, Anger, and Sexuality', *American Journal of Psychiatry*, vol.134(11), pp.1239–43.

Hentig, Hans von (1948), *The Criminal & His Victim: Studies in the Sociology of Crime* (New Haven: Yale University Press).

Hindelang, M., Gottfredson, M. and Garofalo, J. (1978), *Victims of Personal Crime: an Empirical Foundation for a Theory of Personal Victimization* (Cambridge, Mass.: Ballinger).

Hindelang, Michael and Gottfredson, Michael, 'The Victim's Decision not to Invoke the Criminal Justice Process' in McDonald William (ed), *Criminal Justice & the Victim* (Beverly Hills, CA.: Sage Publications).

Inter-University Consortium for Political & Social Research (1978), *National Crime Surveys: National Sample 1971–77*, 7636 (Ann Arbor, Mich.).

LaFree, Gary D. (1980), 'The Effect of Sexual Stratification by Race on Official Reaction to Rape', *American Sociological Review*, vol.45, pp.842–54.

MacDonald, John M. (1971), *Rape: Offenders and Their Victims* (Springfield, IL: C. Thomas).

McDonald, John M. (1975), *Armed Robbery: Offenders & Their Victims* (Springfield, IL: C. Thomas).

Mendelsohn (1956) 'Une nouvelle branche de la science bio-psycho-sociale: la victimologie', *Revue Internationale de Criminologie et de Police Technique*. 11(2), pp.95–109.

Normandeau (1968), Trends and Patterns in Crimes of Robbery. PhD Dissertation, (Philadelphia: University of Pennsylvania) 450pp.

Pittman, D. and Hardy, W. (1964), 'Patterns in Criminal Aggravated Assault', *Journal of Criminal Law, Criminology & Police Science*, vol.55, pp.462–70.

Pokorny, A. D. (1965) 'Human Violence: a Comparison of Homicide, Aggravated Assault, Suicide & Attempted Suicide', *Journal of Criminal Law, Criminology, & Police Science*, vol.56, pp.488–97.

Radzinowicz, L. (1951), *Sexual offenses* (London: Macmillan).

Schafer, Stephen (1977), *Victimology: the Victim & his Criminal* (Reston, VA: Reston Publishing).

Schram, Donna (1978), 'Rape', in Jane Chapman and Margaret Bates, (eds), *The Victimization of Women* (Beverly Hills, CA: Sage Publications) pp.53–80.

Skogan, W. G. (1981) Citizen Reporting of Crime: Some National Panel Data', in B. Galaway and J. Hudson (eds), *Perspectives on Crime Victims* (St. Louis: C. V. Mosby Co) pp.45–51.

Sparks, Richard F., Genn, Hazel and Dodd, David J. (1977), *Surveying Victims: a Study of the Measurement of Criminal Victimization, Perceptions of Crime and Attitudes to Criminal Justice* (New York: John Wiley).

Wolfgang, Marvin (1958), *Patterns in Criminal Homicide* (Philadelphia: University of Pennsylvania Press).

Zimring, Frank, Eigen, Joel and O'Malley, Sheila (1976), 'Punishing Homicide in Philadelphia: Perspectives on the Death Penalty', *University of Chicago Law Review*, vol.43,no2 (winter).

# 11 The Needs of Crime Victims

## Irvin Waller

Surprising to politicians and victim support workers, the majority of reports labelled 'Crime Victims' do not tell them very much about the human impact of crime on victims or what victims need to recover from crime. Most of these reports emanate from large and multi-million dollar surveys to count crime and its dollar costs. These surveys have become known as victimization surveys, though the official – and more accurate – label in the USA is the National Crime Survey (see Block, Prologue).

In this chapter, we will examine first the issues that are becoming a part of the discourse to improve the plight of the crime victim. Then, we will review the knowledge that we have obtained from (a) the large scale 'victim counting' surveys, (b) the many small surveys focused on getting the victim to the 'court on time' – 'victim courting' surveys, and (c) the surveys concerned with improving the plight of the victim – 'victim caring' surveys. In each case, we will try to assess their realized or potential benefits to these crime victim issues. Finally, we will list some of the possible priorities to improve assistance to crime victims, with a view to suggesting areas where victim research could focus attention in the future.

The analysis could be broadened to issues of preventing crime and so reducing the harm to crime victims. However, this review is restricted to immediate effects as crime prevention as well as fear reduction issues have been discussed elsewhere (Waller, 1982). A fuller discussion of the relationship of theory and praxis that focuses on fear reduction, crime prevention, and orientation of the police is contained in several articles (Garofalo, 1977; Waller and Okihiro, 1978; Block, 1984). Further, this chapter does not discuss how surveys of victims can be made effective guides to crime prevention, fear reduction, or orientation of the police (Waller, 1984; Petrunik, 1982). Similarly, the role of victimization surveys for social indicators rather than for programmatic decisions is not treated here (Waller, 1984).

## WHAT IS THE CRIME-VICTIM ISSUE?

The cartoon in Fig. 11.1 says it all. All too often the victims of crime suffer physical, psychological, or financial hardship, where systematic efforts could assist the recovery of victims and their families. Further, victims suffer additional harm and inconvenience when used as tools to identify and punish offenders, yet police, courts, and penal authorities could do much more to respect the dignity of victims and give them a fairer deal (CCSD, 1981; US, 1982; US, 1983).

Crime victims do not have adequate redress, protection, or justice. They have few rights protected by the Criminal Code, legal aid or the Charter of Rights and Freedoms. Referring to apparent progress in humanizing our penal programme for offenders, some say that 'justice' has been dropped from the criminal justice system which leaves a system for the criminal (US, 1983). Whether for or against the criminal it is certainly a system of the state v. the offender – cops, courts, and corrections versus the convict – which excludes and ignores the victim.

However, crime victims are left 'orphaned' by the lack of support from health and social services. Those services that are committed to crime-victims are not only inadequately financed, but are rare, restricted to large cities, not permanently established and operated by non-professionally trained staff at token wages. Compared to more than $100 spent each year per Canadian to try to catch, convict, and incarcerate offenders, we spend less than a dollar on all criminal injuries compensation and rape-crisis centres. If we added to this, all expenditures on transition homes for battered wives and crime-victim support programmes, we still devote less than $2 per Canadian to specific services for victims.

## ROBBERY AND BURGLARY LEAVE TRAUMA

The public discussion of these problems has concentrated on violence against women. Indeed the social movement to improve the status of women has concentrated much of its efforts on rape and wife battering. The insensitivity of the police or doctors to these victims has been regularly discussed in the press. In Canada, the recent parliamentary reports from Ottawa (Canada, 1982) and Queen's Park (Ontario, 1982) recommend immediate action to assist the

Fig.11.1   *Reforms Have Been Directed Toward Protecting the Rights of the Accused – but What About the Victim? (The Citizen: Ottawa, 12 Sept. 1981).*

victims of wife battering by providing better training for the police, police–social worker intervention and permanent funding for transition homes.

We overlook the substantial number of persons who suffer crimes such as robbery, assault, or burglary. These victims face sleeplessness, guilt, fear and suspicion as well as problems of insensitivity and lack of services. From 1965 to 1981 in Canada, the annual proportion of the population who became a victim of these offences doubled. This year, at least one in six Canadian households will be a victim of these crimes (CCSD, 1981).

For residential break and enter in 1983, the Canadians in 340 000 homes will join a similar number from each of the previous years to give more than one million persons victimized within the last 3 years – some for the second or third time. As we shall see, one in twenty of these experiences significant post-traumatic stress disorder (Waller and Okihiro, 1982; Maguire, 1982). So for this offence alone in the last 3 years, there are more than 50 000 persons, who are suffering heightened problems of insomnia, nausea, and fear.

Citizen groups have formed in a variety of Canadian cities to fight for the special interests of crime victims. The best known of these groups have grown around cases of murder and drunken driving. In Toronto, two families, who had had their daughters murdered started 'Victims of Violence'. In Mississaugua, a father of a murdered woman started a petition, to which he has obtained more than 200 000 signatures. In British Columbia, the mother of another murder victim founded Citizens United For Safety and Justice.

## PROTECTION, REDRESS, JUSTICE

The professional groups have also begun to promote reform. In Canada, the Canadian Council on Social Development in *Rights and Services for Crime Victims* proposes many specific measures to give Canadians rights to:

(a) protection from criminal acts;
(b) redress for pain, loss and injury inflicted by crime;
(c) fair deal from police, courts, and correctional authorities.

The Canadian Bar Association, the Canadian Association for the Prevention of Crime, the Church Council on Justice and Corrections and many other groups have begun the task of studying what can be done. Following the major Canadian – NOVA conference in 1981 on Victim Assistance (Leger, 1982), the federal and provincial governments asked a task force of senior public servants to recommend ways to improve the situation. By the summer of 1983, these groups could start to recommend specific action.

Already the federal government is committed to an overhaul of the Criminal Code, based on principles that include promoting and providing for 'reconciliation of the victim, community and offender' and 'redress or recompense for . . . victims'. The Canadian Association for the Prevention of Crime (1982) has recommended specific revisions: to improve restitution, compensation, mediation; to draw up a victim bill of rights and to carry out a study of the French *Partie Civile* system.

## THE NEEDS OF CRIME VICTIMS

The discussion of the needs of crime victims will follow the schema displayed in Fig. 11.2 where the effects of crime are shown to create a variety of different needs for victims. Economic loss, physical injury, and difficulties in criminal justice could be discussed as one group as they are adequately covered in the victim counting and victim courting surveys. Emotional trauma, effects on family, friends, and helpers as well as problems with hospital, insurance, and other general services are less well known, so should be discussed more; our understanding of these has come more from clinical studies and victim 'caring' surveys.

## SOURCES OF INFORMATION

### Counting Victims

One major source of information on the direct effects of crime is the US National Crime Survey, which provides national estimates of losses and injuries due to five categories of theft and assault. This survey has been undertaken each year since 1972 and provides basic

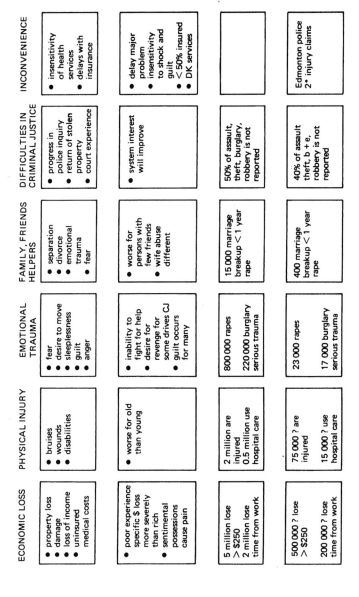

Fig.11.2 *Effects of Crime on Victims*

data for further analysis. Similar data are not available in Canada, though a telephone survey, focused on the same categories of theft and assault, was undertaken in seven cities in 1982. A victimization survey by personal interview was part of a comprehensive analysis of burglary carried out in Toronto in 1974 (Waller and Okihiro, 1978) and a telephone victimization survey of all five categories was undertaken in Vancouver in 1978 (Evans and Léger, 1979; Canada, 1983).

The US National Crime Survey provides useful data on economic loss and physical injury for four of the five categories – robbery, burglary, larceny, and assault. However, the Survey has many limitations (Skogan, 1981; Waller, 1980, 1984). For our present purposes, it does not provide useful data on the emotional trauma, disruption of the support group, or the inconvenience from crime. It does not look at what victims want from the police or courts. It does not measure fear of 'home' crime or states of anxiety. Further, it was not designed to improve victim assistance programmes. Finally, it does not include offences such as murder, fraud, or traffic crime, which in different ways are important for victims.

**Courting Victims**

A second type of approach was pioneered by Knudten *et al.*(1976). The major concern is to understand why victims and other witnesses do not come to court. Its implicit purpose is to get more victims and witnesses to court so that more prosecutions are successful. In Canada, surveys have been undertaken in Waterloo (Brown and Yantzi, 1980) and Winnipeg (Brickey, 1982).

**Caring about Victims**

A third, but less well known, source of information is the special study focused either on a particular type of crime, such as rape or burglary, or on a type of victim, such as women, children, or the elderly. Some of these studies focus on a particular city. These studies are useful to form or improve programmes of assistance to crime victims. Further, they tend to be more complete in analysing the needs of victims by measuring not only physical injury and loss of property but also emotional trauma, the effect on family, friends, and helpers as well as problems with health and social services. Usually they provide data that can be useful for crime prevention. Their major limitations are that they are not carried out on national samples and their reports are not distributed as widely as those undertaken by the governments.

Much of the work on specific types of crime has been focused on the effects of rape on the victim, its prevention and its effect on society (Burgess and Holmstrom, 1974; Brickman *et al.* 1980). The more frequent crimes have not yet received the same public attention, even though researchers have examined residential burglary (Waller and Okihiro, 1978; Maguire, 1982), robbery (Conklin, 1972; Giroux, 1977) and mugging (Lejeune and Alex, 1973). Some authors have examined combinations of burglary and robbery and in some cases assault (Bard, Morton and Sangrey, 1978; Bourque *et al.*, 1978; Friedman *et al.*, 1982; Drennan-Searson, 1982). Baril (1980) compared the effects of each of these crimes with rape.

Another approach to these effects is in terms of the type of victim. Women have been the subject of a number of analyses, particularly as battered wives (US Commission on Civil Rights, 1978; Macleod, 1980; Quebec, 1980; Straus, Gelles and Steinmetz, 1980; *Canadian Association of Social Workers*, 1982; Canada, 1982). Children are the subject of an extensive literature on child abuse (van Stolk, 1978; Cooper, 1979). A growing area of interest is the elderly (Goldsmith and Goldsmith, 1976; Young Rifai, 1977; Jaycox, 1979; Malinchak, 1980).

Calgary (Muir, 1982) and Ottawa (Drennan-Searson, 1982) were the sites for city based surveys as a preliminary to forming new victim assistance programmes. Other surveys are complete or in process for Fredericton, Richmond, and Montreal. Each of these involves a survey of 75 to 300 victims. In some cases a special sample of witnesses is included. Typically, the sample is drawn from recent offences recorded by the police. Sometimes the interviews are done in person and sometimes on the telephone. Each has been designed to orient programmes for crime victims and prepare a base for later evaluation.

A particularly important approach is found in the Victim Service Agency in New York City. Friedman *et al.* (1982) interviewed 274 victims of residential burglary, robbery, and assault and 152 close supporters of these victims in order to understand the problems that victims face and what sources of help they use (see also Davis *et al.*, 1979). It also examines the effects of crime on those supporters.

## LOSS OF PROPERTY – DOLLARS, SECURITY

NOVA (1980) states that economic losses from crime can be staggering. These losses can include property destruction, loss of cash, loss of income, medical, and rehabilitation expenses. However, it is often the sentimental value of objects stolen that is the most traumatizing. Most persons react to a discussion of victim needs in terms of reparation of financial losses. These are visible and relatively easy to measure. Indeed, the principal measure of crime impact in the US National Crime Survey (USA, 1981) are the value of goods and time lost from work. Although financial and property loss occurred frequently in the robbery, larceny, and burglary reported by persons and households in the US National Crime Survey, the amounts of the loss were small. Still, as shown in Table 11.1, more than $50 loss was reported in approximately 17 million events in the USA, in 1979, or approximately 7 incidents for every 100 persons; only 1 of these 7 would have seen recovery from insurance. Further, recovery of property is rare, except for motor vehicle theft. There would also be one incident for every 100 persons where time would be lost from work. Similar data for Canada are not available, though the victimization surveys in Toronto and Vancouver are consistent with the US conclusions.

These figures hide the major dimensions of the impact of economic loss – the poorer the person, the more significant the meaning of a loss of $50 – the more attached the person is to an object, the more shocking the loss. In brief, the loss of a $50 bill to a young millionaire who is insured may be minimal, whereas the loss to a pensioner of $50 or photographs of their youth may be enormous.

## PHYSICAL INJURY AND DEBILITATION

NOVA (1980) indentifies the consequences of criminal assault as ranging from minor abrasions to crippling paralysis to death. Two million Americans suffer injury as a result of robbery or assault each year. Crimes such as robbery and assault can result in serious physical injury to the victim. In practice, violent crime is much rarer than property crime and physical injury is rare among violent crimes. In Table 11.2 USA (1981) is used to identify some key statistics on the incidence of injury and hospital care for three offence categories.

Table 11.1 Value of Economic Loss and Time Lost from Work for Crimes Reported in National Crime Survey – USA 1979

| | Total events N (1000s) | Economic Loss $50–249 N (1000s) | % | $250 or more N (1000s) | % | Recovery From Insurance N (1000s) | % | Time Lost From Work N | % |
|---|---|---|---|---|---|---|---|---|---|
| *Personal* Rape, Robbery, Assault, and Theft | 22 541 | 6 154 | 27.3 | 2 051 | 9.1 | 1 031 | 4.6 | 1 420 | 6.3 |
| *Household* Burglary, Theft, and Car Theft | 18 708 | 4 920 | 26.3 | 3 311 | 17.7 | 1 147 | 6.1 | 973 | 5.2 |
| Total | 41 249 | 11 074 | | 5 362 | | 2 178 | | 2 393 | |
| Rate per 100 total population | 18.7 | 5.0 | | 2.4 | | 1.0 | | 1.1 | |

There were 178 284 000 persons aged 12 and over, 79 499 000 households and 220 099 000 total population in 1979.

Sources: USA (1981) Column 1 – Table 1, p.22; Column 2 – Table 76, pp.68–9; Column 3 – Table 79, p. 72; Column 4 – Table 81, p.73.

Table 11.2    Frequency of Injury and Hospital Care from National
Crime Survey, USA 1979

|  | | *Injured* | | *Hospital Care* | |
|---|---|---|---|---|---|
|  | *1000s* | *in 1000s* | *%* | *in 1000s* | *%* |
| Rape | 192 | 192 | 100 | 25 | 13.3 |
| Robbery | 1 116 | 380 | 34.1 | 108 | 9.7 |
| Assault | 4 851 | 1 392 | 28.7 | 358 | 7.4 |
| Total | 6 159 | 1 964 * | 31.9 | 492 | 8.0 |
| Rate per 100 Total Population | 2.8 | 0.9 | | 0.2 | |
| Source (USA, 1981) | Table 1, p.22 | Table 68, p.63 | | Table 72, p.65 | |

*32.5% of 1 964 000 or 638 000 did not have health insurance or access to public medical services (Table 71, p. 65).

In the USA 380 000 persons sustained physical injury in a robbery and 1.4 million in assaults, of whom more than 600 000 did not have health insurance or access to public medical services (USA, 1981, pp.18,59,61). Of every 10 personal robberies and assaults 3 resulted in an injury. That is, 1 in 150 Americans were injured in this way, of whom 1 in 3 were not covered by health insurance or by public medical services. In Canada in 1979, 8000–24 000 persons were victims of assault (35 to 104 in 100 000), giving 1000–2000 in need of medical care (Solicitor-General, 1979, p.11).

In comparative terms, crime victims are not as injury prone as victims of traffic accidents. In the USA for the 0.9 per 100 persons injured in crime there were 2.6 per 100 injured in traffic accidents (Waller and Touchette, 1982). There are more deaths from impaired driving in Canada, 11 per 100 000 total population, than from murder – 3 per 100 000. In the USA the number of deaths attributable to these two causes is approximately the same for both at 1 per 10 000 total population. These compare with death rates for heart disease of 221 and 301, for cancer of 155 and 175 for Canada and the USA respectively (Waller and Touchette, 1982).

The best known crimes are not necessarily the most injurious. The US literature leaves the impression that the most threatening crime is stranger to stranger crime on the street, but many rapes and burglaries occur in people's homes. Further, it is not necessarily the degree of injury that makes the offence the most frightening.

## EMOTIONAL TRAUMA AND DISTRESS

The emotional trauma or 'invisible wound' is the least evident and understood, but often the most brutal effect of crime, not only on the direct victim but on the victim's dependants, friends and survivors The psychological symptoms can include fear, shame, and guilt, but they can take more forms as insomnia, nausea, inability to manage everyday affairs and, for the elderly, accelerated decline. For some, there is an urgent need to change their residence.

NOVA (1980) identifies (i) stress caused by feelings of humiliation, violation, and fear, (ii) isolation and withdrawal as few persons understand the stress, and (iii) depression and physical ailments from tension. Severe headaches, nausea, and fatigue on the one hand go along with an inability to meet the most ordinary of responsibilities.

The precise explanation of why these symptoms occur is not available. However, it is frequently situated in crisis theory. Authors (Bard, Morton and Sangrey, 1979; Burgess and Holmstrom, 1974) agree that the suddenness and arbitrariness of the criminal event combined with the partial or total loss of personal security are significant elements.

'Post-traumatic Stress Disorder', which is now included in the Diagnostic Standards Manual of the American Psychiatric Association (see Fig. 11.3). This syndrome describes the effect of extreme stressors on ordinary persons. It identifies the similar symptoms that will appear from such wide-ranging calamities as a gang rape, a burglary–vandalism, a dam disaster, or a hotel collapsing (*New York Times*, 1982; USA *Today*, 1982; Fredericks, 1980).

The phases in the trauma have been explored by several authors (Burgess and Holmstrom, 1974; Bard, Morton and Sangrey, 1979; Symonds, 1980; Salasin, 1981). They identify the (a) impact, (b) recoil, and (c) reorganization phases. In the first, the victim experiences shock, disbelief, and numbness. In the second, the victim feels fear, sadness, and anger. In the third, the painful experience is assimilated, as the victims begin to channel their energies into other pursuits.

A. Existence of a recognizable stressor that would evoke significant symptoms of distress in almost everyone.

B. Re-experiencing of the trauma as evidenced by at least one of the following:

   1 Recurrent and intrusive recollections of the event;
   2 Recurrent dreams of the event;
   3 Sudden acting or feeling as if the traumatic event were reoccurring, because of an association with an environmental or ideational stimulus.

C. Numbing of responsiveness to or reduced involvement with the external world, beginning some time after the trauma, as shown by at least one of the following:

   1 Markedly diminished interest in one or more significant activities;
   2 Feeling of detachment or estrangement from others;
   3 Constricted affect.

D. At least two of the following symptoms that were not present before the trauma:

   1 hyperalertness or exaggerated startle response;
   2 sleep disturbance;
   3 Guilt about surviving when others have not, or about behaviour required for survival;
   4 memory impairment or trouble concentrating;
   5 avoidance of activities that arouse recollection of the traumatic event;
   6 intensification of symptoms by exposure to events that symbolize or resemble the traumatic event.

Source: *Diagnostic Standards Manual* (American Psychiatric Association).

Fig. 11.3    Diagnostic Criteria for Post-Traumatic Stress Disorder (DSM III)

The emotional trauma can occur in crimes seemingly not against the person. Many people are surprised that breaking and entering – an offence often seen to be against property – can generate a state of shock. Several authors (Waller and Okihiro, 1978; Bourque *et al.*, 1978; Bard, Morton and Sangrey, 1978) have shown how vandalizing a home or theft of sentimental possessions makes breaking and entering an offence focused more on the person and the possessions they feel are part of them. These authors show how women living alone or older persons tend to be more threatened by the event.

Further, breaking and entering in Canada accounts for nearly as many traumatized victims as rape. In Fig. 11.4, the incidence of indicated symptoms is shown for burglary and robbery (Bourque *et al.*, 1978, pp.30–2). This incidence is used in Table 11.3 to estimate the relative incidence of serious trauma due to rape, robbery, and residential burglary. It assumes that every rape causes emotional trauma and makes several other assumptions, particularly relating to

Table 11.3 Estimated Incidence of Serious Trauma in Rape, Robbery, and Residential Burglary: Canada and USA – 1979/1980

| | National Crime Survey | | Reporting Rate to Police | Police Recorded | | Numbers Estimated Using Reporting Rate | Percentage Trauma | Serious Trauma | |
|---|---|---|---|---|---|---|---|---|---|
| | *No. in 1000s* | *per 100 000* | *%* | *No. in 1000s* | *per 100 000* | *in 1000s* | *Trauma* | *No. in 1000s* | *per 100 000* |
| Rape | | | | | | | | | |
| Canada | 192 | | 10 | 2.3 | 9.7 | 23 | 100 | 23 | 97 |
| USA | | 87.2 | 10 | 80.1 | 36.4 | 801 | 100 | 801 | 364 |
| Robbery | | | | | | | | | |
| Canada | 1 116 | | 52.0 | 24.5 | 102.7 | 47.1 | 3 | 1.4 | 6 |
| USA | | 507.0 | 55.5 | 535.9 | 243.5 | 965.6 | 3 | 28.9 | 13 |
| Residential Burglary | | | | | | | | | |
| Canada | 6 685 | | 62.0 | 209.3 | 876.3 | 337.6 | 5 | 16.9 | 71 |
| USA | | 3 037.3 | 47.6 | 2 111.6 | 959.4 | 4 436.1 | 5 | 221.8 | 101 |

Population: Canada is 23.9 million in 1980; USA is 220.1 million in 1979.
Sources: Crime data: USA (1981); Waller and Touchette (1982).
    Reporting Data: USA (1981); Canada (1982a).
    Trauma: Bourque (1978); Waller and Okihiro (1978).

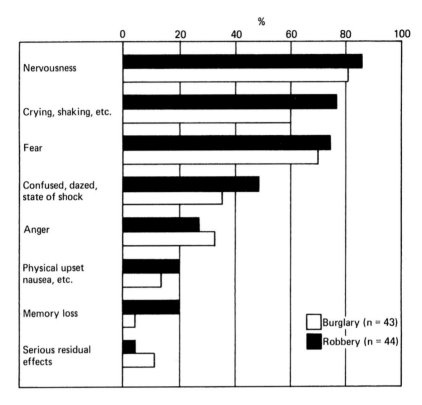

Fig.11.4   *Percentage of Cases Showing Indicated Symptoms*

the reporting of crime to the police and its recording. However, Table 11.3 shows in gross terms that though serious trauma is rare serious burglary trauma is as frequent as rape trauma – even using a 10% reporting rate for rape.

**ANGER**

Anger is one effect which is particularly important for our systems of penal justice. It is anger that underlies the desire for personal revenge. When people are threatened they react by wanting to eliminate the threat or attacking the person who is threatening. It is this desire to do harm to the attacker or offender that is a form of retaliation or revenge. One of the common justifications for criminal justice is that it controls personal revenge. However, it is the state that retaliates, not the victim.

Let us explore anger further in the context of the reaction of the public to residential burglary. Waller and Okihiro (1978, pp.38–9) show that two out of three of the burglary victims experiencing extensive disarrangement in the house wanted a prison sentence for the offender compared to one out of three without such disarrangement. They interpret this reaction in the context of other findings as a reaction to the irrational and potentially violent behaviour of the offender. In the same study, they found members of the public responded to cases of residential burglary involving an offender with previous convictions for assault by wanting sentences that were substantially longer than when the person had no previous conviction.

Hagan (1980, p.333) shows more than half his sample of victims to remain dissatisfied with the court sentences. As shown in the 'Post-Traumatic Stress Disorder', anger is the feeling that can arise from many different sources, such as death, divorce, or even a feeling of unjust treatment as a child. In these contexts, it is the focus of much psychiatric counselling. Talking to friends, relatives, priests or psychiatrists, hitting pillows, going jogging are now advocated as ways of dealing with anger originating from issues other than crime. It is only in the case of crime that we try to channel the anger through the state's prosecution of the offender. From the perspective of the victim, it is likely that civil justice or therapy could be much more effective than state controlled penal justice in relieving feelings of anger.

## CRISIS AMONG FAMILY, FRIENDS AND HELPERS

Many crimes are some form of altercation in an ongoing supportive relationship with such persons as spouse, parents, children, friends, or neighbours. This is not to say that the offenders were justified in their actions, but that victims may be concerned about the effect of police intervention or imprisonment of the offender on their interests or relationships. The crime may be a symptom of a problem that involves both parties and not just a unilateral traumatized victim. In short, both parties may want the relationship and suffer disadvantages when it is in crisis.

A major part of our lives and well-being is influenced by the nature of the love and caring provided by supportive relationships. In some instances, violence or excessive coercion may be symptoms of problems in these relationships. Sometimes the problems can be resolved through conciliation, counselling or therapy. In others, more drastic intervention may be needed. Either way, most victims want such supportive relationships to be adequately repaired or new ones created.

It is difficult to obtain reliable indicators of the impact of crime on the spouse, children, parents or friends of crime victims. It is often stated that 50% of rape victims who were married at the time of the offence will be separated within one year. This statistic has no known source. However, if true, we can assume breakdown in half of the cases of the 29 900 married women raped in the USA in 1979 (USA, 1981). And so we can estimate 15 000 marriages break down each year as a result of rape.

Friedman *et al.* (1982, p.6) reports 80% of supporters suffering many of the same psychological problems as the victims. Most of the symptoms related to increased fear and suspicion. Friedman *et al.* do not report whether anger was significant among supporters of crime victims.

**DIFFICULTIES IN CRIMINAL JUSTICE**

Knudten *et al.* (1976), and several pieces of research following on their work, have shown both the inconvenience and incomprehension associated with court procedures (Davis *et al.*, 1980; Muir, 1982, Brickey, 1982).

Besides the direct effects, most victims experience a wide variety of inconveniences in their life as a result of the crime. In about half of the three types of crime studied in the National Crime Survey, the victims do not report to police (USA, 1981; Canada, 1982). However, if they do, this is done initially over the telephone. It then has to be re-explained to the responding officer. Some victims have to wait some time for the police officer to arrive. Most of the inconvenience and frustration (not directly due to the crime) comes later when the victim tries to recover property from the police or follow the progress of the investigation. As many police departments leave the case with the individual officer who responded, it is difficult for the victim to contact that officer – partly because they do not have the name, partly because the officer is on shift work, and partly because there is often no central file number. If stolen property is recovered, often the victim may not be informed or the property is not released. Sometimes property is kept longer by the police than by the offender. Some police departments, such as Edmonton, Alberta, have instituted a central information system and special police unit to avoid these inconveniences (Liaison, 1982).

## INSENSITIVITY FROM HEALTH, WELFARE AND GENERAL SERVICES

Inconvenience can occur in hospital emergency rooms, in claiming insurance or crime compensation, or in recovering a driver's licence. Each of these means delay to the victim (Drennan-Searson, 1982).

## REFORMS

In the face of these needs there are a variety of specialized and general services that are used by crime victims. The specialized services include rape crisis centres, homes for battered wives, victim support units, compensation, restitution, mediation, and crisis intervention teams. The general services are hospitals, legal aid, crime prevention, police, and welfare. The striking impression left from reviewing the extent to which these agencies meet the needs of victims (Waller, 1982) is that:

1. The services most committed to helping crime victims are the most inadequately financed, rare, restricted to urban areas, least established and with staff, who are rarely professionally trained or paid more than token wages.
2. The general services are well financed, well-established, widely available, with well-paid staff, who have had substantial training – but are insensitive to victim needs, particularly emotional.

The issue for these groups as well as each of us is how to provide human care, professional assistance, and legal reform so that the rights of victims to protection, redress, and a fair deal will take specific form. Many can be made without surveys, but sensitive research activities can make them more effective. The following five areas identify targets for such practical improvements.

### The Police Are First at the Scene

The police are the agency that is best situated to provide crisis support to victims. Because they are often the first officials to talk to the victim of crime, they are able to reassure and refer the victim to the appropriate services in the community (where they exist). So the preliminary training of all police officers should include how to reassure and refer victims, so that victims receive not only emergency medical care, but information and social support.

The police could improve their support for crime victims by requiring the responding officer to provide the victim with a card that identifies the key telephone numbers of services such as the local distress centre, the crime prevention unit and a service that could help or refer the victim to other community services. Ideally this card would identify both the file number of the case as well as the name of the police officer.

Similarly, police procedures could require property to be returned to its owner on recovery. Detectives could be required to inform the crime victim from time to time of action or legitimate inaction on an investigation. This can be done relatively easily through the use of form letters and word processors so as to make the letters individualized.

The Edmonton Police are assisting 3000 victims a month through such procedures, which are supported by a police victim-services unit. One indicator of the effectiveness of this type of outreach and information programme is that it doubled the claims to the Alberta Compensation Board in the first year of operation.

### Victim-Support Centres

Every community could identify or organize a crime victim-support centre. This centre would have two roles. The first would be to work with individual crime victims to ensure they get appropriate assistance from available services. Secondly, it would engage in training, sensitizing, and working for improvements of existing agencies.

The agency could provide support and assistance for the victim to obtain help from agencies such as the hospital emergency room, welfare, legal aid and the police. This agency would also work with the police to identify cases where victims were likely to need 'outreach' services. Many victims do not feel and are not aware that they can be helped. A telephone call, letter, or personal visit can ecnourage victims to seek help and explain what services are available.

The second function of this agency would be to improve services for crime victims. For instance, training is needed for police officers, hospital workers, and related community agencies. They could promote better coordination between existing services and make the public more aware of these services and the need for improvements.

**Traumatic Stress Focus for Health Professionals**

Hospital emergency rooms, local doctors, and psychiatric services could be better organized to assist victims or their families recover from the emotional trauma of crime. The World Federation for Mental Health wants more attention paid to the 'post-traumatic stress disorder'. This is the label given by the American Psychiatric Association to the fear, anger, revulsion, and immobility that consumes some victims after a sudden arbitrary attack threatens their person or their security. The treatment and management of these problems could become part of the basic exams for doctors, nurses, and health workers.

Friedman *et al.* (1982) have shown how this disorder can occur in persons who support victims. So services could be made available to the family, emergency room workers, and police, who deal with severely traumatized victims.

**Participation in Justice**

Canadian governments – Federal and/or provincial – could enact legislation to help crime victims recover civil damages from offenders. Judges could be encouraged to consider restitution by requiring written reasons where it is not ordered. 'Son of Sam' legislation could be enacted to enable the crime victim to recover civil damages from an offender who gains royalties or equivalent income from the sale of books, films, or other publicity arising out of the crime. Further, the victim could attend all major proceedings such as bail, trial, sentencing, or parole hearings. Whether the victim attends or not, a victim advocate or probation officer could be required to provide the court with a victim impact statement, which provides a non-argumentative assessment of the emotional, physical, and financial effects of the crime on the victim. Also, the advocate could keep the victim informed of the proceedings.

## Guidelines

Legislation could be enacted to specify a code of conduct for the fair treatment of victims of crime. This would specify the duties of government and private sector agencies to provide for the victim and, where applicable, witnesses. These standards would be used by victim support centres to encourage police, hospitals, and welfare agencies to improve their services. These would provide guidelines for judges, prosecutors, and correctional officials.

The World Society of Victimology has created a committee to prepare similar standards for adoption as a Declaration by the United Nations. For its 7th Congress on Crime Prevention and the Treatment of Offenders in 1985, the UN decided that two of the five agenda items would be (a) Victims of Crime, and (b) Enforcement and Relevance of UN Standards.

## Commitment Not Cost

These five initiatives need not be costly. Changes in police procedures require only the printing of the card, modification of forms, and the commitment to make it happen. Victim support centres require the funding of a few core staff or the redeployment of existing staff. The stress disorder can be included in doctors', nurses', and psychologists' professional exams. Civil damages require changes in the law, but not a new bureaucracy. The preparation and promulgation of a code of conduct may take time, but does not require the involvement of many staff.

CONCLUSION

In conclusion, the large scale surveys of crime victims have tended to do 'more of the same'. The Canadian government surveys have not cost as much as their American counterparts and have tried to focus more on aspects of crime prevention. Even so, neither provide much information that is useful to assisting victims. There is a need to begin to consider how this research and statistical energy can be harnessed more effectively to meet the needs of public policy.

In this chapter, we have seen the evident need to make improvements in police response to victims, in the emotional support of some victims, in providing civil damages, in financing victim support centres, and enacting general guidelines. Survey techniques can be cost effective in investigating these areas and above all in getting to know the human needs of victims, so that the innovations focus on real needs.

The major benefits to crime victims have .come from relatively cheap, small scale surveys focused on the trauma to the victims, the effect of the crime on their family, friends, and helpers as well as the insensitivity of health, welfare, and general services to their needs. These could be the subject of wider-scale surveys, though likely the greatest benefits for a limited sum of money would come from focused studies executed to assist the effectiveness of services.

One major omission from the work on crime victims is a good study of anger and the desire for revenge. On the one hand, its extent is not known nor the factors that precipitate it. On the other, little is known in the criminal policy area about procedures that can help people live with these feelings. It is not known, whether severe punishment of the offender by the state satisfies angered victims.

**Bibliography**

Bard, Morton and Sangrey, D. (1978), *The Crime Victim's Book* (New York: Basic Books).
Baril, Micheline (1980), 'Rape and Other Acts of Violence', Paper read at meeting of American Society of Criminology in San Francisco, Mimeograph (Montreal: Université de Montréal, Centre International de Criminologie Comparée).
Block, Richard (1984), *Victimization and Fear of Crime: World Perspectives.* (Washington: Dept. of Justice).

Bourque, Blair B., Brumback, G. B., Krug, R. E. and Richardson, L. O. (1978), *Crisis Intervention: Investigating the Need for New Applications*, Mimeograph (Washington: American Institute for Research).

Brickey, Stephen L. (1982) 'Winnipeg Victim/Witness Assistance Program: Planning Phase' (Winnipeg, University of Manitoba). Unpublished.

Brickman, Julie, Briere, J., Lungen, A., Shepherd, M. and Lofchick, M. (1980), 'Winnipeg Rape Incidence Project: Final Results', Paper read at May 1980 meeting of the Canadian Association of Sexual Assault Centres in Winnipeg, Manitoba.

Brown, S. D. and Yantzi, M. (1980), *Needs Assessment for Victims and Witnesses of Crime* (Sententica Inc., Elmira. Ont.) Unpublished.

Burgess, A. W. and Holmstrom, L. L. (1974), *Rape: Victims of Crisis* (Bowie, MD.: Robert J. Brady Co.).

Canada (1982), *Wife Battering* (Ottawa: Standing Committee on Health, Welfare and Social Affairs).

Canada (1983), *Victimization in Greater Vancouver* (Ottawa: Solicitor-General).

Canadian Association for the Prevention of Crime (1982), Recommendations for Revision of the Criminal Code.

Canadian Council on Social Development (1981), *Rights and Services for Crime Victims* (Ottawa: Canadian Council on Social Development).

Conklin, J. (1972), *Robbery and the Criminal Justice System* (Philadelphia: Lippincott).

Cooper, Christine E. (1979), *The Causes and Prevention of Child Abuse* (Strasbourg: Council of Europe).

Davis, Robert, Tichane, M. and Connich, E. (1980), *Victim Involvement Project: First Year Evaluation* (New York: Victim Services Agency).

Drennan-Searson, Phyllis (1982), *Crime Victim Needs and Services: Ottawa* (University of Ottawa, Dept of Criminology).

Evans, J. L. and Léger, G. J. (1979), 'Canadian Victimization Surveys: a Discussion Paper', *Canadian J. of Criminology*, vol. 21, no. 2, pp. 166–83.

Fredericks, Carl (1980), 'Effects of Natural vs. Human-Induced Violence upon Victims', *Evaluation and Change*, Special Issue (spring).

Friedman, Kenneth, Bischoff, H., Davis, R. and Person, A. (1982), *Victims and Their Helpers: Reaction to Crime* (New York: Victim Services Agency).

Garofalo, James (1977), *Local Victim Surveys: a Review of the Issues* (Washington: LEAA, NCJRS).

Garofalo, James and McDermott, M. J., (1979), 'National Victim Compensation – Its Cost and Coverage', *Law and Policy Quarterly*, vol.1 (Oct.) p.456.

Giroux, J. and Hust, L. (1977), *Les petits commerçants victimes de vol à main armée, Enquête de justice*, Report no. 5 (Montreal: CICC).

Goldsmith, J. and Goldsmith, Sharon (1976), *Crime and the Elderly: Challenge and Response* (Lexington, Mass.: D. C. Heath and Co.)

Hagan, John (1980), 'A Study of Victim Involvement in the Criminal Justice System' (Toronto: Centre of Criminology).

Knudton, R. *et al.* (1976a), *Victims and Witnesses: the Impact of Crime and Their Experience with the Criminal Justice System* (Milwaukee: Marquette University – Centre for Criminal Justice and Social Policy).

Knudton, R. *et al.* (1976b), 'The Victim in the Administration of Criminal Justice: Problems and Perceptions' in W. F. McDonald (*ed.*), *Criminal Justice and the Victim.* (Beverly Hills, CA: Sage) pp. 115–46.

Jaycox, V. (1979), 'The Elderly's Fear of Crime: Rational or Irrational', *Victimology*, vol. 3, nos 3–4, pp. 329–34.

Léger, Gerry J. (1981) 'The Role of Research in the Initiation, Management and Evaluation of Victim Assistance Programs' (Ottawa: Solicitor-General of Canada: unpublished).

Léger, Gerry J. (1982), *Victim Asisstance: Canada-USA*, proceedings of conference. (Ottawa: Solicitor General of Canada: Research Division).

Lejeune, R. and Alex, N. (1973), 'On Being Mugged: the Event and its Aftermath', *Urban Life and Culture*, vol. 2, no. 3, pp. 259–82.

*Liaison* (1928), 'Connecting the Victim: Edmonton Police Take the Initiative', *Liaison*, vol. 8, no. 4 (Apr.) pp. 2–6.

Macleod, Linda (1980) *Wife Battering in Canada: the Vicious Circle* (Ottawa: Supply and Services).

Maguire, E. M. W. (1982) *Burglary in a Dwelling* (London: Heinemann Educational Books).

Malinchak, A. A. (1980), *Crime and Gerontology* (Englewood Cliffs, NJ Prentice-Hall).

Muir, Judith (1982), 'Needs and Services for Crime Victims'. Unpublished. Calgary, Police Services.

Norquay, Geoff and Weiler, R. (1981), *Services to Victims and Witnesses of Crime in Canada* (Ottawa: Solicitor-General, Research Division).

NOVA (1982), *Campaign for Victim Rights* (Washington, DC: National Organisation for Victim Assistance).

Québec, Groupe de Recherche sur la Violence Faite aux Femmes (1980) *Recherche sur la Violence Faite aux Femmes en Milieu Conjugal* (Québec: Conseil du Statut de la Femme).

Reiff, Robert (1979), *The Invisible Victim* (New York: Basic Books).

Salasin, Susan (ed.) (1981), *Evaluating Victim Services* (Beverley Hills: Sage).

Schneider, Hans J. (1982), *The Victim in International Perspect* (New York: De Gruyter).

Skogan, W. G. (1981), *Issues in the Measurement of Victimization* (Washington, DC: Bureau of Justice Statistics, Dept. of Justice).

Solicitor General of Canada (1979), *Selected Trends in Canadian Criminal Justice* (Ottawa: Supply and Services).

Straus, Murray A., Gelles, R. J. and Steinmetz, J. K. (1980), *Behind Closed Doors: Violence in the American Family* (New York: Anchor/Doubleday).

Symonds, M. (1980), 'The Second Injury to Victims of Violent Crime', *Evaluation and Change*, Special Issue (spring) pp. 36–41.

Tsitsoura, Aglaia (1982), *The Role of the Victim in the Framework of Crime Policy – International Aspects* (Strasbourg: Council of Europe, Division of Crime Problems).

US Congress (1982), *Victim and Witness Protection Act*, S2420.
US Dept. of Justice, Bureau of Justice Statistics (1981) *Criminal Victimisation in the United States, 1979*, a National Crime Survey Report (Washington, DC: US Government Printing Office).
US Dept. of Justice, Bureau of Justice Statistics (1981) *Criminal Victimisation in the United States, 1973–78: Trends*, a National Crime Survey Report (Washington, DC: US Government Printing Office).
*US President's Task Force on Victims of Crime* (1982), Final Report, Chair: Lois Herrington. Washington, DC: Government Printing Office.
Van Stolk, M. (1978), *The Battered Child in Canada* (rev. edn) (Toronto: McClelland & Stewart).
Vennard, Julie (1978), 'Compensation by the Offender: the Victim's Perspective' *Victimology*, vol.3, pp.154–60.
Waller, Irvin (1984), 'Victim Oriented Social Indicators, Knowledge to Reduce Crime and Its Effects and Improved Use of Victimisation Techniques', in Block, R. (*ed.*) *Victimization and Fear of Crime: World Perspectives* (Washington, DC: US Dept. of Justice), pp. 93–102.
Waller, Irvin (1982a), 'Victimisation Studies as Guides to Action: Some Cautions and Suggestions', in Schneider H. J. (*ed.*) *The Victim in International Perspective* (New York: Walter de Gruyter). pp. 166–88.
Waller, Irvin (1982b),*Crime Victims: Needs, Services, and Reforms* (Ottawa: Dept. of Criminology).
Waller, Irvin and Okihiro, N. (1978), *Burglary: The Victim and the Public* (University of Toronto Press).
Waller, I. and Touchette, L. (1982), 'Canadian Crime and Justice in Comparative Perspective – selected indicators for selected countries: 1900–1980' (Ottawa: Dept. of Criminology, University of Ottawa). Mimeo.
Young Rifai, M. A. (1977a), 'The Response of the Older Adult to Criminal Victimization', *Police Chief*, vol. 44, no. 2, pp. 48–50.
Young Rifai, M. A. (1977b), *Justice and Older Americans* (Lexington, Mass.: D.C. Heath & Co).

# 12 Crime Reporting and Services for Victims

## Eduard Ziegenhagen

### CRIME REPORTING AND PUBLIC POLICY

Crime reporting has received a substantial amount of attention in public policy and criminology largely due to the availability of information secured in the United States through the administration of the national crime survey and various city surveys. Criminologists suspected that police reports account for only a small portion of the actual number of incidents of crime and also may vary greatly in respect to types of crime and reporting jurisdictions (Sellin and Wolfgang, 1964). Police sources of crime data are known to vary as a result of differences in reporting procedures, the intentional manipulation of data that serves a variety of administrative and political purposes, and variation in the criteria employed by police to determine whether incidents reported were considered to be crimes (see LaFave, 1965; Goldstein, 1960; Seidman, 1974).

Most attention was focused on unreported crime, often termed 'the dark figure of crime' by those concerned with the practice of victims exercising great selectivity in reporting. The tendency of victims and bystanders to impose their own personal criteria as the basis for crime reporting is believed to be contrary to the general public interest in having crimes brought to the attention of law enforcement authorities (see, for example, Schneider, Burcart and Wilson, 1976.) Victims seem to perform a type of gate-keeping function exercised in a manner that prevents the police from acquiring information about the occurrence of crime, or at the very least, the actual occurrences of particular types of crime. Crime reporting can be viewed as information about the level of crime in society, but also may be a measure of citizen confidence in the criminal justice system or the performance of the system. The meaning of crime reporting varies substantially with the policy perspectives being advocated.

Under-reporting by victims of crime emerged as an important problem in public policy largely due to national crime panel survey results. It appears that at least 50% of all types of crime and 80% of all property crime of less than $50 are unreported. Furthermore, personal crimes, often involving persons well known to each other, often are not reported. Such under-reporting and selective reporting are often viewed as indicators of the obstinate and uncooperative nature of victims of crime. Among criminal justice professionals, under-reporting and selective reporting of crimes to the police are associated with victims who are believed to share certain undesirable attributes. Persons who engage in unlawful behaviour with others, fail to take precautionary measures to avoid harm, react to harm or threats with force and violence, or are habitual associates of the accused are regarded as not very innocent and most likely not very cooperative victims. Although behavioural criteria may be important in the determination of how cooperative victims are, the determination of an uncooperative victim by criminal justice professionals often seems to reflect a particular point of view. For example, in a study of witness management approaches used by prosecuters' offices, 90% of the victim witnesses regarded by the prosecuter as uncooperative saw themselves as being cooperative (Cannavale, 1975, pp.39-40).

Regardless of varying interpretations of the meaning of victim non-cooperation, there seems to be general agreement that under-reporting is in itself problematic in public policy and that it is necessary to increase levels of crime reporting to some, as yet undetermined, satisfactory level. Therefore, more crime reporting is believed to be better than less crime reporting and citizen involvement is to be the mechanism by which this objective is to be achieved.

Eventually, behaviour of individual crime victims and bystanders emerged as the focus for intervention rather than the practices of criminal justice institutions themselves. Consistent with this focus and drawing upon national crime panel survey data, a series of studies was conducted to identify factors which contribute to crime reporting practices by victims. A display of selected predictors and their relationship to crime reporting is found in Table 12.1.

Crime outcomes, especially whether or not the crime was successfully executed and the extent of the losses sustained by the victim, are closely related to the likelihood that a crime will be reported. Completed crimes and those which have resulted in serious injury or substantial property loss to the victim are more likely to be reported. A second source of influence may be individual attributes which make persons vulnerable or available to crime. For example, men are more likely to report robbery and assault incidents than women although no differences in report behaviour are found in cases of

Table 12.1   Factors Associated with Crime Reporting

|  | *Relationship to Crime Reporting* |
|---|---|
| *Crime Outcomes* | |
| Completion<br>Hindelang, 1976; Hindelang &<br>Gottfredson, 1976; Ziegenhagen &<br>Brosnan, 1982. | + |
| *Seriousness*<br>Hindelang. 1976; Fishman, 1979. | + |
| *Victim Attributes*<br>Income<br>Hindelang & Gottfredson, 1976;<br>Sparks, 1977; Fishman, 1979. | +/0 |
| *Age, Sex, Race*<br>Dodge, 1976; Hindelang & Gottfredson,<br>1976. | + |
| *Social Environment*<br>Population density<br>Gamble, 1980. | + |
| *% of Non-white Population*<br>Gamble, 1980. | + |
| *Police Resources*<br>Per capita Manpower<br>Gamble, 1980. | + |
| *Per capita Expenditures*<br>Gamble, 1980. | + |
| *Attitudes toward Criminal Justice System*<br>Schneider *et. al.*, 1976; Garofalo, 1977;<br>Dukes & Alpert, 1980; Gamble, 1980. | +/0 |

(+) = statistically significant association.
(0) = no association or not significant.

personal larceny. Black victims appear more likely to report violent crimes than white victims although property crimes are more likely to be reported by whites than blacks. Some researchers found a slight relationship between higher income groups and an increased tendency to report crimes (Hindelang and Gottfredson, 1976) but others found no relationship. The third set of factors appears to be related to aspects of the social environment in which the victim lives, especially population density and the percentage of non-white persons in the community. American cities having comparative high percentages of non-white residents, and those cities which have high population densities most often rank high in crime reporting. Factors comprising a fourth set include police resources as measured by per capita expenditures on police services and per capita police manpower. Crime reporting tends to increase as police resources increase. The fifth set of findings is based upon association of ratings of criminal justice services and crime reporting. Schneider (1976), Dukes and Alpert (1980) found high ratings of criminal justice services to be related to comparably high rates of crime reporting but others failed to find this association.

Although the American National crime panel surveys are not very sensitive to disclosing the exact nature of the victim's role in the commission of crimes, the results of empirical studies frequently disclose that victims base their decision to report crimes to the police on a careful assessment of crime outcomes and the additional costs and benefits of becoming involved with the criminal justice system. Aside from conflicting findings that positive attitudes towards the criminal justice system may be related to crime reporting and that police resources are related to crime reporting, none suggests that individual victims are open to public policy interventions. Nevertheless, various types of intervention taking the form of services for victims of crime, emphasize crime reporting as a programme component and give the impression that under-reporting of crime can be addressed from this perspective.

**CRIME REPORTING AND VICTIM SERVICE PROGRAMMES**

The relationship of crime reporting to the structure of other objectives in victim service programmes varies substantially. Programmes vary in the degree to which crime reporting is a functional prerequisite to achieving other programme objectives. For example, crime reporting by victims or bystanders is a functional prerequisite in all programmes which emphasize prosecution of the offender as an ultimate objective (offender restitution, victim witness and victim advocacy). Yet victim compensation programmes require crime reporting as a pre-condition of being considered as a claimant of programme services, although reporting is not a functional prerequisite to awarding compensation to victims of crime. Crime reporting provisions seem to serve different policy purposes in each victim service programme aside from the explicit purpose of increased rates of reporting.

Client populations tend to be defined in terms of the types of crimes sustained. For example, crisis intervention seems more appropriate for victims of violent crimes than victims of property crimes. Therefore, some programmes may have an impact on reporting of particular types of crimes rather than others. The role of crime reporting and five types of victim service programme is displayed in Table 12.2.

## VICTIM COMPENSATION PROGRAMMES

The efficacy of crime reporting and its primacy as a public policy objective is reflected in its inclusion in most victim compensation programmes (see Edelhertz and Geis, 1974). There is a strong official position taken that the 'innocent' victim should be ready to report crimes to the police. Should the victim not be as ready and willing to report crimes as is desired, non-reporting bars the victim from having his/her claim considered by compensation boards. Lack of enthusiasm about crime reporting may be seen as an expression of doubt about the efficacy of the police in providing an appropriate response. Hostility toward the police, in combination with late or selective reporting, can result in the summary rejection of the victim's claim. Similarly, an indication of an interest in revenge against the accused or fear of reprisal by the accused can serve as a basis for the Board's rejection of a victim's claim if coupled with resistance to crime reporting (Meyers, 1978, p.170).

Insistence upon crime reporting as a prerequisite for consideration of a victim's claim by Compensation Boards seems to exclude all those behavioural and attitudinal orientations which are not believed to fit neatly within the legal stereotype of the 'innocent' or 'cooperative' victim. Victims are expected to be ready and willing to conform to organizational demands for crime reporting and witness service to the criminal justice system. Questions of the efficacy of crime reporting for victims are dismissed as inconsequential when organizational priorities are taken into consideration. Insistence upon a good fit

Table 12.2  Crime Reporting Provisions in Victim Service Programmes

| Crime Reporting | Victim Service Programme | | | | |
| --- | --- | --- | --- | --- | --- |
| | *Victim Compensation* | *Offender Restitution* | *Victim Witness* | *Crisis Intervention* | *Victim Advocacy* |
| Prerequisite to achieving client status | yes (in most jurisdictions) | yes | yes | no (varies slightly) | yes |
| Prerequisite to achieving programme goals | no | yes | yes | no | yes |
| Specification as programme goal | yes (in most jurisdictions) | no | yes | no (varies slightly) | no |
| Violent Crimes | yes | no | yes | yes | yes |
| Property Crimes | no | yes | yes | no | yes |

between organizational demands and the situational aspects of the incident experienced by the victim tends to exclude all those cases which are most often cited as the basis for victim's reluctance to report crimes to the police. Those instances in which victims believe that nothing could be done to remedy the situation through police action, and those cases in which victims consider the police unresponsive or possibly harmful are contrary to organizational conceptions of a proper disposition toward the criminal justice system, and such victims are denied the possibility of compensation.

The same factors which contribute to the reluctance of victims to report crimes contribute to the likelihood that compensation boards will reject a victim's claim. The assumption that the possibility of an award by crime victim compensation boards is sufficient to induce victims to report to the police crimes that would ordinarily not be reported seems unwarranted. Even if anticipation of an award were sufficient to induce less than 'innocent' or 'cooperative' victims to report crimes to the police, those same attributes would preclude them from consideration for an award by victim compensation boards. The likelihood of an actual award for victims of this type would be at the most illusory.

## OFFENDER RESTITUTION PROGRAMMES

Crime reporting is not often explicitly recognized as a crucial component of offender restitution programmes, yet the willingness and capability of the victim to report a crime to the police is a prerequisite to utilizing the criminal justice system to force offenders to provide restitution.[1] Offenders are held accountable by restitution programmes only if the incident reported by the victim constitutes a founded crime. A crime is founded when the police make a determination that an incident contains the appropriate fact–law components which are sufficient for intervention by the criminal justice system. No claims for recompense arising out of the offender's acts are honoured if victims are unwilling or unable to conform to the innocent victim stereotype favoured by the criminal justice system.

In offender restitution programmes, victims are expected to take on the additional burden of participating in procedures by which the offender will be obligated to restore the losses sustained by the victim. Crime reporting objectives rarely appear as explicit programme goals in offender restitution programmes. It could be maintained that crime reporting is encouraged because notification of the police of the occurrence of a crime is a prerequisite for the eventual restoration of losses suffered by the victim. If such opportunities inspire victims to report crimes, reporting is likely to be highly selective. Property crime reporting rates may increase as restitution programmes rarely involve violent crime incidents, and only sizeable property losses are likely to be considered worth the victim's investment of time and effort in the restitution process. The reporting increment is likely to be small as victims are more likely to report more costly losses than less costly losses without the inducement offered by restitution programmes.

## VICTIM WITNESS PROGRAMMES

Victim witness programmes are organized to address what criminal justice practitioners perceive as a management problem caused by the victim's unwillingness or inability to participate in proceedings as a witness.[2] Services to victims most often take on the form of administrative procedures designed to secure organizational objectives. For example, verification of witnesses' phone numbers and addresses, and notification of witnesses as to their appearance in proceedings against the accused is most common. To become a witness, of course, the crime must be reported to the police. If the criteria utilized by the police to determine whether a crime has or has not occurred corresponds to the criteria of the prosecutor's office for the determination of whether or not information derived from witnesses can be used effectively in proceedings against the accused, then victims become eligible as clients. Much as victims possess particular attributes drawn upon to establish the existence of a crime, victims also possess, in varying degrees, qualities which contribute to their desirability as a witness against the accused (see, for example, Newman, 1966; Williams, 1976). The ability and willingness of victims to relate information respecting the occurrence of a crime to the police contribute to the determination of whether incidents become crimes from the police viewpoint, and accordingly how these crimes become translated into proceedings against the offender in which witnesses are expected to play a role. The identification of crime reporting as a specific programme goal is often found in victim witness programmes but is actively encouraged only to the degree that crime reporting is consistent with securing the conviction of the accused.

## CRISIS INTERVENTION

The role of crime reporting in crisis intervention programmes varies substantially among programmes as well as within programmes.[3] Most crisis intervention programmes are designed to provide services related to the immediate and most pressing needs of victims who have suffered physical or psychological injuries. Crisis intervention is a particularly common approach to the needs of victims of crimes when addressing problems associated with female victims. Deprivation suffered by women as a result of domestic conflict and problems associated with particular types of crime, especially rape, receive a great deal of attention. Crime reporting generally is not a prerequisite to achieving client status in most programmes but in some instances reporting may be closely associated with particular varieties of ultimate programme objectives. Those programmes focused on dealing with problems experienced by victims of rape may emphasize both public education and punitive responses to the crime through reporting the incident to the police. Programmes of this variety frequently have as programme objectives increases in the number of rape incidents reported to the police and in the number of successful prosecutions of the accused. Reporting of the incident to the organization exists as an alternative to reporting the incident to the police in particular situations, especially those which entail intimidation or revenge directed against the victim.

Crisis intervention programmes by definition are directed to addressing the needs of victims of violent crimes and if there are any effects on rates of crime reporting they would most certainly be in the area of crime of this type.

## VICTIM ADVOCACY

Programmes of the victim advocacy variety are almost as diverse as crisis intervention programmes, in that virtually all lawful strategies which address the needs of victims of crime are employed to achieve some level of satisfaction of victim needs.[4] In practice, however, most programmes are focused on the issue of retribution or recompense for victims and most resources are of a variety appropriate to pursuing remedies within criminal or civil courts.

The major strategy of victim advocates is to introduce the victim as a participant in the decision-making process respecting the disposition of the offender or the victim's property. Within this framework, crime reporting contributes to establishing the role of the victim as a claimant respecting proceedings against the accused. To a great extent reporting the crime to the police is a prerequisite to achieving a desirable course of action against the accused. Crime reporting is not a central goal of victim advocacy programmes irrespective of pursuing specific objectives of interest to the victim.

## CONCLUSION

Relatively little is known about the impact of victim service programmes on the phenomenon of under-reporting of crimes.[5] Although most victim service programmes entail some aspect of crime reporting there is little reason to believe that persons who are least likely to report crimes will be induced to change their behaviour by virtue of opportunities for services offered to victims of crime. Most victim service programmes referred to above provide services to victims who have sustained substantial losses, exactly those persons who are most likely to report a crime to the police.

A small prospect for increases in the reporting of particular kinds of crime may exist as a result of the activities of particular types of victim service programmes. Crisis intervention programmes which contain strong commitments to public education and punitive action against offenders may account for some increase in crime reporting. Crimes involving domestic conflict or sexual misbehaviour are of this variety although there is little systematically collected comparative information available to indicate increases in the predilection of individuals to report crimes of this type.

The incorporation of crime reporting objectives into the design of programmes for services to victims of crime is unlikely to increase general levels of crime reporting. No change is virtually assured by the inclusion of reporting as a prerequisite to achieving client status. This practice excludes prospective claimants having those individual and situational attributes which detract from the idealized 'innocent' victim stereotype. Crime reporting often is not an operational objective in the sense that it induces persons to report crimes which would ordinarily go unreported. It does serve as a screening technique which functions to eliminate victims who do not meet the organizational needs of criminal justice organizations or the internal definitions of clients acceptable to the programme. This limitation exists for victim compensation programme and victim witness programmes but may also be applicable to offender restitution programmes and victim advocacy programmes. By contrast, in offender restitution programmes, victim witness programmes, and victim advocacy programmes, crime reporting is an integral part of the process by which victim needs are served and the justification for the inclusion of crime reporting as a functional programme goal seems well founded.

One must conclude that only a tangential linkage exists between the activities of victim service programmes and opportunities to increase levels of crime reporting. Most victim service programmes provide aid to individuals who are predisposed to report crimes to the police. Ultimately, crime reporting provisions are likely to reduce the number of persons seeking sources rather than increase the number of persons reporting crimes to the police.

## Notes

1. See Burt Galaway and Joe Hudson, *Offender Restitution in Theory and Action*, (Lexington Books, 1977) for a description and assessment of programmes of this variety.
2. For a powerful criticism of courtroom practices respecting the role of witnesses, see M. Ash 'On Witnesses: a Radical Critique of Criminal Court Proceedings', *Notre Dame Lawyer* vol.48, (1972) pp.386–425.
3. For example, see *Child Abuse and Neglect: the Problem and its Management*, vol.3, *The Community Team; An Approach to Case Management and Prevention*, (US Dept. of Health Education and Welfare, 1976) and Elizabeth Ann O'Sullivan, 'What Has Happened to Rape Crisis Centers?: a Look at Their Structures, Members and Funding', *Victimology: an International Journal*, vol.3, (1978), pp.45–62.
4. Fredrick L. DuBow and Theodore M. Becker provide a summary of the victim advocacy approach in 'Patterns of Victim Advocacy' in William F. McDonald (ed.), *Criminal Justice and the Victim*, Beverly Hills, CA Sage publications, 1976) pp.147–64.
5. The few empirical evaluation results that exist are not encouraging. See, for example, William G. Doerner, 'An Examination of the Alleged Latent Effects of Victim Compensation Programmes upon Crime Reporting', *LAE Journal*, vol.41 (1978).

**Bibliography**

Cannavale, Frank (1975), *Witnesses Cooperation with a Handbook of Witness Management* (Lexington, Mass.: D. C. Heath).
Dodge, Richard, Lentzner, H. and Shenk, F. (1976), 'Crime in the United States: a Report on the National Crime Survey', in W. Skogan (ed.), *Sample Surveys of the Victims of Crime*, (Cambridge: Ballinger).
Dukes, Richard L. and Alpert, Geoffrey, P. (1980), 'Criminal Victimization from a Police Perspective', *Journal of Police Science and Administration*, vol.8, no.1, pp.21–30.
Edelhertz, Herbert and Geis, Gilbert (1974), *Public Compensation to Victims of Crime* (New York: Praeger Special Studies).
Fishman, Gideon (1979), 'Patterns of Victimization and Notification', *British Journal of Criminology*, vol.19, no.2, pp.146–57.
Gamble, Darwin (1980), 'In Search of a Linkage: Citizen Evaluation, Police Systems Activity and Unreported Crime', *Criminology*, vol.17, pp.471–76.
Garofalo, James (1977), *The Police and Public Opinion* (Washington, DC: Government Printing Office).
Goldstein, J., (1960), 'Police Decision not to Invoke the Criminal Process: Low Visibility Decisions in the Administration of Justice', *Yale Law Review*, vol.69, pp.543–88.
Hindelang, Michael (1976), *Criminal Victimization in Eight American Cities* (Cambridge: Ballinger).
Hindelang, Michael J. and Gottfredson, Michael (1976), 'The Victim's Decision not to Invoke the Criminal Justice Process', in William F. McDonald (ed.), *Criminal Justice and the Victim* (Beverley Hills: Sage Publications).
LaFave, W. R. (1965), *Arrest: the Decision to Take a Suspect into Custody* (Boston: Little Brown).
Meyers, David (1978), *Responses to Victimization* (Abington, Oxon: Professional Books).
Newman, D. J. (1966). *Conviction* (Boston: Little Brown).
Seidman, David and Couzens, Michael (1974), 'Getting the Crime Rate Down: Public Pressure and Crime Reporting', *Law and Society Review*, vol.8, pp.457–93.
Schneider, Anne, Burcart, J. and Wilson II, L. A. (1976), 'The Role of Attitudes in the Decision to Report Crimes to the Police', in William F. McDonald (ed.), *Criminal Justice and the Victim*, (Beverly Hills, CA, Sage Publications).
Sellin, T. and Wolfgang, Marvin, (1964), *The Measurement of Delinquency* (New York: John Wiley).
Sparks, Richard, Genn, Hazel G. and Dodd, David J. (1977), *Surveying Victims* (New York: John Wiley).
Williams, Kirsten (1976), 'The Effects of Victim Characteristics on the Disposition of Violent Crimes' in William F. McDonald (ed.), *Criminal Justice and the Victim* (Beverly Hills, CA: Sage Publications).
Ziegenhagen, Eduard A., and Brosnan, Dolores (1982), 'Victim Responses to Robbery and Crime Control Policy', paper presented at the Academy of Criminal Justice Sciences Annual Meeting.

# Part IV

# On Services for Crime Victims

# 13 Compensation by Offenders in Canada: a Victim's Right?

## Ab Thorvaldson

### THE PROPOSITION

The central purpose of this chapter is to consider the validity of a deceptively simple proposition: that victims should have a legal right to compensation[1] in the criminal sentencing process. Surely, it is argued, criminal sentencing has become out of balance; it has become far too concerned with maintaining the criminal law on an abstract plane and with protecting the rights of the offender; surely the courts have forgotten that crimes often entail actual or substantive harm to real people and not merely symbolic harm to the social order. Surely, therefore, the victim not only has a right to be heard and to make a claim in the sentencing process but a right to a compensation order, a compensation order enforced routinely by criminal justice administrators. Perhaps the needs and rights of the actual victim of crime should indeed be a matter of priority in our total response to crime. Perhaps the victim should have the right to have all the harm or damage done properly assessed and to legal assistance in court quite separate from the prosecutor and the defence counsel. Surely such proposals are consistent with the common moral principles of our society and a matter of simple justice. Perhaps they are also consistent with the rehabilitation of offenders because they hold offenders morally accountable for the wrong they do.

The first thing to note about such an appealing proposition is the rather sobering fact that essentially the same arguments have been presented, varying only in intensity, for well over a century, and with cogency and conviction by eminent criminologists and social philosophers – Bentham, Ferri (see Hudson and Galaway) 1975), Garofalo (1914), Del Vecchio (1969), and more recently by Margery Fry (1951) in Britain and Stephen Schafer (1960) in the United States. The topic of redress was in fact extensively debated at several world penal congresses late in the last century (Ruggles-Brise, 1901). They were also among the arguments, 10 or 12 years ago, of the Advisory Council on the Penal System in Britain (1970) and of the Law Reform Commission of Canada (1974).

And yet these arguments have conspicuously failed to date to win a significant place for compensation as a criminal sanction or, certainly, for the notion that the victim has a legal right to such compensation. The main reason for the failure is the fact that the proposition raises both a host of fundamental theoretical questions – the nature, aims, and methods of the criminal law, the distinction between public and private law, the distinction between crimes and torts – and also a series of difficult procedural and administrative issues. It turns out that it is one thing to defend the notion of redress for wrongdoing as a common moral precept and quite another to argue that it should be accepted as a criminal sentencing aim or principle. It is one thing to say that the victim has a *moral* right to compensation by some sort of procedure and another to say that a victim should have a legal right to compensation in criminal procedure. Is compensation an appropriate response to a *criminal* wrong? Is it compatible with the modern notion of crime and specifically with the relatively recent historical division of legal procedure in two separate sections: the criminal and the civil?

I am suggesting, then, that while the current rallying cry is victims' rights, essentially the same question has been asked for a long time from the standpoint of sentencing theory. From that standpoint there are three main questions that should be considered, roughly in sequence: 1. can compensation by the offender to the victim be *justified in principle* as a criminal sanction? 2. If so, should compensation, as a matter of sentencing policy, *be a priority* in sentencing? and 3. – to the point of this chapter – should one go so far as to say the victim has a *legal right* to compensation from the offender in the sentencing process?

There are at least five reasonably definable clusters of opinions on these questions. I will label them here the abolitionist, the conservative, the pragmatic, the radical, and what I will call the 'reparativist'. I will briefly describe each position in turn with reference to the three main questions: (a) compensation by offenders in principle, (b) its priority in sentencing, and (c) the victim's legal right to compensation. As regards the victim's rights question, it will often be necessary to sub-divide it into several related questions, as suggested in the opening remarks earlier. That is: Does the victim have a legal right (a) to make a claim (to force the court to consider the matter)? (b) to have the harm or damage entailed in the offence properly assessed by state services? (c) to have the legal assistance of the crown prosecutor or a separate counsel? (d) to compensation itself by the offender in full or in part and this (e) for all the types of harm the offence may entail (i.e. both pecuniary and non-pecuniary)? and (f) to proper administration and enforcement of the order by state services?

## THE ABOLITIONISTS

I mean to describe here the conservative view in its purest form. The view is not in fact reflected in the *Criminal Code* of Canada but will serve here as a limiting position. The position is that compensation is in principle a civil remedy intended to serve the interests of victims in their private capacity. The criminal law, it is argued here, is after all public law, not private. The criminal law represents the values or interests of the state or community as a whole and the crime is by definition a violation of those values or interests.[2] The criminal harm thus consists in the violation of public order, an assault on the rights of all citizens to be protected from certain harmful or exploitive acts, sometimes constituting an outrage to commonly held principles of decency or morality, a 'trespass on the King's peace'.

The 'actual' or material harm to a citizen (or even to the state itself) becomes merely the occasion, the vehicle for the vindication of the ideals of social order and justice which the criminal law is supposed to represent, particularly in a democratic society. To consider compensation directly by the offender to the victim, it would be argued here, is worse than inappropriate. It would jeopardize the total effectiveness of the criminal law for several reasons: Firstly it would becloud the nature and function of the criminal process. It would confuse private and public law, confuse the obvious distinction between a wrong which is left to the citizens involved to settle as they see fit, in their private capacities, and a wrong which is considered to jeopardize or harm the interests of the social group as a whole and concerning which the group as a whole considers it necessary to take action. That distinction, the conservatives might add, is as old as human society itself and one which is readily recognized by the public.

Secondly, compensation to the victim would clearly be, even if not inappropriate, at least insufficient as a response to certain types of crime. How could the highwayman or pirate of centuries ago be expected to be adequately controlled in the public interest simply by being required to give back the booty in those cases where he was caught? Could modern professional crime be controlled simply by requiring the offender, where apprehended, to repay the victim? Would he not treat it simply as a licence to continue? Surely the concept of 'crime' as public wrong developed in part precisely because the 'civil' process was insufficient as a method of deterring or controlling certain types of wrongful behaviour.

There would be frequent conflict between the interests of the community and those of the victim, between the public and the private interest. If the court were obliged to order compensation as a matter of victims' rights it would be faced with a built in, and unsolvable, conflict. It would be serving two masters.

Thirdly, even in cases where no conflict occurred, enormous administrative difficulties can be predicted. The court would presumably be expected to assess and administer compensation orders in a consistent, uniform, just, and competent manner. It would logically be asked to take into account all the types of harm which even a minor crime might entail – pecuniary and non-pecuniary, tangible and intangible, immediate and remote – all of the types of harm which went into defining the wrongful act as a crime in the first place. It would also be required to show due regard for the procedural rights of all parties, rights they would enjoy in the civil process. Such administrative burdens, even if we could afford them, would tend to detract from the administration of other criminal sanctions which are designed appropriately to vindicate the criminal law and to control crime rather than to assist the individual victim.

In short, the abolitionists argue that compensation can have no function as a criminal sanction on grounds of both theory and administration, and, of course, the question of priority does not arise.

Turning to the victims' status, it follows that they have no rights in the process, at least not as individuals or 'third parties' in the criminal process. Their appropriate role is to present the evidence of the violation of public order, to appear when called upon to provide that evidence if the offender disputes the charge. While the victim therefore is extremely important to the process, at the sentencing stage the victim has no more (and no fewer) rights than those of any other citizen. While in some places criminal legislation permits the victim to apply for compensation or obliges the authorities to consult the victim, and in some cases private prosecutions are permitted, from this point of view these are anachronisms, vestiges of the days before the criminal law as we now know it was developed. They are the exceptions which prove the rule.

The abolitionists acknowledge, of course, the *moral* right of the victim to claim compensation from the offender. Indeed, the retributivists among them – those who have placed an emphasis on punishment of the offender according to some notion of equitable justice – can point out that they have always been conscious of the victim's desire to see justice done; that they have consistently resisted the preoccupation of sentencing theory with utilitarian notions which stress the rehabilitation, deterrence, and control of offenders, and have always emphasized the moral aspect of crimes.

They also readily acknowledge the *legal* right of the victim to claim compensation from the offender, but argue that the criminal court is simply the wrong place to make the claim. They would refer the victim to the civil process or perhaps to state victim insurance schemes or community victim assistance programmes. They might suggest that reformers should look in that direction and that such reforms may indeed be long overdue!

In this connection it should be mentioned that abolitionists might also agree in principle with what is called the 'combined trial', the so called 'adhesion process', or, colloquially, 'one-stop justice', the procedure practised in many European countries whereby the victim is permitted to make a claim for damages but where the civil character of such a claim is at least reasonably clear. There is no assumption in such procedures that a compensation order would be a criminal sanction in whole or in part. Abolitionists might object on administrative grounds – the concerns about public perceptions of the nature of the criminal process and administrative burdens mentioned earlier – but a proposal for a combined civil and criminal process does not appear to be under serious consideration in Canada, and so I will not speculate about it further here.

## THE CONSERVATIVES

This more moderate or 'compromise' position would provide for compensation within the criminal sentencing process but only in a very limited way. It is in fact the prevailing one in Canada. Under

Section 653 of the *Criminal Code* the victim must apply for the order at the time of sentence, compensable harm is limited to loss or damage to property, and the victim is obliged to enforce the order 'as if it were a judgement rendered in civil proceedings'. Further, the courts have generally interpreted the powers narrowly (see Burns, 1980). In a recent notable case (*R.* v. *Zelensky*, 1978) the Supreme Court of Canada reaffirmed that a compensation order under Section 653 was acceptable in principle as a criminal sanction but in doing so it also (a) reaffirmed that it should be used with caution and as an ancillary matter in sentencing, (b) that it should be considered only where the property loss or damage was easily ascertainable, and where there is no serious dispute over quantum, and (c) that it should not be used 'in terrorem as a substitute . . . for civil proceedings'. At the level of administration by provincial authorities, current policies might encourage prosecutors to assist victims but at the same time warn prosecutors lest they imply that they are an advocate for the victim or are representing his/her interests.

Compensation is also permitted under Section 663 where it may be ordered as a condition of a probation order. Again it is restricted to 'actual loss or damage' which has been interpreted, for the most part, as denoting pecuniary damages. Here, however, compliance with the order is enforced by state officials rather than by the victim; that is, by the usual breach of probation procedures where required.[3]

What do these legal provisions for compensation imply, then, for the first question posed earlier: is it a criminal sanction or a civil remedy? The Code itself provides no statement justifying their inclusion, a fact frequently pointed out by critics (Law Reform Commission of Canada, 1974; Chasse, 1977). The issue has been particularly controversial as regards Section 653. Critics argue that the fact that compensable harm is limited to loss or damage to property, that the victim must apply for the order and enforce the order as if it were a civil remedy, all imply that the order is in reality a civil remedy offered to victims on the basis of convenience, common sense, or simple humanitarian feeling for the injustice to the victim in the face of the cumbersome, expensive, and probably ineffective alternative of a civil action.

The continuing controversy over the nature of compensation under Section 653 reached the Supreme Court of Canada in the Zelensky (1978) case mentioned above. In effect the court was asked if it found the provision to be justified as a criminal sanction, to provide the justifying rationale. If one assumes that criminal sanctions are justified according to the extent that they can be shown to serve the ends of the criminal law, the court was obliged also to state its assumptions about those ends and to demonstrate, on grounds of penal theory, a logical or at least plausible connection between the sanction and one or more of those ends.

The court did declare that compensation under the sanction was a proper part of criminal sentencing and thus removed the legal challenge. The decision, however, was split (6–3) and no systematic theoretical analysis was provided. The section therefore remains controversial on a theoretical and hence on an administrative level in this country.

As regards compensation as a condition of probation, the courts have held that the order must be consistent with probation and thus, by implication, consistent with the ends of the criminal process. In *R. v. Groves* (1977) it was considered to be in keeping with the aim of probation in 'securing the good conduct' of the offender and therefore justified as part of a criminal sanction. What the connection between compensation to the victim and the rehabilitation or control of the offenders is, however, was not explained.

The difference between this conservative position and the abolitionist position is thus not as clear as it might seem. One gets the impression that many of the conservatives accept the provision for compensation in the Code only grudgingly. They tend to emphasize the practical obstacles (staff, resources, expertise, etc.) to the greater use of compensation but usually show no desire to deal with such administrative problems and thus to explore the significance or potential of compensation within the criminal process. Further, it can be argued that those who accept the notion of compensation only for pecuniary damages or 'easily ascertainable' harm but suggest that more complicated cases 'belong in the civil court' are in fact implying that compensation is really civil in nature, and that they are offering it even in the 'simple cases' only because it is a practical and humane way to meet the victim's private need and *not because in principle it serves the ends of criminal justice.* Moreover, why it is in principle in keeping with criminal justice to require the offender to pay for the pecuniary damages entailed in an offence but not the non-pecuniary is not explained.

In other words, what this position often seems to imply is that what determines the criminal versus the civil nature of a compensation order is the practical difficulty of administering it. If it is simple and easy to adjudicate, then it is acceptable (in principle) as a criminal sanction; if it is not then it becomes a matter for the civil courts. Such an argument is obviously untenable from a theoretical point of view. While complicated or disputed cases would indeed create administrative and procedural problems and might well be excluded on grounds of administrative policy, clearly the choice in principle between the criminal and civil processes cannot turn on the administrative difficulty of assessing harm.

In short, this position provides no clear or consistent answer to the question about the justification of compensation as a criminal sanction. It provides for compensation for only certain types of damages and even here only when there are no serious complicating factors. As for the question of priority it says emphatically that compensation is not to receive priority and even that it is not expected to serve as a sole or independent sanction.

The victim role, accordingly, is also controversial and ambiguous, and victim's rights vary from one section of the code to the other. The victim has a right to make a claim under Section 653 but not under Section 663, and in any event can claim only certain types of damages and has no right to the prosecutor's assistance. The victim has no legal right to have the order enforced criminally under Section 663 or to require that compensation as a condition of probation under Section 663 be properly enforced.

## THE PRAGMATISTS

While the abolitionists and to some extent the conservatives have been concerned about distinguishing compensation as a civil remedy from its possible role as a criminal sanction, and upon reconciling compensation with the aims of criminal sentencing, this group of reformers I'm calling pragmatists fear that we are becoming completely mired in formal and theoretical issues. They fear we will make no progress at all. They place the emphasis – and it is only a matter of emphasis – on reform as an incremental, gradual, experimental trial and error process guided by intuitive judgement. One can mention to them the saying that there is nothing so practical as good theory, but they very much doubt it. The test is not one of formal logic but practical utility.

When they do consider the question *why* a criminal court should order compensation they tend to suggest first that no explanation is needed, that the justification of compensation by the offender is a self-evident moral axiom, a matter of common sense with which all can agree, particularly the average citizen who after all is to be served by the justice system. They speak first, then, in the morally righteous way mentioned at the outset of this chapter.

A further group are those who argue that the distinction between the criminal and civil process is itself not a significant one in actual practice. Thus they also do not concede at the outset that it is necessary to decide whether compensation offered in the criminal process is in the nature of a civil remedy or legitimately a criminal sanction in the traditional sense. Some argue that the difference in this respect between the two processes is not significant. They point out that the civil process does not confine itself purely to settling the dispute between individual citizens for their sake alone but is very conscious of its role in maintaining social order. The civil court may order not only pecuniary and non-pecuniary damages but also so-called 'punitive damages'. Similarly, they suggest, a criminal court should not be restricted to punitive or rehabilitative or other controlling measures but should be permitted to apply reparative measures as well. They argue it is not really necessary to worry whether the claim for compensation is private or public in nature.

But others go further than that. They acknowledge that compensation in the criminal process should somehow be justified in terms of the aims of sentencing. They attack this too, of course, in a pragmatic fashion, and point out that compensation has a number of effects which are consistent with those aims. The Widgery Committee in Britain, for example, deliberately assumed a pragmatic approach (see Hood, 1974 for a critique) and lists several 'views' about the rationale of the concept: the actual benefit to the victim, the possible deterrent effect on the offender or on the public, the possible educative or preventive effect on public morality, the possible 'reformative' effect on offenders, its effect in depriving the offender of ill gotten gains, and the view that compensation has an 'intrinsic moral value of its own' (Advisory Council on the Penal System, 1970). The Law Reform Commission of Canada (1974) also argued in this way, pointing out that compensation was consistent with the 'core values' of the community.

But one can suggest that in the end this approach has *not* in fact been practical. As pointed out at the beginning of this chapter, simple moral idealism has not, over the past century, been able to cope with the arguments of the abolitionists and conservatives that there is a logical and necessary difference, for all the inconsistencies, between a crime and a tort, and that compensation has only to do with settling private disputes. If they are going to argue seriously that there is no valid distinction between the criminal and civil process they must do more than point out inconsistencies.

And when they do attempt in a pragmatic way to justify compensation in principle as a criminal sanction they raise more questions than they solve. If the task is to retrieve ill-gotten profits of crime, the greater use of fines would serve more efficiently (and indeed fines have been used partly for that purpose). Fines also serve more efficiently if it is the deterrent effect of compensation that is desired. Further, if compensation is supposed to reform offenders, precisely what kind of reformation is meant? A garnishee on wages imposed by a criminal court will hardly help them to find jobs or pay the rent. If the order is intended to vindicate 'core values' how are such values related to the ends of the criminal process? The 'multiple-aim' arguments for compensation are not so much in error as they are unsystematic and ultimately ineffective.

The pragmatists, in keeping with their approach, either deny the significance of the theoretical objections to compensation or, when they do enter the fray, fail to convince. In the end, in terms of legislative proposals and practical implications they fall seriously short. The provisions for compensation in the new Young Offenders Act and proposals in Bill C-21 for changes in the Criminal Code, while encouraging greater use of compensation actually have the effect of consolidating, in some respects, the present conservative legislation and practice.

As for administrative implications, while the pragmatists propose that the courts consider compensation in all cases, their failure to win the minds of the many conservatives on the bench will severely curtail the actual use of the sanction. While they would require enforcement by criminal justice agencies, they fail to guide officials in the use of their discretion. While they ask for legal assistance by the prosecutor they fail to answer his/her concerns about his/her vulnerability to a negligence suit. While they ask for damages they fail to ask for non-pecuniary damages which are frequently the essence of a crime. If a home is broken into but by means of an open window and no material damage is done and nothing is taken, the pragmatist has nothing to say! The pragmatist has nothing to say about crimes which merely shock the feelings of a victim or shock the values of us all. Is that not what the criminal law, at least ideally, is all about?

Certainly there is some validity in a pragmatic approach to reform, fired by intuition, in this case a moral and human concern for the victim. We would not have made what progress we have without it. It is obvious that the problems are much too complicated and much too complex to be left to theorists of any stripe. But just as certainly the pragmatic approach to this problem is insufficient. While it can, and apparently already has, resulted in a substantial increase in the use of compensation within the present restrictions, it will suffer the same fate as previous efforts when it suggests major changes in legislation and a substantial shift in sentencing policy and practice. Such a shift would entail major administrative changes, changes which will require a commitment to purpose the pragmatists cannot inspire.

## THE RADICALS

This group has no difficulty acknowledging that theoretical issues are both relevant and significant, but challenge the specific questions asked. Rather than ask how compensation can be reconciled with the concept of crime they question the validity of the current concept and function of the criminal law in our society. Having said that, it is difficult to isolate any particular radical approach. I will attempt here only to outline what I take to be a basic radical position on this topic.

First, the radicals regard the state apparatus and the community of citizens as quite distinct entities. They do not regard the 'government' as being in any real sense accountable to the people, even in our society which is conventionally considered to be democratic.

Second, concerning the concept of criminal law, they point out that the notion of crime is relatively recent in its origins, beginning to dominate jurisprudence in the early 19th century and developing as an accepted paradigm of law only in the latter part of that century. They hold that the essential function of the criminal law is to protect and preserve the authority at one time of the reigning monarch or autocrat and more recently of the 'state', quite independent from the community. The purpose of the criminal law is here to protect and preserve the power of the group or groups in society who control the state. A crime therefore is primarily a violation of the interests of the state in maintaining obedience and social order and not necessarily an expression of the consensus of the people or a reflection of their values.

Further, since the criminal law is justified not in terms of its moral validity or function but in terms of its superior power, it relies, in its methods of application, on intimidation and control. Control would include any prophylactic or rehabilitative methods. In short, the concept of crime is that it is a tool in the sole possession of a central authority seeking, at least mainly, to preserve itself by repressive methods.

In this light, the general notion of redress as a sentencing principle, the idea of compensation to the victim, and the concept of a victim's right to compensation all represent a fundamental challenge to the status quo for several reasons: (a) they imply the concept of a community of citizens distinct from the state, (b) they imply the settlement of disputes between individual citizens leaving state officials in the mediating role of 'peacemaker' rather than 'law enforcer', and (c) they imply that order can be achieved by giving expression to an accepted and rational principle rather than intimidating punishment or other controlling methods.

The radicals thus do not accept the fundamental premises of the abolitionists as to the political justification and function of the criminal law itself. They consider the concept of criminal law as morally bankrupt since it cannot be considered to rest on the consent of the people, and thus is unacceptable in a society which aspires to be democratic, just, and humane. Almost ironically, the radical position is in agreement with the abolitionists and conservatives (and unlike some pragmatists) in associating the concept of criminal law with certain enforcement methods or sentencing principles, i.e. intimidation and control. Like the conservatives they do not recognize the possibility that 'doing justice' by settling disputes through compensation can be seen as a method of keeping the peace. Such a view would be inconsistent with their assumptions about the purpose of the criminal law.

The radicals, accordingly, welcome the concept of redress by offenders, the notion of victim rights and the fact that this requires the participation of both victim and offender in the settlement process, and see this as the primary response to behaviour we now call crime. They would regard it politically as primarily a means of standing the criminal justice system on its head, and forcing this political institution to be accountable to the people and to the moral values of the community.

## THE REPARATIVISTS

This brings me to the last general approach which I have called the 'reparative' or 'justice' approach since, as we shall see, it stresses the importance of 'doing justice' in sentencing and the use of the principle of redress or reparation to that end (see Thorvaldson, 1978, 1979, 1980, 1981).

Turning first to the basic question of the justification of compensation in principle, it is assumed that any action undertaken to administer the criminal law must be justified in terms of some conception of the aims of the criminal law. In this connection, this position takes a conventional stance and assumes that the system was primarily established to keep social order within the limits of a number of limiting social values such as equal justice, equitable justice, humanity, liberty, and democratic control of the process. If it can be shown that requiring offenders to make up for the wrong done will affect their moral attitudes which will in turn affect their tendency to break the law, and if it can be shown that this is a fair and humane procedure, one which does not unreasonably deprive the offender of his individual rights or freedoms, and one which permits a degree of control by citizens, then one can argue that such a sentence is justified as a criminal sanction.

The 'justice approach', then, argues that a shift to the use of compensation, along with other reparative sanctions, represents a renewed emphasis on the vindication and promulgation of the notion of justice or moral accountability for criminal wrongdoing. The position accepts the idea that the criminal sentencing process may function in part as a kind of 'morality play' (Morton, 1962) in the society, and that sentences can be used in part to try to teach moral values and to appeal to the moral sense or conscience in both offenders and the observing public. It acknowledges also that this is certainly not a new idea. The earlier concept of retribution and in the last century the development of the notion of denunciation of crime expressed precisely the same principle. Retribution and denunciation, however, were expressed in the form of punishment according to deserts, that is, making the offender suffer commensurate with some assessment of the seriousness of his offence and his culpability. Reparative sanctions are here seen as methods of serving such moral values in a concrete, material, and constructive or non-punitive way. The approach, in terms of sentencing theory, is neo-retributivist in the sense that it supports the moral position in sentencing (Thorvaldson, 1978; Geis, 1977).

The maintenance of the principle of equitable justice or reciprocity in society in turn can be shown at least theoretically to be directly connected to the maintenance of ordered and peaceful relationships (see Thorvaldson, 1978, for review) and empirical research is beginning to test the effects of redress on offenders' social attitudes (Thorvaldson, 1978). It is the 'master moral norm' regulating social relations (Gouldner, 1960). The essential concept of equitable justice – that doing right should be rewarded and doing wrong should result in some form of atonement – is clearly primeval in its origins and pervasive in society, so much so that it is usually accepted, as the pragmatists and others say, as axiomatic.

The requirement to repay the harm done is also more consistent than many alternative sanctions with several of the limiting social values mentioned earlier: the liberty of the individual, fair treatment, humane treatment, the participation of citizens, and the like. The shift of emphasis to redress as a sentencing principle and to compensation as one expression of that principle, is therefore considered justified in terms of several of the ends of the criminal law.

Turning to the question of priority, the overall priority the courts give to reparative sanctions in general and compensation in particular will depend on how they assess the logic of its rationale and its effectiveness. If, for example, they accept the 'justice aim' in principle, do they see the maintenance of justice as a moral value to be directly related to social behaviour in general and law-breaking in particular? Do they see reparation as an effective (including cost-effective) method of influencing moral values (either in the public or in the offender or in both)? Do they take the court process, capped by the sentence, seriously as a morality play? Considering, as indicated above, the fundamental importance of moral values in society and what evidence there is of the effectiveness of making a moral appeal to citizens or to offenders, the reparativist argues for very high priority for this type of sentence. Compensation directly between offender and victim is a form of redress which exemplifies the justice principle in a palpable and direct manner.

We come then to the initial question of this chapter: should compensation by offenders not only be regarded as a mainstream criminal sanction and be given priority as such but should the victim of crime in fact have a legal right to that compensation. The answer here is perhaps more complicated than at first appears.

The concept of 'crime' as a harm to the interests of the community of citizens clearly implies that it is *not* to be perceived as simply a violation of the interests of the victim as an individual. Thus when the victim makes a claim he does so in his role as the citizen injured, that is, as a surrogate for all citizens whose common interests have been harmed. He makes his claim as 'everyman' and not as an individual protecting his private interests. Failure to appreciate this rather obvious distinction in the roles a citizen may play is the most common error in the literature, and would seem to rest on the implicit assumption that compensation is in the nature of a civil remedy offered alongside criminal sanctions for the convenience of the victim (see, for example, Klein, 1978). The conception of the victim as everyman implies that when the criminal court orders compensation it does so not merely out of compassion for the victim or to provide a 'poor man's justice service' but, again, to vindicate justice as a social value in a concrete, humane, and clear fashion.

Should the victim therefore have a legal right to compensation? On the one hand, this position can be seen distinctly as diminishing the victim's status. That is, if he is indeed simply a surrogate for the harmed community then in principle he is in no sense a 'third party' with interests separate from the other two parties: the offender and the community (as represented by the Crown). In principle he has no more, and no fewer, rights than any citizen, much in the same way that any citizen, victim or not, can report an offence.

Nor does it make sense to provide the victim with legal assistance to protect his interests, since this implies that he has private or at least separate interests to protect. His interests as a citizen are, in theory, the same as those of the community, and the Crown is expected to present them. The victim metaphorically *is* the harmed community, and the Crown is, in this sense, the victim's lawyer.

The reparativist, then, agrees with the abolitionists and conservatives in holding that as a private party the victim cannot have rights in the criminal process. Any consideration or benefits would at best have to be an auxiliary or secondary matter. Such rights would be in direct competition with the interests of society which the criminal process is intended to protect.

But while victims can have no rights in the process as private parties seeking remedies, can they be accorded rights in their public role as the citizen injured? Here a strong case can be made that, *as a matter of sentencing policy*, procedures intended to enhance the status of the victim and compensate the victim might be justified. If the victim is indeed all of us in flesh and blood, representing the injustice to all and the violation of the rights of all in concrete and palpable terms, if the victim is one of the protagonists in this public morality play, then the symbolic power and significance of the role should be apparent. Administrative policy might well require in all cases that the harm be adequately assessed, presented in court and considered by the judge, and that compensation orders are properly enforced.

The point to be made is that the status, role, or consideration accorded victims at all stages of the criminal process will continue to turn, as it has in the past, on assumptions about the relevance of their position to the ends of that process. In the past the victim was regarded mainly as a source of evidence. If justice was to be done the offender was to be punished according to deserts. The reparativist agrees that it is important that justice be done, but suggests that according the victim a high status in the proceedings and requiring compensation by the offender are more effective means of doing it than retributive punishment. Victims accordingly will be considered to the extent that sentencing policy reflects an emphasis on vindicating the concept of justice, and to the extent that such consideration is deemed an effective method of doing justice. Procedures to reflect the victim's status could be left to administrative discretion or could be incorporated in legislation, the latter in effect providing the victim with legal rights.

The reparativists thus do attempt, unlike the pragmatists, to respond systematically to the theoretical challenge raised by the abolitionists. The argument suggests that the abolitionists' fundamental error is not in their conception of the social purpose of the criminal law but their failure – almost ironically considering the numbers of moralists in their ranks (retributivists and denunciators) – to appreciate the potential of the moral appeal as a sentencing principle, and the power of the symbolic role the individual citizen victimized can play in making that appeal. The reparative position challenges the offender and the public to perceive crime as essentially an injustice, a moral wrong rather than disobedience to a greater power. It appeals to their humanity.

## SUMMARY AND REMARKS

It was pointed out at the beginning that the question of the victim's right to compensation by the offender in the criminal process was embedded in the issue of the justification and priority of compensation in sentencing, and that that question had a long history. The various responses to the several questions raised can be summarized briefly as follows:

The Abolitionists would remove provisions for compensation entirely from the criminal statutes, and of course grant the victim no rights concerning it, on the grounds that such provisions are civil in nature and not in keeping with the aims and methods of the criminal law.

The Conservatives would compromise, maintaining the status quo which allows compensation for certain types of harm under certain conditions, but they have not to date provided a satisfactory theoretical explanation for their position. The sanction is seen as an ancillary one and hence low in priority, and the victim accordingly has low status and few rights.

The Pragmatists: I've used that label for a disparate group of reformers because of their doubts about the utility of any attempt toward a theoretical 'breakthrough'. They argue for compensation as a criminal sanction largely on the basis of simple moral principle and count, to some extent, on the political power of that principle. It was suggested that their stance would in the end be insufficient, that their actual proposals were silent on some crucial issues.

The Radicals of course question the questions asked, the political assumptions implied. Like the Abolitionists, they also see the notion of compensation by offenders as essentially incompatible with both the aims and methods of the present criminal law in this country. They strongly support it in principle and as a vehicle for reform of the political foundations of the justice system. Their response is of course entirely relevant to the issue, but can mainly be answered only at the level of political theory.

Finally the Reparativists, as I've described them, attempt to deal with the theoretical issue posed by the Abolitionists within the assumptions of the Abolitionists. They strongly support compensation by offenders and see it as representing a major shift in sentencing theory toward an emphasis on the moral appeal rather than intimidation and control.

The categories of course represent ideal types. They clearly range from muddling through to grand theory, from tinkering to fundamental reforms in sentencing policy. The main point of the chapter is the attempt to demonstrate the nature of some of the controversies. The conservative position, with the Abolitionist close behind, has been a formidable obstacle to reform. While the outcome of this new reform movement for victim rights does not turn only on formal theory, neither can it be supported simply by moral idealism.

## Notes

1. The term compensation (money payment for harm) is preferred here over the term restitution. Compensation is the term used in the *Criminal Code* of Canada and also in the *Powers of the Criminal Courts Act 1973* in Britain, while restitution denotes the restoration of property.
2. For a review of this jurisprudential position see British Columbia (1983).
3. Compensation may also be ordered under Section 388 on summary conviction to a maximum of $50 for destruction or damage to property. This provision is not discussed here since it is little used and is of very minor significance. (Section 388 of the Canadian Criminal Code has since been repealed – 1985, c.19, 5.59 – the editor.)

## References

Advisory Council on the Penal System (1970), *Reparation by the offender*, Chairman: The Rt. Hon. Kenneth Younger (London: HMSO). (*Widgery Report*).

British Columbia, Ministry of Attorney General, Research and Evaluation Division. Federal Provincial Research Program on Reparative Sanctions (forthcoming), *The Justice Approach to Compensation by Offenders* (Report no.1) and *Reparation by Offenders: a Study in Legal Theory* (Report no.3).

Burns, P. T. (1980), *Criminal injuries compensation* (Vancouver: Butterworths).

Chasse, K. L. (1977), 'Restitution in Canadian criminal law', CRNS, vol.36, pp.201–37.

Del Vecchio, G. D (1969), 'The Struggle Against Crime' in H. G. Acton (ed.), *The Philosophy of Punishment: a Collection of Papers* (London: Macmillan, St Martin's Press).

Fry, M. (1951), *Arms of the Law* (London: Victor Gollancz).

Garofalo, R. (1914), *Criminology*, 2nd ed., trans. Robert W. Millar (Boston: Little Brown).

Geis, G. (1977), 'Restitution by Criminal Offenders: a Summary and Overview' in J. Hudson and B. Galaway (eds), *Restitution in criminal justice* (Lexington, Mass: Heath) pp.147–64.

Gouldner, A. W. (1960), 'The Norm of Reciprocity: a Preliminary Statement', *American Sociological Review*, vol.25, pp.161–78.

Hood, R. (1974), 'Criminology and Penal Change: a Case Study of the Nature and Impact of Some Recent Advice to Governments', in Hood, R.

(ed.), *Crime, Criminology and Public Policy: Essays in Honour of Sir Leon Radzinowicz* (London: Heinemann) pp.375–417.

Hudson, J. and Galaway, B. (eds), (1975), *Considering the Victim: Readings in Restitution and Victim Compensation* (Springfield, Ill.: Charles C. Thomas).

Klein, J. F. (1978), 'Revitalizing Restitution: Flogging a Horse that May Have Been Killed for Just Cause', *Criminal Law Quarterly*, vol.20, no.3, pp.383–408.

Law Reform Commission of Canada (1974), *Restitution and Compensation*, Working Paper No.5, Information Canada Cat. No. J32-1/5.

Morton, J. D. (1962), *The Function of the Criminal Law in 1962* (Toronto: CBC Publications).

*R. v. Groves*, 1977, 39 CRNS 366 (Ont. HC).

*R. v. Zelensky*, 1978 DLR (3rd) 179.

Ruggles-Brise, E. (1901), *Report to the Secretary of State for the Home Department on the Proceedings of the Fifth and Sixth International Penitentiary Congresses* (London: HMSO).

Schafer, S. (1970), *Compensation and Restitution to Victims of Crime*, 2nd ed. (Montclair, NJ: Patterson Smith).

Thorvaldson, S. A. (1978), *The Effects of Community Service on the Attitudes of Offenders*, Ph.D. Dissertation, University of Cambridge, Institute of Criminology, 380pp. (Microfilm copy available from the US Department of Justice Reference Service, Box 6000, Rockville, MD 20850, USA).

Thorvaldson, S. A. (1980), 'Toward the Definition of the Reparative Aim', in J. Hudson and B. Galaway (eds), *Victims, Offenders and Alternative Sanctions* (Lexington, Mass.: Heath) pp.15–28.

Thorvaldson, S. A. (1980), 'Reparative Sanctions: Some Issues for Federal Legislation', in J. Laplante (ed.), *Proceedings of the Fourth Canadian Conference on Applied Criminology: Social Control in a State of Crisis* (University of Ottawa) pp.241–53.

Thorvaldson, S. A. (1980), 'Reparation by Offenders: How Far Can We Go?' in B. Pinet, (ed.), *Selected Papers of Canadian Congress for the Prevention of Crime* (Ottawa: Canadian Association for the Prevention of Crime; Winnipeg: Manitoba Society of Criminology) pp.119–28.

# 14 Legal Aid to Crime Victims

## Susan Hillenbrand

In his play *Henry VI*, Shakespeare has Cade the rebel leader fantasizing with the butcher, the smith, and the weaver about how sweet life would be if the king were deposed and he himself were made ruler. Cade is listing a number of 'impovements' he would institute, such as banning money and requiring uniform clothing, when he is interrupted by Dick, the butcher. 'The first thing,' says Dick, 'let's kill all the lawyers.'

Today in the United States, many echo Dick's implied opinion of lawyers if not, perhaps, his solution. Among these are undoubtedly a number of crime victims who, more than most, have had an opportunity to see our justice system at work and who may well have concluded that the system and the lawyers who run it represent everyone but the victims of injustice. Indeed, at a time when the public seems to feel that lawyers have their noses in just about every aspect of a person's life, lawyers for the crime victim are often conspicuous for their absence.

Two basic reasons for this situation lie in the repesentative nature of the legal profession and the paucity of recognized rights for crime victims. A lawyer represents the legal interests of a person (or institution) who has specifically or implicitly been granted certain rights by the US Constitution, a state constitution, or otherwise by law. Those accused of crime, for example, have been guaranteed a number of rights in the Bill of Rights to the Constitution. There is even the right to be represented by Counsel to ensure that the other rights are upheld. Thus the accused are generally represented by attorneys.

Crime victims – as victims –on the other hand, have few explicit constitutional 'rights', either directly or by reference. In fact, victims are not mentioned in the Constitution, the constitutions of most states,[1] or even, until recently, in the laws of most states. (As further indication of the victim's low status in the US justice system, the term 'victim' is not included in the West Publishing keyword retrieval system used in legal research, nor is it included in either of the two

310

most basic reference books, *American Jurisprudence* and *Black's Law Dictionary*.)

Historically, victims have not always been so impotent in our justice system.[2] In Colonial America, crime was conceived of as an injury to the individual victim. It had little relevance to society as a whole. If, on the one hand, the victim chose to apprehend and prosecute the offender, he was free to do so, with whatever assistance he was able and willing to afford. To obtain a warrant and an arrest, the victim would generally buy the services of a justice of the peace and a constable. Similarly, to prepare an indictment and prosecute the case, he was likely to hire a private attorney. While criminal prosecutions were brought in the name of the state, for all practical purposes they were private prosecutions in which the state did not play an active role. Moreover, the victim – not the state – benefited from the usual sentence involving multiple damages from the offender. (If the offender were indigent, the victim might be authorized to sell him into service for a period corresponding to the amount of multiple damages.)

On the other hand, if the victim chose not to follow through on the case, he was under no requirement to do so from government authorities.

The advantages which the colonists had seen in the system of private prosecutions – freedom from the potential of tyranny by government police and prosecutors and an inexpensive criminal justice system – began to fade in importance as the industrial revolution took hold. Increased mobility and size of towns eroded the sense of community which had been so important in the days of raising the 'hue and cry', when the townspeople would help an aggrieved neighbour pursue his offender. The 'social contract' theory of government which became popular in the 19th century held that those who broke the contract by the commission of a crime-injured society, rather than just an individual victim. Therefore society became responsible for deciding which cases to pursue, and for apprehending, prosecuting and punishing offenders in those cases. Paid police and public prosecutors were hired by the state. Any debt the offender owed was now seen as owing to society; use of imprisonment replaced multiple damages to the victim.

Thus, the role of the victim in the criminal justice system had changed dramatically from colonial times to the end of the 19th century. The individual who had originally made all the major decisions, initiated virtually all actions, and was chief beneficiary of a successful case became a mere source of evidence for the state. Admittedly the state takeover of prosecutions removed from the victim a considerable burden and provided considerably greater resources and experience in apprehending and prosecuting the offender. However, crime victims must soon have realized that the broad interests of the state which the police and prosecutor represented were not necessarily the same as their own narrow interests in the case at hand.

## THE VICTIM AND THE CIVIL COURTS[3]

Theoretically at least, the crime victim who had lost access to the criminal justice system could seek redress from the offender through the civil courts. If the victim as victim has few 'rights' in criminal law, he or she shares with everyone else (including offenders) certain rights at civil law. When these rights are violated, the courts may be asked to intervene. Crime victims, as others seeking civil remedies, generally look to the legal profession for assistance.[4]

## VICTIM VERSUS OFFENDER

The most common instance of victim involvement in the civil justice system is as a plaintiff seeking money damages from the offender.

In no jurisdiction is the offender's criminal conviction a prerequisite for a civil suit against him. However, jurisdictions vary as to the relationship between a criminal conviction and evidence of a civil wrongdoing. For example, the Victim Witness Protection Act of 1982 provides that a conviction for an offence that would properly give rise to restitution prohibits the defendant from denying the essential allegations of the criminal offence in subsequent victim-initiated civil proceedings. A Wisconsin statute, however, prohibits the admission into evidence of facts surrounding criminal restitution orders. In any event, the burden of proof is less stringent in a civil case than in a criminal case, the former requiring preponderance of the evidence, the latter proof beyond a reasonable doubt. Moreover, discovery material in the criminal case can sometimes be invaluable in a subsequent civil case, regardless of the outcome of the criminal case.

Therefore, an acquittal in the criminal courts should not, in and of itself, discourage a victim from suing the defendant civilly.

The financial means of both victim and offender may determine in large part whether or not a suit against the offender is brought. The victim may not have the 'up front' means to hire an attorney to handle the case for a fixed fee. Lack of funds is not a barrier to filing a suit if the victim can find an attorney willing to take the case on a 'contingency' fee basis, that is, a fee based on the amount actually recovered. Obviously, however, most attorneys will only agree to these terms if they feel sufficient funds will be forthcoming. This depends on several factors: the strength of the case (i.e. likelihood that the court will award a judgement); the amount likely to be awarded, and the likelihood that the defendant will have the means to make good on whatever judgement is awarded.[5]

It is a fact that many, if not most, defendants are 'judgement free', i.e. without the funds to satisfy a judgement if it is awarded. However, there are a number of offenders who do have the means to make good on a judgement, and victims and their attorneys are increasingly going after such offenders. For example, the Washington Legal Foundation in Washington, DC has estimated that 5% to 10% of offenders are able to provide some money damages to their victims. The Foundation has assisted many victims in civil suits against such offenders.

Within the past several years, a number of states have passed laws to improve the chances of significant victim recovery from at least a small segment of potentially wealthy offenders. These so-called 'Son of Sam'[6] statutes provide that any profit generated by a convicted offender through the sale of books, movie rights, etc. which publicize the crime be held in escrow to satisfy a civil judgement in favour of the victim within a specified time period (usually 5 years). This guaranteed pool of generally quite substantial funds makes representing victims of highly-publicized crimes on a contingency fee basis highly attractive to lawyers.

## DEFENDANT VERSUS VICTIM

Less common than the situation where a crime victim sues the defendant is the situation where the defendant sues the victim. The latter are generally based on violation of the defendants's civil rights as, for example, when a victim mistakenly identifies his perpetrator.

The availability of civil damages to individuals whom victims (or alleged victims) have *intentionally* wrongly accused is, of course, fitting. The courts, however, have usually found in favour of the victim if the false accusation is shown to be the result of the victim's good faith mistake.[7] (Were this not the case, there certainly would be many more such suits – at least until victims and witnesses stopped cooperating with the system even to the extent they do so today.)

As in victim-initiated suits, most victims will seek attorney assitance in civil suits where they are the defendant. Unfortunately, however, they may have more difficulty in retaining counsel for this type of case since the defendant stance does not carry with it the same attractive financial potential which the plaintiff role does.

(Though not in the civil realm, another related circumstance in which victims generally utilize legal aid is that in which they are accused by the state of criminal responsibility for some action against their perpetrator – for example, shooting an unarmed intruder. Ironically, in this instance, if the victim/defendant is indigent, the state will provide legal counsel for him – not because he is a victim, but because he is now an alleged criminal.)


## VICTIM VERSUS PRIVATE THIRD PARTIES

The fact that a victim's assailant is without sufficient funds to warrant a suit against him does not necessarily shut the door on the victim's recovery through the civil courts. Increasingly victims are successfully suing private third parties whose actions or failure to act responsibly have permitted the victimization to occur. Liability may be somewhat more difficult to establish in these cases than in suits against the criminal defendant. To prove negligence, it must generally be shown that the defendant had a duty to the victim, breached that duty, and as a result provided the proximate cause for the victimization. Examples of third parties who have been successfully sued are innkeepers and landlords on whose insecure premises crimes of violence occurred. Perhaps the most famous case was that involving singer Connie Francis who was raped in a New York hotel room with insecure locks. She subsequently recovered some $2.5 million from the hotel.

Again, the availability of a solvent (or even wealthy) defendant in a civil suit makes such suits very attractive to lawyers.

## VICTIM VERSUS THE STATE

In addition to suing private third parties, victims, and their attorneys are increasingly looking to responsible state and government officials as possible targets of civil actions. This is the case, for instance, where government officials are allegedly 'grossly negligent' in releasing offenders who subsequently – and predictably – commit further crimes. Parole boards and correctional officials have been the target of such suits.

Like third party suits against private parties, third party suits against government entities or officials do not face the 'judgement free' problems associated with actions against the offender (though some states, e.g. Minnesota, limit the amount of personal injury awards against the state). However, they often face a major obstacle in the doctrine of sovereign immunity. Under this well-established doctrine, a sovereign cannot be sued in its own courts unless a specific cause of action is established. In other words, unless the state gives permission – through statute or otherwise – for its citizens to bring action against it, no such action may be brought. About half the states have waived absolute immunity, thus paving the way for successful torts under certain conditions. For example, suits can often be brought successfully if it is shown that the official in question was, or should have been, acting ministerially (that is, carrying out the instructions of a superior or higher authority) rather than discretionally (i.e. making state-protected decisions involving issues of judgement). In at least one major case *Payton* v. *US*, CA 5, 2.2.81), the US Supreme Court found the facts of the situation so weighted against release of a specific offender as to render the decision of the parole board ministerial rather than discretionary.

The Victims Assistance Legal Organization (VALOR) in Virginia Beach has been in the forefront of 'gross negligence' suits against the state and its officials, and has provided considerable aid to victims who chose to follow this route.

### Crime-Victim Compensation

While on the whole not nearly as potentially rewarding as third-party civil suits for money damages, crime victim compensation programmes in some 37 states and the District of Columbia provide some compensation for financial costs associated with victimization. Almost without exception, this compensation is limited to expenses associated with personal injury and loss of wages (property damage or loss are rarely reimbursed by these programmes). The upper limit of awards varies considerably from state to state, though $10 000 is a fairly common limit.

The complexity of processing application forms, attending hearings, and appealing the original decision differs from state to state. Moreover, the specific issues involved and the capacity of the individual claimants of course vary from case to case.

The value of attorney assistance to victims seeking state compensation is a subject of some controversy.[8] Supporters of attorney involvement argue that it will ease the programme's administrative burden by ensuring complete and accurate information as well as providing an important spokesperson for victims who are emotionally or physically unable to speak for themselves, or who are not sufficiently familiar with the requirements and language of administrative or judicial organizations to provide effective self-representation. Opponents on the other hand argue that attorneys may encourage complicated and unwieldy procedures, and create a formal and adversarial climate in victim-compensation proceedings. It is also argued that use of attorneys by some victims may work to the detriment of those victims who do not use them, thereby creating inequities in the distribution of the available benefits.

Nevertheless, most states recognize that many claimants may need or desire legal assistance in seeking state compensation, and have accordingly not only allowed attorney participation but have established specific policies concerning the payment of legal fees. Some programmes limit attorneys fees to a stated maximum amount. Others allow a certain percentage of the award. Still others provide for the compensation board to determine a reasonable fee on a case-by-case basis. Attorneys' fees may be included in the amount of the award or paid by the state in addition to the award.

**The Victim and the Criminal Courts**

While victims of crime have been encouraged for many years to look to the civil courts rather than the criminal courts for redress for their grievances, for the past decade or so the criminal justice system has begun to recognize that it, too, has certain responsibilities to the victims whom it has failed, or been unable, to protect. Numerous victim/witness programmes in police stations, courts, and particularly prosecutors' offices now offer a number of services and courtesies to help victims deal with the criminal justice process. These include, for example, increased protection from intimidation, prompt notification of scheduling changes and important decisions in the case, and prompt return of stolen property.

In addition, there has recently been a move to recognize a legitimate victim interest in the outcome of the criminal case. The legislatures and criminal justice practitioners have been increasingly sensitive to considering such interests and in certain cases allowing the victim to participate in the criminal proceedings. Attorney assistance has been requested in many instances.

## LEGITIMATE VICTIM INTERESTS

Court-ordered restitution is the only monetary compensation available to many victims of both personal and property crimes. Of course, some are insured, but many are not. In theory, conventional civil actions against offenders and third parties are available to victims; in practice, however, such actions provide financial relief to few victims. Crime victim compensation programmes, where they exist, generally compensate only for physical injury and loss of wages. Victims of property loss in these states as well as virtually all victims in the states without compensation programmes therefore have a very tangible interest in the court's requiring restitution from the offender.

Most would agree that the vengeance some crime victims seek from the criminal justice system is an inappropriate and unacceptable goal of the system. Such an acknowledgement, however, in no way implies that crime victims are not entitled to a just disposition of their case, in accordance with the US Constitution and the constitution and laws of the specific jurisdictions. As noted above, the legitimacy of this interest has been increasingly recognized by a number of jurisdictions.

## INCREASED VICTIM PARTICIPATION

There are several stages of a criminal proceeding which are of particular interest to the victim, both because of the restitution implications and because of the victim's interest that justice be served. These include dismissal of the case, plea negotiations, sentencing, and parole. Depending upon the applicable rules and laws as well as the receptivity of the individual prosecutor and the court, victims are beginning to participate in these criminal proceedings. Many are utilizing legal assistance in doing so.

For instance, jurisdictions are increasingly allowing the victim to consult with the prosecutor prior to dismissal of the case or submission of a proposed plea to the court. (Indiana, for example, has enacted a statute permitting the victim to present his opinion of the proposed recommendation to the prosecution.) Such consultation ensures that before making a dispositional decision, the prosecutor has before him pertinent information regarding the true nature and consequences of the crime from the victim's perspective. This gives victims the opportunity to inform the prosecutor about any evidence not previously made known to the state. It also brings to the prosecutor's attention information about the crime's physical, psychological, and financial impact on the victim and the victim's family.

Even more than at the dismissal or plea stages, jurisdictions are allowing for use of 'victim impact' statements at sentencing. Some dozen[9] states have enacted legislation providing for victim input at this stage. Most if not all of these statutes authorize or require a written victim impact statement to be included in the presentence report prepared by the probation department. Such reports provide the sentencing body information which might aggravate or mitigate the offender's sentence. At least three of the statutes provide that the victim may appear personally (and at least two, by counsel, as well) at the sentencing hearing to present evidence and express opinions about the crime, the defendant or the need for restitution. Moreover, many jurisdictions not required legislatively to consider victim impact statments are doing so nevertheless.

Parole hearings are another stage of the criminal process wherein victims are increasingly having a say. At least five states (Arizona, Arkansas, California, Massachusetts, and Oklahoma) allow victims to participate in the parole hearing. Most of these explicitly allow such participation to be personally or through counsel.

At any of these stages where the victim is given the opportunity to make his or her views known – dismissal, plea negotiations, sentencing, or parole – attorney assistance may be sought on the preparation of the written or oral statement, whether or not the attorney is allowed to actually represent the victim at the proceeding in question. The attorney may be able to help the victim put his concerns into a form which will be meaningful and helpful to the prosecutor or court. For example, the attorney might suggest that a victim of extensive property damage suggest to the prosecutor the inappropriateness of a plea recommendation involving a plea of guilty to a lesser offence which might preclude adequate restitution, e.g. a charge of robbery reduced to 'attempted robbery'. Prior to sentencing, the attorney may point out restitution possibilities to the victim so that he or she may request adequate restitution. The relevance of threats by the offender may be pointed up by the attorney as of possible relevance at parole hearings.

Victims and their representatives have utilized private legal counsel to influence the course of the case in other ways. Sometimes counsel is retained to gather and present additional evidence to the prosecutor or to exert pressure on the prosecutor not to drop the charges. In some states, statutes specifically allow victims to retain counsel to prosecute petty crimes which the state decides do not warrant its own involvement. In addition, most states have statutes allowing the court to appoint special prosecutors hired by the victim to assist the public prosecutor. While prosecutors are generally wary of even the appearance of limiting their own authority, the rationale behind such statutes was not so much to give victims the 'right' to participate in the prosecution as it was to provide the state with a means of obtaining outside prosecutorial expertise at no charge. Regardless of the original intent, victims may be expected to seek increased application of such statutes in the future.

New legislation may also be in the offing. For instance, a bill introduced into the New York legislature in 1981 would have authorized the court to allow counsel for victims in cases where the defendant alleged improper or illegal conduct of the victim as an affirmative defence. In sexual assault cases, such representation would be as a matter of right. The attorney could participate and offer legal argument in any stage of the criminal proceeding in which the conduct of the victim was at issue. An Ohio bill would have authorized neighbourhood organizations to employ attorneys to assist crime victims who reside in the neighbourhood. While neither of these bills was enacted, they represent the kind of innovative approaches to increased victim representation by the legal profession which are almost surely to be before our legislatures for the foreseeable future.

## SUMMARY

Victims of crime who have been so ignored in both the civil and criminal justice arenas are finally beginning to command the attention of the legal profession. Civil suits for money damages from offenders are increasing. A relatively new area of litigation against private and governmental third parties indirectly responsible for victimization is burgeoning. Attorneys are also assisting victims who are seeking state crime victim compensation benefits.

In the criminal system, victims are being given increased opportunities to have a say or to participate in the proceedings, and in at least some instances are looking for legal assistance in doing so. Both to improve their chances of restitution and to help ensure a just disposition of the case, victims and their attorneys in many jurisdictions may now consult with the decision-makers at various stages of a criminal proceeding. Finally, victims and their attorneys are becoming more aware of existing statutes such as the 'special prosecutor' statutes and pending legislation with a potential for increasing the victim presence in the system.

**Notes**

1. California is an exception, since approval of the 1982 referendum on 'Proposition 8'.
2. See William F. McDonald, 'Towards a Bicentennial Revolution in Criminal Justice: the Return of the Victim', *American Criminal Law Review*, vol.13, no.4 (1976).
3. See Frank Carrington, 'Victims' Rights Litigation: a Wave of the Future?', *University of Richmond Law Review*, vol.11, no.3 (1977).
4. Some bar associations' legal referral services include a list of lawyers particularly interested in representing crime victims. Some of these will take 'pro bono' cases. More generally, however, they will charge for their services, either on a fixed fee or contingency fee basis.
5. It has been suggested by some, including Frank Carrington who chairs the American Bar Association Criminal Justice Section's Victims Committee, that consideration be given to state-funded legal assistance for crime victims who wish to sue their assailants, similar to state-funded legal assistance to those who have been accused of crime. Money considerations aside, one can anticipate the argument that state assistance in defending individuals accused by the state of criminal

charges is a far cry from state assistance for individuals who initiate suits for money damages.

6. Named after a New York statute enacted to preclude David Berkowitz, New York's famed 'Son of Sam' killer and similar felons from engaging in profitable negotiations for the publicity rights to their stories. Other states subsequently passing such statutes include Alaska, Arizona, Florida, Georgia, Illinois, Kentucky, Massachusetts, Nebraska, Oklahoma, South Carolina, and Tennessee.

7. A 1981 bill in the Arizona legislature would have provided that a person who reports a crime is not liable for any cause of action arising out of or in connection with the report unless the person acted with malice and without basis in fact. If the party prevailed in the lawsuit, the court would award reasonable attorneys' fees. The bill did not pass.

8. See Deborah M. Carrow, *Crime Victim Compensation: Program Models* (National Institute of Justice, US Department of Justice, 1980).

9. Arizona, California, Connecticut, Indiana, Kansas, Maryland, Nevada, New York, New Hampshire, New Jersey, and Ohio.

# 15 Victim–Witness Programmes

## Susan Hillenbrand

To say that victims whom the criminal justice system has not successfully protected and witnesses on whom the system depends are due certain considerations from that system is a truism in many jurisdictions today. However, only within the past decade or so has any significant official responsibility for victim/witness assistance been acknowledged. Previously, the criminal justice system – ironically so sensitive to the needs of defendants and offenders – tended to view victims and witnesses as mere sources of evidence whose personal concerns were irrelevant to the processing of the case at hand. Social service agencies helped some victims deal with the direct consequences of the crime. However, their limited access to the criminal justice system precluded significant assistance with the victim's myriad problems which emanated from that system. Moreover, such programmes rarely reached out to crime victims, as victims, or treated those who sought their services differently than they treated their non-victim clients.

Today the situation has changed dramatically. According to the National Organization for Victim Assistance, over 500 programmes around the country provide victim and/or witness services. In California alone, 36 counties have comprehensive programmes, serving over 90% of the population in that state.

Programmes whose primary purpose is to assist victims and witnesses vary considerably in the needs they address. Some programmes' major concern is the crime's psychological and social impact on the victim. Institutionally separate from the criminal justice system, these programmes may or may not work closely with the system. Some provide comprehensive services to victims of any type of crime; others, such as rape-crisis centres and domestic violence shelters, are crime-specific.

What is known as a 'victim/witness' programme, on the other hand, generally functions under the auspices of a criminal justice agency – usually the prosecutor's office, but occasionally the police department or court. Many of these projects also tend to the crime's

322

immediate impact on the victim, though often in a referral capacity. Their prime concern is ameliorating the *indirect* consequences of the crime – that is, keeping to a minimum the further victimization likely to result from the victim's (or witness's) contact with the criminal justice system. Examples of such 'secondary' victimization include:

1. official indifference concerning matters of little relevance to the 'case', but of grave importance to the victim (such as retrieval of stolen property from law enforcement agencies holding it for evidentiary purposes);
2. insensitive, adverse questioning by police and prosecutors who may harbour a 'guilty-victim' syndrome – a feeling that the victim has somehow 'asked' to be victimized;
3. embarrassing and intimidating service of subpoenas by uniformed law enforcement officials;
4. uncomfortable and insecure accommodations at the police station or in the courthouse, often involving close proximity to defendants, associates of defendants, or adverse witnesses;
5. lack of clear, lay explanations of proceedings and decisions during and after the case;
6. poorly coordinated, conflicting, repetitive, and unexplained summonses; and
7. fear resulting from real or imagined intimidating threats and acts by defendants.

Victim/witness programmes seek to address these victim and witness concerns by providing information and services as the case progresses through the system. Increasingly, they are also seeking and facilitating a greater victim participation in the process itself.

## ADVANTAGES/DISADVANTAGES OF CRIMINAL JUSTICE-BASED PROGRAMMES

There are both advantages and disadvantages to criminal justice-based victim/witness projects. A major advantage is the ability of such programmes to encourage internal reforms to *prevent* (or at least to reduce substantially) secondary victimization, rather than merely treating or responding to it after the fact. Institutionalization of reforms in the system will eliminate the necessity of responding to individual victim/witness problems on an *ad hoc* basis. Moreover, affiliation with an official agency often increases the project's credibility with a wide range of outside agencies able to provide specialized services.

Perhaps the major complaint about police, prosecutor and court-based projects is that their loyalty is first to the host agency and only secondarily to the victim or witness. Where there is a conflict between system interests and victim/witness interests, the system interests prevail. In addition, most criminal justice system-based projects only serve those victims and witnesses willing to cooperate. Individuals who decide it is in their better interests not to report the crime or provide testimony about it are generally excluded, whatever the reason for their non-cooperation (e.g. intimidation, embarrassment, family and employment responsibilities, or simple lack of faith in the system). Also generally excluded are those potentially cooperative victims and witnesses who are never informed of the existence of the programme because no offender has been apprehended or prosecution undertaken in the case (this is probably less true of police-based programmes than it is of prosecution and court-based programmes).

**STAFF AND FUNDING**

Victim/witness assistance projects, like non-criminal justice affiliated programmes which assist victims, are staffed and funded in a variety of ways.

Considerable Law Enforcement Assistance Administration funding between 1974 and 1982 enabled a number of police and especially prosecutor-based programmes to hire professional and support staff. Many of these programmes have since become institutionalized, and at least limited funding is being provided through the agencies' general operating budgets. Unfortunately, however, budgetary constraints have required some programmes to be dropped and a number to be substantially reduced in the past year or so. The future for many others is extremely uncertain.

In order to keep the victim/witness assistance projects functioning, a number of innovative steps have been taken. California, for example, funds its extensive statewide network of programmes through fines and penalties levied against offenders. Wisconsin reimburses counties which provide specified services to crime victims and witnesses. Nebraska has established a Crime Victim and Witness

Assistance Fund to receive monies appropriated by the legislature for victim/witness assistance. Oklahoma has authorized its larger counties to appoint a victim/witness coordinator at state expense.

Victim/witness assistance programmes are also receiving substantial support from the private sector. Donations from local businesses and individual citizens are responsible for programmes in some areas. In addition, several national organizations such as the National Council of Jewish Women and the Kiwanis Club, have encouraged their local affiliates to support existing programmes or to develop new ones.

To stretch what dollars are available, most projects rely quite heavily on volunteer support. Volunteers are particularly well-suited for certain aspects of a programme, such as answering 24-hour 'hotlines'; providing escort, transportation, and babysitting services; and staffing witness information centres.

## SERVICES TO CRIME VICTIMS AND WITNESSES

Few victims or witnesses are likely to require every service offered by a victim and witness assistance project. Most, however, will face at least one problem with which they will require assistance. Described below are some of the more typical services offered.

## SERVICES DIRECTLY RELATED TO THE CRIME

As mentioned above, both criminal justice-based victim/witness assistance projects and victim and witness programmes not affiliated with the system offer direct or referral services to address the direct effects of the crime on the victim. Some of these effects are immediate and require emergency attention.

Others may not be so quickly apparent, but may prove to be the more serious of the crime's effects in the long run.

### Emergency Needs

Victims who require assistance at the crime scene have often been victimized by violent crime. They are injured, frightened, disoriented, without shelter, food, clothing, etc.

Assistance to these victims must be immediate. Programmes which serve them therefore work closely with police departments, hospitals and others with whom victims are likely to have early contact and who will alert the project on a 24-hour basis. Services provided include hotlines, telephone counselling services, emergency shelter, food, and financial resources. Police departments are becoming increasingly sensitive to the need for 'on the scene' assistance to crime victims, and are training and providing their own personnel to deliver needed services or to act in a 'stand-by' capacity until appropriate assistance can be summoned.

**Property Loss or Damage**

Victims whose property has been damaged or stolen often need prompt assitance. For instance, broken locks or windows must be fixed; glasses and hearing aids must be replaced.

Some programmes provide such services directly; others refer victims to agencies or individuals who have agreed to provide them in a timely manner.

**Financial Loss**

Medical bills and loss of wages due to violent crime or psychologically damaging crime can be tremendous. Many projects seek to assist the victim in recovering or reducing such losses in several ways. For example, in those 37 states and the District of Columbia which have state-funded victim compensation programmes, the project may alert the victim to the programme and help in completing the necessary application procedures. The project may also inform the victim of the availability of civil remedies, such as suing the offender or a third party indirectly responsible for the victimization. Another sometimes successful tact has been to request the victim's employer not to penalize the victim for missing work while recuperating.

**Counselling Services**

Many victims require counselling to enable them to cope with the fact of their victimization. This is true not only of sexual assault victims (who generally do require considerable counselling) but of other victims as well. The counselling need may be short or long term, depending on a number of factors.

Rape crisis centres and domestic violence shelters often have professional counsellors. Some other victim assistance projects also have in-house counsellors. Others, including most criminal justice-based projects, refer victims to social service agencies which specialize in counselling.

## SERVICES RELATED TO THE CRIMINAL JUSTICE SYSTEM

It is common for victims to think of themselves as victimized twice, once by the criminal and again by the criminal justice system. This system victimization often applies to witnesses as well.

The fact that the goals of the criminal justice system and those of the victim and witness do not always coincide can lead to conflict between them. Some of this may be unavoidable. However, problems can usually be considerably ameliorated by the attitude of the individuals within the system. The attitude which prevailed until relatively recently – and undoubtedly still prevails in a great many jurisdictions – was that victims and witnesses are sources of evidence, that they should be available at the whim of the system, and that their personal concerns are totally irrelevant to the processing of the case and, hence, to the criminal justice system. An increased sensitivity to victims and witnesses and a recognition of some system responsibility to them brings to light a number of ways the system can soften the impact of its legitimate requirements and, in at least some instances, increase victim and witness cooperation as well.

### Subpoena by Mail

The introduction many victims and witnesses have to the criminal justice system is by way of a uniformed police officer or sheriff appearing at their door with a subpoena commanding their appearance at a specified proceeding. At once, the victim or witness is likely to feel embarrassed, intimidated, and defensive at such an intrusion. While the system does need the witnesses' testimony, it does not help the prosecution – in fact, it works to its detriment – to instill in the witness such an initial negative feeling.

Many victim/witness projects have instituted mail subpoena systems in their jurisdictions. Though more private and less threatening from the witnesses' point of view, the subpoenas apparently are equally effective in obtaining the required witness participation.

## Transportation and Babysitting

Once witnesses know they must be available for a specific police or court appearance, many face transportation problems in getting there. This is particularly true for aged or handicapped witnesses. The need for child-care also acts as an impediment in participation by witnesses who would otherwise be attending their children.

To address the transporation problem, victim/witness projects often pick witnesses up at their home or employment, take them to the proceeding, and return them when it is over. Some provide limited taxi or public transportation fares and free, convenient parking for those who are able to drive. The provision of babysitting services not only increases participation but makes for happier witnesses.

## Witness Reception Centres

Victims and witnesses (particularly those involved in serious crimes of violence) are understandably surprised, frightened, and outraged when they are ushered into a reception room to await a proceeding to which they have been summoned and find the assailant in the same waiting room. Until recently this was a common occurrence and undoubtedly still exists in many jurisdictions.

Provision of a separate waiting room for prosecution witnesses is generally a priority goal of victim/witness assistance projects.

## Scheduling Changes

Nothing is more frustrating for a witness who after making the necessary arrangements arrives at a proceeding to find it has been cancelled or postponed. There are many reasons for such calendar changes, many of them unavoidable. What is generally avoidable, however, is failure to notify witnesses in time for them to revise their plans accordingly.

Victim/witness projects have tried to remedy this situation in several ways. Some telephone or mail a notice (if time permits) to witnesses as soon as a schedule change is made. Others provide witnesses with a telephone number to call the evening before the scheduled proceeding to confirm that it is going on as planned. Still others put witnesses who agree to be at a specified telephone number at certain times on 'alert' so that they need not interrupt their personal activities unless called. Once called, however, they are expected to appear within a previously-specified time period.

**Property Return**

Victims whose property has been stolen and then recovered by the criminal justice system are often surprised to learn that the recovery is of little practical use to them. Because the property is 'evidence' in the criminal proceedings, sometimes law enforcement officials retain it for months or even years.

Victim/witness projects have been quite successful in persuading police and prosecutors that photographs of the property in question may be substituted for the actual item for evidentiary purposes. At least one state – Kansas – has enacted legislation deeming photographs competent evidence.

**Witness Fees**

Even though witness fees in most jurisdictions are extremely low, they are still very important to many victims and witnesses. Moreover, even such a minimal acknowledgement of their value can favourably influence a witness' impression of the criminal justice system.

Victim/witness projects often expedite payment of witness fees. They are in a good position to do this, as they usually keep reliable records of witness appearance.

**Intimidation**

Victims and witnesses may be afraid to attend criminal justice proceedings if they have been threatened by the defendant or the defendant's friends. Even the fear of such threats can be terrifying to some.

Victim/witness projects often provide escorts to accompany such individuals to and from proceedings. In especially dangerous situations, temporary relocation services may be provided, or special arrangements made with the police department for extra patrols of the victim's neighbourhood. Where appropriate, victim/witness projects also encourage charges to be brought against those who are intimidating witnesses.

## Information about the Criminal Justice System

Contact with the criminal justice system is an unfamiliar and intimidating experience for most victims and witnesses. They generally do not know what is expected of them or what they can realistically expect from the system.

Most victim/witness projects make it a priority to provide an orientation to the system, explaining its functions and how these relate to responsibilities of the victim and witness. Sometimes this is done by printed materials, sometimes by a film and often in personal discussions with individual witnesses. (A printed brochure is sometimes provided by the police on the scene or included with the initial subpoena so that the victim or witness has some information well in advance of any official proceeding.) Topics to be covered might include the prosecutor's role *vis-à-vis* the victim; reasons a case may be continued, postponed, or dismissed; and the witnesses' responsibilities with respect to defence counsel.

Opportunities for victim participation may be set forth. An Indiana statute, for example, requires the prosecutor to allow the victim to offer an opinion on any recommendation the government plans to file with the court. In addition, at least eleven states (and the federal government) have enacted legislation allowing victims to inform the sentencing court of the crime's physical, psychological, economical and social impact on them or their families. The 'victim impact statement' is sometimes prepared by the victim and sometimes by the probation department after interviewing the victim. It is included in the presentence report containing information about the defendant and the circumstances of the crime which may be relevant as mitigating or aggravating factors in the sentence. Several states (as well as individual jurisdictions in other states) also allow the victim to appear personally or by counsel before the sentencing court to deliver an oral victim impact statement.

Logistical information about the location of the courtroom, the reception centre, relevant telephone numbers, etc. is also generally provided.

## Information About the Specific Case

Most victims and witnesses are understandably interested in the progress of 'their' case, whether or not their appearance is required at certain proceedings. Victim/witness projects almost always, therefore, respond to requests for status information from victims and witnesses. Many take affirmative action in this respect by routinely providing information at certain stages to victims and witnesses who have made a standing request for it and who keep an up-to-date address and/or telephone number on file with the project. Information is generally conveyed through a series of form letters with the particular information regarding the specific case inserted where appropriate. Typical stages prompting notification include arraignment (including the charge and scheduled trial date, if defendant pleads not guilty); outcome of plea negotiation or trial (including sentence, if defendant pleads or is found guilty); and dismissal.

Advance notification of scheduled proceedings is also becoming more commonplace, especially where the victim has an opportunity to have his or her concerns considered.

**Victim Input**

Victims who are allowed (either statutorily or by practice) to provide information to the prosecutor, sentencing court or other official body may be unsure as to what information is relevant. They may also be unsure as to how to present the information effectively.

The victim/witness assistance project which is familiar both with the system and with the victim's individual case is in an excellent position to help the victim prepare either an oral or written statement. It can, for example, explain to the victim the importance of including detailed information about financial expenses associated with the victimization so as to provide the basis for restitution. It can caution against an excessively vindictive attitude which may actually work against the very end the victim is seeking to accomplish. It can also ensure that the statement is clear, accurate, and, where warranted, documented.

**SUMMARY**

Victims and witnesses – until relatively recently left to face the consequences of the crime alone – are beginning to see their concerns addressed by established programmes both within and without the criminal justice system.

Some of these concerns are related directly to the crime. Others come about because of subsequent victim or witness contact with the criminal justice system. Though there are exceptions, generally speaking non-criminal justice sponsored programmes are better equipped to deal with problems resulting directly from the crime, and criminal justice affiliated programmes are better equipped to deal with those 'secondary victimization' problems resulting from participation in the criminal justice process.

Programmes which deal with problems directly related to the crime usually offer emergency services to take care of the immediate physical, psychological, and financial needs of the victim. They also provide counselling services and assist the victim in recouping financial losses.

Services which victim/witness assistance projects offer to those unwittingly involved with the system include mail subpoenas, transportation and babysitting, witness reception centres, notification regarding scheduling changes, protection from intimidation, and assistance with property return, and payment of witness fees. They also provide information about the criminal justice system and the particular case. Finally, these programmes are increasingly helping victims prepare 'victim impact statements' for the prosecutor and the sentencing court.

# 16  Family Violence and Changing Ideologies in Shelter Movement*

## Teuvo Peltoniemi

Shelters (refuges, transition houses, Frauenhäuser, crisis centres) are the first specific institution for the treatment of family violence. Since the first Chiswick shelter in London in 1971 (Pizzey, 1974) their number has grown rapidly. There are now more than 100 shelters in Canada, 200 in Great Britain and at least 500 in the United States (Response, 1983). In Finland there are 15 shelters.

The emergence of family violence as a social problem and the rise of the shelter movement have taken place through different stages in different countries. Family violence discussion has so far remained a Western phenomenon. Little discussion of the theme has emerged in Socialist or in developing countries.

Three groups have been behind the discussion of family violence and shelters: these are 1. the feminist movement, 2. social welfare, and 3. the court system. The birth of shelters was closely related to grassroots movements, such as feminist rape centres activism and social welfare volunteer activity (Tierney, 1982).

The first US shelter in Phoenix, Arizona, was established in 1973 for the wives of alcoholics (Tierney, 1982). The Chiswick shelter was originally founded as a general woman's centre and only gradually developed into a shelter for the victims of family violence (Pizzey, 1974). The same also happened in the Vancouver, British Columbia shelter (Ridington, 1978).

Norquay and Weiler (1981) have suggested that in the United States the Federal government strongly promoted this activity, but in Canada the role of the authorities was more passive. In North America especially, the role of feminist movements has been prominent (Kalmuss and Straus, 1983).

In Norway, Denmark, and Sweden the discussion of family violence came through the radical feminist movement (Snare et al., 1983). This has directed the nature of the discussion in different courses compared to Finland, where family violence discussion originated primarily in voluntary child-care and research circles, and the role of the feminist movement and the criminal justice system has been minor (Peltoniemi, 1984).

There seems to be quite remarkable differences in people's attitudes towards family violence in Finland and Sweden, according to polls made in both countries (Peltoniemi, 1983b). These differences can partly be explained by the cultural and historical differences between the two societies.

The general climate of opinion in family matters differs in Finland and Sweden (Peltoniemi, 1983b). But an important factor is likely to be the way family violence discussion arose in these countries. In this case a varying emphasis in the mass media may have influenced people's opinions on family violence, as may happen when a new issue arises on which no definite general public opinion yet prevails.

In Finland a 3-year experiment with 4 shelters was begun in the spring of 1979 by the First Homes' Federation, a semi-public organization that maintains homes for young single mothers (Leskinen, Mäkinen and Peltoniemi, 1982). The work load of the organization was relieved because of the improvement in the status of unwed mothers and because the Federation was probing into related activities. Thus there were available a ready organization, know-how and other resources that could readily be exploited to serve a new kind of clientele. A similar development has been reported for some US shelters (Johnson, 1981).

The First Homes' Federation had earlier occasionally been confronted by family violence among their clients. The organization had also advocated against physical correction of children (Peltoniemi, 1981, 1983a). These principles were easy to link with new ideas of shelters for the victims of family violence. The child-care emphasis can be seen in the rules of the shelters even if they have not emerged as distinctly in their everyday activities.


## TWO SHELTER IDEOLOGIES

Shelters can be divided into two main groups on the basis of their underlying philosophy: either *feminist or social-welfare and family-oriented.*

The most important feature of the feminist shelter ideology is the emphasis on a non-hierarchical system. There are no specified work roles and the ideology insists that those staying at the shelters be called women, not clients, or anything else. Much of the ideology of the feminist shelter approach resembles the goals of the green movement. Thus it generally receives more public support than appears to be the case at first glance.

The entire ideology rests on one explanatory theory of family violence: the structural theory saying that the phenomenon is caused by a patriarchal society (Dobash and Dobash, 1979). According to Ridington (1978), the Vancouver shelter has only three rules: 'No liquor, no drugs, no men!' In feminist shelters it is feared that the male companions of clients might cause trouble, and the locations of the shelters are consequently often kept secret and strict precautions are taken to keep them that way (Melville, 1978, p.301). Some feminist shelters don't even accept male teenage children of the clients in the shelter (King, 1984).

The family-oriented shelter ideology is in most respects an antithesis of the feminist ideology. Family violence is thought to be directed towards many different victims within the family. Several reasons for violence are suggested, and it is considered that the entire family needs help, not only women. The shelters are organized in a more traditional way and cooperate closely with social care agencies. The differences in the two models are listed in Table 15.1.

In Great Britain, 97 shelters out of 135 fall under the feminist National Women's Aid; the rest remain outside (Response, 1983). In the USA it has been estimated that less than half of the shelters work from the feminist perspective (Johnson, 1981).

The feminist-oriented shelter movement emphasizes the criminal nature of family violence, and the role of the court system (Soler and Martin, 1981). The other direction, in turn, looks for features of social maladjustment, deviance, and illnesses in family violence and emphasizes the significance of treatment and mediation (Lynch and Norris, 1978).

The differences in the two ideologies are illustrated, e.g. by the discussion in the United States of the findings that men are as often victims of family violence as women (Steinmetz, 1978; Straus, Gelles and Steinmetz, 1980), in the debate on crisis intervention systems (Lerman, 1984) and in Great Britain in the social learning theory of family violence as proposed by Pizzey (1974).

Table 15.1　Features of the Two Main Shelter Ideologies

|  | Family-Oriented | Feminism-Oriented |
|---|---|---|
| Term used | Family violence | Battered wives |
| Relation to feminism | Somewhat negative | Strongly positive |
| Reasons for family violence | Relation problems | Patriarchal society |
| Nature of family violence | Social illness | Crime |
| Victims | Both men and women | Only women |
| Children's role | Very important | Less important |
| Openness of the operation | Very open | Very closed |
| Acceptance of men | Accepted as staff | Not accepted at all |
| Working procedures | Personal discussions | Group meetings |
| Object of the work | The family | Women's self-respect |
| Staff | Specialized | Non-specialized |
| Relation to the state | Cooperation | Independent |
| Political involvement | Scant | Extensive |

This table is based on Alfredsson (1980) pp. 157–8; see also Pizzey (1979) and Freeman (1980).

## ACTUAL DIFFERENCES IN OPERATION

Even though there are ideological differences between shelters, the actual work done by them may be much the same. Remarkable similarities in the actual work appear in the descriptions of feminist-oriented shelters (e.g. Vaughan, 1979; Christensen, 1983) and family-oriented shelters (Pizzey, 1974), when certain ideological terms are removed.

Unfortunately, not a great deal is known about the actual working procedures of shelters, despite the fact that research into family violence is expanding (Peltoniemi and Honkavaara, 1981). Most studies on shelters tend to content themselves with looking at the clientele of one particular shelter (e.g. LaBell, 1979; Thompson, 1978) and offer no comparisons or details of the shelter's actual work. Others are more phamphlets than scientific studies (e.g. *Berliner Frauenhaus* . . ., 1978). Notable exceptions are the studies on the shelters of Canterbury (Pahl, 1978) and Copenhagen (Christensen, 1983).

In the following, data from Finnish shelters are based on the Shelter Study Project of the Finnish Foundation for Alcohol Studies. The study analysed the operation and background ideology of the shelters and described everyday activities in them. The data consist of client records, observations, and interviews with the staff and the clients (Peltoniemi, 1981; Leskinen, Mäkinen and Peltoniemi, 1982).

## FINNISH SHELTERS

The Finnish shelters mainly conform to the family-oriented model. This view can be seen in the low level of importance given to the feminist perspective, the emphasis on children, the well-defined work roles of the staff members, and the fact that no attempt is made to keep the location of the shelters secret, unlike many foreign shelters (Peltoniemi, 1981).

All the Finnish shelters list the same fundamental objectives. Unlike a shelter in Jacksonville, Florida (LaBell, 1979, p.259), victims of non-physical family violence are also accepted. As far as sex is concerned, no restriction on admittance exists – both female and male victims of family violence are admitted.

This distinguishes the Finnish shelters from most shelters in other countries. This may partly be a reflection of the equality of Finnish society, which probably stands higher than in the Anglo-Saxon countries. Nearly without exception the shelter clients as well as the staff considered this rule to be right. Male staff members, in addition, were also welcomed as a good balance, especially from the point of view of the children (Leskinen, Mäkinen and Peltoniemi, 1982).

The Finnish shelters are situated in middle-class standard apartments and are by no means characterized by a description of British shelters: 'Poverty is the first thing that strikes you when you visit refuges: invariably there are peeling walls, patched lino, and a general state of disrepair. Conditions are crowded' (Melville, 1978, p.299). This, of course, partly reflects differences in standard of living but also probably different attitudes regarding the importance of outside resources.

## CLIENTS

The four first Finnish shelters can accommodate 36 adult clients along with their children. The combined number of client visits paid to the shelters during the first 2 years of operation was 1192. The number of separate clients during the period was 971. By far the greatest number of clients were women (92%). There were 33 male clients during the period; 57% of clients were accompanied by children with 846 children in all. The average age of the clients was 32 years. Usually, the clients came from the lower social stratus (Leskinen, Mäkinen and Peltoniemi, 1982).

Shelters admit clients at all and any times. Somewhat contrary to what was expected when the shelters were instigated, shelters have not been used only as refuges in emergencies. Most clients did not come to the shelter until the immediate crisis had passed, and not from the crisis situation proper (Peltoniemi, 1981).

Shelters also function as crisis centres and telephones are manned 24 hours a day. During the first 12 months of operation 2362 telephone calls were made by clients. The telephone calls demonstrate how the shelters are used as a type of out-patient clinic. Most callers wanted to know how the shelter was getting on and how it worked.

It was also quite common for a person to telephone the shelter and say that she or he would be coming shortly and then not turn up. Shelter staff felt that these callers were victims of family violence who did not feel capable of making a deliberate effort to improve things, to leave home and come to the shelter.

The clients may stay up to 2 months but most only stayed for a brief period. Half of the clients stayed for less than 24 hours. Only 21% of clients stayed for longer than a week. Clients apparently use the shelter as a kind of out-patient centre. They spend a couple of hours at the shelter and then feel able to cope with things at home.

The crises from which the client came were recorded upon arrival. The most common were physical (44%) and verbal family violence (41%) as well as fear of family violence (32%).

Shelter clients reported twice as much physical violence as that reported in the domestic disturbance call study in Helsinki (Peltoniemi, 1980). And this is to be expected – it would seem safe to assume that the clients who came to the shelters faced exacerbated difficulties. It is important to note, however, that half of the clients came to the shelter because of non-physical violence. This has obvious implications for treatment.

## ALCOHOL

The most apparent single problem connected to violence was alcohol. It very often came up in discussion in the shelters. Nearly half of the clients had clear views as to whether or not alcohol played an important role. Most of them thought that their problems were caused by alcohol (Peltoniemi, 1982). This attitude is shared commonly by the entire population; 86% of the Finns agreed with the following statement: 'Family violence is most often due to the excessive use of alcohol' (Peltoniemi, 1982).

In shelter cases the perpetrator had been drinking in 70% of the situations, and 23% of them had been registered in alcohol treatment agencies (Peltoniemi, 1982). A few clients (9%) even said they had a drinking problem themselves. These results accord with findings of the police study (Peltoniemi, 1980).

When alcohol and non-alcohol client groups are compared the results suggest that when alcohol is involved there are more cases of physical violence. The victim also seems to expect more trouble in drinking situations and leaves before any physical violence develops (Peltoniemi, 1982).

## CHILDREN

When the Finnish shelters were established, the emphasis was on child welfare. Even so, children have been left very much on their own in the shelters. The mothers don't seem to have the energy to pay enough attention to children, and do not respond to their needs. In the same way, the duties of staff members don't allow sufficient time to be with the children.

Many children in the shelters are frightened, cling to their mothers or other adults present. Others are aggressive so that there is a lot of quarrelling among shelter children and sometimes also among mothers because of children (Leskinen, Mäkinen and Peltoniemi, 1982).

Similar experiences have been reported in Canada and the USA (King, 1984; Hughes, 1982). However, in contrast to foreign experiences (King, 1984), violence against children in Finnish shelters is not registered very often. This is in line with the finding that only 7% of the clients reported that children had been abused at home (Peltoniemi, 1983a). In some foreign shelters, the overlapping of spouse abuse and child abuse has been reported to a far greater extent (Brückner, 1982).

## SELF-HELP GOAL

The general philosophy of the Finnish shelters is such that no treatment is given in the therapeutic sense of the word. The shelters offer a safe and non-violent atmosphere where clients can find themselves and cope with matters with the aid of shelter staff and fellow victims. Clients are encouraged to ponder their situation and to help themselves. On this point, most shelters seem to stress similar goals which can be understood as a self-help community ideal (e.g. Ridington, 1978; Pahl, 1978; Christensen, 1983).

The choice of a semi-professional staff in Finnish shelters reflects this goal. The staff generally have educational and employment backgrounds in the social-work field. The combined total number of the staff is 22. The staff are available at all times. Some of the staff of the Oulu and Turku shelters also work concurrently for the local First Home (Peltoniemi, 1981).

Formal weekly meetings are held in the shelters. The meetings discuss practical arrangements and personal problems and all the clients of the shelter are encouraged to attend. The Helsinki shelter also holds a weekly meeting at which the clients' children are present but the only adult is the shelter director.

In all the shelters, the hope was expressed by the clients that there be more opportunities to meet the other party in the conflict and to discuss the situation with the entire family (Leskinen, Mäkinen and Peltoniemi, 1982).

Almost all of the clients regarded the opportunity to discuss the situation with other people with similar experiences to be a positive matter. On the other hand, clients expected a fuller opportunity to deal with their situation with the help of the staff. In the Helsinki shelter, all of the staff members were assigned the task of engaging in discussions with the clients, while in Oulu and Turku, the chance of discussion was restricted to the office hours of the director and social worker.

Observations in Finnish shelters show that as is the case with institutions in general, meal-times dominate the life in the shelters. Otherwise, the day is spent in non-programmed activities and conversations between the clients. Public rooms are often crowded by clients who smoke and talk about their experiences of family violence and other matters. Everybody has his or her own room but very few remain there alone.

In principle, the clients participate in the preparation of the meals and cleaning chores, but in practice there are difficulties in this. The inability of the clients to concentrate on any matter is evident. For example the care of children suffers. Not even television, radio, and newspapers are popular and reading consists mainly of romance stories (Leskinen, Mäkinen and Peltoniemi, 1982).

The most important element in the self-help community seemed to be, not the actual discussions, but the presence of someone who listened. It has been shown that many victims of family violence live an isolated life (Peltoniemi, 1984) and seemingly don't have anyone to talk with about their situation. That is why the clients have a great urge to speak about their problem with anyone in the shelter who cares to listen.

The low occupancy of shelters and the division of work among the staff members make the idea of a self-help community, however, difficult to achieve in small shelters. The Kotka and Oulu shelters have been completely empty on occasion, and quite often there is only one client in the shelter. This automatically leads to the situation in which no self-help community can be achieved, and the shelter begins to resemble a traditional social-work agency (Leskinen, Mäkinen and Peltoniemi, 1982).


**REFERRALS**

In the shelters, the clients are counselled on other places where help can be obtained. Every other client (56%) is put in touch with an agency. The people who stood in need of help were referred to concrete aid as well as to therapeutic agencies. Concrete referrals dominated. The agency to which the clients were most often referred was the Social Welfare Authority. Clients who decided not to rejoin their partners but to begin life on their own often needed municipal housing and the services of an employment exchange.

There were difficulties in referrals. First of all, a fair number of clients (60%) already had recourse to various agencies. Similar results are reported in the studies of LaBell (1979) and Thompson (1978). Also problems like the line-ups of receiving agencies, and motivation problems among clients and shelter staff members posed complications. Quite often a client did not visit the agency in spite of a booking or discontinued visits after a time or two.

## VOLUNTEERS

The Kotka and Helsinki shelters have used volunteer workers on weekends but in Helsinki this practice was discontinued. It was found that the relations between volunteers and clients were not satisfactory. Some volunteers felt unable to cope with new clients. The high turnover of volunteers caused complaints. Over the weekends the clients had to get to know new staff members, whom they probably would not see again.

Similarly in the Copenhagen shelter, there were 12–16 staff members present during 24 hours (Christensen, 1983). For a client, that is an unmanageable number of people with whom the problem is to be shared (cf. also Pahl, 1978).

These problems with volunteers have led in many shelters to the hiring of at least some staff members. This in turn often creates conflicts between the profesionally oriented staff and non-hierarchically oriented volunteers (see e.g. Ahrens, 1980).

## THE FUTURE

In Finland, shelters are included in the long-range planning programmes of the National Board of Social Welfare. It is obvious that the Finnish shelters are becoming integrated with the social care services. This is a universal trend. Shelters do become integrated and institutionalized (Lynch and Norris, 1978). In the USA special bodies were established on the federal level to finance and guide shelters. These activities have, however, been slowed by the Reagan administration (Response, 1983).

Tierney (1982) differentiates between three developments in this process: 1. the social welfare focus increases and the emphasis on feminism decreases; 2. understanding of the family violence problem becomes increasingly medicalized, professionalized, individualized, and depoliticized; and 3. official social welfare organizations emerge as spokesman for the shelter movement.

According to the classification of Tierney, the Finnish shelters have started in a late phase, under a semi-official organization in the First Homes' Federation. The trend towards institutionalization is shown by the fact that most new shelters in Finland have been established by cities.

In general, the shelters are in a period of transition in other ways as well. Many shelters have begun as feminist-oriented but have later become family-oriented. There have been conflicts between the middle-class feminist activists and the lower-class clients of shelters (McGrath, 1979, p.25). Lois Ahrens (1980) describes the change in a shelter in Austin, Texas, where ideological conflicts emerged very clearly.

It is quite important to realize that both types of shelters seem to help. Seemingly the availability of a shelter for family violence is more important than the way the house is run.

The process of transition has given rise to much discussion. Melville (1978, p.306) holds that there is nothing wrong with it as it provides an answer to financial and staffing problems and ascertains continuity of operation. It is indeed a precept of general organizational sociology that voluntary bodies tend to become institutionalized (Etzioni, 1969). Many feminists do not quite see things this way and resist this development (Ahrens, 1980; Morgan, 1981).

In Finland conflicts of this kind have been rare, but still they do exist. A fraction of the feminist movement has criticized the shelters of the First Homes' Federation and founded a separate, feminist-oriented shelter in the Greater Helsinki area (see Germain *et al.*, 1980).

The shelter movement is a grassroots folk movement. Looking at the history of similar movements, one can predict that it will not last forever. A folk movement consists of three elements: the actors, the ideology, and the subjects. The actors will turn to other issues sooner or later, the ideology will change, and the state will take care of the victims of family violence. The This is the usual path most social problems in industrial societies have taken, and it makes the institutionalization development of shelters quite understandable.

At least in Finland, society is now very much in favour of shelters. But, when the wave of support for a 'fad phenomenon' fades, ordinary cost-benefit thinking will prevail. In the present economic situation all activities will be reviewed, and so will the shelters. Those who fight against family violence would do better to prepare for this phase to come, as Pfouts and Renz (1981) and Tierney (1982) also emphasize.

The shelter movement, be it a feminist-oriented or the family-oriented Finnish movement, should be wise to enlarge its scope around other issues in the treatment of family violence. This is partly already the case. In Finland there are plans for crisis intervention systems in conjunction with shelters (Peltoniemi, 1984). In the USA and Great Britain shelters have established special self-help groups for the victims of family violence as well as for the perpetrators (Melville, 1978).

Also the scope of family violence has widened from wife and child abuse to men (Steinmetz, 1978), the elderly (Rathbone-McCuan, 1980), sexual abuse of children (Finkelhor, 1982) and to family violence as a macro-concept (Finkelhor, 1983). This development is, however, very closely connected to the main theories of family violence and shelter ideologies and is still subject to scientific debate.

### Notes

*This study was finished mainly by the Finnish Foundation for Alcohol Studies.

### References

Ahrens, Lois (1980), 'Battered Women's Refuges: Feminist Cooperatives vs. Social Service Institutions, *Radical America*, pp.41–9.
Alfredsson, Karin (1980) Den man älskar agar man? (when one loves one corrects?), (Lund, Sweden: Raben and Sjögren).
Berliner Frauenhaus für mishandelte Frauen (1978), *Erster Erfahrungsbericht: Frauen gegen Männergewalt* (Frauenselbstverlag Berlin-West).
Brückner, Margit (1982), 'Frauenhausliteratur', *Literatur Rundschau*, vol.7, pp.46–53.
Christensen, Else (1983), 'The Danner refuge for battered women – an

Evaluation', Women's Research Centre in Social Science, Working note 5 (Copenhagen).

Dobash, R. Emerson and Dobash, Russel P. (1979), *Violence Against Wives: a Case Against Patriarchy* (New York: Free Press).

Etzioni, Amitai (1969), *A Sociological Reader on Complex Organizations* (New York: Holt, Rinehardt & Winston).

Finkelhor David (1982), 'Sexual Abuse: a Sociological Perspective', *Child Abuse & Neglect*, vol.6, pp.95–102.

Finkelhor, David (1983), 'Common Features of Family Abuse' in David Finkelhor, Richard J. Gelles, Gerald T. Hotaling and Murray A Straus (eds), *The Dark Side of Families: Current Family Violence Research* (Beverly Hills, CA: Sage Publications).

Freeman, M. D. A. (1980) Violence against women. *British J. of Law and Society*, 7(2), pp. 215–41.

Germain, Sinikka, Mattila, Kari, Meyer-Törnroth, Chris and Polkunen-Gartz, Marja-Liisa (1980), *Våld i hemmet: Rapport om kvinnomisshandel* (Violence at home. A report on battered women) (Lovisa: Schildts).

Hughes, Honore M. (1982), 'Brief Interventions with Children in a Battered Women's Shelter: a Model Preventive Program', *Family Relations*, vol.31, pp.495–502.

Johnson, John M. (1981), 'Program Enterprise and Official Cooption in the Battered Women's Shelter Movement', *American Behavioral Scientist*, vol.24, pp.827–42.

Kalmuss, Debra S. and Straus, Murray A. (1983), 'Feminist Political and Economic Determinants of Wife Abuse Services' in David Finkelhor, Richard J. Gelles, Gerald T. Hotaling and Murray A. Straus (eds), *The Dark Side of Families: Current Family Violence Research* (Beverly Hills, CA: Sage Publications).

King, Nancy (1984), 'Children of Abused Women: the Canadian Response', *Response*, vol.7, pp.7–8.

LaBell, Linda S. (1979), 'Wife Abuse: a Sociological Study of Battered Women and Their Mates', *Victimology*, vol.3, pp.258–67.

Lerman, Lisa G. (1984), 'A Feminist Critique of Mediation in Wife Abuse Cases', *Response*, vol.7, pp.5–6, 12–13.

Leskinen, Riitta, Mäkinen, Tuija and Peltoniemi, Teuvo (1982), *Täällä ei tarvitse pelätä – tutkimus turvakodeiesta* (English summary: There is nothing to fear here!: A study of shelters in Finland.) First Homes' Federation of Finland. Report no.1.

Lynch, Catherine and Norris, Thomas L. (1978), 'Services for Battered Women: Looking for a Perspective', *Victimology*, vol.2, pp.553–62.

McGrath, Colleen (1979), 'The Crisis of Domestic Order', *Socialist Review*, pp.11–30.

Melville, Joy (1978), 'Women in Refuges' in J. P. Martin (ed.), *Violence and the Family* (Chichester: John Wiley).

Morgan, Patricia (1981), 'From Battered Wife to Program Client: the State's Shaping of Social Problems', *Kapitaliststate*, vol.9, pp.17–39.

Norquay, Geoff and Weiler, Richard (1981), *Services to Victims and Witnesses of Crime in Canada*, Solicitor General Canada, Research division (Ottawa).

Pahl, Jean (1978), *A Refuge for Battered Women: a Study of the Role of a*

346     *On Services for Crime Victims*

*Women's Centre*, Department of Health and Social Security (London: HMSO).

Peltoniemi, Teuvo (1980), 'Family Violence: Police House Calls in Helsinki, Finland in 1977', *Victimology*, vol.5, pp.213–24.

Peltoniemi, Teuvo (1981), 'The First 12 Months of the Finnish Shelters', *Victimology*, vol.6, pp.198–211.

Peltoniemi, Teuvo (1982), 'Alcohol and Family Violence' in 28th International Institute on the Prevention and Treatment of Alcoholism, München 5–9 July 1982, *Proceedings: International Council on Alcohol and Alcoholism* (Lausanne) pp.562–76.

Peltoniemi, Teuvo (1983a), 'Child Abuse and Physical Punishment of Children in Finland', *Child Abuse & Neglect*, vol.7, pp.33–6.

Peltoniemi, Teuvo (1983b), *Familjevåld i Finland och Sverige – omfattning och attityder* (English summary: Family violence in Finland and Sweden – Prevalence and Attitudes), Research Institute of Legal Policy, Publication 58 (Helsinki).

Peltoniemi, Teuvo (1984), *Perheväkivalta* (Family Violence) (Keuruu: Otava Publishing House).

Peltoniemi, Teuvo and Honkavaara, Pirjo (1981), *A Bibliography of Family Violence and Child Battering*, Central Union for Child Welfare in Finalnd (Helsinki).

Pfouts, Jane H. and Renz, Connie (1981), 'The Future of Wife Abuse Programs', *Social Work*, vol.26, pp.451–5.

Pizzey, Erin (1974), *Scream Quietly or the Neighbours Will Hear* (London: Penguin Books).

Rathbone-McCuan, Eloise (1980), 'Elderly Victims of Family Violence and Neglect', *Social Casework*, vol.61, pp.296–304.

Response No 3 (1983), Center for women studies (Washington, DC).

Ridington, Jillian (1978), 'The Transition Process: a Feminist Environment as a Reconstitutive Milieu', *Victimology*, vol.2, pp.563–75.

Snare, Annika, Olafsdottir Hildigunnur and Peltoniemi, Teuvo (1983), 'Den privata volden: om hustrumishandling' (The Private Violence: on Battered (Women) in Cecilie Høigård and Annika Snare *Kvinners skyld – en nordisk antologi i kriminologi* (Women's Blame – a Nordic Anthology in Criminology) (Oslo: Pax).

Soler, Esta and Martin, Sue (1981), *Domestic Violence is a Crime*, Family violence project (San Francisco, CA).

Steinmetz, Suzanne K. (1978), 'Battered Husband Syndrome', *Victimology*, vol.2, pp.499–507.

Straus, Murray A., Gelles, Richard J. and Steinmetz, Suzanne K. (1980), *Behind Closed Doors: Violence in the American Family* (New York: Doubleday).

Tierney, Kathleen J. (1982), 'The Battered Women Movement and the Creation of the Wife Beating Problem', *Social Problems*, vol.29, pp.207–20.

Thompson, Judy (1978), *Overview of Domestic Violence Between Mates*, Women's Community House (London, Ontario).

Vaughan, Sharon Rice (1979), 'The Last Refuge: Shelter for Battered Women', *Victimology*, vol.3, pp.113–18.

# Epilogue: For a Charter of Rights for Crime Victims

André Normandeau

*Prisoners' rights* were established about 10 years ago, in Quebec as in North America and Europe. These rights are not always respected and the fight to have them upheld must be taken up over and over again. But the breach has been made and the system of criminal justice should take it into account from now on. Three recent events illustrate the credibility of this movement in Canada: (a) in 1980, the Canadian government and the Department of the Solicitor General published a 'manual' of prisoners' rights; (b) the Quebec government and the Department of Justice, in a 'green paper' on correctional policy, recognized the rights of prisoners in 1981; (c) the 'Ligue des droits et libertés' of Quebec and the 'Office des droits des détenus' proposed a 'Charter' of prisoners' rights which was ratified in 1982 during the congress of the International Federation of Human Rights. This movement, moreover, has an international background, starting with the 'Standard Minimum Rules for the Treatment of Prisoners' adopted by the first congress of the United Nations Organization on the 'Prevention of Crime and Treatment of Offenders' at Geneva, in 1955, to the remarkable recent work of Amnesty International.

On the basis of a symbolic and historical parallel with this movement, I would like to propose that you support a more recent movement whose mission, far more pressing than the first, is to radically overturn the 'old' system of justice we now know by the close of the century. It is the movement for *the rights and liberties of crime victims* and a project for a *Charter of Rights for Crime Victims*.

I already hear cries of protest. 'What! more rights! Haven't we got enough?'

Obviously, there are 'too many rights'! but there are also 'too many victims'! Half jokingly, the American sociologist, Robert Nisbet, recently wrote in the *New York Times* (15 August 1982) that there is no end to the continual creation of victims and unlimited recognition of rights. Since the 19th century, 'the Welfare State and American do-gooders have decreed that the poor, the unemployed, the handi-

347

capped, alcoholics, women, blacks, Indians, the Inuit . . . and criminals were actually the victims of society'. At this rate, victimology is no longer a speciality of criminology but the science par excellence of western society. Every citizen is afflicted by it but no one nearly or actually dies from it (save those who are murdered), to paraphrase Jean de Lafontaine and his fable about the plague. And Nisbet reminds us very seriously that, associated with rights, there are *duties, responsibilities, constraints* and *rules of individual and public morality*.

In my opinion, it goes without saying that rights and responsibilities are two sides of the same coin and that any movement in favour of victims' rights, like prisoners' rights, should take this into account in a *search for a balance* between the rights of some and those of others, between the responsibilities of some and those of others, *between rights and personal and collective responsibilities*.

## PROJECT FOR A CHARTER OF RIGHTS FOR CRIME VICTIMS

A project for a Charter of Rights for Crime Victims, which I will call either 'Minimum Charter' or 'Standard Minimum Rules', could be set down in terms similar to certain rights suggested by the Canadian Council on Social Development (1982), the US National Organization for Victim Assistance (1982), as well as other private and public organizations (Norquay and Weiler, 1981), as follows:

## PROPOSED CHARTER OF RIGHTS FOR CRIME VICTIMS

WHEREAS society's main goal may be summarized as liberty, equality, dignity, fraternity, solidarity, peace, and justice for all citizens;
WHEREAS crime victims derive less benefit from this liberty in society;
WHEREAS victims are unjustly subjected to:

(a) *physical injury* (minor, permanent or even fatal injuries);
(b) *financial loss* (loss of money, loss or destruction of property, incurred medical expenses);

(c) *emotional trauma* over a short, medium or long term (stress, distress, tension, anger, fear, anxiety, humiliation, shame, disgrace); and

(d) *secondary psychological and physical effects* (depression, migraines, nausea, dizziness, fatigue), suffering for which they do not receive the proper support and assistance from social resources.

WHEREAS the criminal justice system is inadequate in the following respects:

(a) police and legal *protection* for victims;

(b) *reparation* for injury and wrong suffered;

(c) *information* on how the penal system operates and what the results of the work by officials in the system are; and

(d) humane, personal *treatment* of victims.

AND WHEREAS Quebecers and all other Canadians, imbued with a *sense of justice and fairness*, are prepared to support the legitimate claims of crime victims;

THEREFORE WE PROPOSE A CHARTER OF RIGHTS FOR CRIME VICTIMS and ask that it be recognized by the governments of Quebec and Canada *officially and publicly* once any necessary studies have been conducted and any required amendments made:

**CHAPTER I:   RIGHT TO PROTECTION** from criminals

Quebecers and all other Canadians shall be assured that sufficient effort is being made by government and private agencies to prevent crime. In return, every citizen shall 'do his part' to better protect himself. This personal *responsibility* goes together with his *right* to protection. All individuals have a right to liberty and security. Consequently, they have:

*article* *1* – the right to proper information on the protective measures which each person may take;

*article* *2* – the right to private and government programmes (including municipal programmes) which will improve protection, whether through good police services, urban environmental design policies, community projects oriented toward neighbourhood watch, or citizens involvement.

**CHAPTER II: RIGHT TO REPARATION** for injury, loss, trauma, and other consequences and suffering;
Victims have the right to regain the *physical, psychological, social, and financial* well-being they had before the crime. Consequently, they have:

*article* 3 – the right to the practical support and professional assistance of health and social service agencies;

*article* 4 – the right to the understanding of those providing the services;

*article* 5 – the right to government financial compensation for physical injury and emotional trauma suffered; and

*article* 6 – the right to compensation (in money) and/or restitution (of losses) by the offender/criminal through civil and criminal proceedings at no cost to themselves owing to the *intervention of the Crown prosecutor* and free and universal access to legal aid, if necessary.

**CHAPTER III: RIGHT TO PROPER INFORMATION AND PREFERRED TREATMENT** from the media, police and judicial and penal authorities
Victims are absolutely entitled to be *fully informed* and *kindly protected* and *treated* by the criminal justice system. Consequently, they have:

*article* 7 – the right to privacy, dignity, and courtesy where the media, police and judicial and penal authorities are concerned;

*article* 8 – the right to be fully informed in non-technical language as to how the criminal justice system operates;

*article* 9 – the right to be kept informed of the progress of the police investigation, the progress and outcome of any legal proceedings, including plea and sentence bargaining, as well as correctional measures taken, including the offender's release on probation or parole, for example;

*article 10* – the right to have their say at every stage in the judicial process, including the passing of sentence;

*article 11* – the right to be represented in court by the Crown prosecutor, who would also act as 'counsel for the victim';

*article 12* – the right to a rapid disposition of the case, without a loss of time due to delay and postponement;

*article 13* – the right to prior notification of plans and any changes in court proceedings;

*article 14* – the right to have property returned as soon as it is found;

*article 15* – the right to answer a subpoena without fear of losing income or employment;

*article 16* – the right to receive fair treatment when testifying in court;

*article 17* – the right of protection from any intimidation, threat or aggression resulting from the complaint lodged with police, the arrest, the trial or the sentence.

**CHAPTER IV: RIGHT TO ALTERNATIVES TO THE CRIMINAL JUSTICE SYSTEM** to resolve conflicts arising from a criminal-type problem situation

The criminal justice system has not always been equal to this task in minimizing suffering on the part of both offenders and victims. The conflict has often been taken out of the victim's hands and placed in the hands of a third party, the State. Perhaps it is now time to introduce at least a partial change in *society's reaction* to a so-called criminal *problem situation*, with a *non-criminal, non-penal system for resolving conflicts*. Consequently, individuals and victims have:

*article 18* – the right, *in the short term*, to a criminal justice system in which State intervention would be kept to a minimum with *de facto* decriminalization programmes (diversion), which would involve both the offenders and the victims;

*article 19* – the right, *in the medium term*, to a more comprehensive system for resolving conflicts in civil and administrative law. This system would, by stages, partially or entirely replace the criminal justice system with de jure decriminalization programmes, as well as make substantial and considerable use of conciliation, reconciliation, compensation, restitution, and indemnification measures and educational and therapeutic processes.

## CHAPTER V: RIGHT TO A SOCIAL SYSTEM WITH LESS INJUSTICE AND CONFLICT

In the final analysis, without dreaming of that great revolutionary but utopian world where social classes would be abolished and all people would be equal 'before God, man and woman', there must be a *clear reaffirmation* that in so far as possible social *inequality* shall be *reduced* so as to minimize suffering, injustice, and conflict, which are the poisonous fruits of such inequality. Consequently, Quebecers and other Canadians have:

*article 20* – the right, *in the long term*, to a fairer, more egalitarian socio-economic system likely to reduce the incidence of problem situations, conflicts, and so-called criminal acts, as well as the negative physical, psychological, social and financial consequences for the offenders *and* the victims involved.

*A charter largely supported by public and private organizations*
This outline of a Charter of Rights for Crime Victims is *not an end in itself but a means for humanizing* the social system and criminal justice system. Since in its broadest sense it is part of a relatively recent awareness, a Charter of this kind is necessary to ensure that this awareness will not be transitory and that the presence and point of view of the victim will from now on be integrated in the very heart of the criminal justice system by the end of the 20th century, or of the non-penal system of resolving conflicts of the rapidly approaching 21st century.

This recent awareness is shown at every level of authority in America and it is interesting to trace certain manifestations of it in order to show that the movement for victims' rights is set on a solid foundation. For example:

A.   *The United States of America*
– American Bar Association (1981)
– Omnibus, Victim Protection Bill of 1982 (Washington, DC)
– Crime Victim's Bill of Rights (Proposition 8, California 1982)
– American Civil Liberties Union (1982)
– National Organization for Victim Assistance (NOVA, 1982)
– Victim Advocate Center, Victims' Bill of Rights (New York, 1982)

B. *Canada*
- Constitutional Law of 1982 (Ottawa)
- Federal and Provincial Charter of Human Rights (Ex. Quebec, 1975)
- White paper: 'The Criminal Law in Canadian Society' (Department of Justice, Ottawa, 1982)
- Law Reform Commission of Canada (since 1972)
- Department of the Solicitor General, Ottawa (Norquay and Weiler, 1981)
- Canadian Council on Social Development (Ottawa, 1981)

C. *Quebec*
- Québec Minister of Justice (Speeches, 1981, 1982)
- Annual Reports of the Department of Justice (1981, 1982)
- Green paper on Corrections (Québec, 1981, 1982)
- Health and Security at Work, Victim Compensation (Québec, IVAC, 1982)
- Victim Advocate Center in Montréal and St Jérôme (Baril, Normandeau, 1982)
- Political platforms (NDP Québec, PQ, MCM, 1982)
- Council of Churches on Justice and Criminology (Québec, 1982)

## CONCLUSIONS

Five suggestions for concrete action could be given immediate attention:

1. Ask the Ministers of Justice in Canada (federal and provincial) for the nomination, within 6 months, of a *public protector of victims* (or 'victims' ombudsman') to ensure that the machinery of justice will be geared toward satisfying certain needs of the victims of criminal acts.

2. Demand of appropriate Canadian governments (federal and provincial) a proclamation, within the year, of a *Charter of Rights for Crime Victims*

3. Reallocate 5% per year, for 4 years, that is *20% of the budgets* of the Departments of Justice and of the Solicitor General to *programmes of assistance to victims* at the judicial, financial, psycho-social, and medical levels.

4. Challenge Civil Liberties Unions to take the initiative in creating Victims' Rights Offices in collaboration with victims. Ex-prisoners could sit on the Board of Directors of a victims' Office, and, conversely, an ex-victim on the Board of Directors of a prisoners' Office, in order to clarify and balance the stands taken by each office.

5. Promote the establishment by community organizations of a Canadian *Annual Public Victims Week*, for a period of three to five years. *After* the International Year for women, children, the handicapped . . . but *before* the United Nations prehaps declares an *International Victims Year*, so that this Week would make the public and appropriate authorities aware of the negative consequences of a criminal act for the victim and the community, as well as the victim's rights and need of assistance.

In conclusion, may I call to mind three fundamental elements of our thinking on the justice system of the 1980s. In the *first* place, we reaffirm our conviction that *rights are a corollary of responsibilities* as much for victims and prisoners as for the agents of the justice system and social affairs. In the *second* place, we are persuaded that the defence of *victims'* rights and those of witnesses does not mean a reduction in the rights of the *accused*, prisoners and ex-prisoners. It is a question of *balance*. It is a question of *justice*. In the *third* place, we are in favour of developing *alternatives to the penal system* in order to promote the *resolution of conflicts* by 'minimizing the suffering' (Christie, 1981) of victims and prisoners and 'maximizing' the pocess of arbitration (in *civil and administrative law*) where the focus is on *conciliation, compensation, education* and *therapy*, broadly speaking (Hulsman, 1982; Landreville, 1982). *Decriminalization in practice* (or *diversion*) and *decriminalization by law* are short, middle- and long-term objectives that are totally valid, pertinent and carry with them the hope of change and true justice for all those involved (Council of Europe, 1980).

To balance rights and responsibilities, to balance victims' rights and prisoners' rights, to balance penal intervention, non-penal and even non-intervention; here are three precarious balances that we must ceaselessly keep working on. It is an exciting challenge that awaits us if we expend the energy and put our hearts in it.

To paraphrase some remarks of the greats, there is no glory in winning without a struggle (Corneille) and to fight for one's beliefs is to live (Victor Hugo). And closer in time and space, the Quebec ecologist, Pierre Dansereau, recently wrote that the art of living consists in balancing its contradictions, not resolving them (1981). How true!

In this perspective, we intend, with others, to carry a version of this proposed Charter of Rights for Crime Victims to other International forums such as the IXth International Congress of Criminology in Vienna, Austria (September 1983) and the VIIth United Nations Congress on the Prevention of Crime and the Treatment of Offenders (September 1985).

**Bibliography**

American Bar Association (1981), *Victim–Witness Legislation* (Washington, DC: ABA).
Bard, M. and Sangrey, D. (1978), *The Crime Victim's Book* (New York: Basic Books).
Baril, M. (1981), 'La criminologie et la justice pénale à l'heure de la victimologie', *Revue internationale de criminologie et de police technique* (Dec.) pp.356–660.
Baril, M., Normandeau, A. and Waller, I. (1981), 'Débat: Les services privés et publics aux victims', *Déviance et société* (Sept.) pp.261–92.
Baril, M (1982), 'Les laissés-pour-compte', *Sûreté de Québec* (Jan.) pp.14–18.
Baril, M. and Normandeau, A. (1982), 'Centre d'aide pour les victimes d'actes criminels', projets multiples, Ecole de criminologie, Université de Montréal.
Bédard, M. A. (1981), 'L'humanisation du système de justice et les services aux victimes d'actes criminels', 10pp, *Conférence* du ministre de la Justice du Québec au Congrès de l'American Probation and Parole Association.
Bédard, M. A. (1982), 'Le ministère de la Justice du Québec et les services aux victimes d'actes criminels', 15pp, *Conférence* du ministre de la Justice du Québec au Congrès de la Société de criminologie du Québec.
Bernot de Célis, J. (1982), 'Les grandes options de la politique criminelle: la perspective de Louk Hulsman', *Archives de politique criminelle* (June) pp.11–60.
California (1982), *The Victims' Bill of Rights*. Amendments to the constitution of California, Penal Code, Welfare and Institutions Code (Sacramento: Department of Justice).
Christie, N. (1981), *Limits to Pain* (New York: Columbia University Press).
Commission de la santé et de la sécurité au travail (1981), *Indemnisation des victimes d'actes criminels* (IVAC) (Rapport. Québec: Editeur Officiel).
Commission de réforme du droit du Canada (1974),*Le dédommagement et l'indemnisation* (Ottawa: CRD).
Conseil canadien du développement social (1982), *Les victimes d'actes criminels: droits et services* (Ottawa: CCDS).

Conseil de l'Europe (1980), *Rapport sur la décriminalisation* (Strasbourg: Comité Européen pour les problèmes criminels).

Conseil des Eglises pour la Justice et la Criminologie (1981), *Colloque sur les victimes d'actes criminels, Section-Québec* (Montréal, 6 June).

*Crimonologie* (1980), 'Regards sur la victime' (Montréal: Nouvelle Optique).

Davila, Luis B. (1982), *Protection de la victime* (Ecole de criminologie, Université de Montréal).

Drapkin, I. and Viano, E. (1974), *Victimology*, 5 vols (Mass.: Lexington Books).

Fattah, E. (1981), 'La victimologie', *Déviance et sociét'* (Mar.) pp.71–92.

Galaway, B. and Hudson, J. (1981), *Perspectives on crime victims* (St-Louis, Mosby).

Hulsman, L. (1981), 'Une perspective abolitionniste du système de justice pénale' in C. Debuyst (dir.): *Dangerosité et justice pénale* (Paris: Masson) pp.7–16.

Jacoby, D. (1981), 'L'humanisation envers tous et contre tout', 29pp, *Conférence* du sous-ministre de la Justice du Québec au Congrès des Officiers de justice du Québec.

Landreville, P. (1982), *Notes pour une analyse socio-politique des normes* (Ecole de criminologie, Université de Montréal).

Laplante, L and Normandeau, A. (1980), *Le vol à main armée au Québec Rapport* au ministre de la Justice (Québec: Editeur Officiel).

Ligue des droits et libertés du Québec (1980), *Projet de Charte des droits des détenu(e)s* (Montréal: Office des droits des détenu(e)s.

Ministère de la Justice du Canada (1982), *Le droit pénal dans la société canadienne* (Ottawa: Justice).

Ministère de la Justice du Québec (1981), *'Livre vert' sur les politiques correctionnelles* (Québec: Justice).

Ministère de la Justice du Québec (1981), *Rapport annuel 1980–81* (Québec: Editeur Officiel).

Ministère du Solliciteur Général du Canada (1980), *Compte-rendu de Colloque national sur les services d'aide aux victimes du crime* (Ottawa: Solliciteur).

National Organization for Victim Assistance (1982), *Campaign for Victim Rights* (Washington, DC: NOVA).

Normandeau, A. (1979), 'L'administration de la justice', *Crime et/and Justice*, (June) pp.131–6.

Normandeau, A. (1981), 'Les droits et libertés des victimes', *Revue internationale de police criminelle* (Oct) pp.229–31 .

Normandeau, A. (1982), 'Un changement de cap en criminologie: après les droits des détenus, ceux de la victime', *Le Devoir* (9 Oct) p.13.

Norquay, G. and Weiler, R. (1981), *Les services aux victimes et aux témoins de crime au Canada* (Ottawa: Solliciteur Général du Canada).

Ontario, Canada, Ministry of Correctional Services (1980), *Package on crime Victims* (Toronto: MCS).

*Programmes politiques* du Nouveau Parti Démocratique, du Parti Québécois et du Rassemblement des Citoyens de Montréal (1982). Voir les articles appropriés sur les victimes.

US Department of Justice (1981), *Attorney General's Task Force on Violent*

*Crime* (Washington, DC: US GPO).

US Senate and House of Representatives (1982), *Omnibus Victims Protection Act of 1982* (Washington, DC: US GPO).

Waller, I. (1982), 'Crime Victims: Needs, Services and Reforms', Orphans of Social Policy', 56pp, *Symposium international de victimologie* (Tokyo-Kyoto). Version française (partielle) au Congrès de la Société de criminologie du Québec (20 Oct).

# Appendix: Declaration of Basic Principles of Justice for Victims of Crime and Abuse of Power

*The following resolution was adopted by the General Assembly of the United Nations at its 96th plenary meeting on 29 November 1985.*

**The General Assembly,**

**Recalling** that the Sixth United Nations Congress on the Prevention of Crime and the Treatment of Offenders recommended that the Unitd Nations should continue its present work on the development of guidelines and standards regarding abuse of economic and political power[1].

**Cognizant** that millions of people throughout the world suffer harm as a result of crime and the abuse of power and that the rights of these victims have not been adequately recognized.

**Recognizing** that the victims of crime and the victims of abuse of power, and also frequently their families, witnesses and others who aid them, are unjustly subjected to loss, damage or injury and that they may, in addition, suffer hardship when assisting in the prosecution of offenders.

    1.  **Affirms** the necessity of adopting national and international measures in order to secure the universal and effective recognition of, and respect for, the rights of victims of crime and of abuse of power;

    2.  **Stresses** the need to promote progress by all States in their efforts to that end, without prejudice to the rights of suspects or offenders;

    3.  **Adopts** the Declaration of Basic Principles of Justice for Victims of Crime and Abuse of Power, annexed to the present resolution, which is designed to assist Governments and the international community in their efforts to secure justice and assistance for victims of crime and victims of abuse of power;

4. **Calls upon** Member States to take the necessary steps to give effect to the provisions contained in the Declaration and, in order to curtail victimization as referred to hereinafter, endeavour:

(a)   To implement social, health, including mental health, educational, economic and specific crime prevention policies to reduce victimization and encourage assistance to victims in distress;

(b)   To promote community efforts and public participation in crime prevention;

(c)   To review periodically their existing legislation and practices in order to ensure responsiveness to changing circumstances, and to enact and enforce legislation proscribing acts that violate internationally recognized norms relating to human rights, corporate conduct, and other abuses of power;

(d)   To establish and strengthen the means of detecting, prosecuting and sentencing those guilty of crime;

(e)   To promote disclosure of relevant information to expose official and corporate conduct to public scrutiny, and other ways of increasing responsiveness to public concerns;

(f)   To promote the observance of codes of conduct and ethical norms, in particular international standards, by public sevants, including law enfocement, correctional, medical, social service and military personnel, as well as the staff of economic enterprises;

(g)   To prohibit practices and procedures conducive to abuse, such as secret places of detention and incommunicado detention;

(h)   To co-operate with other States, through mutual judicial and administrative assistance, in such matters as the detection and pursuit of offenders, their extradition and the seizure of their assets, to be used for restitution to the victims;

5.   **Recommends** that, at the international and regional levels, all approrpiate measures should be taken:

(a)   To promote training activities designed to foster adherence to United Nations standards and norms and to curtail possible abuses;

(b)   To sponsor collaborative action-research on ways in which victimization can be reduced and victims aided, and to promote information exchanges on the most effective means of doing so;

(c)   To render direct aid to requesting Governments designed to help them curtail victimization and alleviate the plight of victims;

(d)   To develop ways and means of providing recourse for victims where national channels may be insufficient;

6.   **Requests** the Secretary-General to invite Member States to report periodically to the General Assembly on the implementation

of the Declaration, as well as on measures taken by them to this effect;

7.  **Also requests** the Secretary-General to make use of the opportunities, which all relevant bodies and organizations within the United Nations system offer, to assist Member States, whenever necessary, in improving ways and means of protecting victims both at the national level and through international co-operation;

8.  **Further requests** the Secretary-General to promote the objectives of the Declaration, in particular by ensuring its widest possible dissemination;

9.  **Urges** the specialized agencies and other entities and bodies of the United Nations system, other relevant intergovernmental and non-governmental organizations and the public to co-operate in the implementation of the provisions of the Declaration.

**Notes**

1.  Sixth United Nations Congress on the Prevention of Crime and the Treatment of Offenders, (United Nations publication, Sales no. E.81.IV.4), chap.1, sect.C.

## ANNEX: DECLARATION OF BASIC PRINCIPLES OF JUSTICE FOR VICTIMS OF CRIME AND ABUSE OF POWER

### A.  Victims of Crime

1.  "Victims" means persons who, individually or collectively, have suffered harm, including physical or mental injury, emotional suffering, economic loss or substantial impairment of their fundamental rights, through acts or omissions that are in violation of criminal laws operative within Member States, including those laws proscribing criminal abuse of power.

2.  A person may be considered a victim, under this Declaration, regardless of whether the perpetrator is identified, apprehended, prosecuted or convicted and regardless of the familial relationship between the perpetrator and the victim. The term "victim" also includes, where appropriate, the immediate family or dependants of

the direct victim and persons who have suffered harm in intervening to assist victims in distress or to prevent victimization.

3. The provisions contained herein shall be applicable to all, without distinction of any kind, such as race, colour, sex, age, language, religion, nationality, political or other opinion, cultural beliefs or practices, property, birth or family status, ethnic or group origin, and disability.

*Access to justice and fair treatment*

4. Victims should be treated with compassion and respect for their dignity. They are entitled to access to the mechanisms of justice and to prompt redress, as provided for by national legislation, for the harm that they have suffered.

5. Judicial and administrative mechanisms should be established and strengthened where necessary to enable victims to obtain redress through formal or informal procedures that are expeditious, fair, inexpensive and accessible. Victims should be informed of their rights in seeking redress through such mechanisms.

6. The responsiveness of judicial and administrative processes to the needs of victims should be facilitated by:

(a) Informing victims of their role and the scope, timing and progress of the proceedings and of the disposition of their cases, especially where serious crimes are involved and where they have requested such information;

(b) Allowing the views and concerns of victims to be presented and considered at appropriate stages of the proceedings where their personal interests are affected, without prejudice to the accused and consistent with the relevant national criminal justice system;

(c) Providing proper assistance to victims throughout the legal process;

(d) Taking measures to minimize inconvenience to victims, protect their privacy, when necessary, and ensure their safety, as well as that of their families and witnesses on their behalf, from intimidation and retailiation;

(e) Avoiding unnecessary delay in the disposition of cases and the execution of orders or decrees granting awards to victims.

7. Informal mechanisms for the resolution of disputes, including mediation, arbitration and customary justice or indigenous practices, should be utilized where appropriate to facilitiate conciliation and redress for victims.

*Restitution*

8.  Offenders or third parties responsible for their behaviour should, where appropriate, make fair restitution to victims, their families or dependants. Such restituion should include the return of property or payment for the harm or loss suffered, reimbursement of expenses incurred as a result of the victimization, the provision of services and the restoration of rights.

9.  Governments should review their practices, regulations and laws to consider restitution as an available sentencing option in criminal cases, in addition to other criminal sanctions.

10.  In cases of substantial harm to the environment, restitution, if ordered, should include, as far as possible, restoration of the environment, reconstruction of the infrastructure, replacement of community facilities and reimbursement of the expenses of relocation, whenever such harm results in the dislocation of a community.

11.  Where public officials or other agents acting in an official or quasi-official capacity have violated national criminal laws, the victims should receive restitution from the State whose officials or agents were responsible for the harm inflicted. In cases where the Government under whose authority the victimizing act or omission occurred is no longer in existence, the State or Government successor in title should provide restitution to the victims.

*Compensation*

12.  When compensation is not fully available from the offender or other sources, States should endeavour to provide financial compensation to:

  (a)  Victims who have sustained significant bodily injury or impairment of physical or mental health as a result of serious crimes;

  (b)  The family, in particular dependants of persons who have died or become physically or mentally incapacitated as a result of such victimization.

13.  The establishment, strengthening and expansion of national funds for compensation to victims should be encouraged. Where appropriate, other funds may also be established for this purpose, including those cases where the State of which the victim is a national is not in a position to compensate the victim for the harm.

*Assistance*

14.  Victims should receive the necessary material, medical, psycho-

logical and social assistance through governmental, voluntary, community-based and indigenous means.

15. Victims should be informed of the availability of health and social services and other relevant assistance and be readily afforded access to them.

16. Police, justice, health, social service and other personnel concerned should receive training to sensitize them to the needs of victims, and guidelines to ensure proper and prompt aid.

17. In providing services and assistance to victims, attention should be given to those who have special needs because of the nature of the harm inflicted or because of factors such as those mentioned in paragraph 3 above.

## B. Victims of Abuse of Power

18. "Victims" means persons who, individually or collectively, have suffered harm, including physical or mental injury, emotional suffering, economic loss or substantial impairment of their fundamental rights, through acts or omissions that do not yet constitute violations of national criminal laws but of internationally recognized norms relating to human rights.

19. States should consider incorporating into the national law norms proscribing abuses of power and providing remedies to victims of such abuses. In particular, such remedies should include restitution and/or compensation, and necessary material, medical, psychological and social assistance and support.

20. States should consider negotiating multilateral international treaties relating to victims, as defined in paragraph 18.

21. States should periodically review existing legislation and practices to ensure their responsiveness to changing circumstances, should enact and enforce, if necessary, legislation proscribing acts that constitute serious abuses of political or economic power, as well as promoting policies and mechanisms for the prevention of such acts, and should develop and make readily available appropriate rights and remedies for victims of such acts.